Legal Theories

in principle

LAWBOOK CO.
HEAD OFFICE: 100 Harris Street PYRMONT NSW 2009
Tel: (02) 8587 7000 Fax: (02) 8587 7100
For all sales inquiries please ring 1800 650 522
(for calls within Australia only)

INTERNATIONAL AGENTS & DISTRIBUTORS

CANADA
Carswell Co
Ontario, Montreal,
Vancouver, Calgary

HONG KONG
Sweet & Maxwell Asia
Hennessy Road, Wanchai

Bloomsbury Books Ltd
Chater Road, Central

MALAYSIA
Sweet & Maxwell Asia
Petaling Jaya, Selangor

NEW ZEALAND
Brooker's Ltd
Wellington

SINGAPORE
Sweet & Maxwell Asia
Albert Street

UNITED KINGDOM & EUROPE
Sweet & Maxwell Ltd
London

UNITED STATES
Wm W Gaunt & Sons, Inc
Holmes Beach, Florida

William S Hein Co Inc
Buffalo, New York

JAPAN
Maruzen Company Ltd
Tokyo

Legal Theories
in principle

by

MARETT LEIBOFF
BA (Qld) Grad Dip T (KGCAE) MA (NSW) LLB (Hons)(QUT) LLM (Lond)
Barrister of the Supreme Court of Queensland
Lecturer, Faculty of Law, Queensland University of Technology

MARK THOMAS
BA (Hons)(Qld) LLB (Hons)(QUT)
Barrister of the Supreme Court of Queensland
Associate Lecturer, Faculty of Law, Queensland University of Technology

LAWBOOK CO. 2004

Published in Sydney by

Lawbook Co.
100 Harris Street, Pyrmont, NSW

First edition 2004
    second impression 2005

National Library of Australia
    Cataloguing-in-Publication entry

Leiboff, Marett.
    Legal theories in principle.

    Includes index.
    ISBN 0 455 21944 3.

    1. Law – Philosophy. 2. Law – Interpretation and
    construction. I. Thomas, Mark, 1955-. II. Title.

    340.1

Editor: Catherine J Page
Product Developer: Georgiana Pringle

Typeset in Rotis Serif, 10 on 11.5 point, by
RE Typesetting, Woy Woy, NSW

Printed by Ligare Pty Ltd, Riverwood, NSW

Dedication

My contribution to this book is dedicated to my brother Jonathan Leiboff (1967–2003), a brilliant legal scholar, who died during the final stages of its writing. He was never able to read this book, though he knew it was about to be finished. I suspect it would have amused him; he would never have needed it himself.

Marett Leiboff

My contribution to this book is dedicated to my mother, Hilarie Thomas (1921–2002).

Mark Thomas

Preface

If you open the pages of this book hoping to find a new standard legal theory textbook, we know you will be disappointed. Instead, this book does something new, original, and unique by embedding a learning strategy in a book devoted to uncovering the mysteries of legal theory. We have written a book designed to help readers *learn* legal theory by providing examples of the uses of legal theory in practice, an explanation of its methods, and an overview of aspects of the content of legal theory.

This book does not and cannot stand alone. It has been written to complement and supplement two existing texts – Margaret Davies' *Asking the Law Question* (2nd edition) and *Lloyd's Introduction to Jurisprudence* (7th edition). It cannot be used in isolation, as it has been designed to be used with one or other of those texts. In this sense, our book is co-dependent, for want of a better expression. We have supplemented the material in these existing texts where we needed to build on content of one or other of Davies or Lloyd:

- Where we *complement* these existing texts, some of our own 'text' operates as a commentary and direction back to the existing texts. We have eschewed conventional narrative or descriptive form in order to direct readers back to the source material.

- Where we have *supplemented* the content of the existing texts, our own text adopts a more standard narrative form, usually through historicising and contextualising the legal theories, and through the addition of relevant political philosophies.

In order to explain the legal theories we have covered in this book, we have *mapped* their content through our own original diagrams, illustrations, tables, and charts. We use these in different ways. We begin the book with an overarching historicised and contextualised timeline. Each chapter includes a more intimate timeline that charts the relationship between the theory and other contemporaneous theories or events. Sometimes, diagrams and illustrations are used to explain the theory, and readers will need to consider the diagram with the reading of the original theory or theorist. In other cases, we will use diagrams or tables to illustrate our own explanation or description of the legal theory in question.

To an extent, we assume that readers of this book will start at the beginning and finish at the end. We thought we would set out the integrated teaching and learning strategy we have used in the book so that if you do not follow this structure, you will understand why things are as they are:

In Chapters 1 and 2, we set out what we mean by legal theory, how it is used, and how to go about learning legal theory.

Chapter 3 is an 'amplified template' for the rest of the book. It also starts off the process of learning that will apply to the first half of the book: it looks at the themes and methods of the theories in one section, and the 'content' of the theories in a second section. *These are merged in the rest of the book.*

We provide a brief description of the theory before we send readers back to the original texts or source materials. *In later chapters, we return to a more conventional footnoting style to do the same thing.*

Chapter 3 covers a large range of theories and theorists to give readers a taste of the breadth and scope of theories within one school of thought. *We do not repeat this in the rest of the book because we anticipate that readers will begin to explore the content of the original texts or source materials to which they have been referred, beyond our own use of the theory.*

We hope these images will be kept in mind throughout the remainder of the book, and that readers will start to map out their own ideas and thoughts on the theories.

Chapters 4 to 7 supplement the content of both existing texts. These chapters hone in on and magnify the legal theory in question, by marrying an underlying philosophy with a related legal theory. This means that aspects only of a theory are considered, and readers will be left to return to the existing texts to fill out the content of related aspects of the theory.

Chapters 8 and 9 mark a turning point in the book, by changing its theoretical focus, and taking the learning process and methods of legal theory to a new and higher level. We return to overviews of the theories in Chapters 10, 11 and 13. Again, all these chapters assume that readers will return to the original source materials.

The final phase of the learning strategy and use of the methods of legal theory is found in Chapters 12, 14 and 15. We end where we hope our readers will be able to continue learning themselves.

This book was prepared jointly, though for the record, Marett Leiboff wrote Chapters 1, 2, 3, 8, 9, 12, and 15, we worked together on Chapter 14, and Mark Thomas, of course, wrote the remaining chapters.

MARETT LEIBOFF

MARK THOMAS

Brisbane, December 2003

Acknowledgments

In a sense, this book is the product of many hands. Marett would like to thank all of her students over the past seven years, whose annoyance, impatience, irritation and fear about learning legal theory would turn into relief, delight and surprise at being able to understand it after all (usually after the exam). They fill these pages in more ways than they could appreciate. Scott McConnel has played his part as well. She would also like to thank Margaret Davies for her invaluable comments in relation to one chapter of this book, colleagues Sally Sheldon and Tracey Carver, student Scott Edwards, and the other students who read drafts of part of the book (and who wanted an advance copy!).

Mark would like to thank all of his students (who similarly inhabit the book), as well as Bernard Thomas, Glyn Davies and colleagues Ros Macdonald and Nigel Stobbs for their encouraging comments, and his partner, Jill Shanahan, for putting up with him while his chapters were being written.

Table of Contents

Preface vii

Acknowledgments ix

Chapter 1   Explaining Theory 1

Chapter 2   Learning Theory 25

Chapter 3   Natural Law Theories: Speaking to the Sky or
Looking in Ourselves? 43

Chapter 4   Modernism and the Scientific Method:
Law's Search for Certainty 83

Chapter 5   Liberalism: Explaining Why We Think As We Do. 109

Chapter 6   Correcting Irrationality: Positivism and Law's Commonsense 137

Chapter 7   Doing Common Sense: Positivism in Action 167

Chapter 8   Marx and Law: Breaking Down the System 185

Chapter 9   Law Meets Society 203

Chapter 10   Reconceptualising the Practical: Postmodernism. 227

Chapter 11   Feminist Legal Theory 251

Chapter 12   Critical Legal Theories 271

Chapter 13   Critical Race Theory and Postcolonialism 293

Chapter 14   Case Studies: Theories in Action 309

Chapter 15   Concluding, Only to Begin All Over Again 323

Index 331

CHAPTER 1

Explaining Theory

Reading 1
Aim. 1
Principles 1
Introducing legal theory. 1
Mapping legal theories. 8
Introducing the theories. 16
Taking charge — reading theories texts 21
Questions to think about 22
Further reading. 23

READING

DAVIES, *Asking the Law Question: the Dissolution of Legal Theory*, 2nd edition, Chapter 1
FREEMAN, *Lloyd's Introduction to Jurisprudence*, 7th edition, Chapters 1 and 2

AIM

This chapter will:
- introduce you to the ideas and practices of legal theory;
- provide you with a historical and contextual overview of legal theories;
- give you a snapshot of the different theories we will look at in this book;
- introduce you to the Davies and Lloyd books.

PRINCIPLES

Introducing legal theory
Finding the starting point

Have you ever wondered why you think the way you do, or why you make the assumptions you do? Or have you ever thought about why you may accept the politics or values of our society, while others of you not only don't accept them, but may even actively oppose them? And, especially for those of us immersed in law – the judiciary and other legal decision-makers, legal practitioners, legislators and law students – have you ever wondered why we think the way we do about life, the universe and everything,[1] or law's empire,[2] and how this impacts on our understanding of the law, and our responses to its values, politics and assumptions?

You've never thought about these sorts of questions?

Maybe you have, but haven't stood back to think about them.

Let's think about whether we make assumptions or express values by taking a fairly common view expressed by lawyers:

1. Law does not reflect a political standpoint, and law would never prefer some societal values over others.

Clearly, the alternative view is that:

2. Law *does* reflect some form of political standpoint and it *does* prefer some values over others.

Which view do you prefer or agree with?

There isn't a right or wrong answer here. But you have certainly made a *value judgment* or *assumption* about the way law works, and whether you realised it or not, have found yourself caught up in the ideas that have informed the practice of law in the Western world for centuries, through *legal theory*, *jurisprudence*, or *legal philosophy*.

Let's take these ideas a step further. Having a view is one thing, but you need to be able to support that view or idea, or alternatively, to find ways to argue against the view or idea.

Simply saying that you think view 1 is right, or that view 2 is completely wrong, is only half an answer.

Why do you like VIEW 1 and dislike VIEW 2, or vice versa?

You can't say 'because', or that you 'like it', or that it is 'what you believe'. And you can't say that you are repeating what you were told by a practitioner or lecturer – these are just different versions of 'because'.

Instead, you can argue or support your view by basing it in the theory or philosophy that underlies each view.

This book will introduce you to some of the significant legal theories and related political philosophies that have influenced the creation and development of legal doctrine, the practice of law, and the formation of legislation in the Western world, to give you an understanding of where our ideas came from, and where they may lead. This book will not discuss our own views about legal theories, legal philosophies, or jurisprudence. We will leave our own arguments, ideas and thoughts aside, to provide you with an overview and explanation of some of the most significant jurisprudence, legal theories, and legal philosophies, and their influences on the practices of law in Australia, and to give you an insight into the arguments of some of the significant theorists in the field.

---

1 Adams, Douglas, *Life, the Universe, and Everything* (Pan, London, 1982).
2 This is also the title of an influential legal theory work by Ronald Dworkin: see Chapter 5.

This does not mean that we will be uncritical of the theories in their conception or their practical effects, or that through our choices we won't give you an impression of our ideas or thoughts, which you may glean from what we say. What we will do is give you the language and methods to know something about the theories, what they are saying, their methods, and the way they have been used by legal practitioners, the courts, and policy makers. We hope you will enjoy finding your way through law's hidden language!

Sourcing your views

Why do we say law's *hidden* language? Well, some of these theories have merged with the way we think about law, so that we often don't know where our ideas have come from, or why we think the way we do. These theories have become *internalised* into legal thinking, so if you agree with **view 1** without knowing why, it is likely that you will have absorbed this point of view from the way you have learnt different areas of doctrine throughout your law course. Whether you know it or not, you are expressing the views of *liberal political philosophy*, which have found their way into the pre-eminent legal theory of the 19th and 20th centuries: *legal positivism*. The ideas found in **view 1** have become part and parcel of the way many lawyers think, and they may have forgotten, or never known, where their ideas came from. Later in this chapter we will give you a brief overview of all the theories we will cover in this book. If you want to know more about liberalism and positivism, then you might like to go directly to Chapters 4–7.

> Once you have thought about these ideas more fully, you will be able to explain why you agree with **view 1**. Or you may find that you can't support this position, and that you now agree with **view 2** instead. But you will have to understand the reason behind your changed view.

What if you prefer **view 2**? You may have disliked, or found yourself uncomfortable with, some of the assumptions contained in some of the rules or doctrines you have learnt, especially those formed in the 19th century, or you may be concerned about the relationship between law and justice. By adopting this stance, you have brought an *external standpoint* to bear on your understanding of law, which seeks to question the internal standpoint reflected in **view 1**. This external standpoint is found in a range of critical theories, which we look at in Chapters 8–13. Again, if you want to argue in support of your views, you will need to rely upon a theory to show why you think the way you do. A number of these theories (through a range of different ideas and methods), provide a critical response to accepted values of law. For this reason they overtly challenge the deeply-embedded ideas found in **view 1**.

> Once you have thought about these ideas more fully, you will be able to ask questions about the basis on which a theory is established, or the *methods* the theory or theorist uses. If you are going to argue for or against a theory, you will have to demonstrate a good understanding of the theory before you can argue against its validity or usefulness.
>
> **We will be talking about the methods used by the theories or theorists throughout this book to help you uncover why a theory says what it says.**

Using legal theory

While a legal theory can help us understand why we hold the views we do, legal theories can also be used *instrumentally*. When we say that something is 'instrumental', we mean that the theory can be useful, such as showing the underlying basis of a rule, or to justify a judicial decision. When a theory is used instrumentally, you can put your personal views aside, and use the theory to achieve some kind of outcome, such as the development of a new argument or reinterpretation of the law.

Sometimes the courts will overtly rely upon a theory in this way. For instance, in *Garcia v National Australia Bank Limited*,[3] the High Court used *feminist legal theory* to examine the status of bank guarantees provided by a wife for a husband.[4] When used in this way, a theory becomes part of the *language of the law*, through its acceptance or use in a judgment.

Law's secret language

In other cases, the theory itself will disappear once it has been used to frame an argument by counsel, or as part of the creation of new legislation. All we are left with is the outcome. Sometimes, the only way we will know that a theory has been used is for us to *know* the theory, its language and its method. If we don't know this language, we will miss out on a wealth of ideas and concepts which drive the judgment, legislation, or counsel's argument.

Legal theories let us into this *secret language*. Once you know some of the more significant theories, you will be given the key to the door of aspects of law you may never have been able to make sense of, particularly where novel questions of law have to be considered.

DID YOU KNOW THIS?

Contract law is based on the assumptions of human behaviour found in the political philosophy of 'liberalism'. This philosophy assumes all of us to be 'free-thinking' individuals who are all capable of making rational decisions about their lives. It disregards the differences between us, like power or money. For instance, a corporation, as a *legal person*, is treated the same as an individual human, natural person. If we think about the basic rules establishing the formation of a contract — offer and acceptance, consideration, intention to create legal relations, capacity to contract — we can see how it constructs a world where free-thinking individuals come together to make decisions about the transaction into which they enter: see Chapter 5.

Knowing this may help you understand what the law is trying to achieve.

Understanding the basis of a rule will guide law reform. Provisions like s 52 of the *Trade Practices Act* 1974 (Cth) were a Labor government response to the power imbalance faced by consumers in a mass market economy dominated by corporate entities.

---

3   [1998] HCA 48.

4   At fn 21, references included Howell, " 'Sexually Transmitted Debt': A Feminist Analysis of Laws Regulating Guarantors and Co-borrowers" (1994) 4 *Australian Feminist Law Journal* 93; Fehlberg, "The Husband, the Bank, the Wife and Her Signature — the Sequel" (1996) 59 *Modern Law Review* 675; Fehlberg, "Women in 'Family' Companies: English and Australian Experiences" (1997) 15 *Company and Securities Law Journal* 348.

These reforms had their origins in the theories of Marx, and the provision directly challenged the liberal foundations of contract law. The law has developed dramatically since it was enacted. It is used by corporations against corporations, as well as by consumers, and it is now hard to trace the ideas that lay behind the origins of the provision.

**Reaching back into the history of a statute,
rule or principle will give you the tools to argue for change.**

Sometimes the secret language is used in argument before the court. In the appeal in *Re Kevin*,[5] a case dealing with a transgender marriage, counsel's submission included the phrase 'equal concern and respect'. This sounds like a normal phrase, but if you are in the 'know', then it will have been obvious that counsel was relying on a key phrase found in the rights-based theories of Ronald Dworkin, who you will meet in Chapter 5.[6] This is only one of a number of examples we will refer to in this book. You will find more and more examples for yourselves once you know what to look for.

Encountering concepts

You will also come across legal theories that, at first glance, are apparently unconcerned with any 'useful' function. They appear to operate purely in the abstract, or in the world of the imagination. This type of *conceptual thinking* occurs across the spectrum of legal theory. When theorists engage in this type of theoretical work, they try to uncover some of the profound questions that drive our thought processes, or which seek to explain the basis of our legal system. Just as scientists engage in 'pure' research, which seemingly has no practical application, legal theorists also undertake this sort of work. However, as you will know, this sort of pure scientific research will ultimately flow through to the day-to-day, because intermediate researchers will apply it to problems in the field. The same applies to conceptual thinking in law.

When you encounter these theories, many of you will be entering into alien territory, where a completely different language and method is used to explain concepts that may seem to have no connection with law at all. This form of theoretical work will eventually flow through to other legal thinkers, who will use these insights to explore the use of the *conceptual* theory in a more practical or applied way. This type of theoretical work takes a long time to seep into the practices of law, so its influence is long term, and not short term. Sometimes it never enters the legal profession directly, but provides a language and technique to analyse, evaluate or assess the effectiveness of law and its practices.

For instance, in Chapter 10, we will introduce you to some of the theories of postmodernism and poststructuralism. They originated outside law, but flowed through into legal thought during the 1980s. These theories operate at a conceptual level, but can have highly practical consequences. There has been ongoing conceptual work in this area, but *other* theorists are using the insights of postmodernism and poststructuralism by applying them to practical situations.

**With time, you will find it easier to understand the more conceptual
theories, why they are written as they are, and their ultimate usefulness at
ground level.**

---

5 [2003] FamCA 94, http://www.austlii.edu.au/au/cases/cth/family_ct/2003/94.html
6 Mark Thomas was present at the appeal hearing, 18 and 19 February 2002.

Jurisprudence, legal theory, and legal philosophy

There are no hard and fast rules governing the terminology we will use in this book. At least three different words or phrases can be used to encompass the topics we will be looking at: jurisprudence, legal theory, and legal philosophy.

Throughout this book, we will use the term LEGAL THEORY to cover all three concepts, but we will use a specific word in appropriate circumstances

Jurisprudence is a term that can be used interchangeably with legal theory or legal philosophy. More particularly, it is concerned with explaining law within its own boundaries. In another sense, jurisprudence provides the guidance for good or wise judging and lawmaking.

Legal theory considers law within its own framework, and critical responses to the operation of law.

Legal philosophy, in its narrowest sense, considers questions about law within its own framework, disregarding associated political, moral and ethical questions. A broader concept of legal philosophy contemplates an understanding of law using a diverse range of philosophical inquiry.

You will be studying courses with different titles, and you should go with the meaning used by the academics teaching your course.[7]

What you will be reading

This book is only the first port of call for you in any study you undertake in this area. It has been written to introduce you to the legal theories we are covering, and to act as an *introduction* and a *supplement* to two other books: Margaret Davies' *Asking the Law Question, 2nd edition*, and MDA Freeman's *Lloyd's Introduction to Jurisprudence, 7th edition*. (We will call these texts Davies and Lloyd throughout the body of this book.) If you are familiar with the *In Principle* series, of which this book is a part, you need to be aware that this book has some differences, brought about by the specific needs of legal theory:

• Legal theories do not form any settled body of doctrine or rules which can be neatly summarised under formalised principles or headings. You will see that Davies and Lloyd differ markedly in their treatment of some theories, sometimes don't cover the same theories, or rely on completely different material to explain what a theory does. We have tried to steer an even path through the two books so that we can introduce you to as many theories as possible. You may find yourselves reading material set for your course that we have not included in this book. In other words, there are no hard and fast rules about what you will be looking at!

---

7   Harris, JW, *Legal Philosophies* (2nd ed, 1997) pp 3–4, for example, comes up with different explanations for these categories.

- An *introduction* to legal theory can only ever scratch the surface of the ideas and thoughts underlying the different theories we will be looking at in this book. We cannot emphasise enough that you will need to read Davies and Lloyd, and any other material you are asked to read for your own course. We have written *this chapter* assuming that you will also be reading either (or both) of Davies Chapter 1 and Lloyd Chapters 1 and 2. Those chapters will introduce you to the insights, intricacies, complexities and subtleties of legal theory we cannot cover here.

- When we say that this book is a *supplement*, we mean that we will be adding, at times, to the way a topic has been dealt with by other writers or thinkers. We will do this, mostly, to help your understanding of a topic, by giving you some historical or contextual background, or where we think an additional extract of a theory could be useful for you. We will therefore sometimes provide you with original material that may not be readily available to you from other sources.

- Some of you may be taught legal theory as a source of study in its own right. This book can only ever act as a very basic starting point for you, in your quest to engage with complex conceptual questions that can only be grappled with after detailed and engaged study of original texts, other thinkers and theorists. Our use of practical examples (especially where they deal with theoretical methods) will be helpful to your thinking about the *conceptual* questions you will be asked to consider. Others of you may look at legal theory to be 'applied' to the law, or to assess the practices of the law. This book will provide you with the start you need. Others of you will be exposed to *both approaches* to learning legal theory, and we have written this book with this style of learning in mind.

- Legal theories are rarely dealt with in the same way as standard 'legal problem solving'. However, we will refer to the use of theories in practical settings throughout this book, and will provide you with questions to spark off your own thoughts about the theories we will look at. In Chapter 14, we will specifically look at the way that theories are used in practice.

We will be talking to you more about LEARNING about legal theory
in Chapter 2.

Where we stand

We said earlier that we wouldn't be discussing our own views about legal theories, legal philosophies, or jurisprudence in this book. What we mean is that we are not intending to, nor will we, develop our *own* theory in this book, unlike, for instance, Finnis,[8] Hart,[9] Dworkin,[10] or Margaret Davies. You will very easily find Davies' argument in her book, because she tells you directly where she stands and why her book is written the way it is. But other thinkers, like Finnis, are less direct in identifying their viewpoints, and you will have to learn to read between the lines to find them. We aren't doing either of these things, because of the intended aim of this book, which is to introduce you to the

---

8 See Chapter 3.
9 See Chapters 3 and 7.
10 See Chapter 5.

body of theoretical work that has influenced law. We are also concerned to show that we respect the differences in views that different people have (so long as they are supported and are not simply opinion, invective or polemic, which may otherwise be called unsubstantiated grandstanding).

We won't be trying to tell you what to think 'between the lines', but you may have started to ask questions of us: why do we use the examples we do, why do we provide the supplementary material that we do, and why do we describe the theories the way we do? Or have you started to make other connections for yourself, or begun reading other things into what we have said? If you have asked these questions then you will know that any author is never divorced from what they think important, where they may stand politically or socially, or what they think about the law. We acknowledge that it is virtually impossible to avoid this, but we will be doing our best to fairly and accurately treat all the theories we cover, whether we like them or not, or agree with them or not. Having said that, we do know that we may inadvertently let our guard down – see if you can find where we may have done it, and you will be making great progress in your reading and understanding of legal theory.

We will be talking to you more about READING AND WRITING about legal theory in Chapter 2.

Mapping legal theories

Setting the scene

As you can see, we haven't, as yet, *described or discussed* the detail of any of the theories we will look at in this book. We will come to a brief overview of them shortly, but before we do, we thought we would map out the different theories for you. It is sometimes easier for us to make sense of new concepts and ideas by setting out or 'mapping' them, as we will do here through *timelines*, to give you a broad picture of the subject area you will encounter. In an area like legal theory, where we will skip across thousands of years of Western thought, it is also helpful to be able to place a particular theory in its historical, societal and legal contexts. Each chapter of this book will have its own timeline, applicable to the theory to be considered in that chapter. In this chapter, we have set out a *consolidated timeline* which provides you with a reference point for you to track all the theories we will consider in this book, and for you to place any other theories or theorists you may learn about that we don't consider here.

Let's look at the first map, Figure 1.1, which is a broad and schematic timeline that puts together, or juxtaposes, the main groupings of theories we will be looking at. You will see there that one of the theories – natural law – has been around more or less continuously for 2 500 years, an incredibly long time.[11] This theory has a gap in it, where it fell out of favour from the beginning of legal positivism, but came back into favour after World War Two. The next 'oldest' of the theories – the philosophies of modernism and liberalism – have

---

11 We will look at natural law theory in Chapter 3.

only been around for the last 500 or 600 years,[12] followed by legal positivism, which is only 200 years old.[13] You will remember that liberalism and positivism were the theories that informed the ideas in view 1 above.

FIGURE 1.1: MAPPING THE EPOCHS

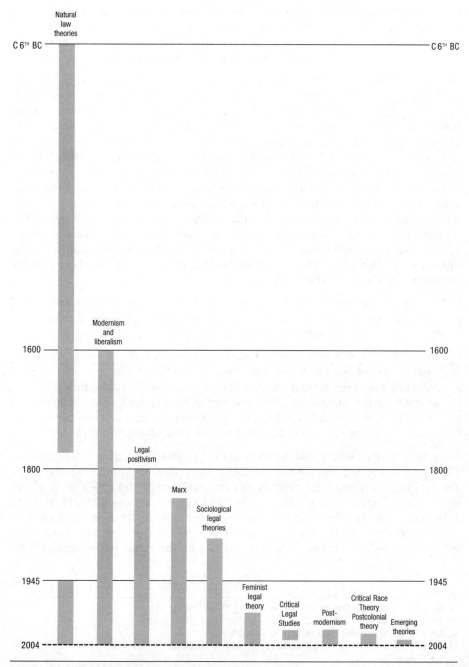

---

12 We will look at these theories in Chapters 4–6.
13 We will look at legal positivism in Chapters 6 and 7.

We don't have enough pages in this book to correctly 'scale' the timeline in Figure 1.1. You will have to imagine the gap between natural law and the other theories for yourself, or draw your own timeline if you can't do this in your mind's eye, to illustrate the length of time that natural law theory has been around, compared to the other theories.

This first part of the timeline covers the types of legal theory we will call CONVENTIONAL LEGAL THEORY. These legal theories are the ones that have become part and parcel of legal thought, and which generally do not dispute the accepted structures or assumptions of law.

Let's look at the next part of the timeline in Figure 1.1, which covers the last 150 or so years. Two of the theories have been around for about this length of time — Marxism and its later offshoots,[14] and sociological legal theories (and other associated theories, like the American Legal Realists).[15] But most of the other theories which cluster around the bottom part of the timeline have only developed over the last 5–30 years: feminist legal theory,[16] Critical Legal Studies,[17] postmodernism,[18] critical race theory and postcolonial legal theory.[19] There are also the mysterious 'emerging' theories — the theories that are currently being thought about for the first time, which either build on or adapt existing legal theories, or which build on or adapt ideas from outside law.[20] All of the legal theories in the bottom part of the timeline have grown from a source *outside* the 'accepted' boundaries of legal thought, before finding their way into discourses about the law. You will remember that *critical* aspects of these theories informed the ideas in **view 2** above.

The categories of legal theory are not closed, and will continue to change as new thinkers and theorists provide new insights into the way we think about the law in all its guises.

The later part of the timeline in Figure 1.1 generally includes the types of legal theory we will call NON-CONVENTIONAL LEGAL THEORY. While some of these theories have been accepted within conventional legal thought, they look at law from the 'outside in'. Other theories which also look at law from the outside in, but call into question the accepted structures or assumptions of law are not always accepted by conventional legal thought.

Now, let's look at where this timeline ends, in 2004. We can see that most of the theories are still in operation. Throughout this book, we will find new theories being created, and older ones continually used and revitalised. At the end of her Chapter 1, at pp 26–31, Margaret Davies contemplates the state of legal theory at the beginning of the 21st century. Apart from finding that many more legal theories exist than set out in this timeline and book, you might want to ask yourself whether *our* use of the terms 'conventional' and

---

14 We will look at the influence of Marx in Chapter 8 and Chapter 12.
15 We will look at these ideas in Chapter 9 and Chapter 12.
16 We will look at feminist legal thought in Chapter 11.
17 We will look at the critical legal studies movement in Chapter 12.
18 See Chapter 10.
19 See Chapter 13.
20 We will look at the way new theories emerge in Chapters 12 and 15.

'non-conventional' legal theory matches up with her use of 'mainstream' and 'resistance' legal thought, or 'traditional and universalist' and 'critical, postmodern, deconstructive' legal thought?[21]

Situating the theories

We have now identified, or named, many of the theories we will look at in this book. We will now provide you with one *more* map, which we hope you can use now to place the theories into some kind of context. You will also be able to use it throughout your study of legal theory. Figure 1.2 is a 'consolidated timeline', which acts as a 'next stage' to introduce you to legal theory. It fills out the very flimsy timeline we have already seen with a more fully sketched picture of the theories. This consolidated timeline also gives you the names of influential theorists, some key ideas of the theory, the society in which the theory developed, and some contemporary common law legal events.

USING THE TIMELINE

This timeline is here for you to use as a resource tool, and cannot be used as an end in itself. At this very early stage of your study in legal theory, you will find that the names, dates, times and ideas will not mean anything specific for you, but will look like a vague set of details that you won't be able to relate to. How did we know that that's what you'd be thinking? Let's use a common example — have you ever walked into a classroom where unfamiliar content is written and drawn on the board? The content is virtually meaningless because it is dependent on the text that accompanies it — student answers, teacher notes and diagrams to assist with the explanation of concepts. If you had been in that class, though, the meaningless material would make perfect sense, though to a outsider, it is confronting because it is strange and difficult.

So we know that even when we map out ideas in a very simple form, there are always considerable gaps in how you will read the map or timeline, because the map is always constructed on the basis of *our* knowledge, which, at least at this stage, is likely to be greater than yours. But once you've, say, read the chapter on natural law theory, some of the key ideas of the theories will become obvious to you. You will then find that this timeline is really just a schematic way of looking at the more detailed material in the chapter, and what had once looked like isolated ideas will now have some meaning for you, and you will be able to situate the theory more fully in the broader scheme of things. An even fuller understanding will come from your reading of Davies and Lloyd, and any other material you are required to read for your course.

As you work through different theories, you will make stronger connections and comparisons between different theories and within the theories themselves. Through this process, you will find yourself entering into a study pattern, where you stage your progress using a range of resources and materials. If you drop in and out of the timeline throughout different stages of your study of legal theory, you will find yourselves revising, rethinking, and reappraising your understanding of the theories simply by looking at them in a slightly different light.

---

21 Davies, *Asking the Law Question: The Dissolution of Legal Theory*, 2nd edition, p 31.

FIGURE 1.2: CONSOLIDATED TIMELINE

Century	C6TH BC 500BC	C5TH BC 400BC	C4TH BC 300 BC	C3RD–C1STBC 200–100BC	1 AD–400	400–1000	1000–1200	1200–1400
Where	Ancient Greece: Athens, Sparta			Roman Empire	Europe, North Africa, Middle East	Europe, North Africa, Middle East	Spain and North Africa	Italy and Western Europe
Who		Socrates	Plato Aristotle	Cicero	Birth of Christ	St Augustine	Avicenna Averroës Maimonides	St Thomas Aquinas
Influence on legal theory	Western ideas of philosophy begin here	Created the dialectic method Wanted to establish the source of truth	Reason as the way to seek truth Natural Law 'The Politics' 'The Ethics' (Aristotle)	Stoic method and the role of reason in natural law 'De re publica' 'De legibus'		Neo-Platonism: law derived from God, human law was not connected to God's laws	Revitalised Aristotle Influenced St Thomas Aquinas	'Summa Theologica' Law derived from God now guided human law
Influence on law and legal thinking	The provision of moral guidance for humans, based in the need for society to function well. These guiding principles meant that law would be created for the good of the community.							
What else was happening	The source of ideals of Western culture: science, arts, poetry, democracy, law			Roman government throughout the 'world'	Roman Empire ended Early Christian Church	Dark Ages Influence of the Church	The Norman conquest in England Feudal society Cathedrals Crusades	Crusades The Black Death Catholic Church as the centre of the world
Events in law in the common law world					Saxon law: custom, shires and courts; writs	Time immemorial (custom) Trial by ordeal (procedure) Trial by battle (procedure) Assizes (court structure) Trespass (tort) Doctrine of tenure (land) Sub-infeudation (land)	Trial by ordeal abolished 1215, juries created Magna Carta 1215 Law Merchant *Statute of Quia Emptores* 1290 (land)
				Natural law: Chapter 3				

Century	1400–1600	1600–1700	1700–1800
Where	Western Europe and the American Colonies		
Who	*Rene Descartes*	*Hobbes* *Locke*	*Hume* *Kant* *Hegel* *Smith* *Rousseau* *Paine* Blackstone
Influence on legal theory	*A shift from the monarch to the citizen; law is used as the basis to exercise rights of free thinking, unconstrained individuals. Government cannot interfere with these rights unless the individual agrees. Law facilitates commerce and liberty*		
Influence on law and legal thinking	*Rationality* *Reason* *Science*	Natural rights *Property rights, human rights, liberalism, democracy*	
What else was happening	Renaissance in Italy Printing Spanish Inquisition Henry VIII Columbus Shakespeare Great Fire of London	The Enlightenment Charles I beheaded English Civil War The Restoration Sir Christopher Wren Glorious Revolution	American and French Revolutions Enclosure of the commons Invention of the watermill and early steam engine 'Great voyages of discovery' Australia 'discovered' and 'settled' Mozart Dr Johnson's dictionary Publication of Paine *The Rights of Man* (1791) – charged with sedition – fled to France
Events in law in the common law world	*Statue of Frauds* 1528 (property) *Statute of Uses* 1535 (land) Rule against perpetuities: 1598 (property)	'Statute of Elizabeth' – *Statute of Charitable Uses* 1601 (charitable trusts) *Statute of Tenures* 1660 (property)	Statute of Anne 1709 (Copyright) *Armory v Delamirie* 1722 (finder's case) Lord Mansfield: *Miller v Race* 1758 (commercial law derived from the law merchant) *Entinck v Carrington* 1765 (unlawful detention and seizure of property) *Payne v Cave* 1789 (contracts)
	Natural law: Chapter 3		
		Modernism and liberalism: Chapters 4–6	

Century	1800–1830	1830–1870	1870–1900	1900–1930	1930–1945	1945–1960
Where	Western Europe, England		United States of America and Western Europe			
Who	BENTHAM AUSTIN	Marx	Ehrlich Durkheim Weber Holmes	Pound Weber James Dewey	Frank Llewellyn Kelsen Fuller HART	
Influence on legal theory	CREATED LEGAL POSITIVISM	Identified the relationship between law and economics and society	Sociological legal theories		Frank – American Legal Realism – fact skeptic Llewellyn – American Legal Realism – rule skeptic Kelsen – new conceptualism Fuller – new natural law HART – REVIVED POSITIVISM	
Influence on law and legal thinking	BENTHAM AND AUSTIN: LAW IS CONSIDERED WITHIN ITS OWN BOUNDARIES DISSOCIATED FROM SOCIAL OR OTHER FACTORS Marx: Highlights the gaps between law and justice, and provides methodologies for law reform			American realists: Practical insights into the way law works, to assist with prediction of decisions and managing judging. Provided impetus for law reform Kelsen – analytical method enabling a clear conceptual framework for law and legal change Fuller – new natural law revived thinking about law and human rights HART – REVIVED POSITIVISM TO ENABLE AN EXPANDED UNDERSTANDING OF LEGAL CHANGE		
What else was happening	The Romantics (music and literature) Industrial Revolution	Dickens Industrial Revolution Queensland split from NSW Lord Shaftesbury – exploitation of women and children in the mines in England	Boer War Shifts in population from Europe to USA, Australia, and other countries End of reign of Queen Victoria	Shifts in population from Europe to USA, Australia, and other countries Australian Federation World War I Russian Revolution	'New Deal' social reforms in the USA Edward VIII abdicates Nazi Germany World War II	Nuremberg Trials Creation of the United Nations Elizabeth II Negotiations for the creation of the International Covenant on Civil and Political Rights
Events in law in the common law world	Trial by battle abolished 1819	Roscorla v Thomas 1842 (contracts) Bridges v Hawkesworth 1851 (finder's case) Rylands v Fletcher 1868 (torts) R v Jack Congo Murrell 1836 (Aboriginal crime)	Judicature Acts 1873, 1875 Carlill v Carbolic Smoke Ball 1892 (contracts) Smith v Baker 1891 (torts – volenti) South Staffordshire Water Company v Sharman 1896 (finders)	Constitution of Australia	Statute of Westminster 1931 Donoghue v Stevenson 1932 (torts)	Penfolds Wine v Elliot 1946 (torts) Searle v Wallbank 1947 (torts) Leaf v International Galleries 1950 (contracts) Bolton v Stone 1951(contracts)

Modernism and liberalism: Chapters 4–6 POSITIVISM: CHAPTERS 5–7	Natural law: Chapter 3

Marx: Chapter 8 *Sociological theories: Chapter 9*

Century	1960–1970	1970–1990		1990–2000	2000 >
Where	England, USA	USA, Australia, England			
Who	HART Fuller *Kelsen* *Sociological legal theorists* **Theorists reliant on Marx**	FEMINIST LEGAL THEORISTS CRITICAL LEGAL STUDIES THEORISTS Finnis HART POSTMODERNISTS **Theorists reliant on Marx** *Sociological legal theorists*		Finnis FEMINIST LEGAL THEORISTS CRITICAL LEGAL STUDIES THEORISTS CRITICAL RACE THEORISTS *Sociological legal theorists* **Theorists reliant on Marx** POSTCOLONIALISTS NEW POSITIVISTS POSTMODERNISTS *Emerging legal theorists*	
Influence on legal theory	see previous entry	THE EMERGENCE OF A RANGE OF CRITICAL THEORIES PROVIDES CRITIQUES OF THE FAIRNESS, JUSTICE AND EFFECTIVENESS OF THE LAW AND ITS ASSUMPTIONS			
Influence on law and legal thinking		Finnis' revived natural law creates the foundation for a neo-conservative foundation for law, marrying positivism with natural law in its most explicit form since St Thomas Aquinas			
What else was happening	Freedom rides in outback NSW to highlight lack of rights of indigenous Australians Women's lib, Gay liberation The Beatles Moon landing Woodstock	Federal Labor Government for the first time in over 20 years Punk The Dismissal of the Whitlam Labor Government by the Governor-General Federal Labor returns to power		Gulf War Federal Liberal coalition returns to power Waterfront dispute	
Events in law in the common law world	*Shaw v DPP* 1962 (conspiracy to corrupt public morals) *Hedley Byrne v Heller* 1964 (torts) International Covenant on Civil and Political Rights 1966	*Racial Discrimination Act* 1975 (Cth) *Trade Practices Act* 1975 (Cth) *Bernstein v Skyviews* 1979 (trespass to air) *SGIC v Trigwell* 1979 (torts)	*Parker v British Airways Board* 1982 (finders) *Jaensch v Coffey* 1984 (torts) *Australia Act* 1986 (UK and Cth)	*Mabo* 1992 (native title) *Native Title Act* 1993 (Cth) *Lange v ABC* 1997 (defamation)	*Annetts v Australian Stations Pty Ltd* 2000 (torts – shock cases) *Re Kevin* 2003 (family law – transgender marriage)

Natural law: Chapter 3

Modernism and liberalism: Chapters 4–6

POSITIVISM: CHAPTERS 5–7

Marx: Chapter 8

Sociological legal theories: Chapter 9

CRITICAL THEORIES (FEMINIST LEGAL THEORY, CRITICAL LEGAL STUDIES, POSTMODERNISM, POSTCOLONIAL LEGAL THEORY AND CRITICAL RACE THEORY): CHAPTERS 10–13

Introducing the theories

The purpose of knowing legal theory

If you like acquiring knowledge for its own sake, then you will think that we have taken an incredibly long time to get to the heart of the issue — knowledge and content about the theories themselves. We know that lengthy ways into material can be frustrating, but unfortunately, the content, or knowing, legal theory is only part of the story — how you approach it can be as, or more, important than the knowledge itself. We will touch on the importance of understanding the methods used by theory or theorists in the next chapter.

> **Knowing what a theory says is important.**
>
> Without this knowledge, you will miss out on a wealth of understanding of the law, where it came from, and guidance for its development.
>
> **However, this knowledge is not an end in itself.**
> **We will explore how you can use, analyse, think about, apply, and discuss the theories throughout this book.**

The way we will introduce the theories to you here is a 'cheap and cheerful' snapshot of the main ideas of the theory, following a rough chronological order. You may like to refer to the consolidated timeline in Figure 1.2 while you are looking at the brief descriptions set out here. If you like the look of the theory, you might like to read ahead to the chapter that contains the theory, to consider the ideas more fully.

Natural law

Natural law theory is the most ancient of all the theories we will be looking at in this book. With a 2 500 year history, its has had a considerable and nearly constant relationship with our law and legal system. The ideas of natural law have influenced Western thinking since the ancient Greeks and Romans, and the time of the early Christian church. The most influential natural law ideas we have inherited came from medieval church thinking, and its influence on law comes from a historical connection between the law, the state, and the church. Natural law provides guidance for the creation of the law from derived from God, using *reason* as the method to derive principles to guide the development of good law. Natural law is closely connected to what can be called 'morals', in this case meaning 'what is good'.

By the 19th century, natural law fell out of favour because of the effects of the 'Enlightenment'; you will see where this happened in 'the gap' in the timeline. Law became concerned with knowing that law was correctly and validly enacted and applied, through the theory known as legal positivism. After 150 years in abeyance, natural law re-emerged in the aftermath of World War Two. The most recent reinvigoration of natural law comes from John Finnis, a contemporary natural law theorist who has had a considerable influence on current ideas and responses to natural law thought.

You now might want to look at Chapter 3,
which deals with natural law theory.

CHAPTER 1

Modernism and liberalism

While they would play a major part in its eventual demise, the new ideas of the philosophy of modernism (and its twin political philosophy, liberalism) overlapped with natural law theory in the 16th–18th centuries. These new theories were instrumental in shaping the 'modern' world, replacing the old reliance on the irrational beliefs with rational, scientific, and observable findings. Observation, provability, and verification were key to this new way of thinking. This was most famously expressed through the ideas of the 17th century French philosopher, Descartes, 'I think therefore I am', meaning that proof of existence could only be sourced within or from the individual.

The new scientific method which resulted from these observations wanted verifiable 'facts': it could be proved that the earth now revolved around the sun, and not the other way around. Legal theories that could not 'pay up' in observable facts (like natural law) were dismissed as nonsense.

You now might want to look at Chapter 4, which deals with the theories of
modernism and the scientific method.

You might also want to look at the beginning of Chapter 6,
which deals with the ideas of the Enlightenment.

Even more profoundly, these ideas shook up the world politically. Kings had the divine right to rule directly from God, and men could be ruled, as subjects, without their having a say in the way they were governed. But in England in the 17th century, these beliefs began to be questioned: individuals now saw themselves as having the freedom to direct their own lives. They had unassailable rights, conceived of through the concept of 'property', which could not be interfered with by the sovereign or government without permission. The system of commerce, economics and capital that we now know arose in this climate, and shaped many of the fundamental assumptions we have about the way the world works.

What we have described here is liberal political theory. This political philosophy has profoundly influenced the law in all its respects, from the law affecting our interactions with the State, to our rights of property, and the assumptions of liberty and freedom underpinning our society. While many legal thinkers rely on liberal theory, we will focus on Ronald Dworkin, and his theories about law, judging and rights.

You now might want to look at Chapter 5, which deals with liberal theory.

Legal positivism

A specifically *legal* theory owes its origins to modernism and liberalism: legal positivism. Positivism, meaning 'placed down' or positioned, emerged at the beginning of the 19th century and continues to exert a strong hold on the legal mind at the beginning of the 21st century. Especially in the common law world, positivism's scientifically based, formularised explanation for law 'as it is' displaced natural law theory for nearly 200 years. In the 19th century, the London-based Jeremy Bentham and John Austin, the 'fathers' of positivism, were especially concerned to analyse law 'as it is'. They wanted to understand whether the law applied to us and our actions, and whether it was validly constituted and constructed. In Austin's version of positivism, which maintained its influence for common lawyers until the 1960s, law was only ever considered within its own boundaries, and never concerned itself with morals, society or other factors. (Bentham's version *did* consider these matters, though.)

You now might want to look at Chapter 6, which discusses the theories of early positivism.

While positivism is a very useful theory to *analyse* law, Austin's version was not good at providing explanations for, or accommodating changes in, the law. HLA Hart reinvigorated positivism in England in the 1960s by providing scope for legal change through the identification and explanation of the points in the legal system where change could be accommodated. His identification of the open texture of language explained how new interpretations of words could be accommodated by law, while his explanation of the system of rules showed how new law could be created through the legal system, through 'rules of change, adjudication, and recognition'.

You now might want to look at Chapter 7, which discusses the work of HLA Hart.

There are many other versions of legal positivism (which is sometimes also called 'analytical jurisprudence') in the common law world, which we won't be looking at in this book. However, we will touch on some developments in this area, and you will come across these ideas throughout your reading in Davies and Lloyd.

Legal conceptualism

While legal positivism relied on what can be observed and identified in a legal system, another type of modern thinking developed through European legal systems, derived from the philosophy of Immanuel Kant. Concerned with explaining how we understand and organise thought into categories, Kant's influence can be found in the work of Hans Kelsen, an Austrian legal thinker whose body of work covered over half a century from the 1930s until the publication of his final, posthumous work in 1991.

Kelsen sought to explain law through a *conceptual theory* of law. What this means is that he wanted us to understand the law *not* through what we could touch and see and feel, but instead to understand the system and structure within which it is located. Kelsen's theory, in very basic terms, tries to organise law into its own categories of thought, and to set out a framework that explains how the legal system works from its most basic level to its highest guiding principles. A conceptual system like Kelsen's is dependent on our having to accept structures without content, ideas without form and law without laws.

You now might want to look at Chapter 4, which deals with the theories of Kant and Kelsen.

Marx and law

We now drop back in time to England in the 19th century, where we encounter the theories of Karl Marx. Marx provided explanations for the relationship between law and economic and social forces. These observations were instrumental in fracturing the idea that law was not affected by these sorts of factors, an assumption deeply embedded in legal positivism. Marx's theories functioned as a springboard for a range of theorists in the 20th and 21st centuries, who took his ideas and developed them into a set of critical theories about law, its practices and effects on society and individuals in society.

There is another level at which we will look at Marx and his influence. As a 'modern' thinker, Marx created a 'big picture' theory, but one which broke down the idea that there could ever be one unified explanation for the way the world worked. His theories cleared a path for thinkers who were to more fundamentally disturb an image of the world cut from the clean template of modernism in the late 20th century: those who developed the theories of postmodernism and poststructuralism.

If you like, go to Chapter 8, which introduces you to Marx's theories and the flow-on effect of Marx's ideas to other theorists. These will be picked up again in Chapter 12.

Theories about law based in social thought

Alongside Marx, other forms of social thought were emerging in the 19th century in Europe, including the new science of sociology, through Ehrlich, Durkheim and Weber. New philosophies were emerging in the USA at the same time, especially pragmatism, which explained the 'can do' approach of a new powerhouse nation. It was in the USA, not Europe, in the latter part of the 19th century and the early 20th century, that a new set of legal theories based in 'social thought', started to emerge. In this early phase, 'sociological jurisprudence' was created by Roscoe Pound. A form of pragmatics influenced Justice Oliver Wendell Holmes, who influenced a new movement, the American Legal Realists, which was influential from the 1930s until the 1950s. It was only by the latter part of the 1960s that other parts of the common law world started to adopt an interest in 'sociology' or socio-legal research, especially in the UK.

Currently, it is virtually impossible to place fences or defined limits around these theories, which are incredibly diverse in their interests, methods and approaches. Sometimes they can become defined theories in their own right, like the offshoot of American Legal Realism, the now defunct 1970s Critical Legal Studies movement. Like a number of the contemporary theories we will look at, these theories should be seen as works in progress, which is a challenge in its own right – the idea that theories never close down means that you can never stop learning!

You now might want to look at Chapter 9, where you will find the main ideas of these theories set out, while contemporary versions are included in Chapter 12.

Insights for law from postmodernism

There is no 'one size fits all' explanation for the range of ideas and theories that fall under the umbrella of postmodernism, and its twin theory poststructuralism. However, as we have already suggested, these theories have unsettled established images of the world. For law, these theories are used in a number of ways: to uncover hidden histories that underlie rules and doctrines, to explore the contingent, unstructured way our law develops, and to uncover the differences between the law and justice. The techniques and methods used by these theories operate at another level, by throwing out challenges to the accepted practices of law, and overtly questioning the fundamental bases on which the law is structured.

You now might want to look at Chapter 10, where you will find out how postmodernism and poststructuralism have influenced law.

Feminist legal theories

Law, because of its basis in liberal thought, has always assumed that it treats everyone the same. Feminist legal theories have shown that this is not the case, and that law has historically been constructed from a 'male' standpoint. What these theories try and do is find out why this has happened, and set out strategies to change the law and its assumptions. Not all feminist legal theories are alike. Some simply argue for equality with men, so that women are treated the same as men by the law. Others argue that the fundamental basis on which society is constructed discards women's experience. Therefore, society needs to change, and law has to play a part in this change. Yet others argue for the vast array of women's experiences to be accommodated. These are only some of the feminist legal theories that have developed since the 1960s, all of which, along with feminists since the 18th century, have actively sought to practically change the way law and society approaches women and their experiences.

To find out more about these theories, go to Chapter 11, where we look at a range of the different types of feminist legal theory.

Critical Legal Studies

Some legal theories have their place in the sun and then disappear from the radar, as happened with the American Legal Realists. The movement known as Critical Legal Studies (CLS) had its own time of furious activity from the 1970s until its dissipation in the 1990s. The CLS theorists, also US-based, were known as the 'crits'. They sought to uncover the problems sourced in the 'liberal' foundation of law, or 'liberal legalism'. Chief in their sights was the gap between law's rhetoric — what it said it stood for — and its reality — what it actually did. Using methods like 'trashing', the crits uncovered law's hidden values, but using techniques of postmodernism and poststructuralism led to the eventual demise of CLS. Its proponents moved on, having opened up new theoretical horizons within other critical theories.

We look at the crits in Chapter 12.

Postcolonial legal theory and critical race theory

Law's liberal ideals are also questioned by other theories, including postcolonial legal theory and critical race theory. The liberal subject was allowed all the freedoms and rights society offered, but some people were denied this access because of their race, religion, or ethnic difference. At various times in history, law has been used to deny individuals or groups of their humanity, and in its most extreme form has led to slavery, genocide, and the denial of rights accorded to everyone else in society. We can see this in terms of the impact of law on indigenous Australians, laws against Jews in Nazi Germany, and the denial of civil and political rights to African Americans.

While a number of theories, including natural law, have tried to deal with these issues, postcolonial legal theory and critical race theory instead mark out a space for those previously denied access to law and the rights accorded to the rest of the community to speak, specifically indigenous Australians, indigenous people in colonised countries, and African Americans. Critical race theory (CRT) sprang out of the civil rights movements in the USA in the 1960s, and the Critical Legal Studies movement. CRT is specifically concerned with articulating the effects of law on people previously denied access to law's benefits. Postcolonial legal theory works at a more generalised level.

You can read more about this topic in Chapter 13.

Emerging legal theories

No, there is no school of legal theory called 'emerging' legal theories. What we want to do is alert you to the constantly changing nature of legal theory, and touch on some of these developments, including some theoretical dead-ends. Perhaps more important than obtaining knowledge about these theories is the idea that theory never stands still, and for you to know that the theory you learnt at law school will change and develop over time.

For more on this topic, go to Chapters 12 and 15.

Taking charge — reading theories texts

You will have noticed that we suggested that you read Davies Chapter 1, and Lloyds Chapters 1 and 2, but that we haven't told you what these chapters say! We think that you're the only ones who can tackle the ideas set out in these introductory chapters, which we hope you will read bearing in mind our own introductory guidance for you. However, we'll give you some clues to reading the chapters. Both Davies and Lloyd use their introductory chapters to set the scene for their books, and to mark out the scope of their own 'take' on legal theory. But as you will see, their approaches, though perhaps not their arguments, differ markedly.

Davies clearly tells us that her book operates as a postmodern critique of law and the methods of conventional legal theory. While traversing some of the mainstays of conventional legal theory, like 'what is law', she takes these ideas and turns them on their head, to draw attention to the gaps, assumptions, and inconsistencies found in these theories. What you won't get in this chapter is description, overview and explanation — what you get instead is methodology, argument, and deconstruction, the inside and outside of law. What you will have to do when reading her argument is to understand that it *is* an argument, deeply studded with references to theories, theorists, and non-legal philosophies. When you first start reading the chapter, don't try to acquire any knowledge, but try to immerse yourself in Davies' underlying argument, and come back again and again to the chapter throughout your studies of legal theory (just as we have suggested you return to the consolidated timeline in Figure 1.2).

An argument is also set out in the first two chapters of Lloyd, emphasising the relevance of jurisprudence — legal theory — for lawyers, and the need for lawyers to be aware of and alive to the influences of external factors in under-standing and considering law. Like Davies, Lloyd also makes extensive reference to the broad range of legal theory, and sets out the foundation for the structure of the book. Lloyd also considers the question 'what is law', and though seemingly taking a conventional legal theory approach to the question, also slips in a considerable amount of argument about the scope of the legal enter-prise. Unlike Davies, the argument is in the third, not the first, person and may be difficult to spot if you are not used to finding arguments written in this way. As a 'casebook', Lloyd also includes detailed extracts of texts for you to dip into, so that you can read the arguments from the authors themselves, and not only how someone else explains what they are saying (as we are doing here; our brief overview cannot take the place of reading the originals).

Though Lloyd is written in a vastly different style from Davies, you may be surprised to find that one or two of their arguments are not so far removed from each other, and you might like to see where they have the same views. To get there, though, you will have to uncover the differences in their arguments and methods, and why they have taken such different paths to get to *some* similar conclusions. Your task may not always be clear — Freeman has been involved with, co-edited and edited Lloyd since the 1970s, and Lord Lloyd died early in the 1990s. It seems that the two early chapters in the current 7th edition of this book have not been changed for many years (the book itself has been in publication since 1959), and you may want to ask yourself: does a later, different writer or editor change the flavour, argument and content of a book like this, and does it matter, in any event?

We will take up these questions, and more,
in the next chapter of this book.

QUESTIONS TO THINK ABOUT

Yes, this is the world of legal theory where you get all the questions and none of the answers. This is not because we want to be difficult, but because we can't provide you with an answer to these questions! That's because there are many answers, arguments and ideas in legal theory, rather than one, perfect answer to a set body of knowledge. So, think about these questions as the start, and not the finish (and in any case, we are only at the beginning of the book).

1. What is legal theory?

2. Can you think of any examples of law's secret language?

3. What are the differences between conventional and non-conventional legal theory?

4. If you have decided you agree with a particular theory, what are your reasons or arguments for taking this standpoint? Think about how you would try to convince another person that your view is right.

5. Following on from the last question, how would you go about justifying your views in the face of criticism?

6. Why do you think Davies and Lloyd are so concerned with explaining where they see the boundaries of legal theory?

7. What do Davies and Lloyd say that 'law' is? Why do you think they look at theories outside law, like Lloyd's use the 'language' theories of Wittgenstein, and Davies' reliance on poststructuralism, to consider these questions?

8. Why do you think different people gravitate to one type of theory in preference to another?

9. Why do so many legal theories exist, and why are they continually changing?

10. How can legal theory influence the development of the law?

FURTHER READING

Bix, Brian, *Jurisprudence: Theory and Context*, 2nd ed (Sweet & Maxwell, London, 1999).

Davies, H & Holdcroft, D, *Jurisprudence: Texts and Commentary* (Butterworths, London, 1991).

Dias, RMW, *Jurisprudence*, 5th ed (Butterworths, London, 1985).

Cotterrell, Roger, *The Politics of Jurisprudence: A Critical Introduction to Legal Philosophy* (Butterworths, London, 1989).

Harris, JW, *Legal Philosophies*, 2nd edition (Butterworths, London, 1997).

Kelly, JM, *A short history of Western legal theory* (Clarendon Press, Oxford, 1992).

McCoubrey, H & White, N, *Textbook on Jurisprudence*, 2nd edition (Blackstone Press, London, 1993).

Morrison, Wayne, *Jurisprudence: from the Greeks to post-modernism* (Cavendish Press, London, 1997).

Riddall, JG, *Jurisprudence* (Butterworths, London, 1991).

Wacks, R, *Swot: Jurisprudence*, 5th edition (Blackstone Press, London, 1999).

CHAPTER 2

Learning Theory

Reading 25
Aim. 25
Principles 25
Starting out 25
The process of understanding. 29
Reading legal theory 38
Questions to think about 40
Further reading. 41

READING

There is no additional reading for this chapter.

AIM

This chapter will introduce you to:
- the challenges you will face when you start learning legal theory;
- the processes of understanding legal theory;
- the techniques of reading legal theory.

PRINCIPLES

Starting out

Levelling with you

Depending on your background, your interests, and your inclinations, you will have found Chapter 1:

☐ really difficult – can't you use normal words?

☐ patronising

☐ boring

☐ not related to reality

☐ a really interesting way into a topic that I thought had nothing to do with law

☐ Don't ask questions — give me the answer!

☐ None of the above — fill in your own response

_____

☐ Is this on the exam?

Introducing legal theory to law students is fraught with pitfalls and uncertainties — you are a diverse range of people with widely varying backgrounds. Some of you will have studied philosophy and political theory or other areas of the humanities at postgraduate level before starting your law studies; others of you will have combined law with courses like information technology, engineering or accountancy; others still will be doing law with humanities. Again, the point at which your law course introduces you to legal theory will vary — some of you will be in first year and be fresh to university level study, others will be studying this area later in your courses, and have a firm idea of what the law is, what you need to know and how to acquire that knowledge.

This chapter is written for those of you who are theory beginners, who are not quite sure how to read legal theory, how to understand it, how to write about it, and how to link it back to the rest of your law studies. We think theory beginners includes you if you are new to university study, or if you are later year law students who already know how to problem solve well, and are being introduced to legal theory at a later stage of your course. The type of course you are studying will influence your understanding of legal theory, so if you are also studying 'technical' courses, you may have had less exposure to these ideas than your peers. We have another aim in mind in this chapter — to give you some *insights about yourselves* so that you can find the best way into the different legal theories.

We will step back a few levels in this chapter from our starting point in Chapter 1, to give you some basics to help you engage with legal theory. While all of you are welcome to read this chapter, it will be apparent that it is not directed to those of you who are already well versed in the language, ideas and methods of theory, including those of you who have had theory integrated into your substantive law subjects. We appreciate that your needs differ from your peers, but you may find it helpful to work out how to adapt your under-lying abilities to the different interests of a specifically *legal* theory.

Reading

Reading legal theory for you will be:

☐ a breeze

☐ a challenge

☐ OK

☐ impossible

☐ a waste of time

☐ something in between any or all of the above.

One of the challenges you may face when studying legal theory is *why* theorists write and think the way they do. It can be utterly frustrating when you first start reading legal theory when you are confronted with words and ideas you don't understand, or you are left wondering why someone has written a *whole book* simply to develop an argument which they could say in one paragraph.

> We have to assume that all of you have acquired, or are in the process of acquiring, the skill of reading statutes, cases, and associated legal material. We assume you can find the *ratio* or *obiter* of cases (or are learning this technique), and that you have found new meanings for words you thought you understood in everyday parlance (language), like negligence or property. Law French and Law Latin are now familiar, or becoming familiar, to you: words and phrases like tort, consensus ad idem, res ipsa loquitur, and mens rea. You have acquired knowledge and understanding of new language and concepts during your law studies, through the processes of learning. What was strange, odd, challenging and new is now clear and obvious to you, though the first time you encountered these concepts they were meaningless.

Reading legal theory is no different:

- Just like when reading law, you will come across familiar words used differently, and a range of new, strange words that you have never encountered before. As you become used to reading legal theory, new and strange words will become familiar to you.

- Meanings of phrases, passages, or whole articles and books have to be understood, which is the same skill as understanding the meaning of a provision of a statute or the substance of a judgment. You will become adept at finding your way through the text of an article or book to find out what the theorist or theory is arguing, or to be able to find out the position they are adopting.

Unlike the sort of reading you do to acquire information (like the type of reading you need to do to read a shopping list or a set of summary notes), though, you will have to use a *different* reading skill to read legal theory: the skill of discerning or uncovering the argument, ideas and thoughts of the theorist or theory. A theorist will construct an argument using different legal theories or other forms of knowledge to support their standpoint or argument, and you will acquire the ability to find their argument. Even this skill shouldn't be strange to you, because a theorist's argument is nothing much other than the legal theory version of a *ratio* or *obiter*. A whole book or article can be compared to a judgment with its analysis of the facts, the law, the arguments of the different parties, and the analysis by the court of the different facets that lead to the conclusion reached.

The methods used by legal theory give us an insight into the arguments of the theorist. Understanding how a theory is constructed, which includes knowing the method used to establish the theory, tells us a lot about the validity of the theory, how well it stands up to critical examination, and how far it conforms to its own aims. Understanding these methods will also guide your own writing.

Just as with anything else, the more you practice reading to find out arguments, ideas and thoughts, the better you will be at it. If you are studying legal theory late in your course and have relied on lecture outlines and other people's notes, and have never read a case up until now, you have lost some important opportunities to develop your ability as a thoughtful, critical reader. You need this skill to understand legal theory, and you should treat this new challenge as an important part of your development as a lawyer.

We will spend more time later in this chapter talking about what you will be reading.

What do we mean by learning?

Learning legal theory means that I will:

☐ develop my own understanding of the theories through the tasks I set myself

☐ give up because it is too hard

☐ have to work hard and smart

☐ rote learn this book because it is easier than anything else I have to read

☐ get notes from my friends.

Learning is something *you* do. It isn't a passive activity where you ingest and memorise information from books or lectures, to be regurgitated later in an exam or assignment. Getting notes from your peers isn't learning either, because all you see is the end result of *their* process of learning, and you will have missed the *active* work they have done to turn raw material into their own notes.

Learning is an *active* process, where you take responsibility for acquiring knowledge about and comprehension of a topic — any topic — and then move on to higher level analytical understanding and appreciation of the topic. No one else can do this for you, because only *you* can find your own starting point into the topic, and then develop your knowledge and understanding from this entry point. Only you can make sense of it for yourself, whether the topic be cricket statistics, fashion, or legal theory. The people teaching you can give you the key to start this process for you, but it is only ever a starting point which you develop for yourself. No one else can learn for you.

This book may help you find your starting point, but we know that not all of it will make sense to you on a first read of a topic. We illustrated this process for you in the last chapter, where we suggested that the consolidated timelines will only make sense to you once you have undertaken your own developed reading and understanding of the theories.

We will talk about understanding and thinking about legal theory shortly.

What do we mean by writing?

Writing about legal theory means that I will:

☐ repeat all the theories I have learnt and not answer the question because I will still pass anyway

☐ answer the question I have been asked, supporting my argument using the theories I have learnt

☐ just write anything — something will stick

☐ copy out notes or lecture slides or the text of this book

☐ get an answer from another year and adapt it.

Up to this point we haven't said much about writing, though the words 'exam' and 'assignment' have been mentioned, both of which require you to write. Legal theory writing is usually essay or essay-type writing, in which you will have to set out a reasoned argument to answer a question or to support an assertion.

If you are used to writing essays, then you will know how to write to construct this type of reasoned and thoughtful argument. The way you write to solve legal problems is not the same as essay writing. If you don't know how to write essays then you may want to hide behind 'knowing' the theories and repeating your knowledge of them without thinking about why you are including them in your essay. If you write an answer like this, you would have written something like a judgment that only contains other people's descriptions of the law, with no analysis of how the case is decided.

> The method of 'I don't know much about this but if I write something down something will stick' doesn't work very well in legal theory, because the people reading what you write will be looking for your reasoned and thoughtful argument based on your knowledge and understanding of the legal theories.

On the flipside, you cannot just come up with your own ideas and write whatever you feel like, because you will be expected to place your ideas into the framework and pedigree of the theory. You can compare this type of writing to a judgment that does not refer to the law on which a decision is based — we would not accept its reasoning. You have to crawl before you can walk, and you have to *know and understand* the theories before you can begin to analyse or critique a theory. Writing outside the framework will leave a reader of your work wondering if you actually understand the topic, and your work will fail to meet the required standard needed to pass your exam or assignment.

> Writing is one way you express your arguments, ideas and thoughts. It is the other side of reading: writing gives you the chance to explain your *informed* ideas and arguments. Knowing this may help you understand why the people you are reading write the way they do!

The process of understanding

Understanding legal theory can be hard work

We cannot pretend that understanding legal theory is an easy task, unless you are a 'natural'. Nearly everyone has to work at reading, thinking, and writing about legal theory, even if you are an incredibly gifted thinker. But what might surprise you is that even the people teaching you will never finish this process of hard work: they will also have worked hard to acquire knowledge and understanding about the theories they teach you. No one is born with theory in their head, and the processes you are going through are no different from our own. We would never ever accept that our knowledge or comprehension of a theory or theorist is complete or perfect, because there is always something new to read into or see about a theory or a theorist. It is through this process of reading, thinking, analysing and critiquing that new insights into theories can be developed.

When you are new to legal theory, we want to assure you that you are not alone if the words on the page don't make immediate sense to you. Be reassured that you will need to make the effort to read and re-read a chapter, article, or book. You will be rewarded by returning to read the material again after a few weeks. You will be astonished to find that you understand the material easily, and that you will find your way into new topics easily.

Finding your best way to understand legal theory

What we have described here is a perfectly normal process of learning. However, the way we *approach* that learning is unique to us, and the summaries that help your best friend get excellent grades may be poison for your own learning. Knowing that your messy highlighting of text in different colours may be just right for you, and your friend's summaries just right for them, may help you on your way to understanding legal theory. Others of you will have to find your own way into learning theory.

All of us learn differently and respond to material presented to us in diverse ways. You might like to think about how you responded to the choices we gave you at the beginning of this chapter. If your response was 'just get on with it', this says a lot about who you are; the same goes if you thought 'I like having my brain teased — this is fun'. All of you learn differently and respond differently to different styles of teaching and learning. In writing this book, we have attempted to accommodate your preferred learning style, through a mix of different approaches to the topic, and through suggesting different starting points for you at the beginning of each chapter.

Even though we use a variety of different strategies and methods to acquire new knowledge and understanding, we tend to prefer one of four *main* styles of learning.[1] These styles can be described as being more like points on a continuum than strict categories. There is no right or wrong style for learning legal theory — but knowing your dominant style will help you find the best way to make sense of reading, writing and understanding legal theory.

So who are you? If you know the Harry Potter books, you will know that a magic hat gleaned information about the pupils before sorting them into their correct school house. Each of the four houses was populated by pupils whose dominant characteristics matched the house. We can't 'sort' you, because this is a book about legal theory, and we suggest you access specialist resources about learning styles if you want to find out more about your dominant style. What we will do is briefly outline some characteristics of different styles, to help you find out the best way into learning legal theory.

Don't think that knowing your dominant style will be the pathway to getting a perfect answer in an exam or assignment — it is just there to help you find out how you should best approach reading, writing and thinking about legal theory.

---

1 Atherton, JS, *Learning and Teaching: Learning from experience* [Online]: http://www.dmu.ac.uk/ ~jamesa/learning/experien.htm (2002), accessed 17 June 2003; Smith, Donna M and Kolb, David, *User's guide for the learning style inventory: a manual for teachers and trainers* (1986); Briggs-Myers, Isabel, *Introduction to type: a guide to understanding your results on the Myers-Briggs Type Indicator* (5th edition, c1993).

Style A: You like getting a single correct answer or solution

Is this you? You are most comfortable acquiring a set body of knowledge, obtaining information, and want to know the right answer.[2] When you learn legal theory, you will find yourself confronted with a range of different theories with completely different approaches within a theory. We think you will find some theories more easily digestible because they follow a formula, while other more 'argumentative' theories will be more of a challenge for you.

You will probably find it easiest to learn legal theory in bite-size segments, slowly and methodically acquiring knowledge of the theory, and feeling comfortable with that knowledge before coming back to think about some of the complexities of the theory. When you read a new chapter or article, we suggest that you keep asking yourself 'What is the main idea of this writer?', and not 'How much information am I meant to know?'. Try this out with Chapters 1 and 2 of Lloyd and Chapter 1 of Davies. Every time you find a clue about the idea, make a note for yourself, and see what you have by the end of the chapter or article. You should find you have set out a nice summary of the theory: to see the summary we have done of Lloyd and Davies, go back and have a look at pages 21–22 in Chapter 1.

> In terms of reading this book, if you are a Style A learner you will want to work through the detail of each part of each chapter rather than looking through the whole book first. In Chapter 3, you will probably find that you feel like looking at Section B before Section A.

Style B: You want to know 'why'

Is this you? You are most comfortable being creative and imaginative, and coming up with original ideas.[3] You may not be so good at the detail that underpins these ideas, and you are not practically oriented. When you learn legal theory, you will find yourself comfortable with the arguments and ideas used by the different theories, especially the more socially oriented theories. You will find the more abstract impersonal theories harder to engage with.

You will probably find it easiest to learn legal theory by dipping in and out of the theories, comparing them, and placing them into a bigger picture, and you probably love those highlighting pens and hate summaries. You will like the timelines we have given you, and you will refer to them from time to time. You will find it harder to pin yourself down with the detail of a theory, and we know that you will need to jump in and out of chapters, topics, and different writers. When you read a new chapter or article, we suggest that you keep asking yourself 'How does this argument fit into the rest of the theory, or how does it compare to another theoretical framework?', and use this as a basis for filling out the basic knowledge you need to acquire. Try this out with the different versions of natural law theory in Chapter 3 of this book, and see if you can set out a framework for understanding the theories.

---

2 Based on the Kolb classification 'assimilator'.
3 Based on the Kolb classification 'diverger'.

In terms of reading this book, if you are a Style B learner you will want to scan the whole book before looking at the detail of individual chapters. If you have a look at Chapter 3, you will find that you probably want to look at Section A before Section B.

Style C: You want to know how to apply the legal theory

Is this you? We're not talking here about the practicalities of 'applying law to facts', but the dominant learning style that finds it easiest to learn by relating what you learn to how it works or how you will use it.[4] Because of your practical bent, you may have already found the use of the word 'theory' off-putting – the word 'practical' makes sense, but 'theory' doesn't. You will need to make sense of how legal theory fits into the 'real world' and how you can 'use' it. That's not such a tough ask, because while legal theory can be treated in a purely theoretical frame of reference, it is also used in a practical sense. When you read a new chapter or article, we suggest that you keep asking yourself **'Where have I seen this idea in a case or legislative policy?'**, and not 'Is this on the exam?'. You should find yourself making the connections between theory and practice, and your outlines and summaries will be full of these thoughts. We have given you examples of the practical uses of theory in Chapter 1, and you will see examples throughout this book.

You will probably find it easiest to learn legal theory by first acquiring knowledge of the theories' uses in practice. This means you will find all types of theories useful, ranging from the most conventional to the most non-conventional theory, so long as you can see a use for them. Your main challenge will come from within the methods of theorists themselves: you may find it difficult to understand why method matters. We think that you will find it easier to work out why internal theoretical differences matter if you think about a theory as being like the rules of a sport – if the rules change, the game will change – and if the theory changes, the practice of the law will change.

In terms of reading this book, if you are a Style C learner you will want to work through the detail of each part of each chapter rather than looking through the whole book first. If you have a look at Chapter 3, you will find that you probably want to look at Section B before Section A.

Style D: I want to discover what legal theory is about

Is this you? You are happy to find your way through new material and ideas, and to take charge of your own learning.[5] You have to find your own connections between what you know already and how any new material fits into the framework within which you already work in. You like 'doing', and flying by the seat of your (intellectual) pants. When you learn legal theory, you will intuitively connect to what a theory is doing, but you will find the idea of following the logic of the theories, well, tedious.

You will probably find it easiest to learn legal theory by worrying about the detail later and getting the big picture first. You will have to know the detail though, because you can't use theory without knowing it to start with.

---

4 Based on the Kolb classification 'converger'.
5 Based on the Kolb classification 'accommodator'.

When you read a new chapter or article, we suggest that you keep asking yourself 'What can I do with this?'. Make the connections in a set of notes which repeats this question, or which takes a real example from your other law subjects and traces the theory through. Make that the basis for the acquisition of your knowledge. From this point, try and find a way of making sense of the different arguments of the theorists to see how you can use them differently. Talk your way through the theories with your peers, but you will also have to do some reading.

> In terms of reading this book, if you are a Style D learner you will want to scan the whole book before looking at the detail of individual chapters. If you have a look at Chapter 3, you will find that you probably want to look at Section A before Section B.

While you now have an insight into the best approach for you to learn legal theory, and know why your best friend's notes won't work for you, you have to remember that you still have to work hard to understand any new topic — you now know why some aspects of your reading and understanding will be more or less comfortable for you.

Blooming marvellous

One of the main challenges for your learning of legal theory is trying to work out what is expected of you, especially if you are learning legal theory later in your course and have spent most of your time solving problems rather than writing essays. We think a helpful way for you to understand what we expect of you can come from the idea of the *Blooming* Tree. The Blooming Tree (Figure 2.1) is our visual adaptation of educationalist Benjamin Bloom's categories of thinking skills.[6]

Bloom identified six different categories of thinking, which are inter-related and interdependent on each other, as we illustrate through the tree itself, where all parts are connected together. We think the categories will help you understand the processes you need to go through to develop your understanding of a topic. When you start reading legal theory, some of you will be analysing and synthesising while you read, while others of you will be knowledge based, and only then start moving up through the more complex modes of thought. The categories are:

- Knowledge
- Comprehension
- Application
- Analysis
- Synthesis
- Evaluation

---

6   Bloom, B, *Taxonomy of Educational objectives, Vol 1: The cognitive domain* (1956).

FIGURE 2.1: THE BLOOMING TREE

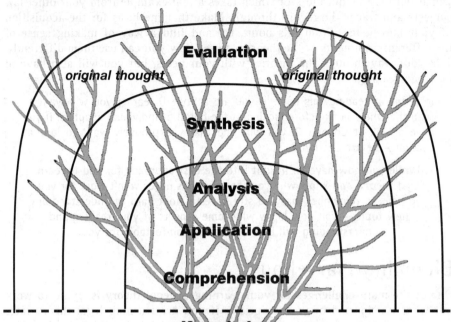

Evaluation

original thought   *original thought*

Synthesis

Analysis

Application

Comprehension

Knowledge

Description and comprehension is only part of the process

Some limited understanding of the knowledge underlying the theory

No connection between theory and analysis
Unsubstantiated assertion unrelated to theory
No basis for opinion, argument, or point of view, polemic

Knowledge

You will have noticed throughout this chapter that we have said that in legal theory you need to do more than acquiring knowledge or repeating that knowledge. *But you must also have knowledge of the legal theory*, its main ideas, who the theorists are and what they say. If you mixed up natural law with positivism, or Finnis with Foucault, then a reader of your work would be concerned that you did not know the theory you were learning. You can think of knowledge as being the tree trunk in Figure 2.1.

> For legal theory, treat your acquisition of knowledge as a basic building block for the rest of your learning.

Comprehension

Beyond this basic level, you need to show that you understand or comprehend the theories. When you comprehend a theory, you will show that you are able to draw out central ideas of a theory, or show how a theory might be adapted to different contexts, or to compare two different theories. You will have to show an understanding of the theory or theories to complete this task. You can think of comprehension as sitting in the lower branches of the tree in Figure 2.1.

> Your comprehension of a legal theory relies on your knowledge of the theory, but you will find yourself interconnecting both activities as part of your process of learning.

Application

You can apply the theories you are learning in a number of ways, whether it be in a 'practical' application or problem solving, or whether you have to reconceptualise a theory in a different setting. The ability to apply requires you to use your knowledge and comprehension skills and adjust to the expected use of the theory. You might be asked to use a theory to develop an argument in a difficult case, such as turning off life support. You will have to rely on the ideas you take from the theories and transform them to this situation. You can think of application as relying on the tree trunk and lower level branches of the tree, growing higher into the new branches of the tree in Figure 2.1.

> Your ability to apply a legal theory relies on your knowledge and comprehension of the theory, and you will use all of these facets to assist your understanding of a theory.

Analysis

An analysis of the theories requires you to demonstrate higher level thinking, which shows a deep understanding of the underlying ideas or connections that drive a theory and its method. You might be asked to analyse a theory to find any deficiencies in the theory, or you might be asked to analyse a body of law using a theory to uncover gaps or identify assumptions in the law. Your knowledge and comprehension of the theories will underscore your analysis – you cannot analyse without them. You can think of analysis as relying on the tree trunk and lower level branches of the tree, growing higher into the new branches of the tree in Figure 2.1.

> Your ability to analyse a legal theory relies on your knowledge and comprehension of the theory, and you will use all of these facets to assist your understanding of a theory.

Synthesis

The ability to synthesise means that you can draw from a variety of sources, make connections between different areas of knowledge, and start to create original thought based on an existing body of knowledge. Through this process, you will be able to construct an argument leading to a conclusion, or propose soundly argued proposals for change in a theory or the law. Examples might include drawing together justifications for and against the legal regulation of euthanasia based on competing theoretical arguments, or constructing a new interpretation of an existing theoretical insight, like Finnis did with St Thomas Aquinas (see Chapter 3). Synthesis relies on your ability to analyse, and cannot occur without a deep understanding of the theories. Synthesis grows from its base in the tree trunk and lower level branches of the tree, into the newer and higher branches of the tree in Figure 2.1.

Your ability to synthesise legal theory allows you to start to think originally and creatively about law and legal theory.

Evaluation

Evaluation draws on all your abilities. Through the process of evaluation, you will find yourself constructing original insights into a legal theory, undertaking an assessment of the validity and methodological soundness of a legal theory, and being able to discern how well an argument has been constructed. As you can imagine, you cannot do this without a full and well-developed understanding of the legal theory or theories under consideration, and again relying on the tree trunk and lower level branches of the tree, evaluation is found in the highest and newest branches of the tree in Figure 2.1.

Your ability to evaluate legal theory shows that you can think originally and insightfully about legal theory at all levels.

Falling out of the tree

Beneath the tree in Figure 2.1 is a basket with some branches in it. We felt we needed to show you what would happen if you did not meet the basic requirements we have shown you here. For instance, if you try to criticise a theory, which is an evaluative skill, without showing or using any knowledge or comprehension of the theory, then you will find yourself in the basket. You have tried to do something at a high level without having the basic tools at your disposal. You may want to do something like this if you think you know what the theory means, if you want to be 'original', or if you have decided that the theory is wrong, without having understood it first.

When we talked in Chapter 1 about 'opinion, invective or polemic, which may otherwise be called unsubstantiated grandstanding', we wanted to alert you to the problems that arise if you do not locate your work or ideas within the body of knowledge in which you are working. At a simpler level, if you do this, you will no longer have a connection with the tree trunk, if you ever did (the branches might have come from another tree).

The higher reaches of the tree

You can see that we have added the words 'original thought' at the top parts of the tree at Figure 2.1. When you write assignments or exams, you will be judged in terms of your overall abilities and the extent to which you demonstrate a connection with the question and the ideas that come out of the question. Original thinking is the mark of the highest level abilities in legal theory, and one which not all of us will be able to meet.

It is a mistake for you to try to be original and miss the basics.
Being original is not 'externally original' but relies on deep understanding and thinking, as we can see in Figure 2.2.

It is a challenge for us to know how to balance our description and explanation of a theory with the other tasks we need to perform in our writing, like analysis or evaluation. If your original ideas are grounded in the theory on which they are based, it should be apparent to the people reading your work. You may be able to reduce the description of a theory, so long as reference points are made which show us that you understand the basis for your ideas.

Putting Bloom into practice

Let's look at how you can shift thought processes from a basis in knowledge to a high level form of evaluation. Have a look at Figure 2.2, using the British monarchy as a topic.

FIGURE 2.2

	What you know or can do	What is the effect?
Knowledge	You will know the names and dates of all the monarchs, and all the important events that occurred during their reign.	You can enter a trivia quiz.
Comprehension	You can extract the main features that characterised the reign of a monarch, or compare the effects of different reigns on the country.	You can set the scene for further work in the area.
Application	You can structure recommendations for the continued functioning of the British monarchy for the 21st century based on your knowledge and understanding of the monarchy and its effects on the country.	You can see the connections between the base knowledge and what you can do with it.
Analysis	You can consider the underlying impact of the monarchy on the social fabric of Britain, by critically appraising its development from its feudal origins, and its ongoing changes in light of political development, especially since the 18th century with the emergence of constitutional monarchy and the demise of the divine right of kings.	You can take a core body of knowledge, and look beyond the surface to provide insights into the operation of a political and legal system.
Synthesis	You will draw on a range of materials from differing sources, including theory, politics and law, to understand the relationship between the monarchy and the emerging rights of individuals in a post-Enlightenment Britain.	You can adapt your understanding of the topic to find new insights into the development of law at a critical stage in history — this is original thinking.
Evaluation	You will be able to consider the future role for the monarchy and its relationship to the political and legal institutions in a post-Europe Britain.	You have broadened out the knowledge in the field to set out a thesis or new argument based on the pedigree of knowledge that has gone before you.

This, of course, is only one reading or set of ideas that can spin out from a topic like this. In your reading of legal theory, you will encounter multiple readings and interpretations of a single theory, and criticisms and critiques of that theory. How well you read, interpret and understand legal theory will open doors for you not only as a legal theory student, but will also assist you in the critical thought processes that are the hallmarks of a clear-thinking and innovative legal practitioner.

Reading legal theory

Reading non-legal material: inside law's way of thinking

One of the challenges you will face when reading legal theory is that you will find yourselves reading all sorts of new types of material with which you are not familiar. We suggested some strategies above (pp 26–28) to you to help you understand how to adapt your reading skills to read legal theory, but thought we would devote a separate section to explain to you *why* you will be expected to read this material.

> As you will have seen from the consolidated timeline in the last chapter (Figure 1.2), for centuries law has existed alongside, and been dependent on, ideas that have come from outside law itself. At various stages in history, perhaps typified by the medieval period, law, the monarch, and the church were virtually one and the same, and law was not a separate entity apart from those influences. It drew upon the learning and ideas that came outside law. You may be familiar with the close connection between the church and equity, which illustrates the relationship well. Through these connections, philosophy and religion came to be embedded into legal thinking, to the extent that they have almost become part of law itself, like natural law, which is intricately woven into the fabric of law through centuries of judging and legislation.

For this reason, reading and understanding this conventional legal theory has become part of the accepted training for lawyers, so that you can acquire law's hidden language and become part of the community of lawyers. *But it does mean that you will have to read material outside law's standard framework*: the Ancient Greek and Roman philosophers who influenced natural law, and Catholic saints like St Thomas Aquinas. You will become familiar with the political philosophers of the 16th and 17th centuries, whose ideas have become intertwined with law. You will be reading translations of these works, or the fragments and reconstructions of them, and will need to understand how to work out how whole theories were constructed from a very small body of material. You will find yourself reading 'olde' English, which you will have to try to understand, but more importantly, you will need to immerse yourself in the ideas and thoughts of the people you are writing about. The techniques we have suggested to you throughout this chapter will help you in this task.

You will also be reading English lawyers of the 19th century, like the reformer Bentham, a social theorist as well as the creator of legal positivism, and John Austin, professor of jurisprudence at London University, who took Bentham's ideas and reconstructed them into a form that remained popular until the 1960s. To read this material, you will be faced with an 'old-fashioned' form of English, very similar to the type of writing you will have read from late 18th and early 19th century cases. You will find it helpful to work out why the positivists were trying to explain law as an entity in its own right, compared to the theorists that preceded them, and why at this stage of history, legal theory became the sole preserve of lawyers. However, by the mid-1960s, even positivists such as Hart began to think about the external influences on law, and you will have to read to understand why he shifted the ground from the positivism derived from Austin. In reading this material, you will encounter *lawyers* who write within a legal framework, but who have picked up ideas from outside law, and you will be faced with the challenge of reading to understand and comprehend *how* their theories work, but also why and how they relied on *ideas from outside law*.

Reading non-legal material: outside law's way of thinking

Other theories you will read will seem, without further reflection, to have no connection with lawyer's methods and mindsets at all, but are clearly concerned with ideas *about* law. A little after positivism took over legal thought in the early 19th century, a range of new ideas about law, and the society in which it functioned, began to emerge from the theories of Karl Marx, who, coincidentally, was also trained as a lawyer. Marx's theories opened the path for a broad range of social thought, which looked at law from the outside. However, a number of *American lawyers* of the early and mid 20th century took up these theories, to give them guidance in their quest to improve the way the law worked. These new ideas brought a wider range of ideas back into law, and broke down the isolationist model of law that had been the legacy of 'Austinian' positivism (from John Austin). You should be prompted to ask yourself: why did these lawyers look outside law in the first place, and how did they understand these theories enough to adapt them to their own ideas? If you can't make the connections, then go back to 'The process of understanding' above (pp 29–33).

You will meet some new challenges when reading these theories. When you read Marx, you will find yourself drawn into his new way of looking at the world, the world of the production of goods and the impact on society, and law's role in supporting the capitalist system. That's one hurdle. But you will also find yourself reading theorists who have drawn strands of ideas from Marx and developed new interpretations of his theories, specifically dealing with law. Later theories, like the Critical Legal Studies movement, built on a range of theories, all of which drew on the insights that originated from Marx. Reading the range of critical, non-conventional theories will take you into a completely new form of thinking, which differs markedly from the ideas with which you are familiar from law. You will have to immerse yourself in a new set of ideas and language, which will be hard to start with; with ongoing work, you will find out more about the theories, and their relationship with the law.

Reading something for the first time

What do you do if you don't understand something, like a new word, or a whole paragraph? We think you can do a few things to help yourself, but the best method for you will match up to your dominant learning style:

Words

Check a standard dictionary or the meanings we've explained in this book. You can also make some sense of new words by reading ahead and building your understanding from the context of the sentence.

Sentences

Try scanning over the next few sentences or paragraph to see if the writer explains their ideas further. Sometimes a sentence will not be clearly expressed, and it is not your fault if you can't understand it. Read ahead, return to it later, and you might find that it makes sense after all.

Paragraphs

If a paragraph is not making sense, then you might want to spend some time asking why the theorist is including it as part of their argument or development of their ideas in their book. You may be reading it the wrong way — if is part of the development of an idea and you are trying to find information in it, then you will probably be lost. Try stepping out of the paragraph and coming back to it after reading a page or so further.

A whole section, an article, or a chapter

Try returning to the beginning of the chapter or article to see what the writer is telling you there. You might want to make connections to the writer's theoretical school of thought and make comparisons between your existing knowledge and the new idea. You may be blocking out their argument because you have 'locked down' your own reading of the topic, or have a preconceived idea about the theory itself.

If this doesn't work, the theory may be very difficult and you will have to read an explanation first, and then return to the text. We suggest you don't jump into more complex reading as your first port of call, but work up to this kind of reading.

Reading the original

We made the last point to you because, as well as reading this book, Davies' arguments and/or Lloyd's commentaries, you will also be reading original material, or the words of the theorists themselves. You need to do this because another person's explanations of a theory or theorist can never be the same as reading the original material itself. So after reading an explanation, you should always look at the original, and try to read it from your standpoint, bearing in mind that the text itself is always mediated by any knowledge or understanding you bring to the reading. If you read in this way, you will find yourself using the different categories of Bloom to help you understand the text, and your thought processes will assist you on the way to a highly developed understanding of legal theory.

Now, go back and re-read Chapter 1.

QUESTIONS TO THINK ABOUT

Rather than ask you a set of specific questions, we thought you would like to think about the way you would approach the following scenarios, based on your new understanding of Bloom and your learning style, along with the material you read in Chapter 1. You will also find it helpful, when thinking about your responses to these questions, to discuss these ideas with a peer or with a group of your peers, to see how well you can support your own understanding. Try to construct an explanation for each of your answers, which will demonstrate the level of understanding you bring to the question.

1. Imagine starting a new society: would law come first or second?

2. What should the law in that new society deal with?

3. Should the law guide society or should society guide law?

4. Think about changing an existing society: should this be done through law or through society? Why?

5. What role should the law take in developing a new society?

6. How do lawyers respond to changes in the law driven by societal change? Do we just apply the law without thinking about the consequences?

7. Think about changing an existing legal system. What should be the source of that change — law or society?

8. Think about changing a precedent or how the law deals with a novel case. What factors do lawyers bring to bear when dealing with changes in society?

9. What role does legal theory play in these situations?

10. Rethink your answers to the questions at the end of Chapter 1.

FURTHER READING

Atherton, JS, *Learning and Teaching: Learning from experience* [Online]: http://www.dmu.ac.uk/~jamesa/learning/experien.htm (2002), accessed 17 June 2003.

Bloom, Benjamin S et al (eds), *Taxonomy of educational objectives: the classification of educational goals, Volume 1: The cognitive domain* (Longman Group, London, c1956).

Briggs-Myers, Isabel with Peter B Myers, *Gifts differing: understanding personality type* (Consulting Psychologists Press, Palo Alto, California, c1995).

Briggs-Myers, Isabel, *Introduction to type: a guide to understanding your results on the Myers-Briggs Type Indicator*, 5th edition, revised by Linda K Kirby & Katharine D Myers (Consulting Psychologists Press, Palo Alto, California, c1993).

Smith, Donna M & Kolb, David, *User's guide for the learning style inventory: a manual for teachers and trainers* (McBer and Company, Boston, 1986).

Wacks, R, *Swot: Jurisprudence*, 5th edition (Blackstone Press, London, 1999).

CHAPTER 3

Natural Law Theories: Speaking to the Sky or Looking in Ourselves?

Reading	43
Aim	44
Introducing natural law theories	44
What are natural law theories?	44
Natural law method	49
Natural law theories	53
Back to the beginning – Ancient Greece and Rome	53
Connecting society to law in medieval Europe	57
Natural rights – the natural law of persons, property and promises	61
Mind the gap	66
Rekindling natural law – Fuller's secular natural law	67
Justifying posited law – HLA Hart's minimum content of natural law	71
Reviving Aquinas – John Finnis' conception of natural law	72
Critical responses to natural law theories	80
Questions to think about	80
Further reading	81

READING

DAVIES, *Asking the Law Question: the Dissolution of Legal Theory*, 2nd edition, Chapter 3 (pp 67–90, 108–112)
FREEMAN, *Lloyd's Introduction to Jurisprudence*, 7th edition, Chapter 3

AIM

This chapter will introduce you to:

- the main ideas and themes of natural law theory;
- the ways that natural law is used by lawyers;
- the methods used by natural law theory and theorists;
- the influential natural law theories from the Ancient Greeks to John Finnis.

This chapter is set out in two sections. It is a little like two separate chapters in one. Section A will introduce you to the ideas underlying and informing natural law theories. Section B will provide you with an overview of a number of influential natural law theories. It is up to you how you choose to read through this chapter — some of you may want to look at the content of Section B and then read through Section A, while others of you will follow the order of the chapter.

We will set out the assumptions of these theories, or the claims made on their behalf, on their own terms. We will leave criticisms and critiques of the theories to the end of this chapter, and to your reading of Davies and Lloyd.

Before you start to work through this chapter, please re-read pages 8–17 in Chapter 1.

SECTION A: INTRODUCING NATURAL LAW THEORIES

What are natural law theories?

Where does law come from? This seems like such an easy question, with such an easy answer. Law is what the legislature says it is, or judges say it is, and we can find what it says by looking at statutes and decisions of the courts. But is the answer that easy? When you start to think about it, the law that we can find and apply so easily has actually been guided by some underlying philosophy, and for much of the history of Western legal systems, the guide has been *natural law theory*.

It is possible to trace the principles that hover around criminal law, tort law, and principles of property law to natural law foundations. More recently, natural law theories turn up, whether identified or not, in situations where 'moral' dilemmas have to be solved, such as euthanasia or abortion law.

THE CLAIMS OF NATURAL LAW

Natural law theory is based on unchanging guiding principles, including those which come from God, which are discovered by reason, to which human laws are expected to conform. Natural law theory therefore guides how human law should be created and interpreted. Natural law is not a theory about nature — we will come back to this point a little later.

It has been said that natural law is the place where law and morals intersect,[1] so what does this mean? Natural law is a structure used to create law that conforms to notions of *good*, *morality* or *ethics*. When you read about natural law, you will see lots of references to 'morals' or morality. The word is not used in this context in its day-to-day meaning, but is more broadly focused. It is concerned with right and wrong, good and evil, duty, responsibility, obligations, and virtuous behaviour.

Natural law themes

Let's now set out a few questions to help us identify *some* of the themes of natural law, which can be found in various forms through different natural law theories:

- *What is law's relationship to individuals and communities?* Natural law says that law does not exist in isolation, but relates to or connects with a society and the needs of that society.[2] Natural law provides a set of guiding principles, ethics or 'morals' for the law.

- *But where do we draw the line between my desire for a law to benefit me, and the way it may impact on other people in the community?* This question draws out another issue that turns up in natural law theories — that the needs of a society may override a personal desire of an individual in certain situations.[3] However, some natural law theories do not accept that people's fundamental human rights should be devalued.[4]

- *But what if that law is a bad law?* Some natural law theories say that it would be wrong for us to disobey such a law, if such disobedience would adversely affect the community.[5] Other natural law theories do not tolerate bad law, and require concepts of 'right' or 'good' to overcome a bad law.[6] Some natural law theories say all of us have natural rights which cannot be taken away from us.[7]

- *What is the role of the legislature and the courts?* The day-to-day face of natural law is known as *human (or posited) law*. Natural law theory says that when natural law guides human law, that human law will be *good* law.[8] Some natural law theories provide guidance for the legislature and the courts to assist with the creation or interpretation of human law.[9]

These are some (but not all) of the questions that natural law theories pose and try to answer, to make the *best law* for us as individuals and society.

The subject matter of natural law

One of the things we have not discussed with you yet is the *subject matter* of natural law theories. In Section B of this chapter, we will look at natural law

CHAPTER 3

---

1   D'Entrèves, in R. Wacks, *Swot: Jurisprudence* (5th ed, 1987), p 99.
2   Based in Aristotle (pp 53–56), Finnis (pp 72–79), Fuller (pp 67–70).
3   Based in Aquinas (pp 57–61), Hobbes (pp 62–63), Hart (pp 71–72), Finnis (pp 72–79).
4   Based on Fuller (pp 67–70), theories of natural rights (pp 62–67).
5   Based on Finnis.
6   Based on Fuller.
7   Fuller, theories of natural rights.
8   Based on Aquinas and Finnis.
9   Based on Finnis.

theories by topic, in chronological order (see Figure 3.1). Before we move on, we thought you might find it helpful to see some ways that natural law theories connect to the law you will have learnt at law school:

- Natural law theories are used to ensure that good human law is made so that an individual, community or state will flourish, as seen through Aristotle, Cicero, Aquinas and Finnis.

- Natural law theories have been used to support and maintain the basic principles of the legal system, by providing a way of explaining the need for the protection of 'persons, property and promises'. We will look at these ideas through Hobbes, Locke, Hart and Finnis.

- Natural law has mutated into a notion of natural rights to protect fundamental human rights (we won't be exploring this topic, but we thought you should be aware of the connection).

As you can see, the *subject matter* and *themes* of natural law theories overlap.

Do natural law theories have a standpoint?

Natural law theories are the most ancient of all the Western-based legal theories, with a history stretching back over 2 500 years, as we can see in Figure 3.1. Except for a short 150–200 year period in the 19th and 20th centuries, these theories have exerted an ongoing influence on the legal landscape, especially up until the end of the 18th century. Because they have been around for such a long time, they have become part and parcel of how we think in law, which makes it more difficult to stand back from them and ask questions about what they stand for. As we will see in this chapter, a number of claims are made by or about natural law theories, in support of their legitimacy, validity, usefulness and correctness.

It needs to be remembered that these theories cannot be dissociated from their contexts and circumstances, even though they claim to be timeless, universal, and unchanging. They have supported: slavery, the denial of civil and political rights to women, and the denunciation of groups of people who do not conform in some way because of their sexuality, their religion, or racial backgrounds. Many natural law theories can be characterised as being politically, religiously and socially conservative. Margaret Davies uses the example of the anti-contraception stance of the Catholic Church, based on natural law edicts sanctifying life, which ignores the practical effects of overpopulation.[10] On the other hand, some natural law theories have been used to support revolutionary ideas like parliamentary democracy, and the French and American revolutions.

But the colourful idea that natural law is at the disposal of everyone, 'like a harlot',[11] perhaps sums up the idea that natural law can be used to support any standpoint at all. At the end of this chapter, we will spend a little time considering the range of critiques of natural law theories.

---

10 Davies, M, *Asking the Law Question: The Dissolution of Legal Theory* (2nd ed, 2002), p 77.
11 Alf Ross in Wacks, op cit, p 100.

FIGURE 3.1 NATURAL LAW TIMELINE

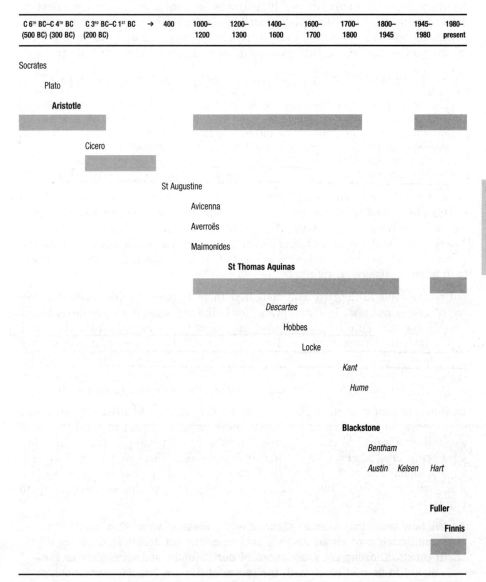

This timeline pulls out the natural law components of the detailed timeline set out in Chapter One. We have juxtaposed natural law with positivism and marked the theories we will consider in detail in this or later chapters: **Natural Law**, *Modernism and Positivism*.

Using natural law

How do lawyers use natural law theory? In 2000, Northern Territory judges were bound to impose prison sentences for certain property offences. The judge was not free to exercise discretion in the case. The laws caused considerable disquiet, and were eventually repealed after a change of government. While they were still in effect, Michael Maurice QC, a former Justice of the Northern Territory Supreme Court (in the 1980s), was so concerned about the effect of the laws that he stated that if he had had to apply them as a member of the bench, he would have been forced to resign, because 'Those laws, in my view, are so profoundly unjust that as a point of conscience, I couldn't do it.[12]

SO WHERE DID HE GET THESE WORDS FROM?

The notion of an 'unjust law' and of 'conscience' was not simply his own justification as to why he could not apply the laws. Let's trace their source. Michael Maurice was referencing 1000 years of natural law theory, from Saint Augustine to St Thomas Aquinas and more recently John Finnis. (You might like to check the timeline in Figure 3.1 to situate these theorists.) St Augustine had said 'there is no law unless it be just', while Aquinas said that if human law varies from the natural law 'it is a corruption of law'.[13]

Let's take this one step further. What are the consequences for a judge placed in this position? Can she or he simply say that the law is unjust and not apply it? Let's see what Finnis says. On a surface reading of Finnis, it may seem permissible for the courts to read down a human law which does not conform to the natural law, because Finnis suggests that that human law has to conform to fundamental human rights.[14]

 But as we read further, we will find that there is more to this reading of 'an unjust law is not law'. In Finnis' view, an individual cannot simply disregard or disobey the law. Finnis tells us that if an unjust law is important for the fabric of the laws of a community, an individual or official of the legal system may have to obey the law, even if they are 'diminished' morally by having to do so. In effect, it would harm the entire legal system if the law were disobeyed. Instead, the ruler who made the bad or unjust law would be bound to correct it.[15]

So from the simple starting point, where we saw Michael Maurice rely on words of a theory, we have moved into some more complex aspect of legal theory. If we follow Finnis, Michael Maurice would have to apply the mandatory sentencing law, however unjust it may be. As an official of the legal system, he would have been bound to conform to the law so that the legal system would not be brought into disrepute. However, the government, according to Finnis, was obliged to fix the law.

We now know that Michael Maurice was expressing views that have a long tradition, but which are also the subject of current debate amongst legal theorists. Knowing the foundations of our thoughts and ideas gives us the ability to keep in touch with the source of our law and its assumptions.

You may have found it hard to make the connections we have set out here. This is absolutely normal — it is very difficult for anyone to grasp new concepts without a background understanding of a topic. As we said to you in the last chapter, you will often have to read things a few times over to start to make the connections yourself. So, you will probably want to come back and look at this discussion again after you

---

12 'Justice continues to divide Northern Territory', The 7.30 Report, ABC Television, 24 February 2000, http://www.abc.net.au/7.30/stories/s103127.htm
13 Freeman, Lloyd's Introduction to Jurisprudence (7th ed, 2001), p 146.
14 Ibid, pp 182−184.
15 Ibid, pp 185−191.

have spent some time working through this chapter and undertaken your readings of natural law. You will find that you will be able to see some of the connections set out here, and if you return to this chapter in a few weeks time, you will surprise yourself with how easy this will be.

Natural law method

All legal theorists use *methods* to guide their thought processes, as we explained in Chapter 2. As we have seen from the discussion of the themes, not all natural law theories are the same and one reason they differ is that they use different *methods* to explain how they reached their conclusions. One way of understanding what we mean by *methods* is to think of them a little like a formula or recipe. One method will lead you in one direction, while another will point you down another path.

Why do we need to find out what methods a theorist uses?

If we know the basis on which a theory is constructed, we will better understand what it is trying to do. If we understand a theorist's *method*, we will understand what she or he is arguing. If you go on to write about, criticise, or use a theory to support your standpoint on an issue, you can only do so effectively if you know where the theory is 'coming from':

- We should understand the basis on which a theory is established, so that we know where the theory is coming from, and can understand the basis on which others have criticised the theory and its approaches.

  Aristotle, for instance, observed the state of nature to draw conclusions about how communities should live, be governed, and be subjected to law. A 'modern', rational Enlightenment theorist like Hume criticised natural law because you cannot observe nature and then say what law ought to be. He examined the claims of the theory and only then worked out how to criticise it. (You will look at Hume's problem of deriving an 'ought' from an 'is' in the next chapter and in Chapter 6.)

- Later theorists can then find a way out of a 'methodological' problem by taking on the criticisms, to strengthen and support a natural law theory that answers the criticisms. A theorist will also want to justify or support their argument to show why their theory, or interpretation of a theory, is correct.

  When Finnis published his major work on natural law in 1980, he sought to show that the criticisms like Hume's could be overcome. His new method says that <u>self-evident human goods are the source</u>, in part, of his natural law theory. Because these goods are self-evident, they do not have to be supported or proved, which gets around the problem of deriving an 'ought' from an 'is'.[16] However, other theorists do not accept that Finnis' 'self-evidence' method is correct,[17] and so new interpretations of the theory will follow.

---

16 Davies, op cit, p 80.
17 Ibid, p 84.

- If we are to critique or criticise a theory, we should only do so if we understand what the theory is saying, and we need to understand the method used by the theorist before we can engage in that critique or criticism.

  Margaret Davies' discussion of Finnis is structured as an argument against Finnis' entire theory: its content, its assumptions, and its method. Her criticism is directed against his claims of universality, his use of the concept of reason (which we will come to shortly), and his world view. Along with other theorists, she takes Finnis to task, but she does so having shown an understanding and appreciation of his views as the springboard for her own arguments.[18] You too will need to show that you understand a theory before launching into an argument for or against it.

The methodological basis of this theory: what is natural about natural law?

You have probably been wondering what makes natural law theory 'natural', but may have worked out that it is not the 'natural' world or the law of the jungle, nor what we colloquially think of as being 'natural' as opposed to being 'artificial'. Instead, natural law is a *system or a structure* which enables us to derive forms of law based in observations about human nature, which we have used as the title of this chapter: *speaking to the sky or looking in ourselves*.

1. **Structures and systems derived from** 'SPEAKING TO THE SKY':

   - Some natural law theories observe the processes that occur in nature to explain the development of society, which we will see in Aristotle and Cicero. These theories also use the process of 'reason' or rational methods to understand what will constitute the guiding principles of natural law. The guidance provided by these theories will be used by those responsible for running the community, and cannot be used by individuals.

   - Religion-based natural law theories use a deity as the basis on which natural law is constructed. Natural law then guides the creation of the human law we use day-to-day. The theories also employ reason, as we will see through St Thomas Aquinas. The guidance provided by these theories is meant for the ruler of the community, and cannot be used by individuals.

   - Natural rights theories created by Hobbes and Locke presume the existence of a deity, from which our natural rights are given. These theories were part of a new political movement which emerged in the 16th and 17th centuries. Individuals argued that they were now free from arbitrary actions of the monarch, and would only give up their rights under the *social contract* in return for some benefit, such as the protection of their property or their rights. You will meet these ideas again in the next four chapters.

2. **Structures and systems derived from** 'LOOKING IN OURSELVES':

   - While 20th century natural law theories rely on the heritage of natural law method, they use methods designed to appeal to a legal world brought up on legal positivism and the rational approaches of modernism.

---

18 Ibid, pp 79–86.

- Fuller's use of a form of 'proceduralism' as the basis for his natural law, and Finnis' use of 'self-evidence' are designed to make natural law work in a legal environment dominated by the methods of legal positivism. Hart's minimum content of natural law looks within the legal system itself. By 'looking in ourselves' they find a way to get around the criticisms of positivism (which we talked about under 'Natural law themes' on page 45), or ways to work and co-exist alongside positivism.

- These theories employ 'reason' to determine what constitutes natural law. They also use reason to show how the theories are useful for real world law, and how they can be used by lawyers, the legislature and the judiciary in framing arguments, policy and judgments.

Keeping your distance

You will have to keep in mind that natural law theory is a structure and system, which is effectively designed to provide governments and courts with a set of guiding principles for the creation of good law for the community. We will see shortly how the structures established by Aristotle and St Thomas Aquinas did not allow for a personal response to a deity. We sound a particular word of caution here — while some natural law theories are based in religion, they do not function as a way for individuals to construct their own 'natural law'. You should be conscious that an individual's personal ideas of what is or is not 'natural' are not part of the structure or system of natural law theory.

Another way of explaining the structure of natural law as we have inherited it is to build on Margaret Davies' use of Sophocles' Greek tragedy *Antigone*.[19] Davies is using the example of Antigone to explain the differences and inter-relationships between non-human and human law. We will use this example for a different purpose: to illustrate the difference between natural law and personal responses to the gods. Creon, the ruler, is empowered to make posited law, which should conform to the natural law. Antigone argues that his edicts against the burial of her brother do not conform to the natural law. But the systems we will see shortly do not permit an individual to conceive of the natural law,[20] so Antigone's plea to the gods is not 'natural law' but prayer. She should obey Creon's law for the good of the community in the natural law system, however unjust the law is.[21] It is up to Creon to fix up his posited law to ensure it conforms to the natural law.

Reading and writing about natural law theories

While you should be aware of the structures of these theories, you should not think that you should shy away from a critical or appreciative reading of them. Some of you will respond to these theories optimistically, and will be heartened by the idea that the law we apply day-to-day comes from a foundation of goodness or good intentions. At the other end of the spectrum, others of you

---

19 Ibid, pp 68–71.
20 Lloyd, pp 142–143 (Aquinas — who has the right to promulgate law).
21 Ibid, p 146 (Aquinas — the subordination of human laws to the natural law).

will think the structures of natural law are simply a smokescreen to conceal an oppressive legal system under the guise of goodness. Whatever standpoint you take, though, you will have to show a good understanding of the theories before you support or criticise them.

Your starting point, as with all of the theories you will study, will be your reading. In the rest of this chapter, we will give you some ways into the reading of natural law theories, but think of our treatment of the theories like a 'guidebook' to a city you are visiting for the first time. The guidebook will give you some information about where to go, how much things will cost, what the place looks like. But it can only give you so much information, and can only give you some ideas about what the city is like. You are the only one who can fill in the details while you are in the city, and you will create your own impressions, find out why you disagreed with the views expressed in the guidebook, and so on.

Finding your way through natural law theories, like all theories, is much the same. But we know that for anyone new to these areas of study, adapting to the reading can be a real challenge, so our guidebook is designed to be the way into the reading for you, but cannot replace your own thoughtful, critical reading of the material. In going through some of the theories that follow, we will be your guide to the ideas and thoughts you find in Lloyd and Davies. We will fill in some gaps for you as well, and encourage you to delve into the details and complexities of the theories. Having said that, any first read is going to be a major challenge. The second time you read anything will always be much easier if you have made an effort to try to read and understand what a theory is saying the first time around. Again, using the visit to the city as an example, your second visit will be easier because you know your way around, at least at some level, but you will see far more detail than you saw the first time you visited it.

And as with all courses you study, you will be subjected to some form of assessment: an exam, a seminar, or an assignment or essay. It is unlikely that you will be asked to 'describe' Aristotle's concept of natural law or Finnis' basic goods. You will need to do more than simply repeat the subject matter of the theory. Some of you will be expected to engage in a detailed analysis or critique of the theory, while others will be asked to 'apply' the theory or see where it has been used by the legislature or the judiciary. These are only a couple of examples, and we will look at some questions at the end of this chapter and in Chapter 14.

Why do you have to do more than repeat the theories? Let's go back to the guidebook example. When you come back from your visit to the city, what will you tell your friends about your trip? How many of you would read out what the guidebook said? We would think none of you would do this — instead, you will say what you liked, why you liked it, what you didn't like, what you agreed with and why. You will probably give examples of what you liked. Now translate this idea to thinking about a theory. The same thing goes — repeating the guidebook, lectures, tutorial content, lecture outlines, or this chapter, is not the same as providing a thoughtful, considered answer.

We will refer to extracts or materials from Davies and Lloyd within the
body of the text where we expect that you should read this material.
We will use footnotes where we are setting out an argument or where the
books don't include the material we refer to.

SECTION B: NATURAL LAW THEORIES

Back to the beginning — the natural law theories of Ancient Greece and Rome

We will begin looking at natural law theories by going back to where these ideas emerged: Ancient Greece and Rome (also known as the classical world). These two civilisations have profoundly influenced the way Western societies see the world, and their conceptions of natural law have had an ongoing influence on the ideas guiding later natural law theories, including the more current natural law theories. The timeline in Figure 3.1 will help you place these theories of natural law into their historical contexts.

Ancient Greece: Aristotle's good life — natural law and society

This part of the chapter will supplement the material in Lloyd and Davies and does not stand alone.

Ancient Greece has been held up as the ideal society, and has influenced a broad spectrum of Western culture, philosophy, literature, and politics, among many other achievements. Ancient Greece was not a single entity, but was made up of a number of different city-states — Athens and Sparta among many others — though larger empires formed at the end of this period, known as Hellenism, between 800 and 300 BC.

> Athens was the most famous of the city-states, reaching its pinnacle in the 5th century BC. From the 6th century BC, rule by tyrants was replaced by democracy, with freeborn men — the citizens — responsible for the running their society (it should be pointed out that fewer than 20% of Athenians were citizens — women, foreigners and slaves were excluded). As their society and its political structure developed, citizens sought answers to the ethical and political questions affecting them. The Athenian philosophers, whose initial aim was to provide guidance for their own community, left a rich tradition of ideas, which became the source of Western thought. Some of these ideas may be commonsense to us, but these philosophers asked the questions that we now take for granted. Among the ideas which they created were the origins of a natural law theory, the most famous for natural law being the 4th century BC philosopher, Aristotle.

Before we look at Aristotle's conception of natural law, we need to briefly touch on the ideas of the philosophers who directly preceded him.

- Socrates (470–399 BC) inquired into what was meant by truth, justice, and the notion of 'good'. He was the inventor of the 'dialectic' or questioning method of enquiry, with which we are familiar in law.
- Plato (c428–347 BC) provided us with three main ideas which have influenced thinking about law, though none directly related to natural law theory. The first was his use of reason as a device to uncover truth. Second, he provided us with a model for law in the *Republic*, through his ideal city-state, which combined monarchy with democracy. People would be ruled by the

'philosopher king' who would engage in an exercise of reasoned 'wisdom' instead of law. Thirdly, in terms of our obligation to obey law, in the *Crito* he argued that individuals were under an obligation to obey the law based on their choice to reside in the society in which they lived.

Aristotle

Aristotle (c384–322 BC), Plato's pupil, lived at the end of the classical era and the city-state, and the beginning of the period known as 'Hellenism'. He was the last of the stars of Greek philosophy, a prolific thinker who developed the method of logic called the syllogistic method, and the categorisation of knowledge into subject areas. He studied topics ranging from biology and metaphysics to poetics. He also developed a notion of natural law theory that has been taken up as the key source of current natural law thought.

> Aristotle's ideas about natural law can be gleaned from two very brief sources — *The Ethics* and *The Politics*. But neither text sought to provide an explanation of natural law alone.
>
> Extracts from *The Politics* and *The Ethics* are found in Davies (pp 75–77) and from *The Ethics* in Lloyd (p 140).

The Ethics sought to explain how humans can achieve the 'good life', through the use of practical wisdom, or *active reason*. The adoption of *active reason* will ensure that choices made by a person will be correct. The correct choice will be the *mean* between one extreme of conduct and another extreme. To guide reaching decisions about your behaviour, a good or virtuous person will use *practical wisdom* or *practical reasoning*, which will lead to the achievement of the good life.

> **Reason is a key concept in natural law theory. Aristotle's notion of reason is picked up and developed by later natural law theorists.**

In *The Politics*, Aristotle argued that the city-state was the ideal form of political entity. He argued that a balance between tyranny and democracy would lead to the strongest form of political stability, reflecting the wisdom of the many individuals of the society. A person not meeting up to the ideals set out in *The Ethics* would not be suited to being a citizen of the city-state.

Teleology

Aristotle developed a method of *reasoning* called teleology to understand the best way for communities to live. Teleology can be used to uncover the 'good' or *perfect* form to which we should aspire (that acorns will become oak trees). What we mean by 'perfect' here is that the thing has completed its aims (like growing to its full form), an idea not far from our usual understanding of the word. It is good for humans to live in communities because it is a natural good; as we can see in Figure 3.2:

- the good of a couple is to become a family,
- the good of a family is to become a community,
- and this leads in the end to a perfect form of society.

In this way we will best achieve the good life.

FIGURE 3.2: ACORNS TO OAK TREES: THE NATURAL ORDERING OF HUMAN LIFE IS TO LIVE IN SOCIETY

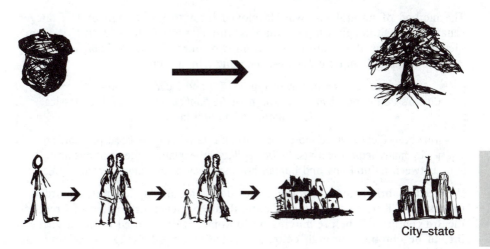

City–state

CHAPTER 3

Law will enhance this ideal society by supporting the virtuous life. In Book V of *The Ethics*, Aristotle identifies two types of law, or 'political justice', which he contrasts with the more particularised 'household justice'.[22] The 'natural' is universal and applies in all circumstances to all communities or societies. The 'legal', which is also known as 'conventional' law, simply applies as needed to an individual society for its own needs.[23] He sees that people may be confused by this observation, for they see 'that which is by nature is unchangeable and has everywhere the same force while they see change in the things recognized as just'.[24] While accepting some truth in this observation, it is not as stable a duality as it might seem, but sees a connection between what is 'just and lawful' and the 'universal'. Justice is, though, essentially something human.[25]

How do the legal and conventional connect? We can get a clue from Aristotle's discussion of the role of 'equity', which is to be used as a correction of legal justice. Equity is needed because while 'all law is universal', it is not always possible to make correct universal statements in all cases, as gaps may exist in the law, which will need to be adapted to the circumstances of the case.[26]

So the two types of justice are needed to make for good law. It will be guided by natural justice, through the agency of the *ideal citizen* capable of acting with wisdom.

---

22 Aristotle, *Nicomachean Ethics Book V*, Translated by WD Ross, http://classics.mit.edu/Aristotle/nicomachaen.5.v.html
23 Ibid, Book V, 7.
24 Ibid.
25 Ibid, Book V, 9.
26 Ibid, Book V, 10.

Ancient Rome – expressly adding reason to the mix of natural law

The method of natural law was developed through the Roman orator, lawyer, senator, and Stoic philosopher Marcus Tullius Cicero (106–43 BC). We have gleaned his ideas about natural law from two sources – *De Re Publica*, meaning 'On the Republic', and *De Legibus*, meaning 'On the laws'.

> As you will see in Davies (pp 73–75) and Lloyd (pp 140–141), Cicero's definition of natural law, in *De Re Publica*, represents the classical formulation of natural law.
>
> However, Cicero wrote more about natural law than has been popularised by many legal theorists. In *De Legibus*, he explained the relationship between natural law and human law as a way of guiding a virtuous life.

We need to briefly consider the basic ideas of Stoic philosophy, in order to understand Cicero's conception of natural law. Stoicism originated in Greece in the 3rd century BC, before moving on to Rome. Stoics aspired to live a virtuous life, to be obtained through courage, justice and right living. To achieve this virtuous life, they created an ethical framework to guide their behaviour. The framework relied on *reason* in combination with the natural order of things, and the cosmic order of the world.

Relying on this foundation, *reason* would then lead a person to an understanding of what was *naturally* appropriate behaviour to reach the life of virtue. All of these factors, but in particular the use of *reason*, can be found in Cicero's exposition of natural law. We should also be aware that Cicero's statements about natural law were part of a wider political agenda aimed at restoring Rome to a virtuous life.[27]

Cicero's use of the methods of Stoic philosophy led him towards a new understanding of natural law – as explained in *De Legibus*, it was discoverable through *reason* derived from the cosmic or divine order of things.[28] Law was derived from an 'eternal principle' governing the universe, and natural law combined with divine reason results in true (or virtuous) law. So the use of reason enables us to discover the principles of justice, on which law is based. That law will reflect virtue, and the 'human' law that results will be valid. The law of a tyrant, which does not adopt these principles, will not be valid law.[29]

The statement from *De Re Publica* (Davies pp 73–75 and pp Lloyd 140–141) operates as a set of principles, on which the further explanation in *De Legibus* is based. We probably only need to pull out two points from this statement, and through Cicero's explanation of natural law, we can see the Stoic principles speaking to us:

---

27 Cicero, *De Re Publica*, III.xxxii.33.
28 Cicero, *De Legibus*, I.xx.4–5.
29 Ibid, I.x.28–32.

TRUE LAW = RIGHT REASON + NATURE

Law which leads to a virtuous life comes about through the use of properly ordered reason derived from the order of things. By comparison, tyrannical law cannot meet these requirements, and promulgators of such law, who deny their human nature, will 'pay' in the long run. If we think about Cicero's political agenda, which sought to restore Rome to virtue, we may like to think about the targets of these comments.

TRUE LAW = UNIVERSAL, ETERNAL AND UNCHANGEABLE

Natural law that is derived in this way is universal and unchanging because it has come from the cosmic order. If we think about the Stoic's belief that the cosmic order, combined with reason, led to a virtuous life, we have to accept that the universal law is unchanging.

Connecting society to law in medieval Europe

We will now skid through 1200 years of history, and return to natural law theory in medieval Europe, where the Italian Dominican, St Thomas Aquinas (1225–1274), created a structure in which natural law operated as the basis for human, or posited law, through a connection back to the laws of God. In doing so, he relied on Muslim and Jewish philosophers who introduced Aristotle's philosophy to Christian Europe.

Aquinas' predecessors

We should be aware of some of the ideas that preceded Aquinas, to be able to place them into context, chiefly because many (but not all) of the concepts of natural law that we have already seen disappeared from the realm of human thought after the emergence of the Christian Church.

Instead, a new set of influences, particularly those of St Augustine (345–430) set the tone for the Christian conception of law, in which 'good' was guided by God's eternal law. Good, honourable people could be guided in their actions by the eternal law, while human law was only to be used for sinful people. There was no necessary connection between the eternal law and the human law, though a human law that conflicted with the eternal law, and created evil, would not bind a person in a moral sense. Therefore, the law derived from God existed in a different sphere from the law derived from humans. The problem that resulted from this 'dualism' was that human law was inherently untrustworthy – humans themselves were untrustworthy because of the belief in their inherent sinfulness.

These ideas lasted until Aquinas found a way to connect the law of God with the law of humans. However, other philosophers who came from the Muslim world paved the way for him to make this connection. Unlike Christian Europe, Muslims had continued to use Aristotle's philosophy. In particular, Averroës (1126–1198), who came from Andalusia,[30] revered Aristotle, and through his

---

30 In the medieval period, parts of Spain were Muslim, not Christian.

work, found a way of using reason as the means to identify God. His contemporary, the Spanish Jewish philosopher Moses Maimonides, also relying on Aristotle, took these concepts further, and in the *Guide of the Perplexed* found a way to bridge the gap between God and humans, using the human intellect or reason. His 'two planes of cognition', a process which showed how reason could be used to connect humans with God, directly influenced St Thomas Aquinas and his new Christian Aristotelianism.

St Thomas Aquinas — linking God with human law

Like the other thinkers we have considered so far, St Thomas Aquinas' work was vast, and was concerned with far more than questions about law. He wrote widely, but his two major works are his two theological 'summations' — the *Summa contra Gentiles* (an argument for the conversion of Spanish Muslims and Jews to Catholicism) and the *Summa Theologiae*, or summations on theology, which contains his ideas about law. Through his work, he made Aristotle (who he called 'The Philosopher') acceptable to Christian Europe, in a climate where the Muslim connections with Aristotle made him suspect.

> Before we go further, we need to make a connection between Aquinas' theology and natural law. Theology can be described as the study of God and the relationship between God and humans and the universe. In a medieval world, based in bounded feudal society and newly emerging independent communes or towns, God and Church guided human existence, and theology informed government, law and other forms of human life. Aquinas created a new type of theology, connecting it with Aristotelian reason, order, virtue and community, and these ideas are relevant to his ideas about law and its role.

At another level, he relied on *reason* to find ways for humans to engage with and connect with God, and for our purposes, God's law, and therefore to find the way to perfect human existence, and we can see how he relied on Maimonides among others to make these connections. He therefore found the way to bridge St Augustine's gap between the law that came from God and human law, by the use of human reason. The result was natural law, which could then be used to guide the creation of good human law.

> Having mapped out where Aquinas will take us, and before entering into a consideration of how natural law is created, we need to see how he understands the role of law. If you look at his original text, you will see that he sets out his ideas in a series of questions, which follow from the general to the particular, and internally within each question, a dispute and then answer to his own questions, especially where he has disagreed with St Augustine. You will find it helpful to look at the extracts of *Questions 90–97* in Lloyd at pp 142–146; Margaret Davies describes Aquinas' conception of natural law, including two short extracts from *Questions 90* and *95*, at pp 77–79.

We will rely DIRECTLY on these questions in the following description of Aquinas' ideas.

So, what is law?

The first point Aquinas considers is the what law is meant to do, and its role in relation to the needs of the community (in *Question 90*). His starting point is to explain *The Nature of Law*, which he says is a binding set of obligations on people to achieve virtue, which is directed by reason. The will of a ruler will become law, so long as it is based in reason; otherwise, it will be an evil – not law. Law has to have the wellbeing of the community as its purpose (relying on Aristotle's *Ethics* and *Politics*). The promulgation or creation of law has to be undertaken by the community *or the political person who is responsible for caring for the community*. However, a private person cannot do this, because law has to have *compelling* force, which either the community or the ruler has. Additionally, Aquinas used Aristotle's teleology to explain that one person and their interests has to be subordinated to the common good, as found in the perfect community, the city. So, Aquinas tells us:

> Law = rational ordering of things concerning the common good
>
> Law is made by the ruler of the community
>
> (the ruler uses PRACTICAL REASON to rule the PERFECT community)

Now we know what law is and who is able to make law for us. But how is that law to be created? This is where Aquinas' structure, relating God and human law, has to be established.

We have to ask: what are the various types of law?

We can find out what the various types of law are by having a quick look at Figure 3.3 (overleaf), which sets out the various laws in Aquinas' structure, and how the different components interrelate. He explains the different types of law in *Question 91*, and we can see here how he has been able to make the connections between God's law and human law.

The source of guidance for all of us is the *eternal law*, which is given to us by God. God governs the entire community of the Universe, using divine reason. The eternal law guides all existence, but humans, as rational creatures, are able to participate in aspects of the eternal law through their use of reason. The result of this 'participation' in the eternal law is that *natural law* comes from intelligent understanding – human reason. Natural law comprises principles, which can then be taken further to create human law, which will fill out and detail the natural law for day-to-day purposes. So, by using reason, a ruler can use the natural law to create good *human law*. Aquinas' structure includes one other type of law not relevant for this process – *divine law*.

What are the characteristics of natural law?

Aquinas sets out a detailed explanation of natural law in *Question 94*. He firstly explains that the precepts (or instructions, or prescriptions) of natural law equate to our natural inclinations. So, we have natural inclinations to good, to preserve human life, to produce children, and – relying on our rational nature – to know the truth about God and to live in society. Natural law therefore closely corresponds to Aristotelian teleology.

Aquinas explains the universality of natural law based on our use of *reason* to guide our behaviour. There are two types of reason. *Speculative reason* leads to finding indisputable truths. *Practical reason* (a concept we first came across with Aristotle), is used where no clear outcome can be found. It deals with contingent or changeable aspects of human life, which rely on the use of reason to work out the correct outcome in a particular case. For example, Aquinas explains that while it is usually proper to repay debts, in certain cases it may be wrong to do so.

For most situations, some known *first principles* will guide our conduct, though some people can never know what will be right behaviour because their reason is flawed by depravity or evil; at one time, the Germans did not consider robbery to be wrong, though clearly Aquinas tells us it is against the natural law. Aquinas also tells us that the natural law can change by having additions made to it. However, 'first principles' and 'secondary precepts' are unchangeable where they have become a general rule. Exceptions can be made in unusual circumstances, where general principles don't apply.

FIGURE 3.3: AQUINAS' STRUCTURE

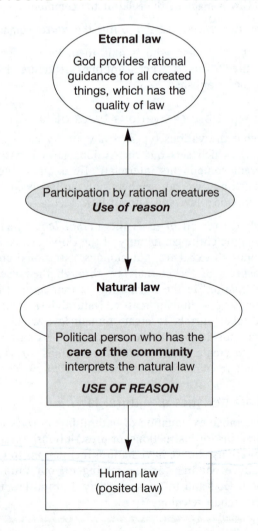

How does human law connect to natural law?

Aquinas explains why human laws are needed, but why they are subordinate to natural law, in *Question 95*. He tells us that humans naturally aspire to live a virtuous life, but for most of us to achieve that, we need guidance through human law. He explains that some of us need more guidance than others, for the good of the community. These people can only be compelled to good behaviour through the force of human law, which 'compels under the fear of penalty'. He concludes that law is therefore necessary to enable a peaceful and virtuous life, especially because of our intellects; reason can be a 'good', but in its worst form, can be used to exploit base desires and cruelty. Here, we can see Aquinas finding a way to link the gap between human and natural law inherited from St Augustine.

However, when it comes to the details of the law, what happens if a human law doesn't bear any relationship to the natural law? Aquinas recognises that situations exist where natural law does not contemplate the needs of human law. Here, natural law will be used as a set of *general first principles* under which the human law is made, using *reason*. He assumed some gaps would need to be filled, like the specific rules of conveyancing. These rules are needed to make land transactions work well, for the benefit and good of the community. So using natural reason will lead you to the creation of good human law to deal with the needs of practical situations not expressly covered by natural law.

However, if a human law completely transgresses a natural law, Aquinas tells us it will be a *corruption of law*, and not legal. He tells us that the natural law gives us the precept 'do harm to no man'. A human law against murder follows, derived from the natural law. However, a human law that ignored or went against this precept would be a *corruption of law*. You might want to think about Margaret Davies' criticism of the Catholic Church's use of this precept to ban contraception. Within the confines of the Catholic Church, this human law is derived from natural law to continue all life.[31]

> Did Aquinas mean that you could ignore a law that did not conform to the natural law? It has been claimed that his observations about 'law that is a corruption of law' meant that he said you could ignore an unjust law because it was not law ('lex injusta non est lex'). However, it seems that Aquinas was more concerned with maintaining the good order of the community, in an Aristotelian sense, than permitting a person to disobey the ruler's law.[32]

Natural rights — the natural law of persons, property and promises

Changing circumstances, new ideas

While Aquinas' influence on natural law thinking continued through to the 18th century, a new take on natural law thinking emerged in 17th century England, at the same time that new ideas were starting to sweep Europe, which

---

31 Davies, op cit, p 77.
32 Wacks, op cit, pp 102–103, relying on *Summa Theologica*, I/II, 96, 4.

has had significant influence on the structure of our contemporary understanding of law and its relationship with society and the needs of individuals.
To locate these changes, though, we have to briefly look at science. You will
see why in a moment. The new science which developed around the time of
Copernicus and Galileo sparked the 'modern' world, in which observation,
experimentation and verification of what could be seen and proved became
paramount (this method is known as *empiricism*). The Enlightenment science
of the 17th century starred Newton, Boyle and Hooke, and Thomas Hobbes,
who as we will shortly see, retained his fame as a political philosopher. The
new science coincided with the new philosophical modernism of Descartes, who
you will meet in the next chapter.

> But other ideas were also influencing English philosophers of the 17th century, which
> was also a period of immense civil turmoil. The English Civil War, between 1642 and
> 1649, led to the overthrow of the monarchy and the beheading of Charles I in 1649,
> to be replaced by Oliver Cromwell's Commonwealth, or Republic, from 1649 to 1660,
> followed by the Restoration of the Monarchy in 1660. However, the Stuarts − Charles II
> and James II − were distrusted because of their Catholic and absolutist tendencies,
> and in 1688−1689, the Glorious Revolution deposed James II. He was replaced by
> William and Mary, who agreed to a new constitutional framework based in
> parliamentary supremacy. The latter development was a consequence of the rise of
> liberalism and associated concepts of democracy. An emerging middle class of this
> period pursued political representation and the enhancement of property rights, in
> association with the beginnings of early capitalism and the development of commerce
> and industry.

The political philosophers of this period responded to this mix of factors in
seeking to develop a new relationship between individuals and the state, or
political entity, in which they lived. You will look at these ideas in more detail
in the next two chapters. One of these factors was the belief that people had
natural rights as individuals against the state, a concept which relied on natural
law to support its assertions. We will look at the two most influential political
philosophers − Thomas Hobbes and John Locke. You will find some discussion
of their philosophies in Lloyd at pages 111−118, and extracts of their writings
at pages 146−150.

Hobbes, the Leviathan, and natural rights

Thomas Hobbes (1588−1679), who we met briefly earlier, was a monarchist and
was strenuously opposed to the Civil War. His *Leviathan* (1651), written in the
immediate aftermath of Cromwell's Commonwealth, was an argument in support
of 'absolutism', or a strong monarch, and against individual liberty where there
was a conflict with the needs of strong government. He created the idea of the
social contract, in which we give up certain of our interests in order to live in
society.

> Hobbes tells us that the natural state of humans is enmity − so what effect does this
> have on our lives? It is clearly not a nice existence, for it means that in we are in a
> state of 'Warre'. In the state of Warre, he says, 'the life of man (is) solitary, poore,
> nasty, brutish and short'. Life improves when, under the *social contract*, we give up
> certain liberties and rights to the monarch, in return for protection.

What happens to us in the state of Warre? For a start, there is no law, no justice, no concept of right or wrong (in the sense of good and bad), and everyone just does what they want, governed by their own 'reason'. Everyone has rights to everything, including the bodies of other men, and for this reason, no-one has any security for themselves or their possessions.

But Hobbes tells us that certain fundamental laws of nature will overcome this state of affairs – that everyone really wants to live in peace, and that if we give up some of our rights we will ensure that peace will prevail. Whatever liberties we lose will be made up with the protection that we will have in the guise of the Common Power or ruler to impose peace on us. This is what we know as the social contract, which Hobbes called an *artificial covenant*, based on the natural agreement of the people entering into the agreement.

FIGURE 3.4: LEVIATHAN:
THE ARTIFICIAL MAN AND THE COMMONWEALTH

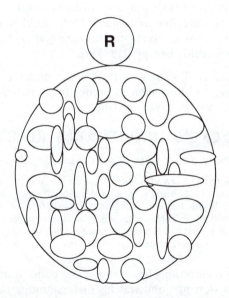

WHO WILL BE THE PERSON THEY HAND OVER THEIR RIGHTS TO?

A Sovereign, who is not simply an individual ruler, but an *artificial person*, artificially made up of all the individuals of the society. The sovereign, or Leviathan, is *a unity of all of them*, or a common-wealth, with whom we have entered into mutual covenants, for peace and common defence. The sovereign therefore exercises sovereign power to which everyone else is subjected. To break the social contract created in this way would be illogical, because we have given up our interests to the sovereign. He used this argument to claim that revolution and rebellion was untenable – after all, we had agreed to be ruled, hadn't we? It also meant that we had to accept the law imposed on us.

Locke, property, and rights against government

John Locke (1632–1704) took a different tack, supporting the rights of individuals against an unfair and absolute monarchy. His two *Treatises on Government* were published in 1689 and 1690, around the time of the Glorious Revolution, whose *Declaration of Rights* and *Bill of Rights* (1689) redefined the relationship between monarch and subjects. The monarch was no longer allowed to suspend and dispense with law and was forbidden to levy taxation or maintain a standing army in peacetime without parliamentary consent, among other matters designed to enhance the rights of subjects. Parliament was now dominant, and the constitutional monarchy formed its modern persona.

Lockes' treatises go hand in glove with the newly emerging society in which individuals were assumed free and equal, with rights in property, and limited government intervention. He argued for the separation of powers, and the supremacy of the legislature over the monarchy. Locke used natural law to justify property rights, which were at the heart of *his* explanation of the social contract with government. The role of government was to act as a commonwealth of men for the preservation of their property. It could never act arbitrarily against men, because all men were free and equal. They could not to be subjected to the will of any other person, except to the extent they had given away their rights to the commonwealth (see pp 113–114).

Government, law and civil society were to exist under a social contract, the purpose of which was to allow men to enjoy their inalienable rights (ie those that cannot be taken away), given by God.

LOCKE'S INALIENABLE RIGHTS

The rights to life, liberty, property (and to rebel against unjust rulers and laws).

'The state of Nature has a law of Nature to govern it ... reason, which is that law, teaches all mankind ... that being all equal and independent, no one ought to harm another in his life, health, liberty or possessions; for men being all the workmanship of one omnipotent and infinitely wise Maker; all the servants of one sovereign Master, sent into the world by His order and about His business; they are his property, whose workmanship they are made to last during His, not one another's pleasure'.[33]

How can we see the connections between Locke's conception of rights, property and natural law? His starting point was his understanding of the state of nature, which differed dramatically from that proposed by Hobbes. Nature was an idyllic place, given to us by God, but it did not provide for the protection of property. We are not allowed to claim anything from nature as our own unless we mix our *labour* with nature, and transform what we have taken.

Locke did not just mean the physical work or intellectual work people do themselves. For Locke, labour meant the work of your labourers, your animals, and anything over which the property owner possessed control. From this position, you can see how the idea of rulers or governments taking property without compensation is contrary to the law of Nature, as is taxation without representation.

---

33 Extracted in Lloyd, p 148.

WHAT YOU CAN DO WITH THESE RIGHTS

You have the power to preserve your property (your life, liberty, and estate).

'Man being born, as has been proved, with a title to perfect freedom and an uncontrolled enjoyment of all the rights and privileges of the law of Nature, equally with any other man ... hath by nature a power not only to preserve his property ... that is, his life, liberty, and estate, against the injuries and attempts of other men, but to judge of and punish the breaches of that law in others, as he is persuaded the offence deserves, even with death itself ... because no political society can be, nor subsist, without having in itself the power to preserve the property'[34]

The state of nature therefore justified private ownership and the ability of the property owner to protect his property. Punishment can follow when property is violated. In civil society this occurs through the law and judicature, exercised by the men authorised by the community to determine punishment. But where this is not established, *a person can exercise this right for himself.*

CREATING HUMAN LAW AND THE LAW OF CIVIL SOCIETY — TRACES OF AQUINAS

'The obligations of the law of Nature cease not in society, but only in many cases are drawn closer, and have, by human laws, known penalties annexed to them to enforce their observation. Thus the law of Nature stands as an eternal rule to all men, legislators as well as others. The rules that they make for other men's actions must ... be conformable to the law of Nature — ie to the will of God ... the fundamental law of Nature being the preservation of mankind, no human sanction can be good or valid against it'[35]

Reimagining property, society and rights

The type of property, and the rights associated with it, that Locke had in mind differ markedly from our own concept of property. This is because *landed* property was the pathway to the creation of law in England. Only landowners were entitled to vote — at the beginning of the 19th century, this constituted around 6 per cent of the population. A series of Reform Acts eventually extended the right to vote to men during the 19th century. The first, in 1832, granted rights to men who owned property like a house. The second, in 1867, gave the vote to every male adult householder living in a town, including lodgers paying £10 per year for unfurnished rooms, which meant that some working class men were entitled to vote. By 1884, the final reform extended this right to rural working men.

As we will see in Chapter 8, the societal impact of property rights and their impact on workers spawned Marx's social theory, based in and around the inequalities produced by property.[36]

---

34 Ibid, p 149.
35 Ibid, p 150.
36 Ibid, pp 116–117. Lloyd proposes that Locke was not seen as an apologist for capitalism — he was against the rise of a money based economy, and supported welfare rights.

Mind the gap

The Age of Reason, the decline of natural law, the rise of positivism

The 18th century, the Age of Reason, the Enlightenment and Revolution, saw a decline of natural law and a mistrust of the methods of the social contract, with their reliance on what could not be proved. The rational, scientific methods of empiricism had taken hold, and if claims could not stand up to scientific rigour, they were dismissed, as you will see in Chapters 4 and 6. But Hume (1711–1776), a leading light of the Scottish Enlightenment (famed for his sceptical analysis of natural law claims that an 'ought' could be derived from an 'is'), suggested that natural law was an idea of 'justice', and preceded human law.

While this new philosophical thought was developing, it initially did not affect the acceptance of the natural law derived from Aquinas, and the natural rights of Locke. Indeed, in the 18th century, natural law was sanctioned through *Blackstone's Commentaries on the Laws of England*, in *Of the Nature of Laws In General*.[37]

> From *Of the Nature of Laws in General*:
>
> > 'These are the eternal, immutable laws of good and evil, to which the creator himself in all his dispensations conforms; and which he has enabled human reason to discover, so far as they are necessary for the conduct of human actions. Such among others are these principles: that we should live honestly, should hurt nobody, and should render every one its due'.

If you look back at Figure 3.1, you will find a gap between Blackstone and the middle of the 20th century in terms of the influence of natural law theory. The influences of the new scientific approaches began to influence legal thinking by the early 19th century, through the work of Bentham, and Austin's adaptation of Bentham's ideas. Legal *analysis* became dissociated from any concerns about the consequences or effects of that law. It was only concerned with that the law was validly enacted, and validly interpreted through the conventions established by the legal system. We will look more closely at the methods of early legal positivism in Chapter 6.

World War Two and its aftermath, and the rise of a new natural law

An awful consequence followed — could validly enacted law be used to deny people's human rights, and to facilitate murder and genocide?[38] During World War Two, the validly enacted laws of Nazi Germany sanctioned the taking of property of Jews, the denial of their citizenship, and the use of regulatory devices to ultimately allow for genocide. This prompted a rethink of the premises of the positivist method and a revival of natural law thinking in the aftermath

---

37 *Blackstone's Commentaries on the Laws of England*, Introduction, Section the Second.
38 See Alexy, R, 'A Defence of Radbruch's Formula' in Lloyd, pp 374–391; Schauer, F, 'Positivism as Pariah', in Lloyd, pp 441–451 considers the idea that positivism contributed to bad decisions.

of World War Two, and a new conception of natural law as the basis of fundamental human rights.

But the new natural lawyers of the 20th century faced a number of challenges, not least the methodological problems they had to overcome. To start with, they had to find ways around the now entrenched scepticism of natural law in a legal world profoundly influenced by positivism, especially in England and the Commonwealth common law world. They had to overcome the problem of 'is' and 'ought', and get around the metaphysics (God-based or other non-rational methods) that natural law was associated with. As we will see shortly, one method used by these thinkers was to get around the idea of a higher law by relying on what looked like legal procedure (Fuller), on what already existed in the legal system (Hart), or on what did not have to be proved — the concept of 'self-evidence' (Finnis). In other words, the new natural law was secularised and avoided any reference to religion, even if there was a religious base to the theory. We will look at these three theorists because of their influence and importance, but you should be aware that new natural law ideas are continually developing.

Rekindling natural law — Fuller's secular natural law

A legal world dominated by the influences of legal positivism

A new post-war natural law emerged in the United States, through the work of Lon Fuller (1902–1978), who was Professor of General Jurisprudence at Harvard University from 1948 to 1972. His 1969 work *The Morality of Law*, sought to demonstrate that some legal systems, such as that of Nazi Germany, were not legal systems because they failed basic rules needed for a legal system. We can get an idea of Fuller's natural law project in his ongoing debate with HLA Hart,[39] about the legal consequences of the Nazi grudge cases.[40]

> ## THE GRUDGE CASES
>
> The grudge cases were tried in West Germany, and were cases in which citizens of Nazi Germany used repressive Nazi laws to get back at people. The Hart/Fuller debate concerned a case in which a wife reported her husband for criticising the Nazi regime, which was unlawful under Nazi law. He was sent to the Russian Front, which was tantamount to a death penalty, but survived. After the War, she was convicted for having unlawfully deprived him of his liberty, under the German Criminal Code of 1871. A report of the case suggested, apparently incorrectly, that the decision was made on the basis that the Nazi law was immoral (ie bad law). This sparked the debate between Hart and Fuller, even though the decision was based in the Criminal Code, and not on a question of morals. Fuller argued that Nazi Germany did not have the internal morality needed for a legal system to be valid, which meant that moral issues *should* be

---

39 Hart is a legal positivist we shall consider shortly, who will be considered in detail in Chapter 7.
40 Davies, p 109; Lloyd, pp 367–374.

considered by the courts. Hart argued that moral issues *should not* be considered within the boundaries of a legal system; a law should not be invalidated on the basis of a moral question, and retrospective law should be enacted to overcome the problem of the bad law.

This debate shows us the main ideas underlying Fuller's procedural natural law in *The Morality of Law*. He wanted to show that if a legal system was *morally* flawed, then it was not a legal system at all. If there was no valid legal system, then, clearly, the laws made in that system could not be valid. So-called laws could therefore be considered in terms of their morality or lack of morality. An overview of Fuller's ideas can be found at pages 124–129 of Lloyd, and an extract of *The Morality of Law* is located at page 157–171.

Reviving the Aristotelian community

At the heart of Fuller's natural law theory is his revival of the importance of *community* and the common good as the basis of natural law thought,[41] through a reconceptualisation of Aristotle and his ideal community. His concept of natural law was far removed from the religious ideas of natural law we have seen. Instead, he sought to create a secular, human, anti-metaphysical natural law, using procedures of legal systems and rules as his language and method. Fuller was keen to connect morality with how law was practised. He tried to show how 'doing' law was derived from the needs of the common good. Law, in effect, was the means by which the community would flourish, through a system of rules.

The story of Rex: a parable

Rex was the king that Fuller used to illustrate the problems that come from a failed legal system. Rex tried hard to improve the legal system of his country, but ended up making the whole system worse. Leading citizens planned a revolution, but Rex died before anything happened. Rex II, his successor, replaced lawyers with psychiatrists and PR people. Fuller tells us this story as a parable for a legal system without rules, which failed to provide for a flourishing community under law. (Do you recall Aristotle here?)

A SUMMARY OF EIGHT WAYS TO RUIN A SYSTEM OF LEGAL RULES (REX DID ALL OF THEM)

1. There are no rules at all — this means cases are decided ad hoc
2. Rules aren't made available to people affected by law
3. Retrospective legislation is used in an abusive sense, leaving people unsure about what will happen to any law[42]
4. Rules can't be understood
5. Rules are contradictory
6. Rules that require you to do something that is impossible
7. Laws that change so often that you can't work out your actions
8. A gap between publicised laws and their administration[43]

---

41 Lloyd, pp 124–125.
42 Fuller calls these 'retroactive'.
43 Lloyd, p 160.

A ruined legal system, in Fuller's theory, leads to a ruined society. The community will be adversely affected by these rules, and he tells us that a total failure of any one of them means there is *no legal system at all*. Nor is there a moral basis to obey these rules, and where the bond between government and citizen breaks down, there is no basis on which a citizen is under a duty to obey these laws. The situation in Nazi Germany left citizens without rules to guide their lives, which instead were replaced with rules designed to do the opposite — to frighten them. This left people unable to act, and in a position where they did not know whether to obey bad laws or whether to disobey them on moral grounds — Fuller does not give guidance on this point, but suggests that respecting 'constituted authority' does not equate to 'fidelity to law'.[44]

PERFECTION — ASPIRING TO EXCELLENCE

(Rex didn't do any of these, but if he had, he would have created a good society under law.)

1. Rules are clear
2. Rules are consistent with each other
3. Every citizen knows them
4. Rules are never retrospective
5. They can be understood
6. They remain constant
7. They only demand what is possible
8. They are observed by courts, police and administration

The inner morality of law — how to make a legal system work for the good of the community

The inner morality of law is Fuller's guide to the operation of a legal system, so that it will conform, at least at a basic level, to the needs of a good community. The legal system and its rules should do more, in order to achieve the good life in the community, than merely protect people against harm. The rules should also be affirmative, requiring the legal system to move towards achievements constituted by the 'morality of aspiration'. Fuller proposes a kind of *balancing act* which sets out an invisible pointer to mark out the point where a legal system fails.[45] Figure 3.5 (overleaf) might help you understand Fuller's balancing act.

Fuller tells us that the inner morality of law is a variety of natural law. It meets this definition as a form of human undertaking, which originates on earth. He calls his natural law a lower (not higher) law, and compares it with the natural laws a carpenter would use to make sure a building would hold up. The inner morality of law compares to the 'external morality of law', which concerns larger policy questions, and which should be the subject of legislation.

---

44 Ibid, pp 160–161.
45 Ibid, pp 161–163.

FIGURE 3.5: WHAT DOES FULLER'S BALANCING ACT LOOK LIKE?

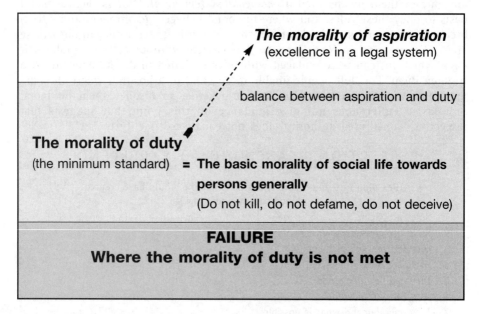

Fuller calls his natural law 'procedural natural law' to make it clear that it is not concerned with the substantive aims of law (the subject of the external morality of law), because it is concerned with how the 'system of rules governing human conduct' should be constructed and administered.[46] He does acknowledge that there can be instances where there can be an interaction between the internal and external moralities of law, where the substantive aims of a law can lead to ill-effects for the internal morality of law. He uses the example of symbolic laws denying contraception which are effectively disobeyed and cannot be enforced. He says legal morality is consequently affected, because one action of this type will spread to the wider system. But as well, because legal morality is designed to serve the community and human life; to depart from law's inner morality is an affront to human dignity.[47]

Communicating

The upshot of Fuller's natural law is to improve how the community functions, through a simple use of the morality of aspiration, which can provide for a substantive Natural Law (with capital letters, as he put it). How? By people *communicating* as a way to achieve the good life, rather than simply meeting the requirements of the minimum aspects found in the morality of duty, which was no standard to aspire to at all. Fuller decried the approach towards law by HLA Hart (who came up with the idea that posited law should contain a minimum content of natural law) as barely meeting the *morality of duty.*[48]

---

46 Lloyd, pp 163–164.
47 Ibid, pp 167–169.
48 Ibid, pp 170–171.

Justifying posited law — HLA Hart's minimum content of natural law

Clashing theories

Fuller's dispute with HLA Hart (1907–1992) had continued from the Hart/Fuller debate into a new arena — Hart's construction of a minimum content of natural law.[49] But why was Hart, a legal positivist, using natural law? As we will see in the next three chapters, the positivist method denies that moral questions can be used to consider 'legal' questions. But we get some clue from the Hart/Fuller debate, that Hart acknowledges that moral questions are relevant to legal questions, so long as retrospective legislation is enacted to overcome an evil — rather than moral arguments. In Chapter 9 of *The Concept of Law*, his major exposition of his positivist method, Hart expounds his ideas for a minimum content of natural law to be found in the legal system.

> A description of the minimum content is set out in Lloyd (pp 129–132). While Hart is a positivist theorist, Lloyd has considered this aspect of Hart's work within the framework of natural law theory.

As part of his overall approach in *The Concept of Law*, Hart engages in quasi-sociological observations of the way that societies live, and the law that those societies create. Hart claims that certain rules of conduct required to maintain a society are 'pre-legal' — that is, they precede the existence of law and a legal system. We saw Hume express similar views above (p 66). These rules are necessary because of the facts of the human condition that, in effect, make us vulnerable. Because of this, we need these rules, as a minimum for survival, to enable us to live together and to be able to continue our existence with each other, rather than live in a 'suicide club'.

It is the 'facts', 'truisms', or observations about the human condition that require some sort of rule, the content of which is not prescribed. Thus, they are not aspirational, but set out a minimum standard of conduct, to ensure human survival continues. Indeed, Hart acknowledged that they could justify an appalling set of human conditions, such as slavery or racial or religious discrimination, so long as survival was maintained:

HART'S FIVE FACTS OF THE HUMAN CONDITION[50]

1. Human vulnerability: this means that it is necessary to proscribe major crimes of violence — think about murder and genocide.
2. Approximate equality: this means that though humans have different capacities, no person can be allowed to be so powerful to permanently dominate — think about constitutional democracy.
3. Limited altruism: this means rules of mutual forbearance are required to secure a balance between altruism and selfishness in life — think about contract.
4. Limited resources: this means that necessities can only be acquired through labour, which means that property rights follow.
5. Limited understanding and strength of will, which leads individuals towards deviant and antisocial behaviour, which requires the imposition of sanctions.

Can you trace the source of these ideas?

49 Ibid.
50 Ibid, pp 129–131.

Protecting persons, property, and promises

Consequently, rules are needed for the protection of persons, property and promises, and to ensure that sanctions can be imposed for transgressions of these rules.[51] These ideas are not far removed from a description of the English legal system of the 1960s, the time at which Hart was writing. We can also see in this description a revival of the social contractarianism of Hobbes and Locke. He has 'locked down' their ideas into his minimum content – you might like to look at these ideas again at pages 62–65 above. Hart's minimum content of natural law has spawned a broad range of critical responses to its assumptions, its methods, and its understanding of society, many of which are summarised by Lloyd.

One other aspect of the minimum content should be pointed out: its relationship with the continuation of a legal system. How a legal system survives is connected with the *acceptability* of the rules under that system. Hart argues that if the system is fair towards those to whom it demands obedience, then stability will follow. If not, and laws favour some dominant group, supported by repression and instability, then the potential for upheaval will follow. At a less extreme level, if laws fail what is needed for the maintenance of the survival, then they will ultimately be changed by some means or other.[52]

This looks like Hart's response to an evil legal system, and perhaps his answer to the problem of Nazi law that we first saw in the Hart/Fuller debate at pages 67–68 above. His response as a positivist to evil law is to accept that a person may say that the law is evil and not obey it, but that it is unacceptable for a claim to be made that the law was not law at all,[53] as played out in the Hart/Fuller debate. A conceptual gap between natural law and legal positivism continued with Hart, but was overcome with the work of John Finnis.

Reviving Aquinas – John Finnis' conception of natural law

Situating Finnis

Making natural law acceptable to legal positivism has been the outcome of Finnis' contemporary reconceptualisation of natural law theory.[54] We thought we would briefly introduce you to Finnis and his broader work before looking at his theory. Finnis was born in 1940, brought up in Adelaide, and studied law at the University of Adelaide before being awarded a Rhodes scholarship in the early 1960s. Hart was his doctoral supervisor at Oxford. Finnis has been Professor of Law and Legal Philosophy at Oxford University since 1989. As a natural lawyer, Finnis has been involved in Catholic legal philosophy, and has

---

51 Hart, *The Concept of Law* (1st ed, 1961) p 199.
52 Ibid, p 197.
53 Ibid, p 205.
54 Lloyd, p 132.

expressly adopted, in a number of his writings, a clear Catholic position on issues ranging from cloning to homosexuality.[55]

A 'NON-RELIGIOUS' NATURAL LAW

Having said this, Finnis' major natural law statement, *Natural Law and Natural Rights*, is not cast in religious terms at all. Instead, Finnis has constructed a form of natural law that dispenses with any connection with a deity, with observations about nature, and with morality in the sense of goodness. It also finds a way of getting around the methodological problems of natural law, of deriving 'ought' from 'is', by creating a new method of understanding how natural law is derived — on the basis of a set of 'self-evident' basic 'goods' on which human existence is based.

Relevant extracts of his core theory are included in Lloyd (pp 171–191 and 192–195). We will try to outline his ideas for you as descriptively as possible so that you can follow the criticisms and critiques which his work has spawned and which are now a vital part of any understanding of Finnis' natural law. In a sense, it is difficult to divorce Finnis' theory from the arguments against it, the arguments for it and the responses and developments in this ongoing work. Indeed, Finnis' natural law theory has provoked very strong responses, as you will see in the overview in Lloyd (pp 132–139) and in Davies (pp 79–86) — and as you will see, the criticisms of Finnis' theory start from the very outset! You may find it hard to unravel the criticisms and critiques from a base understanding of his theory — we suggest that you don't engage in any 'criticisms of the criticisms' until you have got a handle on what Finnis has said.

Reviving Aristotle and Aquinas — individuals, community and law

Finnis' theory proposes that natural law is 'the set of principles of *practical reasonableness* in ordering human life and human community'[56] (emphasis added). What does this mean? Finnis argues that the aim of natural law theory is to provide guidance to the living of a good life which will lead to a good and harmoniously ordered community. Through this notion, Finnis is reviving the natural law theory of Aristotle and Aquinas, which looks at the role of individuals and their actions, and the impact these have on the rest of the community. Within this approach, individuals and their own interests will give way to the community. The role of law is to preserve the good of the community and the common good.

Finnis' structure

Finnis has constructed a multi-layered method to uncover natural law (published in *Natural Law and Natural Rights*),[57] supplemented by the identification of a

---

55 These are a very few of his current writings: 'Natural Law: the Classical Tradition', in Jules L Coleman & Scott Shapiro (eds), *The Oxford Handbook of Jurisprudence and Philosophy of Law* (2002), pp 1–60; 'Some Fundamental Evils in Generating Human Embryos by Cloning', in Cosimo Marco Mazzoni (ed), *Ethics and Law in Biological Research* (2002), pp 99–106; 'On the Incoherence of Legal Positivism', in Dennis Patterson (ed), *Philosophy of Law and Legal Theory: An Anthology* (2003), pp 134–143.

56 Finnis, *Natural Law and Natural Rights* (1980), p 280.

57 Ibid, p 23.

first moral principle which guides choices in connection with the basic goods.[58] See Figure 3.6 for a representation of the method.

FIGURE 3.6: FINNIS' MULTI-LAYERED METHOD

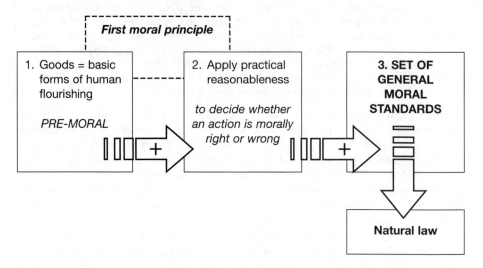

Starting at the beginning: Finnis' basic goods

Finnis starts off by identifying *seven innate basic human goods* that are shared by individuals and the community — the first box in Figure 3.6 (see also Figure 3.7).

> We'll identify those goods in a moment, but we want to explain to you why he has established these goods in the first place.
>
> 'Getting around the methodological problems of is and ought'.
>
> Finnis tells us that criticisms of natural law are wrong, because natural law has never claimed that you could find 'an ought from an is'.
>
> **SELF-EVIDENCE MEANS YOU NEVER HAVE TO PROVE A THING.**
>
> He gets around the problem by showing how the goods are self-evident — *they do not need to be proved*, so they can never be derived from anything. Therefore, you never have to worry about getting an ought from an is — it never has to be proved.[59]

The basic goods are those things all reasonable people strive to achieve, and they exist before moral questions are ever contemplated. What this means is that people will, as individuals, know what is good for themselves through an understanding of their nature. It will then be understood as being good for everyone else, so long as there is an acceptance that the good should be shared. Finnis relies on Aquinas to reach this conclusion that practical reasoning begins

---

58 Finnis et al, *Nuclear Deterrence, Morality and Realism* (1987) in Lloyd, pp 192–195.
59 Finnis, op cit, pp 33–34.

by understanding your nature from within.[60] But in other cases, what we may *want* as individuals may never accord to the good of everyone, and these wants cannot be good for the community.

So what is the starting point? Finnis tells us that the seven goods, which are set out in Figure 3.7 (p 77), exist in some form in all human societies, irrespective of cultural difference. Finnis says that it is possible to identify the goods from the work of psychologists and anthropologists, but that it is fairly clear that all forms of human society value the goods, which are directed to the common good. In combination, the goods make up the sum of all forms of human experience that will ever be needed.[61] *No good is more important or better than another.* You can find the goods and their rationales set out in Lloyd (pp 171–178).

Listing the goods isn't hard, but understanding what they are used for is not as easy to grasp. Let's look at three of the basic goods and what they tell us about the basic forms of human flourishing. A little later, we will combine the goods with the methodological requirements of practical reasonableness to try to see how the structure works.

CHAPTER 3

THE GOOD OF LIFE

Life is such an obvious choice, because who would argue to not preserve life and do everything possible to live a good and fruitful life? Finnis includes health, road safety, food, and all matters connected to vitality and living well. He includes *procreation*, the creation of a new life through vital (living) means. From this basis, we can see how Finnis would argue against euthanasia, homosexuality, abortion, cloning, and other forms of artificial reproduction, all of which are contrary to the good of 'life' because they are not directed to the maintenance of life. Obviously, the arguments against such a position are strong, as you will see in Davies' critique of Finnis.

THE GOOD OF KNOWLEDGE

How can you argue against knowledge? The moment you do, you fall into the trap of accepting that knowledge is a good, simply on the basis of your argument — it is there and it is a good in its own right.

THE GOOD OF PRACTICAL REASONABLENESS

This is the same practical reasonableness that you use to turn the *pre-moral* basic goods into the *moral* natural law. Finnis tells us that it is a good to bring an intelligent and reasonable order into our actions, habits and practical attitudes, which drive how we freely order our decisions. This good also involves the use of reason, and it has a strong family resemblance back to Aquinas.

---

60 Ibid, p 34.
61 Ibid, p 90.

The first moral principle: guiding choices in the basic goods

Finnis expanded on the goods and how they work in the extract from *Nuclear Deterrence, Morality and Realism* set out in Lloyd (pp 192–195). You will see this principle in Figure 3.6, located behind boxes 1 and 2. This principle adds an additional component, which assists with choices by humans, in terms of how they will make decisions. Using it will lead to the best moral outcome in any situation — in effect, it will assist in deciding the difference between right and wrong for the good of the community, and in filling in the blanks of yet unknown circumstances. The first moral principle seems to be self-evident, but is clothed by an *intermediate principle* of the Golden Rule. Its use leads to a correct moral outcome through 'modes of responsibility'.

THE FIRST PRINCIPLE OF MORALITY IS:

- in voluntarily acting for human goods
- in avoiding what is opposed to them
- one ought to choose and otherwise *will* those and *only* those possibilities whose will is compatible with integral human fulfilment

It denies individualistic self-fulfilment and partiality but looks to the good of all persons and communities.

Adding in the nine basic requirements of practical reasonableness

To work out the uses of the nine basic requirements of practical reasonableness, we need to refer to the second box in Figure 3.6. The requirements are then listed out in Figure 3.7, where they are connected back to their 'good' of practical reasonableness. The requirements provide a set of moral and ethical criteria attached to the actions that guide the goods. In combination with the goods, they make up natural law. So, building on the example of the *good of life*, how might we make decisions to end our lives because we cannot continue to live a healthy, pain-free life? Such a decision would be negated by a number of the requirements of practical reasonableness, not least the common good, and the dictates of our conscience. Through the process of reason, we would want to maintain our life not just for ourselves but for the good of the community.

Natural law follows, and a general set of moral standards: LIFE.

Let's look at the third box in Figure 3.6, through which we can derive guidance in the creation and interpretation of law. More particularly, a principle which drives the natural law must be reached through this process, which requires that life be maintained at all costs.

FIGURE 3.7: THE RELATIONSHIP BETWEEN THE BASIC GOODS AND THE REQUIREMENTS OF PRACTICAL REASONABLENESS

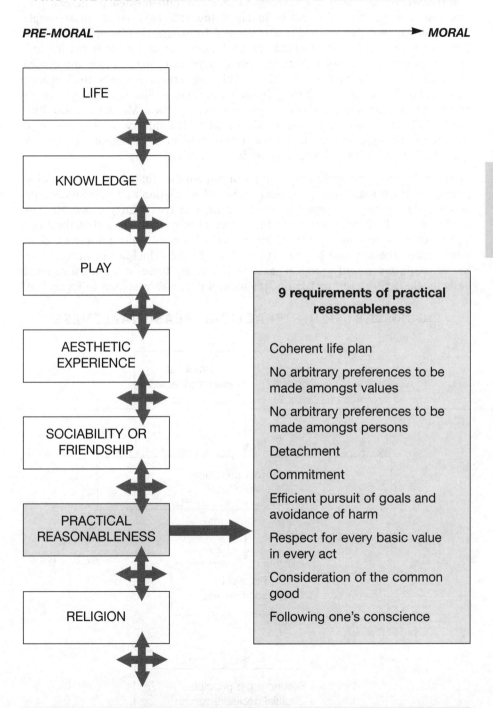

PRE-MORAL ⟶ *MORAL*

LIFE

KNOWLEDGE

PLAY

AESTHETIC EXPERIENCE

SOCIABILITY OR FRIENDSHIP

PRACTICAL REASONABLENESS

RELIGION

9 requirements of practical reasonableness

Coherent life plan

No arbitrary preferences to be made amongst values

No arbitrary preferences to be made amongst persons

Detachment

Commitment

Efficient pursuit of goals and avoidance of harm

Respect for every basic value in every act

Consideration of the common good

Following one's conscience

First principle of morality

CHAPTER 3

The role of law, natural law and human law

Finnis provides guidance for turning natural law into posited or human law. You can find out how this works in Lloyd (pp 180–185). At its most simple level, we can find that posited law is derived from natural law in combination with the requirements of practical reasonableness, or as Finnis terms it, 'first order principles'. First order principles are derived from natural law and guided by 'second order principles', which provide the practical effect to decision-making. Legal rules connect closely to the natural law — Finnis uses the example of murder to show the close connection between the two. Murder is proscribed because life is a basic value and to kill someone is contrary to the seventh of the nine basic requirements of practical reasonableness. A regime of property is a requirement of the common good for human wellbeing.

In effect, the creation and interpretation of human law follows a set of guiding principles which assist with both the creation of legislation and judicial decision making. He assumes an aspect of reason is used to create human law. He tells us that a legislator who ignores a first order principle will find that their law will be challenged and overturned by the use of second order principles, or in other words, the law will be made to conform to the principles of natural law. So, the requirements of practical reasonableness are there to 'afford a rational basis for the activities of legislators, judges and citizens', as set out in Figure 3.8.

FIGURE 3.8: USING PRACTICAL REASONABLENESS

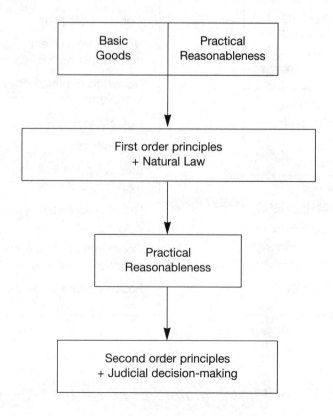

However, these principles can be outweighed or overridden by the 'absolute rights or man'. Finnis identifies natural rights derived from the basic goods, which include the right not to be deprived of life as a direct means to an end, not to be deceived in the course of factual communication, not to be condemned on false charges, and not be denied the ability to procreate.[62]

Obeying law – denying lex injusta non est lex

You need to connect the application of law by officials, as discussed under the last heading, with a citizen's obligation to obey the law. You will see Finnis' discussion on this point in Lloyd (pp 185–191). In Finnis' conception of the good community, it is necessary for an *unjust law* to be complied with, for the common good. A citizen is morally obliged to obey the law, because otherwise the legal system would be weakened.

The only person who can make changes to the law is the ruler, who will have to find out through the application of the principles of practical reasoning. However, the ruler has the responsibility of repealing, not enforcing the unjust law. The ruler does not have a right for it to be conformed to, but until this occurs, citizens and officials *will have to obey it*. Finnis denies that St Thomas Aquinas ever said that an unjust law could be disobeyed.

Critical responses to Finnis

A considerable body of contrary viewpoints are arrayed against Finnis' natural law. You will see these included in both Lloyd's overview and Davies' arguments about Finnis. When you read any criticism or critique of a theory, be sure to know why the criticism is being levelled against the theory, because different arguments are established for different reasons (also see Chapter 9). Here are just a few derived from Davies and Lloyd – you can draw out more for yourselves:

He has discarded all the underlying principles of natural law.

How can you be a natural lawyer if you actively deny principles of good as the basis on which your theory is constructed?

He is simply imposing his world view on all of us through the guise of practical reason.

The claim that Finnis is simply replicating his own world view, but dressed up in universal claims of reason, forms a large part of Davies' critique of his theory.

Read Valerie Kerruish's parable in Davies (p 86) and you will pick up contrary images of the basic goods, and how Finnis' theory excludes people who are marginalised from society.

Is his theory a self-portrait as Kerruish suggests?

---

62 Ibid, p 225.

He is embedding Catholicism in the guise of universality.

Finnis' ideas must take you towards a particular world view, through
the methods he uses to lead you to particular points.
Despite his theory's expressed denial of a religious standpoint,
it supports a particular set of moral principles and denies others.

Critical responses to natural law theories

We have tried to leave questions and criticisms of natural law theories until
the end of this chapter so that you will have had an opportunity to read, digest,
and think about the underlying theories, and what they are saying. If you have
picked up any underlying sense that what we have said about theories may
not be as 'clean' as we have tried to make it, you may be right. Language is
not and can never be unmediated by a writer or a reader, however hard we
try to keep our distance from a topic.

Some of the arguments against natural law theory are:

- Its claim to be universal and immutable, when principles of human conduct
  are so clearly driven by context, politics, and historical circumstance. You
  may have picked up some of these ideas during our discussion of the pre-
  20th century versions of natural law, from our use of historical and
  contextual references in which to place the theory.

- Natural law is simply an argument for personal, conservative views. Natural
  law supports unfair laws, and is based on political structures designed to
  prop up inequalities. These are the kinds of criticisms levelled against Finnis,
  and we have already raised some of these views. We also saw them when
  we looked at the natural rights theories.

- The theory just doesn't 'work'. This is a type of criticism levelled against all
  the 20th century theorists in one form or another.

- The theory is irrational, and questions of law never need to be concerned
  with morals. These ideas will form the basis for modernism and positivism's
  criticisms of natural law, which we foreshadowed in this chapter, and which
  you will now look at in more depth in the next four chapters.

QUESTIONS TO THINK ABOUT

These are not questions to which we will provide you with answers, but are
questions designed to start you thinking about different facets of natural law
theory:

1. Can you explain the role of reason in natural law theory?

2. Is it relevant for natural law to be concerned with the needs of the common
   good or community?

3. At the beginning of this chapter, we suggested that principles found in areas
   of law like crime, tort and property can be traced back to natural law
   foundations — can you think of any examples which illustrate this point?

4. How can posited or human law be based on natural law? You should think about this question using Aristotle, Cicero, Aquinas and Finnis.

5. Is it valid to argue for rights in property using natural rights theories based in natural law, and Finnis' conception of property?

6. What advice would you give to a government considering introducing legislation to allow sperm donation for single women and lesbians? Your advice will need to either support or refute Finnis' natural law theory.

7. Should natural law theory be concerned about the validity or goodness of laws and legal systems?

8. Does Finnis convince you of the ability to find natural law using his methods?

9. Is his method of first and second order principles a viable one to be used by judges when confronted with difficult cases?

10. How valid are the criticisms of Finnis' natural law theory?

FURTHER READING

Beyleveld, Deryck & Brownsword, Roger, *Law as a moral judgment* (Sweet & Maxwell, London, 1986).

Davies, H & Holdcroft, D, *Jurisprudence: Texts and Commentary* (Butterworths, London, 1991).

Douzinas, Costas & Ronnie Warrington, with Shaun McVeigh, *Postmodern jurisprudence: the law of text in the texts of law* (Routledge, London, 1991).

Finnis, John, *Natural law and natural rights* (Clarendon Press, Oxford, 1980).

Finnis, John (ed), *Natural Law: International library of essays in law and legal theory* (Aldershot, Dartmouth, 1991).

Harris, JW, *Legal Philosophies*, 2nd edition (Butterworths, London, 1997).

Kelly, JM, *A short history of Western legal theory* (Clarendon Press, Oxford, 1992).

McCoubrey, H & White, N, *Textbook on Jurisprudence*, 2nd edition (Blackstone Press, London, 1993).

Morrison, Wayne, *Jurisprudence: from the Greeks to post-modernism* (Cavendish Press, London, 1997).

Ward, Ian, *An introduction to critical legal theory* (Cavendish Publishing, London, 1998).

CHAPTER 4

Modernism and the Scientific Method: Law's Search for Certainty

Reading 83
Aim. 83
Why we think the way we do 84
    The shift to modernism 84
    Modernism's method 88
Modernism in law. 96
    Law as science — a product of
    Enlightenment thinking 96
    Hans Kelsen 97
    Critical responses to Kelsen 105
Questions to think about 106
Further reading. 107

READING

DAVIES, *Asking the Law Question: The Dissolution of Legal Theory*, 2nd edition, Chapter 3 (pp 96–102), Chapter 4 (pp 113–131), Chapter 8 (pp 297–300)
FREEMAN, *Lloyd's Introduction to Jurisprudence*, 7th edition, Chapters 1, 2 and 5

AIM

This chapter will introduce you to:

• why we make the assumptions we do about law;
• the main ideas and themes which emerged at the beginning of the modern world;
• the way in which lawyers think about law now, and how this is based in these early ideas; and
• the methods used by lawyers which are derived from these ideas.

This chapter is set out in two sections. Section A will look at the historical context surrounding the way in which views of law have changed between the classical and medieval world and the modern world, as well as introducing some of the basic underlying concepts which inform scientific approaches to law. Section B will look more closely at how these ideas are expressed in law, focusing on one particular theory of law, that of Hans Kelsen, which is one of the major results of this way of thinking.

SECTION A:
WHY WE THINK THE WAY WE DO

The shift to modernism

At the end of the medieval period, religious natural law began to lose its influence, to be replaced eventually by a way of thinking which we now identify as modernism. Modernism produced, as its principal way of looking at law, the legal theories described as 'positivist'. We will look at these theories in detail in Chapter 6.

FIGURE 4.1: MODERNISM TIMELINE

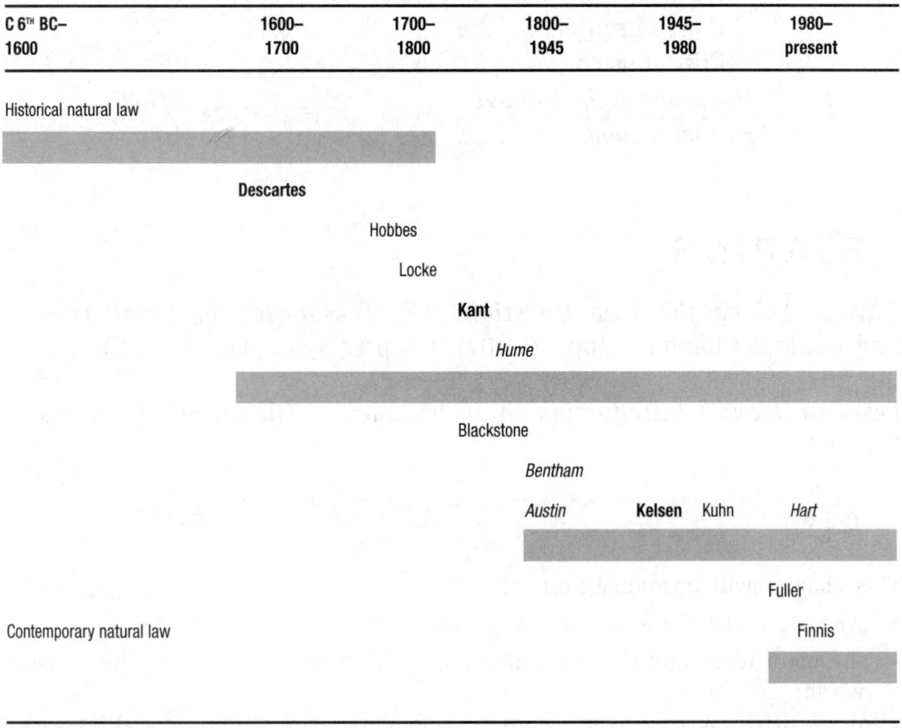

C 6ᵀᴴ BC– 1600	1600– 1700	1700– 1800	1800– 1945	1945– 1980	1980– present
Historical natural law					
	Descartes				
		Hobbes			
		Locke			
		Kant			
		Hume			
		Blackstone			
		Bentham			
		Austin	Kelsen Kuhn		Hart
				Fuller	
Contemporary natural law					Finnis

This timeline pulls out the modernist components of the detailed timeline (Figure 1.2) in Chapter 1.

We have juxtaposed modernism with positivism and a broad timeframe for historical natural law and marked the theories we will consider in detail in this or later chapters: **Modernism**, *Positivism*, Natural law.

MODERNISM

Modernism has become the dominant way of thinking in Western society. It is a view of the world that insists on the existence of an overarching or organising theory, called a metanarrative, from which objective principles can be derived. These objective principles form the basis for all inquiry as to how the world works. Modernism is concerned with finding an *absolute* ground of knowledge, which itself can not be the subject of further inquiry.

Modernism in history

The broad sweep of history, as the old ideas and ways of thinking gave way to what we recognise as modern modes of thought, includes a number of historical periods which overlap, or are in some way interconnected.

FIGURE 4.2: SOME ASPECTS OF MODERNISM

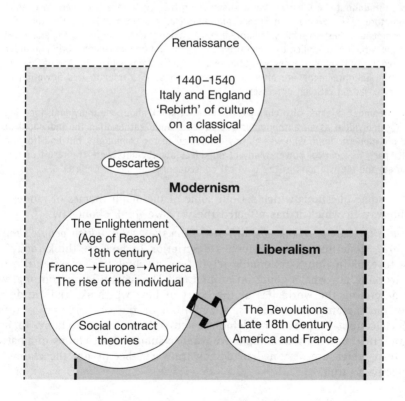

THE RENAISSANCE

The Renaissance describes a period during which Western culture was reborn after a long period of dormancy — indeed the word means 'reborn'. The Renaissance looked to the Greeks as a model of culture, and so the art and literature of the time reflected this classical flavour. There was also a reinvigoration of philosophical speculation, again based on the Greek spirit of critical inquiry. People undertook voyages of discovery which set the stage for the great imperial powers of France, England and Spain. Science as we know it began to take the place of superstition — for example, astrology began to be replaced by scientific investigation in the form of astronomy. While the Renaissance was beginning to develop some of the things which are characteristic of modernism (like the renewed interest in science), because it also looked back to the classical period for inspiration, it remained in some ways limited by those ideas.

THE ENLIGHTENMENT

The Enlightenment refers to a period around the 18th century when our understanding of the world was breaking free from ignorance and superstition. Enlightenment ideas began in France, but spread quickly to the rest of Europe and to America. These fresh ways of thinking were breaking down the ideas of traditional institutions like the Church. The Enlightenment saw the spread of the then new liberal and progressive ideas throughout the Western world — spawning the revolutions that were to change the nature of government in France and America, and ultimately set the tone for government in Western society. Enlightenment thinking is characterised by the analytical method, which was applied to the entire field of thought and knowledge, bringing order and regularity through the analysis of observable facts. Phrases like 'The Age of Reason' and 'The Enlightenment' are often used interchangeably to refer to this flowering of inquiry based on rational processes.

Enlightenment thinking also changed the way we think about the individual, focusing on the individual as an autonomous and rational unit,[1] rather than the individual of the pre-modern world, who was closely connected to the community, but had (for the most part) no political power. Many of our ideas about rights were the result of this change, and we will look at the political consequences of this in Chapter 5.

Here are some questions which set out some of the major themes of modernism and the way in which it has affected the way we think about law:

- *How is the way we think now different from the way in which people thought before?* Modernism is very much a description of how we think today. We try to explain things rationally, relying on an analytical or scientific way of working out what's going on around us.[2] This scientific and rational way of describing the world lies at the heart of how we think, and we do not rely on explanations based on superstition or the supernatural — things which cannot be proved or demonstrated. When someone claims to have paranormal powers, for example, we want to subject those claims to a battery of tests which are designed to demonstrate whether or not the claims are objectively 'true'.

---

1   Davies, M, *Asking the Law Question: The Dissolution of Legal Theory*, 2nd edition, (Sydney, Lawbook Co, 2002), p 300.
2   Davies, p 298.

- *What is different about the way modernism thinks about the individual?* Modernism is characterised by a view, derived from Rene Descartes (1596–1650), that the individual is a rational, free and autonomous unit – the 'I' that thinks. (Believe it or not, this was a very radical departure at the time.) This view has altered the way in which we think about ourselves and how we are governed. For example, the old relationship between autocratic rulers with unlimited power and their subjects has given way to the ideas of modern democracy (via the social contractarians), where individuals do not give away their rights without getting something in return.

- *How does this way of thinking affect the way in which courts operate?* Within the modernist tradition, we expect courts to make their judgments scientifically and analytically – relying on objectively determined facts, rather than on subjective impressions. A modern criminal trial tries to prove objective facts which show the offence charged has been committed, rather than relying on something other than rational argument (like divine intervention) to show guilt or innocence. The rules of evidence are designed to make the evidence which is admitted in a trial objective and value-free – so evidence (such as identification evidence) is acceptable, but subjective evidence (such as a witness's opinion) is usually not. This way of thinking also means that we tend to be sceptical of some types of personal stories, believing them only when they come from an objective source.

- *How does this way of thinking influence the way in which legal theory thinks about law?* The shift to a highly analytical and objective way of thinking about law can be seen in the theory of Hans Kelsen. Kelsen describes his theory as a 'pure theory of law', and tries to remove anything which is not objective from legal analysis – creating a *legal science*. He is trying to establish a conceptual framework in which law can be analysed according to the scientific principles which came to prominence during the Enlightenment.

If you think all of this makes perfect sense, it is because we are describing many of the current ideas and assumptions about the world. What will become obvious is that law as we know it tries to do much the same thing as other disciplines or branches of knowledge do under the influence of modernist thinking – to bring itself under the umbrella of rational, objective inquiry, leaving aside the reliance on things which are not able to be demonstrated according to modernist ideas.

Creating the world as we know it

In Chapter 3, we suggested that the 'easy' answer to the question 'Where does the law come from?' was that it is what the legislature says it is, or what the judges say it is. It is no accident that we see this as the obvious answer to the question, because we are the product of the modernist tradition, which tells us that this is the right way to assess this question. The ideas of modernism generally (and positivism specifically, as a type of legal theory) are those ideas to which, as Davies says, we have been trained to turn, imagining them to be 'instinctive'.[3] We have been brought up with many of these ideas so deeply

CHAPTER 4

---

embedded in our thinking that we are often not aware that we are thinking in this way, which makes us imagine, if we consider the question at all, that we have not adopted any sort of standpoint.

> Think about a fish. If it could talk, it would probably have a great deal of difficulty trying to explain what water was. It spends its entire life immersed in water, to the extent that it never really thinks about what it is. (It only ever becomes important when there isn't any!) We are pretty much the same when it comes to air. We breathe it in and out all the time, without ever giving it much thought. Oxygen, which keeps us all alive, wasn't discovered until the 1770s — right in the middle of the Enlightenment!
>
> The characteristic ideas of modernism are a bit like oxygen to us, or water to a fish. They are so much an intrinsic part of life that we rarely give any thought to them, assuming that they must always have been there. And when they are taken away — or challenged — we often feel the same sort of discomfort as a fish out of water.

Modernism's method

Rene Descartes

Descartes and method

Descartes is often thought of as the first modern thinker, in that his work provides the philosophical framework and methodology which forms the basis of modern scientific approaches to understanding the world. Descartes tries to find a fundamental set of principles about what constitutes knowledge so that we can be certain about what is true.

> ## COGITO ERGO SUM — I THINK, THEREFORE I AM
>
> At the heart of this process is the concept that for us to be certain that something is true (that is, for it to form an *absolute* foundation of our knowledge) it should able to be verified, leaving no room for doubt. So Descartes began to think about what he could be absolutely certain of — by doubting everything. As far as what he perceived with his senses, he imagined that he might be tricked by his senses (such as in dreams, which appear real), or that he might be being deceived by a 'wicked demon'.
>
> Eventually, he concluded that there is a single proposition which can be relied on — that is beyond doubt — and that is the existence of the individual who was thinking about the problem. This principle is summed up in the famous phrase 'cogito ergo sum', or 'I think, therefore I am'.[4]

In this formula, the idea of the individual is linked to the idea of rationality — the concept of the individual as a rational being, capable of reasoning. Once the existence of this thinking individual is established, the existence of reason follows logically, and is equally beyond doubt. This principle forms the basis of Descartes' approach to the methodology of all intellectual inquiry — specifically that of a science.

---

4 Davies, p 298.

CARTESIAN METHODOLOGY

('Cartesian' is the adjective derived from Descartes)

The methodology which Descartes proposed included these steps:

* use only clear ideas as the basis for your analysis;
* divide a problem into as many parts as you need to analyse it;
* work through from the simple to the complex; and
* always check thoroughly for things you might have missed.

All in all, this is probably good advice for doing law exams! Courts take great care (and a great many words) to try and frame a legal rule as precisely as possible. The idea of breaking up a cause of action into elements is an example of Descartes' method of dividing a problem up. We then usually try to state the basic concepts which are relevant to a legal problem before embarking on an examination of the subtler and more difficult issues which are raised in the detail of a problem. And, finally, we should always check over our work (whether it be an assignment or submissions to the court) before we can feel secure in our conclusions.

We ought, Descartes argues, to start from a position of doubt, not accepting the facts which are handed down to us by authority, or even our own observations, until they have been verified by a logical process of deduction and reason. Descartes argues that it is, in fact, this *method* which allows us to assert that our conclusions are true. The method itself excludes doubt. By starting with clear ideas, and proceeding step by step through logical deductions, we can be certain that, in the end, what we assert is true.

Descartes' individual

But this process also places substantially more emphasis on the individual. Because the individual is seen as the basis for understanding the world – individuals can look at the world, analyse what they see, and decide things for themselves – it is now less possible for external authorities and institutions to impose their views on the individual. This new view of the individual gives rise to the idea of the Cartesian 'subject' – autonomous, free and independent.[5]

We are accustomed to thinking about society (and law) from the perspective of the individual. For example, our ideas about contract start from the proposition that individuals go into the market with the freedom to work out their own bargains. A contract is made when two such free individuals achieve consensus ad idem – agreement. Contract law is said to create a neutral environment in which they can make their own *independent* decisions about whom they will contract with, and on what terms. For instance, in contract law, you will probably know that law generally does not intervene when an individual makes a poor decision about whether a contract represents a good bargain – law requires *sufficient* consideration (a legal concept), not *adequate* consideration (an economic or social one).

Furthermore, it was these ideas of autonomy and freedom which were used by the social contract theorists as the model of the individual, and this Cartesian subject forms the basis of modern liberal interpretations of the world.

---

5 Davies, pp 299–300.

CHAPTER 4

FIGURE 4.3: WHAT'S DIFFERENT ABOUT DESCARTES' INDIVIDUAL — THE THINKING 'I'

Pre-Cartesian individual

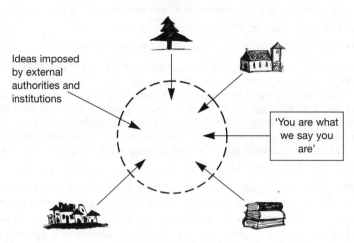

Ideas imposed by external authorities and institutions

'You are what we say you are'

Cartesian individual

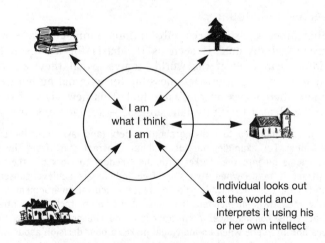

I am what I think I am

Individual looks out at the world and interprets it using his or her own intellect

DENNIS WANTS DEMOCRACY

If you get the chance, watch the film *Monty Python and the Holy Grail*. Pay particular attention to the scene in which King Arthur tries to explain to Dennis the Peasant *why* he is king. Arthur tells the story of the Lady of the Lake, who gave him the sword Excalibur as a symbol that he was to rule the Britons. Arthur is to rule by Divine Right.

Arthur's world is of a community ruled by an autocratic sovereign, deriving power from something beyond the legal system — the mystical figure of the Lady of the Lake. In such a society, individuals have little or no freedom or autonomy.

Dennis, however, rejects this as a basis for legitimate authority, arguing from ideas which derive from this period, and which reflect the assumptions about society which we find as familiar as Arthur's justification seems strange and unconvincing. Dennis argues that relying on the supernatural — gifts from 'strange women in ponds' (or Divine Right?) — is not a valid basis for power. Dennis thinks of power as emanating from the will of the people (a very democratic idea for Dennis's time, strongly reminiscent of some of the liberal or social contract theories about the legitimation of the power of the state).

Dennis then goes on to make observations about social organisation that owe much to the theories of Karl Marx (which will be dealt with in Chapter 8), finally calling on on-lookers to witness his repression at the hands of Arthur.

In many ways, this scene is a graphic (and funny) demonstration of the clash of world views that was to work itself out as the 'old' world — the classical and medieval world dominated by religion and superstition — gave way to the modern world in which ideas of individual autonomy and freedom, together with a participatory role in political power, hold sway.

Along with the desire for a scientific or objective approach to inquiry, modernist thought gave rise a change in the assumptions about government, the development of the now familiar concepts of rights, and the political beliefs which we think of as 'liberal'. (These will be considered in more detail in Chapter 5.)

'POLITICAL' AND 'LIBERAL'

Like many words, 'political' and 'liberal' have a somewhat different flavour from their ordinary meanings when used in the context of legal theory. While 'political' might include the ideas of politics as it relates to political parties, it also has a general and wider meaning, encompassing everything about the relationship between citizens and government. 'Liberal' — with a small 'l' — refers not to any political party (although there is often some relationship between political parties which use the term and the underlying ideas of liberal philosophy), but to the consequences which followed the rise of ideas about individuals' self-interest, and their right to pursue that interest with a minimum interference from government.

FIGURE 4.4: A DIFFERENT VIEW OF GOVERNMENT

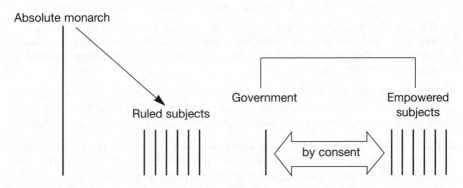

While liberalism involves a series of complex and sometimes contradictory ideas and ideals, it is essentially the political outgrowth of the new emphasis on the individual, as the nature of society changed from feudalism (in which most individuals had very limited freedom) to a market-based economy (in which individuals could operate to their own best advantage). Liberal theorists argued that this could best be done where the state's role in the organisation of society was minimal (see Chapter 3, p 62).

You will come across many descriptions of the individual of the Enlightenment tradition. While they will not be identical, they will tend to list a core of characteristics which this new, Cartesian subject is assumed to possess — unity, atomism, freedom, equality, autonomy, rationality, self-determination and enlightened self-interest.

Many of these characteristics form the foundational assumptions which lie (often unstated) behind the way in which many branches of law have developed.[6] As we have seen, contract law operates from the presumption that individuals in the market possess many, if not most, of these characteristics. Contract law assumes that adults are competent, that they can make rational choices about what contracts they want to form, and on what terms they want to enter those contracts.

Modernism and scientific method

The changes that were being forged during this period were, eventually, to diminish the significance of the church and state in governing our lives. The Renaissance and the Enlightenment were founded in a very different world-view from that which had gone before. Rather than looking to God (or gods) for meaning or justification, the catch-cry of the Enlightenment was that man, not God, was the measure of all things. What this means is that we began to look outwards at the world, rather than having a view imposed by external authorities. Ideas which could not be proven were rejected in favour of those which could be demonstrated by what came to be called the scientific method.

THE SCIENTIFIC METHOD

The 'scientific method' refers to a process of discovering and validating propositions based on: observation and collection of data; the framing of a hypothesis (or theory) to explain the data; and the subsequent testing of the theory by further observation to verify whether the theory does in fact predict the outcomes of such experiments.

This view of science (and its claim to objectivity) is based in the belief that it removes from the process the personal beliefs and subjective aspects of the enquirer, substituting a detached and value-neutral observer whose results are not infected by those subjective elements.

In the modern world, this method finds expression in the use of scientific approaches in a range of disciplines, including law. Our current thinking — not just what we think, but *how* we think — is a direct consequence of these changes.

One of the best illustrations of this changing view, which we referred to briefly in Chapter 3 (p 62), is the clash between the official, Church view of the solar system, and the view about the place of the Earth in that system that was being formed on the basis of observations and calculations about the movement of the stars and planets. A number of astronomers — Galileo was perhaps the most famous of them — were arguing that the official view was wrong.

6   Davies, p 300.

Careful and precise measurements of planetary motion suggested that it was, in fact, the Earth which revolved around the Sun. Church authority, and most particularly the Holy Inquisition, objected to this proposition on the grounds that the Bible clearly stated that the sun moved through the sky.[7] So they denounced Galileo's teachings, maintaining that the Earth was the centre of the solar system and that the Sun revolved around it.

For maintaining and teaching the view that the Earth revolved around the Sun, Galileo was called before the Inquisition. Not wishing to meet the same end as another astronomer, Giordano Bruno (who had been burned at the stake in 1600 for insisting this was the case), Galileo recanted. He escaped being burned, but spent the rest of his life under house arrest, prevented by the Inquisition from further teaching.

While the old way of thinking appears to have won *that* battle, it was the new way, based in observation, experiment, and scientific verification which won in the long run. Because we are the direct inheritors of this new way of thinking, we probably find it strange to think that someone could be burned alive for insisting that they could demonstrate what we take for granted – that the Earth revolves around the Sun!

Modernist thinking in law

In the modern world, the underlying assumptions about law, and the practices which flow from these assumptions, reflect the type of thinking which emerged at the Enlightenment. Examples of modernist thinking in law are everywhere. However, one idea which has developed in the way law thinks about resolving issues clearly illustrates the debt which law owes to Enlightenment thinking: the use of objective tests.

OBJECTIVE TESTS

Many of the tests which are used in law are described as 'objective' tests. Here is an example from the law of negligence. In determining whether a defendant has breached their duty of care, the courts apply an objective test of 'reasonable foresight' – what (if any) steps would a reasonable person, in the position of the defendant, have taken to avoid a foreseeable risk of injury to another person?[8] Because individuals, and their response to perceived risk, vary widely, the courts have used a test based on a hypothetical person – originally the 'man on the Clapham omnibus'. (At the time this phrase was used to denote the hypothetical reasonable person, Clapham was thought of as a very 'ordinary' suburb of London, where respectable people lived, commuting to their respectable jobs by bus.)

In putting the ideas of Enlightenment thinking into practice, the courts have settled on an objective, 'reasonable' person test (rather than just an 'ordinary' person test, or a subjective test, based on the defendant's actual foresight and perception of risk). This hypothetical individual is an ideal who embodies the spirit of objective enquiry, precisely because they are free of the subjective biases, vested interests (or even irrational views) which real people, even judges, can have. Most particularly, the courts rejected a test

---

7   For example, the story of Joshua and the sun standing still in the sky was theological or scriptural 'proof' that the sun moved, not the earth (Joshua Ch 10, 11–14).
8   See, for example, *Wyong Shire Council v Shirt* (1980) 146 CLR 40 at 47, per Mason J.

based on whether the defendant, who actually faced by the situation, could foresee the risk. As the defendant, they will have a vested interest in claiming that they did not foresee sufficient risk to warrant taking precautions. Vested interests are very unscientific.

In many ways, the 'reasonable person' is the voice of the Enlightenment, being used by the court to bring an objective and scientific mode of inquiry into legal thinking.

As we have said, modernism, as a description of a way of thought, has been the predominant influence in the Western world since the Enlightenment. Modernist philosophy insists that there is an overall organising principle or theory (referred to as a *metanarrative*), from which objective principles can be derived.

As an illustration, consider that throughout this period (and right on into the 20th Century), physicists who were working out the details of a mathematically-based view of how the universe worked believed that it would be possible to construct a theory which would explain everything about the universe — one single, self-consistent and overarching set of principles (or equations) from which everything else could be derived.[9] We tend to do something similar in law, by looking at underlying *abstract* legal principles to explain legal significance, rather than focusing on the specifics of a case. So too, courts try to rationalise law into a consistent and coherent set of legal principles.

Modernism and legal theory

In the second half of this chapter and in the chapters following (as far as Chapter 9), we will be looking at the major legal theorists who write within the modernist tradition. Because this chapter is principally about the changes which brought about the primacy of science as the method by which truth is located, though, we will only look at Hans Kelsen in this chapter. Kelsen sought to develop a 'pure theory' of law, uninfected by any subjective considerations — an objective, scientific analysis of what law is.

In Chapter 6, we will look at the theorists who made a significant contribution to the way in which we understand law today: Jeremy Bentham and John Austin. Their theories form the basis of a school of thought known as 'legal positivism'.

LEGAL POSITVISM

Legal positivism describes an approach to law which is primarily concerned with 'posited law' — that is, law which has been laid down, or 'posited', by the institutions which are authorised to make law, like Parliament and the courts. One of the features of legal positivism is that it looks at law as it is, rather than how it ought to be.

This approach is related to the ideas of David Hume (1711–1776), an influential Enlightenment thinker, who argues that what 'is' and what 'ought to be' are different, and that it is not possible to derive prescriptions for human behaviour (what they ought

---

9   Physicists currently appear to be split on the question of whether any such overarching theory is possible. Some believe that a 'grand unifying theory' is a possibility, while others think that the fundamental contradictions in the major theories of the universe will not be resolved by the discovery of any such unifying theory.

to do) from descriptions of the world (as it is).[10] Hume's approach is linked to the idea of empiricism — that we can know, and prove, that some things happen by a process of observation. The bubbles which form as water boils verify that the water *is*, indeed, boiling. But no such process of observation can verify that something is 'good', and therefore something which we *ought* to do.

Subsequent legal writers took up this idea, and sought to focus on law 'as it is' and as it could be observed, separating it from other fields of enquiry, particularly morality, which dealt with what people thought human behaviour ought to be.

While you may not have come across the term 'legal positivism' before, you may well recognise this idea of separating questions of law from questions of morality as being the basis for the way in which you have been taught law.

Does modernism have a standpoint?

Modernism has had a considerable effect on the way we think about law, as well as the way in which we learn law, to the extent that its ideas often sit unnoticed in the background. We tend not to think about them at all, unless something happens which conflicts with what we think of as the normal — or perhaps, the only sensible — way of looking at things.

One of the major ideas of modernist thinking is that it is based in an objective and scientific approach, and as a result, that it is neutral or value free. It claims to have no 'point of view'. The conclusions which are arrived at using these approaches are valid precisely *because* they do not rely on unverifiable or undemonstrable assumptions, or a particular point of view, but are rather created through the dispassionate and detached analytical processes which are the hallmark of science and the scientific method. In this form of analysis, the beliefs, values or opinions of the person are not relevant to, or incorporated in, their results.

Our preference for this type of knowledge — knowledge based in objective and scientific methods of inquiry and analysis — is illustrated, as Davies observes,[11] by the increasing tendency of academic disciplines to characterise themselves as 'sciences'. This in itself speaks volumes about the way in which we consider scientific approaches as the best way of being certain that we know what we know — we know this is 'true' because the method we have used to arrive at our conclusions is one which excludes superstition, or the subjective opinions and biases of the inquirer.

But in one sense, the assumption that there is one, proper, way in which to assess knowledge is, in fact, to take up a particular point of view about how it is that we know what we know, to the exclusion of other possibilities.[12]

CHAPTER 4

---

10 Davies, p 105.
11 Davies, p 116.
12 Davies, p 124.

SECTION B: MODERNISM IN LAW

Law as science — a product of Enlightenment thinking

As we have seen, one of the major changes that accompanied the Enlightenment was the shift to looking for a foundation for knowledge by using the scientific method — basing our understanding in the objective observation and analysis of what it is we are studying. Davies observes that 'scientific' proof is thought of as the standard way of determining all knowledge.[13] This move to detached, objective approaches can also be seen in the way in which law developed.

We are accustomed, in the 21st century view of law, to want to prove facts as part of doing law (rather than relying on the supernatural), and as far as possible, we try to remove the individual (with their idiosyncrasies and subjective feelings) from the law equation. We have already mentioned the rules of evidence (which try to replicate a process of deciding the 'facts' of a case from a neutral, detached and objective perspective). This replaces earlier forms of trial — like trial by ordeal or trial by battle — which relied on divine intervention to indicate guilt or innocence.

Furthermore, if you think about the way in which you have been taught law, you might realise that in analysing legal problems, you have been taught to strip away the personal and the subjective elements of a legal scenario, and to concentrate on placing the people and events into formal legal categories. Most of you will have picked up the habit of stripping away even the names of the individuals who play a part in a legal scenario, referring to the offeror and the offeree in a contract problem as, say, 'A' and 'B' — and your examiners may well have encouraged this by giving the characters in the scenario names with suitable initials.

This is the end product of Enlightenment thinking, and the insistence on a scientific way of approaching what it is that we can know.

But, as Davies points out,[14] science in this sense is not really as objective or detached as it first appears — science (or scientific thought and process) is often based on underlying assumptions which are the product of social and cultural contexts, rather than being value-neutral. Examples include what Davies calls 'androcentrism' (the tendency to use males as the basis for determining 'facts' about human beings), and the Western-oriented racial and cultural assumptions which have sometimes formed the basis for, or at least lay underneath, scientific analysis.[15]

Thomas Kuhn, a physicist and science historian, drew attention to the fact that, far from proceeding as a smooth, detached development of ideas, science

---

13 Davies, p 115.
14 Davies, p 117ff.
15 At the end of the 19th century, reputable (indeed, eminent) scientists formed theories about intelligence which reflected and reinforced the prevailing assumptions about the general superiority of Europeans. See Chapter 13 below.

progresses in fits and starts, with major developments characterised by a change in the *beliefs* of the scientific community as a whole, and the underlying conceptual structures of science – its 'paradigm'.[16] Kuhn argues that science often suppresses new ideas which threaten to subvert the basic commitments of science as they appear at any given time.[17] Science (and scientific beliefs), then, are inseparable from the society in which they arise and are maintained.

COMPETING SCIENTIFIC EXPLANATIONS

We are accustomed in Western society to think of evolution as the scientific explanation for how human beings came into existence, and how different species of animals and plants develop in the way in which they do. But it was not the only possible explanation put forward, and in the nineteenth century, two theories – Darwinism and Lamarckianism – struggled for acceptance within the scientific community as a way of explaining biological diversity. Western science opted for Darwinism, while the Soviet scientific community accepted Lamarckianism (which suggests that species change as the result of direct action by the environment, so that the children of a blacksmith will have stronger arms). Natural selection – Darwin's idea of the survival of the fittest – maps well to the underlying assumptions about society which prevailed in the capitalist West, while the 'inevitability' of change within Lamarck's theory fitted the assumptions which underpin Marxist thought.

Hans Kelsen

A scientific approach to legal systems

The line of reasoning which emerged in the Enlightenment – the insistence on scientific detachment which characterises modern thought about law – reached its apex in the theories of Hans Kelsen (1881–1973).

Kelsen was born in Prague, but at the age of three moved with his family to Austria, where he studied law, and later taught at the University of Vienna. He drafted the Austrian Constitution, and sat in the Constitutional Court from 1921 to 1930. Political controversy over the issue of remarriage under Austrian law led to his being removed from his position in the Court, and eventually forced him to move to Cologne. When the Nazis came to power in Germany in 1933, however, Kelsen (who came from a Jewish family) was removed from his job at the University of Cologne, and he found it necessary to move again, this time to Switzerland. At the outbreak of World War Two, fearing that Switzerland would become involved in the war, Kelsen moved yet again – this time to the United States.

Kelsen's theory is the end product of trying to look at law scientifically. For the purpose of the theory, he rejects anything which is seen as subjective, and is looking for the underlying objective structure of legal systems.[18] For this reason, Kelsen is often described as a 'conceptual'[19] – as well as a 'neo-Kantian'.

---

16 Davies, p 120.
17 Kuhn, Thomas, *The Structure of Scientific Revolution*, (Chicago, University of Chicago Press, 1962) in Lloyd, p 33.
18 Davies, p 96.
19 Davies, p 127.

CHAPTER 4

Kelsen's modernism

Kelsen's is a modernist theory, because it is trying to construct a self-contained theory about legal systems, which does not need to look outside itself (or the legal world) to explain or justify itself. He is looking for the absolute grounds of knowledge about law and legal systems, which are themselves not then the subject of further inquiry.[20]

His roots in modernism extend to his determination to create a theory which deals with law entirely objectively — rejecting subjective concepts which would detract from its scientific purity. While he recognises that law is a social phenomenon,[21] he insists that the values which are promoted by laws should not themselves be the subject of legal analysis — that is the territory of moral philosophers, sociologists etc. Kelsen does not deny the connections between law and these other disciplines, but rather seeks to make the theory pure (and objective) by looking at law and legal systems in themselves — not in the light of those other disciplines (which he considers to be subjective, and hence unscientific).[22]

Kelsen therefore calls his theory a 'pure theory of law', and to that end is concerned with the accurate definition of the subject matter of legal analysis, law and legal systems, without any reference to its political or moral aspects. All these things must be determined objectively, so that questions such as the intention of the legislature in formulating a particular law — questions which are based in psychology or politics — have no place in the theory.

Kelsen's conceptualism

Kelsen is *conceptual* because he is concerned to develop an underlying structure to law — a concept of law — which can be applied without any reference to the values which are contained in law, and is not based in empirical observation about human or social behaviour (as we will see Hart's positivism is). Kelsen is trying to create a model of legal systems which can describe and define *any* legal system, regardless of what values it promotes or enforces, or how it is arranged politically. He does this using, as the basis of the legal system, a series of interrelated 'norms', and the application of sanctions when a norm is not followed. Such a theory can explain primitive and sophisticated legal systems alike, and even loose affiliations such as international law, where sanctions might take the form of embargoes (which are, in fact, frequently referred to as economic sanctions) or even military force (as was recently the case in Iraq).

To retain this objective requirement, the theory is concerned with the relationships between the component parts of a legal system, and not with what individual laws say about human conduct under the legal system, or whether they promote justice. Kelsen's legal theory is primarily about order, rather than any abstract (and subjective) notions of 'justice'.[23]

---

20 Lloyd, pp 257–258.
21 Kelsen, *The Pure Theory of Law*, in Davies, p 128.
22 Kelsen, *The Pure Theory of Law*, quoted in Davies, p 128.
23 That is not to say that Kelsen himself thinks these things are unimportant. He has in fact written extensively on political philosophy, justice and similar topics. It's just that these things do not form the substance of *legal theory* or *legal science*.

Kelsen as 'neo-Kantian'

Kelsen is often described as a 'neo-Kantian' because the method he applies to understanding law relies very much on some aspects of Immanuel Kant's philosophy. Immanuel Kant was an 18th century German philosopher who exerted an enormous influence on the development of Western thinking in relation to the nature of human knowledge and reason, as well as moral philosophy.

For Kant, it is impossible to know anything in itself. We become aware of things through our senses, but our sensory impressions or experiences in themselves do not provide us with any understanding or knowledge of what we perceive. It is impossible to understand or know anything about the world around us without constructing a set of concepts or *categories* which allow us to make sense of that world. Human understanding is the result of our ability to organise the mass of information which floods into our minds as we contemplate the world, by creating a conceptual map which defines and makes sense of that information.

While there might be a real world out there, our knowledge of it is a product of the conceptual map which we use to arrange the information we get from our senses. Davies uses Foucault's description of a fictional classification of animals from the work of Borges to illustrate how dependent we are on such conceptual maps in framing our ideas about the world – how natural our own schemes appear, how important they are to our understanding, and how confronting it is to come across a different set of concepts.[24]

Kelsen's theory is an attempt to provide these categories when we look at law – a way of interpreting events as part of a self-contained *legal system*.[25] For Kelsen, something which happens in the world cannot be understood in terms of law unless it can be fitted into the conceptual structure which the theory provides. Indeed, the process of fitting an event into the conceptual structure is what gives the event legal meaning or significance.

> Take a relatively common event – Tom is driving his car down a suburban street. We might observe, via our senses, that Tom's car is travelling very quickly. With the aid of technology, we might be able to tell that it is travelling at 70 kilometres an hour. But this information has no legal significance in itself. It is only when we think about this information in terms of a legal concept or category – exceeding the speed limit – that the event in the real world takes on any legal significance.[26]

Kelsen's theory

Norms – at the centre of Kelsen's scheme

The central component of Kelsen's theory is the 'norm'. Law, for Kelsen, is a normative science, concerned with propositions about what 'ought' to happen.[27]

24 Davies, pp 9, 23.
25 Lloyd, p 255; Davies, pp 8 and 298.
26 Davies, p 127.
27 Lloyd, p 258; Kelsen, *General Theory of Law and State*, in Lloyd, p 291.

CHAPTER 4

Norms, however, are not 'ought' propositions in the sense that they define how people 'ought' to behave in any moral sense. The scientific face of law — Kelsen's legal science — is not there to pass judgment on the moral value of the norms, but to interpret them objectively as parts of the legal system.[28] So, rather than being statements that a person ought not to behave in a particular way, they are framed as legal statements about what ought to happen if a person behaves in that way. They do not say, 'Thou shalt not kill', but rather, 'If you do kill, you ought to be punished'.[29]

Neither are norms statements about what actually happens in real life — obviously, the norms of human behaviour (legal or otherwise) are frequently ignored by people, and when they are, they are not always caught and punished. Yet the norm remains valid.[30] Legal science is not concerned with describing events in the real world, but about formulating a conceptual framework in which events can be understood as part of a legal system.[31]

For Kelsen, norms are descriptions of, or statements about, what ought to happen within a legal system. They may include statements about required behaviour (such as the norm, common to most societies, which proscribes the killing of another person, except in certain circumstances), or they may authorise institutions, bodies or individuals to create or enforce these norms.

EXAMPLES OF NORMS

A norm created in the Constitution: that legal norms, backed by sanctions, should be created for the peace, welfare and good government of a country only by Parliament or the courts.

A legal norm created by Parliament: that vehicles should not be driven on suburban streets at a speed greater than 50 kilometres per hour.

And when Tom breaks the speed limit?

A legal norm created by the Magistrates Court: that Tom, having been caught by police travelling at 65 kilometres an hour on a suburban street, should pay a fine of $150.

And when Tom refuses to pay the fine?

A legal norm: that a warrant for Tom's arrest should be issued and that Tom should be imprisoned for a specific period.[32]

Sanctions — what happens when a norm is not followed?

Not all statements of what 'ought' to happen are norms. Davies gives an illustration of a statement which, in a formal sense, appears to lay down a norm (or a guide to required conduct) — 'you must hand in a 3 000 word essay'.[33] This may just express a wish ('my subjective will'). But, as Davies explains, such a statement becomes 'objective' (in Kelsen's terms) only by

---

28 Kelsen, *The Pure Theory of Law*, in Lloyd, p 278.
29 Lloyd, p 256.
30 Kelsen, *General theory of Law and State*, in Lloyd, p 285.
31 Kelsen, *The Pure Theory of Law*, in Lloyd, p 278.
32 This example is loosely based on the law in Queensland relating to the creation and enforcement of speed limits in the *Transport Operations (Road Use Management) Act* 1995 and relevant Regulations and the *State Penalties Enforcement Act* 1999.
33 Davies, p 101.

reference to its relationship with other statements which are connected to the statement about handing in the essay itself. These, in this illustration, take the form of the other statements which go to make up a *system* of assessment for the university subject which the essay is part of, and go towards creating a system of related statements about what ought to happen in the administration of the subject.

What is critical for Kelsen is that a legal norm, once broken, attracts a sanction.[34] This is implied by the way in which we characterised a norm as being a statement about what ought to happen when someone acts in a proscribed way. (Kelsen's word for this is 'delict'.) In a very mathematical way of describing this relationship, we can illustrate the relationship by an equation. We can say:

$$\text{norm} + \text{delict} \rightarrow \text{sanction}$$

or use the formula: 'if a person conducts themselves in a manner which is contrary to that which is laid down in a valid norm, then a sanction ought to be applied'.

Law, in this model, is a mechanism for describing the legitimate coercive force in social organisation which we understand law to be. Punishment can be imposed when the norms, which have their practical appearance as laws, are not adhered to. And statements which appear to be legal norms (for example, which appear in Acts of Parliament) will not be relevant to Kelsen's legal analysis if they cannot be formulated according to this model of 'if X, then a sanction'.

The validity of norms

The structure which Kelsen describes as making up a legal system is composed of a multitude of norms. Remember, while these norms are descriptions of prescribed human behaviour, Kelsen is not at all concerned with what the content of these norms might be. The speed limit of 50 kilometres an hour could just as easily be 40 or 60, and indeed, the content of many legal norms, like those about driving on public roads, is constantly changing.

In Figure 4.5 (overleaf), the norms are represented by 'empty' circles. They are empty because, as far as Kelsen is concerned, any of these circles representing norms within the system can have any substantive content. What is significant is not the conduct which is prescribed by the norm, but the fact that a norm forms part of a structure – the hierarchy represented by the triangle and the relationships by the lines connecting them.[35] Norms do not exist in isolation, but form part of a complex interlocking structure which is defined by the relationships each norm has to the others in the legal system.

Any norm, in order to be valid, must be validated by a norm further up the hierarchy. This validation by a higher norm is represented in the diagram by the lines which connect upwards from the lower norms to the higher norms. What 'fills' the circles in the diagram – it may be a proscription against murder, or a norm which requires a particular form to be used when applying for a government grant – is a valid law not because of anything about what it says, but because it has a specific relationship with a higher norm.

34 Lloyd, p 261.
35 Kelsen, *The Pure Theory of Law*, in Lloyd, p 294.

FIGURE 4.5: A HIERARCHY OF NORMS

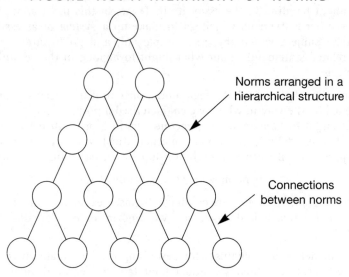

Norms arranged in a
hierarchical structure

Connections
between norms

If you look back at the examples of norms relating to Tom's speeding offence, you might have noticed that they follow a pattern:

- the first norm (p 100) – created by the Constitution – is in a very general form, relating only to the general power of Parliament and the courts to create norms;

- the second norm – specifying a speed limit of 50 kilometres per hour – is more particular, relating not to the general formula of 'peace, welfare and good government', but to quite specific forms of conduct promoting safety when we are driving on public roads;

- the third norm – that Tom should pay a fine for breaking the speed limit – is quite specific. It relates to a particular individual and their conduct with respect to a higher norm;

- and the last norm – about imprisoning Tom for non-payment of his fine – is now very 'real'. It impacts directly on Tom, who gets carted off to jail.

Figure 4.6 illustrates the nature of the relationships between these norms in terms of the original illustration of the hierarchy of norms. We can now fill in the circles – give them some content – not because we approve of the values they embed, but because they fit into the conceptual pattern which Kelsen describes as the structure of legal systems.[36] Norms at the top of the triangle are very general norms which specify that a particular institution – Parliament and the courts – ought to (or are authorised to) create more particular norms. And as we trace down from the top of the hierarchy to the bottom, the norms become increasing more specific, or 'concrete'. The hierarchy describes a system in which norms at the more general levels are translated into very 'real' norms which impact on individuals, in a process of 'concretisation'.

---

36 Kelsen, *The Pure Theory of Law*, in Lloyd, p 295.

FIGURE 4.6: SPECIFIC CONTENT AND THE RELATIONSHIP OF SOME NORMS

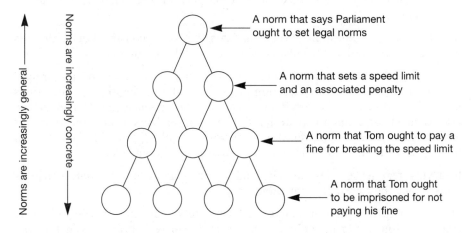

Lower level norms – 'concrete' norms

The Grundnorm — German for 'basic norm'

Norms, as we have seen, are validated by other norms – higher norms – by virtue of the relationship that they bear to each other. The norm which says that officials can throw Tom in jail is related to (and validated by) a higher norm about what the court ought to do if Tom doesn't pay his speeding fine, and so on.

But if norms are only valid because of this relationship – if they are validated only by a higher norm – what happens when we reach the top of the triangle? Do we just keep asking 'What validates this norm?' further and further up through the hierarchy, without end, in what philosophers would call an infinite regression?

Not really. Because Kelsen's theory is a theory of *law* – because sociology, psychology and politics have no place in this scheme – we can only keep asking that question while we remain *within* the legal system. Ultimately, when we ask questions about what validates a norm, we can backtrack as far as the 'first constitution' of the legal system we are investigating.

THE FIRST CONSTITUTION

The 'first constitution' of a legal system is the original legal entity – it may or may not be a written document like Australia's – which brought that legal system into existence. Constitutions may be amended, and they usually have a mechanism for achieving just that purpose, such as s 128 of the Commonwealth Constitution. When we track up the hierarchy, we will come, at some point, to the constitution as-it-currently-is. But the part which validates the norm we are concerned with may be one of these amendments. In that case, what validates that norm in the current constitution is the norm contained in the original, or 'first constitution', which says how the constitution ought to be amended.[37]

---

37 Kelsen, *General Theory of Law and State*, in Lloyd, p 286.

The constitution of a state is a legal document, so we are still within what Kelsen would think of as legitimate *legal* enquiry – relying on things which can be objectively determined, and form part of the legal system under investigation.

But if we ask the question, 'What validates this "first constitution"?', there is nothing *within* the legal system which can provide an answer.

Some countries have formed their governments as a result of an orderly transition of power (like the creation of the Australian federation), while others have been formed as the result of a war of independence (the United States, for example), or a unilateral declaration of independence (Rhodesia as it was at the time – now Zimbabwe). Other governments, like that of Saddam Hussein in Iraq, have been toppled by military force from the outside.

In a very real sense, these are the underlying issues which validate constitutions – but they are *not* legal things.

The answer to the question about what validates a constitution will ordinarily come from the world of 'politics' (in a very broad sense), and given the way in which Kelsen describes legal systems (and excludes from consideration matters which are not *legal*), there can be no *legal* answer to the question, 'What validates the "first constitution"?'.

To prevent either an infinite regression or the necessity to look outside the legal system for validation (and in doing so importing subjective material into the otherwise objective analysis), Kelsen uses the idea of the *Grundnorm* or Basic Norm.

The *Grundnorm* is not a legal norm in itself, because it cannot be validated, as all norms must be, by another norm further up the hierarchy.[38] Neither is it a legal norm in the sense that all other legal norms are created by a law-creating institution, using a legal procedure.[39] It is, as Kelsen suggests, a fiction – just an *assumption* or *presupposition* that the first constitution is valid. It has no legal content in the sense that ordinary legal norms do, but is merely a necessary part of a theory which seeks to isolate questions about law – legal science – from questions about other things, like politics or history. These are important questions – it is just that they have no place in Kelsen's conceptual scheme.[40]

The Constitution is NOT the GRUNDNORM.

Why?

---

38 Lloyd, p 264.
39 Kelsen, *General Theory of Law and State*, in Lloyd, p 287.
40 Lloyd, p 265.

FIGURE 4.7: SPECIFIC NORMS AND THE GRUNDNORM

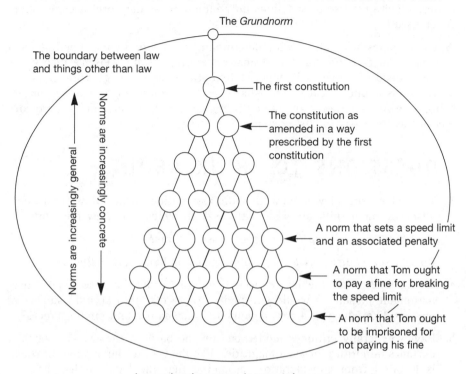

The *Grundnorm* is shown in Figure 4.7 as a point (actually a smaller circle) right at the top of the triangle. As the Basic Norm, it is the proposition from which all other norms within the system gain their validity. But because it is not really a legal norm in the sense that all the other norms are – it does not itself depend on a superior norm for *its* validity and it is not created in the same way as legal norms – it appears on the large circle, at the boundary of the self-contained legal system, and things which are not part of the legal system.[41]

Critical responses to Kelsen

As an expression of modernist thinking, Kelsen's theory seems to rest on a contradiction. Rather than something which is beyond doubt – the heart of modernist appeals to absolute knowledge – the centrepiece of the theory, the *Grundnorm*, is acknowledged by Kelsen to be a fiction, or a mere supposition.[42]

Critics also point to Kelsen's emphasis on the relationship of a norm to the sanctions which enforce it, arguing that there are many laws which do not attract a sanction. This gives rise for the need to assume that the sanctions

---

41 Davies, pp 341–342.
42 Lloyd, pp 264–265.

may be indirectly related to the norm — particularly for the higher, more abstract norms, which give rise to sanctions only indirectly, as the norm becomes more concretised.[43]

When it comes to dealing with determining which of two competing legal systems is, in fact, the 'lawful' system governing a state, Kelsen's theory has to step outside its own self-imposed limitations, and engage with empirical observations about efficacy — to what extent the norms of a legal system are being followed — rather than staying in the conceptual frame which the theory sets out as the basis for its existence.[44]

QUESTIONS TO THINK ABOUT

1. To what extent do you think that the assumptions which flow from liberalism and modernity are part of the way in which you view the world?

2. How hard is it to step outside these assumptions?

3. Do you see yourself as a free, autonomous and rational individual?

4. Would you rather the law expected you to behave like the hypothetical reasonable person, or would you prefer law to take into account subjective matters, like who *you* are, and your personal nature and circumstances?

5. Davies generally critiques modernism on the basis of the way in which it excludes minorities (or even majorities, like the 51% of the population which is female!) from consideration, assuming that the legal subject has the 'objective' characteristics we've considered. Is this a convincing position?

6. By creating an objective frame of reference, does modernism deny justice?

7. In this chapter, we have used some examples from torts law, contract law and the laws of evidence to illustrate the way in which some of the fundamental aspects of modernism have become embedded in substantive law as we know it. Can you think of other examples of laws which reflect this attitude to the world? Are there any examples of law which seem to run counter to these assumptions?

8. Does Kelsen's hierarchy of norms provide a sufficient explanation for all the things we would instinctively think of as laws?

9. What use has been made of Kelsen's theory in actual legal cases?

10. Many revolutions put a new regime in place immediately, and the norms of the old system which survive are then said to derive their validity from the new *Grundnorm*. What can Kelsen say about a situation (as in Iraq) where there is an interregnum — a period after the fall of one regime and before the new 'government' is in place and operating effectively? How would this fit into Kelsen's view of the *Grundnorm*?

---

43 Lloyd, pp 261–262.
44 Lloyd, pp 268–269.

FURTHER READING

Descartes, R, *Meditations on first philosophy*, 2nd edition, (Bobbs-Merrill, New York, 1960).

Kelsen, H, *General theory of Law and State*, translated by Hartney (Russell & Rusell, New York, 1961; Oxford University Press, Oxford, 1991).

Kelsen, H, *General theory of norms*, translated by Hartney (Oxford University Press, Oxford, 1991).

Kelsen, H, *Introduction to the Problems of Legal Theory*, translated by Paulson & Paulson (Clarendon Press, Oxford, 1992).

Kelsen, H, *Pure Theory of Law*, translated by Knight, (University of California Press, Berkeley, 1967).

Moore, R, *Legal Norms and Legal Science: a Critical Study of Kelsen's Pure Theory of Law* (University Press of Hawaii, Honolulu, 1978).

Murphy, J, *Kant: The Philosophy of Right* (Mercer University Press, Macon, Georgia, 1994).

Paulson S & Litschewski Paulson, B (eds), *Normativity and Norms: Critical Perspectives on Kelsenian Themes* (Clarendon Press, Oxford, 1998).

Raz, J, *The Concept of Legal System: An Introduction to the Theory of Legal System*, 2nd edition (Clarendon Press, Oxford, 1980).

Tur, RHS & Twining, W (eds), *Essays on Kelsen* (Clarendon Press, Oxford, 1986).

Want, C & Klimowski, A, *Introducing Kant*, edited by Appignanesi (Allen & Unwin, St Leonards, 1999).

CHAPTER 4

CHAPTER 5

Liberalism: Explaining Why We Think As We Do

Reading. 109
Aim. 109
Liberalism 110
   What then is liberalism?. 112
   Some characteristics of liberal thought 113
Ronald Dworkin 122
   Who is Ronald Dworkin? 122
   Where does Dworkin fit? 123
   Some detailed aspects of Dworkin's theory . . . 125
   Is Dworkin's world real?. 133
   Critical responses to Dworkin. 133
Questions to think about 134
Further reading. 134

READING

DAVIES, *Asking the Law Question: The Dissolution of Legal Theory*, 2nd edition, Chapter 2 (pp 64–65); Chapter 3 (p 73)
FREEMAN, *Lloyd's Introduction to Jurisprudence*, 7th edition, Chapter 7 (pp 540–548, 593–614), Chapter 17 (pp 1391–1403, 1428–1466)

AIM

This chapter will introduce you to:

- how the main ideas and themes which emerged at the Enlightenment translate into the form of political thought known as liberalism;
- some of the main ideas which go to make up liberal thought; and
- major aspects of the theories of Ronald Dworkin, which are closely associated with liberal thought.

This chapter is also set out in two sections. Section A will look at some of the more important ideas that are associated with the dominant form of political organisation in the western world, liberalism. Section B will look at one important theorist, Ronald Dworkin, and the way in which his theory embeds some of these ideas.

SECTION A: LIBERALISM

The twin forces of modernism and the Enlightenment eventually gave rise to the assumptions about social organisation that we take very much for granted in the form of liberalism.

FIGURE 5.1: LIBERALISM TIMELINE

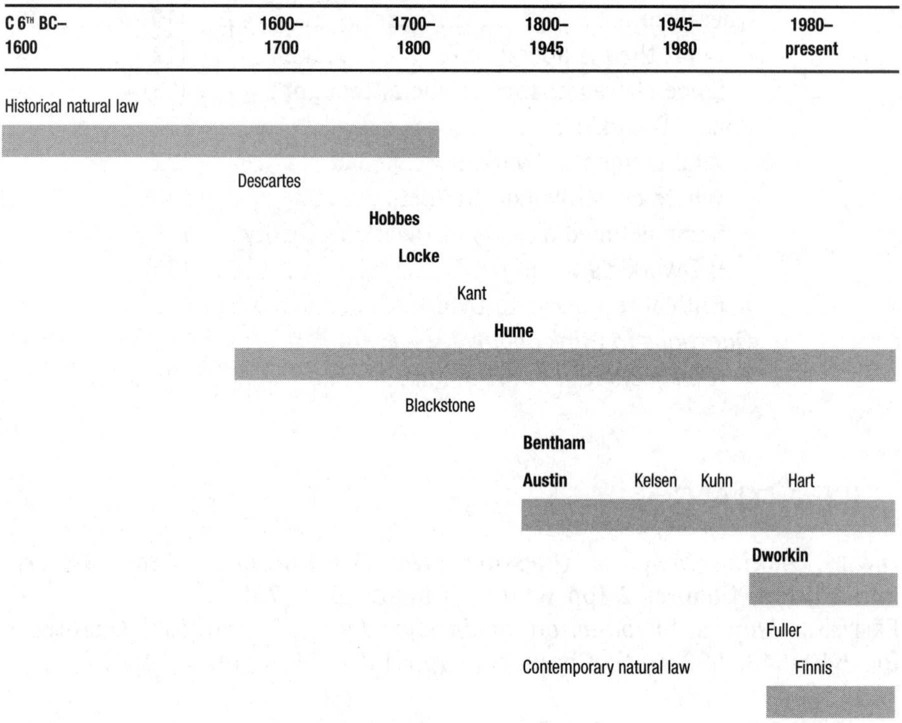

C 6TH BC– 1600	1600– 1700	1700– 1800	1800– 1945	1945– 1980	1980– present
Historical natural law					
	Descartes				
		Hobbes			
		Locke			
			Kant		
			Hume		
		Blackstone			
			Bentham		
			Austin	Kelsen Kuhn	Hart
					Dworkin
					Fuller
			Contemporary natural law		Finnis

This timeline pulls out the liberal components of the detailed timeline (Figure 1.2) in Chapter 1.

There is, of course, considerable overlap between theorists and the parts of legal theory which they are associated with.

Here, we have identified the major writers who influenced the development of liberal thought, or who write predominantly in a **liberal** tradition in bold.

However, Dworkin represents a considerable departure from the early liberal writers like Bentham and Austin, who had written about law from a positivist perspective.

The old view of government — the arbitrary imposition of a ruler's will on the subject — could not be sustained in a world in which the individual (courtesy of Descartes) had assumed a great deal more significance, and was now thought of as autonomous and independent, able to make up their own mind about things, and to make decisions about how they would organise their life.

The autonomy and independence of this newly constituted individual limited what governments could do, and, as Locke argued in his later writings, people were entitled to resist unjust authority where the power vested in government was abused.[1] This was not a general support for resistance to legitimate authority, which Locke saw as a human good.[2] Rather, it was a last resort, justified only in response to a continuing course of action which showed that government was tyrannical, and had abandoned its side of the social contract (see pp 64–68).

In effect, this liberal conception of government imported what we might call constitutional limits to the power of government, which were designed to protect the values which had become important to the emerging and influential commercial classes.

Using this justification for overthrowing tyrannical governments, revolutions had been fought in France and America to establish ideas such as the inherent freedom of individuals from arbitrary rule, and their right to make independent choices about what goals they would pursue.

The revolutions were indicative of the view that all human beings were, as the US Declaration of Independence of 1776 put it, 'created equal, and that they are endowed by their Creator with certain inalienable Rights, that among these are Life, Liberty and the Pursuit of Happiness'. The listing of these rights closely follows Locke's claim that each individual possesses certain fundamental inalienable rights pertaining to 'life, liberty and property', and that the role of government was the protection of these rights.

Similarly, the Declaration of the Rights of Man and Citizen in 1789, written following the French Revolution, provided a description of the ideals which lay at the core of liberal society. Specifically, government existed in order to preserve human rights, which were explicitly listed in Article 2: 'liberty, property, security, and resistance to oppression.'

Each of these documents states the ideals which went into the framing of the *liberal* political order which was in the process of being established in America and France at the end of the 18th century.

Behind the rise of liberalism was the assumption that government was there to serve the citizen (rather than the other way round). Certainly, government necessarily implied the imposition of limits on behaviour in the form of coercion, but these could no longer simply be just what a ruler might want. The power of governments was constrained, for example, by theories of a social contract, which limited government power to what people consented to.

CHAPTER 5

---

1 See Locke, J, *Two Treatises on Government* (edited by P Laslett), 1967, p 209.
2 Locke, op cit, p 220; see also Lloyd, p 115.

DENNIS THE PEASANT — AGAIN

In Chapter 4, we talked briefly about the ideas which Dennis the Peasant was expressing to Arthur in the film *Monty Python and the Holy Grail*. Dennis believes in a system where government is accountable. Its authority does not reside in the ruler, but is based in the will of the people who are governed. This idea of government operating within constitutional limits reflects liberal ideals about the nature of government.

Both the American Declaration of Independence and the French Declaration of the Rights of Man and Citizen also express the mistrust which their authors had of government as an institution. They believed that governments tended to encroach on people's rights as a matter of course, and that something was needed to limit this tendency, which would protect the rights citizens enjoyed. In the United States, this cynicism about government was expressed in the Bill of Rights — a series of Constitutional Amendments which prescribed the rights which individuals had which could not be overridden or removed by government.

Liberal societies assume that governments should protect certain basic aspects of life — for example, life itself (in the form of the protection of the individual's person), or the ability to engage in commerce (which was becoming more important with the rise of the merchant class). One of the *most* important assumptions was that among the rights which citizens of a liberal society possessed was the right to private property (and that governments should protect that property).

In 1765 in *Entick v Carrington* (a case we will look at later in this chapter when we consider the rule of law), Lord Camden CJ observed that:

'[t]he great end for which men entered into society, was to secure their property. That right is preserved sacred and incommunicable in all instances, where it has not been taken away or abridged by some public law for the good of the whole.'[3]

PROTECTION OF PROPERTY IN AUSTRALIA?

Even the Australian Constitution, which otherwise has very little in the way of effective protections for citizen's rights embedded in it, prevents the government from abusing its power with respect to private property. While the Federal Government is given the power to acquire property for Commonwealth purposes, it can only do so 'on just terms' — (s 51(xxxi)) — guaranteeing that a citizen whose property is acquired by the Commonwealth will be compensated.

What then is liberalism?

You will often read that liberalism is the dominant way of thinking, particularly political thinking, in modern Western society. In some ways, liberalism is like modernism as we discussed it in Chapter 4 — we are so accustomed to living in a world in which liberal ideas are assumed that we rarely think about what actually goes to make up this way of thinking about law and government.

Liberalism, however, is not something which can be easily defined. Even when different shades of liberal thought agree on basic propositions, like freedom,

---

3   (1765) 19 Howell's State Trials 1029.

equality or the rule of law, they often mean something slightly different, or see it as being put into practice in slightly different ways.

However, there are a number of characteristic ideas which together form the core of liberalism, and which make their appearance in the social and political beliefs of all liberal societies. The mix of these characteristics, the particular way that each is understood and the weight which each of them assumes, however, frequently differs.

The characteristics which we will deal with in this part of the chapter are not exhaustive, but include some of the most important beliefs and concepts which go into making up the idea of liberalism.[4]

Some characteristics of liberal thought

Liberty

The words 'liberty' and 'liberal' come originally from the Latin meaning 'free', although they have come into English through the French. The slogan of the French Revolution was, after all, 'liberté, fraternité, egalité' — freedom, brotherhood and equality.

Underlying liberal thought is the proposition that human beings are free (although just what this freedom entails will, of course, differ among liberal societies). This freedom generally includes an economic sense of the word (in that we are free to enter into economic relations which other people, being bound only as far as we agree that we should be bound). But liberal societies may stand for a large range of freedoms — freedom of speech, freedom of religion, freedom of political association, freedom to contract.

Positive and negative liberty

Liberty has acquired two distinct meanings within liberal thought — characterised as positive and negative liberty. Negative liberty describes a state of being free *from* constraint. Classical liberalism focuses on this idea of negative liberty, particularly in providing limits on the role of government, and the extent to which government can intrude in the lives of its citizens.

A RULE OF STATUTORY INTERPRETATION?

You can see this idea of minimal government intrusion within the rules of statutory interpretation. Where a statutory provision is uncertain or ambiguous, it is assumed by courts *not* to interfere with the liberty of the individual. Certainly, governments have the power to restrict an individual's freedom, but courts have taken the view that to do so, Parliament must be clear and unambiguous in limiting freedom (and any ambiguity should be resolved in favour of the individual rather than the state).[5]

---

4   For a more detailed discussion of the many aspects which go make up liberal thought, see generally Bottomley, S et al, *Law in Context* (Federation Press, Leichhardt, 1994), Chapter 2 — 'Liberalism, Formalism and the Rule of Law', p 9ff.
5   *Baker v Campbell* (1983) 153 CLR 52; *Williams v R* (1986) 161 CLR 278.

In contract law, this idea is seen in the lack of interference by government in people's negotiations — leaving them free to work out their own deals (even if, in the end, they are not particularly good bargains for the individual concerned). In this sense, government plays a minimal, and essentially passive, role. It sets the stage, but does not intrude, and it does not take positive steps to help individuals achieve their desired outcomes, other than making sure 'the playing field is level'. (It may, of course, be that the playing field only appears level from some perspectives, while from others it looks decidedly slanted.)

Liberty, however, also has a positive meaning, in which the role of government is to actively promote a range of freedoms which are thought of as important aspects of liberal society.[6]

A major characteristic of the Enlightenment individual was that they were autonomous — able to make their own decisions and act upon them. While negative liberty was a principle which prevented government intrusion on individuals, it did not, in itself, promote autonomy.

To be truly autonomous, an individual must have a range of choices available to them.

A MAN IN A PIT — A WOMAN ON AN ISLAND

The theorist Joseph Raz proposes two imaginary scenarios to explain that choice, in itself, does not amount to autonomy.[7]

Imagine a man who is confined in a pit and unable to get out or call for help. There is an adequate supply of food and water for his physical survival. Raz suggests that this man can, in fact, make a series of choices. He can eat when he chooses. He can drink when he chooses. He can sleep when he chooses. Or he can make any number of essentially meaningless choices about how he spends his days and nights, and to that extent, he is 'free'.

For gender equity, there is a female equivalent. Imagine a woman stranded on a desert island, constantly under threat from a vicious predator. She can elude the predator, but to do so uses up all of her (considerable) resources, so that the entirety of her life is bound up in survival and escape. But she, too, is in a limited sense, 'free'.

While each of these individuals has some choices available to them, however, neither can be described as autonomous in the sense that they are in control of their destiny, and can make *effective* choices about how they will live their lives. They have no real choice as to what goals they want to pursue or in how they can go about achieving those goals.

Positive liberty sets about establishing autonomy for the individual by actively intervening in the social order to create or increase the range of real and effective choices which are necessary for an individual to be thought of as truly autonomous. Legislation supporting affirmative action in employment (such as providing access) is an example of positive liberty, since it is an intrusion by government into the 'neutral' field of the labour market, which sets about creating opportunities for real choice about careers where, unchecked, the labour market has produced a decidedly uneven playing field.

---

6 You can read a detailed description of positive and negative liberty in Isaiah Berlin, 'Two Concepts of Liberty' in *Four Essays on Liberty* (Oxford, OUP, 1969).

7 Joseph Raz, *The Morality of Freedom* (Clarendon Press, Oxford, 1986), p 369.

FIGURE 5.2: WHAT AUTONOMY MEANS

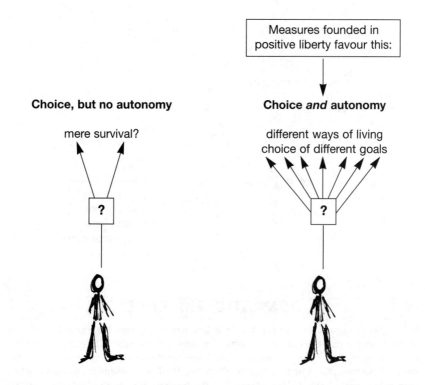

Positive liberty necessarily involves government encroachment in the individual's liberty, and so runs counter to the idea of negative liberty, which suggests that individuals should be left to work out their own destiny, free from government regulation.

The private and public spheres

The idea of minimal government intrusion into human affairs can also be seen in the traditional liberal split between the right of government to interfere in public affairs, contrasted with the limits which are assumed about its right to intrude into private matters. Regulation of private affairs — particularly matters which occurred in a domestic setting — was outside the proper role of government. Historically, they were areas where the 'King's writ did not run — a 'man's home was his castle'.

In Figure 5.3, the larger circle represents the boundary between the private and the public domain. Within the circle, A is free to act how he or she likes, without the intrusion of government or law. Later in this chapter, when we look at the theory of Ronald Dworkin, we will see how he applies his theory of rights to questions like the distribution of pornography in a way which gives effect to this idea of a lack of interference by government in the private domain.

FIGURE 5.3: PRIVATE AND PUBLIC SPHERES

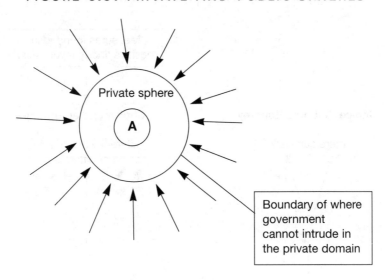

Boundary of where government cannot intrude in the private domain

---

DOMESTIC VIOLENCE

It is only comparatively recently that the law has recognised the existence of, and begun to make its presence felt in, what we now call domestic violence. Acts which, if committed against strangers, would quite clearly constitute assault were, until recently, rarely made the subject of legal action. Certainly, there are evidentiary problems when such events occur behind closed doors. But the inclination of law to 'not get involved' in domestic matters is a direct descendant of the division of human actions into public and private spheres — and the liberal idea that law should not intervene in purely private matters. It was also assumed that a wife was the possession of the husband, and that no-one should interfere (see Chapter 10, p 246).

JS Mill and the 'harm principle'

The illustration of domestic violence, however, shows how the question of freedom becomes complicated when someone's actions involve a relationship with someone else. Human beings are social animals, and their actions generally have some effect on other people. Obviously, then, it is impractical to allow individuals complete freedom, and some mechanism needs to be devised to place a limit on what individuals can do, while leaving them with the maximum amount of personal freedom or liberty.

One theory which has been used to provide this limit is John Stuart Mill's 'harm principle'. Mill proposed that the *only* basis on which individual liberty could be curtailed — the only legitimate justification for the state to intrude on the individual's freedom of action — was to prevent harm to others. An individual was free to act in any way they liked, as long as they were not harming someone else in doing so.[8]

---

8   Davies, p 187.

FIGURE 5.4: MILL'S 'HARM PRINCIPLE'

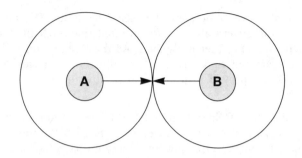

A and B are free to act however they like within their
respective circles. However, A's freedom is limited when
A's actions intrude on B, to the extent that they cause
B 'harm', and B's actions are similarly limited.

This principle lies behind 'liberalising' laws which seek to decriminalise behaviour (like sodomy or marijuana use) which is said to be victimless – that is, to cause harm to no-one.

Individualism

Modernism and the Enlightenment signalled a change from a world in which the individual was largely insignificant. The individual in the classical and medieval worlds was bound up in their relationship with their community, and as political subjects, individuals were, for the most part, subject to the arbitrary power of political rulers.

The change in political sensibility which accompanied these movements placed the individual as the centre of society. Rather than a strongly community-oriented picture of society, liberalism centres on the importance of the individual. The community is thought of as nothing more than the sum of all the independent individuals which make it up. Partly, this is an outgrowth of the increasing complexity of societies as they moved from a predominantly rural and feudal organisation to an urban commercially-based structure. Liberal views of society saw social organisation as being composed of atomistic individuals who formed a series of relationships at all levels, such as family, social or economic relationships. While these were constantly shifting, there remained a constant 'centre' in the form of the individual.

Again, contract law provides a good example of how this emphasis on the individual shows up in liberal thinking. Contract law provides, as we have said, a neutral field. What is significant (and what is protected) is the capacity of individuals to determine for themselves what goals they wish to pursue. Subject to some form of intervention based on avoiding harm, an individual could set themselves whatever commercial goals they wished, and expect to be allowed to pursue them free from government intrusion. Law would say nothing about the goals which each individual chose for themselves. (This idea is obviously also connected with the ideas of liberty and autonomy.)

Equality

Liberal societies all have some sort of basis in equality. The historical forces which shaped liberal society all took for granted that each individual counted exactly as much as every other individual. As the Declaration of Independence said, 'All men are created equal'. (We will see in Chapter 11, on feminism, that all too often, this has proved in practice to be literally true — men are equal, but women aren't.)

But like other aspects of liberal thought, this dedication to equality is not without its problems, and can take different forms. On the one hand, a liberal society may operate on the principle that everyone is equal in a *formal* sense. There are no legal barriers put in the way of someone achieving their goals. On the other hand, equality may be described as substantive — there may be no formal barriers, but in practice, some are 'more equal than others' and can more readily achieve their goals. It is only when government regulates an activity like this that these disadvantaged individuals can achieve actual equality.

LUNCH AT THE RITZ

The distinction between formal and substantive equality is illustrated by the observation that 'everyone is free to have dinner at the Ritz' — a very expensive hotel in London. Certainly, from a formal perspective, this is true and everyone is, in this narrow sense, 'free' to have dinner at the Ritz. But, because the Ritz is a very expensive hotel, dinner isn't cheap, and for practical purposes, most people can't afford to eat there. The substantive reality is that, despite the absence of formal barriers, only some people can actually afford the enormous bill!

The writer Anatole France put this is a decidedly legal context, when he wrote (ironically of course) that the egalitarianism of law 'forbids rich and poor alike to sleep under bridges, to beg in the streets and to steal bread.'[9] Of course, the rich don't need to do those things, so the equality is really illusory.

Rights

As we have seen, the idea of rights was a significant development, arising out of modernist and Enlightenment ideas of the individual as an independent and autonomous being. Rights made their first appearance in the form of natural rights — a product of social contract theory, given political shape in the assumptions of the French and American Revolutions that people were born with certain 'inalienable' rights. We will see in Chapter 6 that the idea of natural rights gave way, in positivist thought, to the idea of rights which were created by law.

However, since World War Two, the increasing role played by international law has seen a resurgence of the idea of certain rights being intrinsic to being human. Many United Nations covenants describe human rights which are thought of as being the birthright of everyone, rather than simply arising because one person happens to live in a society whose laws give them certain rights, while someone else lives in a society which denies them those rights.

---

9 *Le Lys Rouge* (1894), Chapter 7.

Two views about rights

Two versions of the source of rights persist in liberal thought. One sees rights as existing simply because an individual is a person. The other sees rights as arising because the consequences of giving people rights are seen as being good, or at least contributing to a good or desirable outcome. Figure 5.5 illustrates the two views.

FIGURE 5.5: TWO VIEWS OF RIGHTS

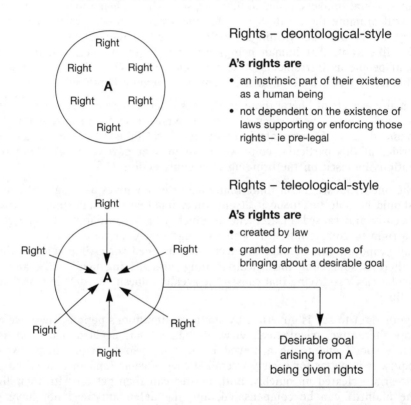

Rights – deontological-style

A's rights are

- an instrinsic part of their existence as a human being

- not dependent on the existence of laws supporting or enforcing those rights – ie pre-legal

Rights – teleological-style

A's rights are

- created by law

- granted for the purpose of bringing about a desirable goal

Desirable goal arising from A being given rights

We discussed Immanuel Kant briefly in Chapter 4, looking at his views about the nature of human knowledge. Another of the significant contributions Kant made to modern thought was his argument about the nature of the individual. For Kant, individuals were 'ends in themselves' – not simply cogs in a machine, to be used as a means to someone else's, or society's, ends. Rights exist, for Kant, because an individual is human. Such rights are not the result of any law which gives these rights to the individual – they are *pre-legal* and exist independently of whether or not they can be found in any law or act of government. Such a view of rights is described as *deontological* – a word derived from the Greek for 'being bound' or 'under a duty' – and the rights which are claimed under this view exist simply because it is 'morally right' to see human beings in this way.

The opposite view of rights is that their existence depends on their being associated with positive consequences. If individuals are given a particular right, will it lead to a desirable outcome? If so, the rights are justified, and should be incorporated in law. If not, they are inappropriate. Such a view is described as *teleological,* referring to the end-purpose to which something is directed. (You will remember that classical natural law theories, like those of Aristotle, were also described as coming from a teleological view, in that the absolute transcendent principles of natural law were directed to humanity's natural end of forming political societies.)

So some liberal thinkers, called utilitarians, see rights as being important because they will promote the greatest good for the greatest number of individuals in society, rather than being things which are good in themselves. Anyone who thinks, like Kant, that human beings are ends in themselves, will reject this view of people as instruments of social policy. (We will look at utilitarianism in Chapter 6, when we look at the theories of Jeremy Bentham).

Like many aspects of liberal thought, there is often a degree of conflict between these two views — both sides of the argument seem to have something to recommend them. As an example of where liberal thinking has to balance the two sides of this particular coin, we might look at how we think about time limitations imposed on the bringing of a court action.

On the one hand, we might think that where the law gives us a right of action, we should be able to pursue it at any time. Imagine that someone has driven negligently and caused an accident in which you were injured. The law gives you a right to compensation. It seems strange that your right to compensation should evaporate just because the accident happened some time ago. We think that there is something intrinsically wrong with driving negligently, and the particular careless driving that caused the accident doesn't become less negligent over time!

But your right to sue is governed by statutory limitations periods. Here, we can see an alternative, teleological, view. Parliament has decided that there is a valuable social end to be achieved by making people begin their lawsuits promptly. It is better for society overall if these events (and their legal consequences) are cleared up quickly. Both parties can then get on with their lives — the plaintiff can be compensated, and the defendant need not have the constant threat of litigation hanging over them.

So a time limit is imposed to promote this desirable social goal, but we probably remain uneasy about the 'moral' aspects of leaving a plaintiff uncompensated, and a defendant unpunished.[10]

The rule of law

You will undoubtedly have heard the expression, the 'rule of law', many times as a law student, usually in the context that it is something which is basic to the way law operates in Western democratic societies.

---

10 For this and other examples of the tension between these two views, see Bottomley, S et al, op cit, p 27.

The rule of law has been defined in a number of ways, and is often used to mean different things.[11] For our purposes, we will take the rule of law to refer to the proposition that governments should operate within the rules. As such, it is very much an ideal arising out of the social and political beliefs which arose at the Enlightenment, and which find their expression in the establishment of liberal societies. The two great 18th century revolutions in France and America were fought largely against the exercise of arbitrary power by governments which were not accountable.

So, built into the liberal view of government is the idea that the exercise of power should not be, as it was before the influence of these Enlightenment ideals, based on the whims of an absolute ruler, but controlled by laws which limit government. In exercising power, governments themselves should be subject to the law.

GOVERNMENT ACCORDING TO LAW

A decade before the American Revolution, English law recognised the principle that when the state exercised its power, it could not do so in any way it liked, but must, itself, obey the rules. The case was *Entick v Carrington*.[12] Entick was closely associated with a critic of the King, John Wilkes. Two of the 'King's messengers' forced their way into Entick's house, broke open his desk and seized papers to use as evidence in criminal proceedings against Entick and Wilkes.

No legal authority could be found to legitimate the search and seizure. The warrant that had been issued was invalid. Entick therefore succeeded in a trespass action against the King's messengers. The state had not acted lawfully in breaking into Entick's house, and so the individuals responsible for the break-in and seizure of Entick's papers were liable in the general law of tort for the interference with his property.

FIGURE 5.6: THE RULE OF LAW

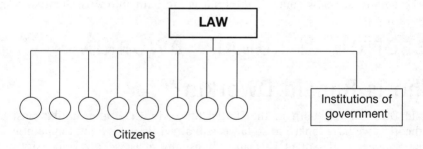

Law operates to constrain government actions in the same way that it applies to individuals. 'Lawmakers should not be lawbreakers'

CHAPTER 5

---

11 For two interpretations of what constitutes the rule of law, see Bottomley, S (op cit) at pp 43–44, and Harris, J, *Legal Philosophies*, 2nd edition (Butterworths, London, 1997), p 150.
12 (1765) 19 Howell's State Trials.

The rule of law is quite distinct from any idea of 'law and order' (although in general conversation, the two are often confused). The rule of law imposes duties on, or constrains, the way in which government (including the judiciary) behaves — something quite different from the prescriptions of 'law and order' which suggest that individuals should obey the law and that the coercive power of the state is justified in enforcing law strictly.

AN EXAMPLE FROM THE LAW OF EVIDENCE

As a general principle, police are expected to abide by the law — both the general law and the specific laws which have been made controlling the way in which they exercise their powers. Sometimes, they exceed those powers, and gather evidence in ways which are not completely legal — for example, by using unauthorised listening devices.

When that happens, courts have a discretion to exclude the evidence which has been gathered illegally — providing an incentive for the state to comply with limitations on its power.

In Australia, the exclusion of illegally obtained evidence is a balancing act — weighing such factors as the capacity of the evidence to prove the guilt of the accused, and the seriousness of the infraction of the rules governing police powers.[13] On one hand, we see an inherent rightness in making sure that the state exercises its power lawfully. But we can also see a desirable social goal — that of punishing the guilty — which sometimes outweighs the intrinsic 'right'.

In the United States, the law takes a much stricter view of the application of the rule of law in this context. Any evidence which flows from a breach of the rules governing the exercise of police powers is inadmissible — the so-called 'fruit of a poisoned tree' doctrine.

While these aspects of liberal thought are, as we have said, not a complete prescription of what liberalism entails, they should have given you a picture of some of the main things that liberal societies think are important. You should also be able to see how some of these ideas are built into Australian society.

SECTION B: RONALD DWORKIN

Who is Ronald Dworkin?

Ronald Dworkin was born in the United States in 1931, and, unlike most of the theorists we have looked at so far, is still alive! He holds a joint appointment as the Sommer Professor of Law and Philosophy at New York University and Quain Professor of Jurisprudence at University College, London.

One feature of Dworkin's approach to law is that he takes an active role in public debate about controversial matters — like pornography and sexuality.

THE OZ TRIAL

In 1971, Richard Neville, Jim Anderson and Felix Dennis, had published an edition of their magazine, *Oz, edited by* schoolkids. The British government had brought charges against the three, including that they had 'conspired to corrupt the morals of young

---

13 *Bunning v Cross* (1978) 141 CLR 54.

children and other young persons', by publishing pornographic material in the magazine. Had they simply been charged with obscenity, they would have faced a maximum penalty of £100 or 6 months imprisonment. The somewhat archaic conspiracy charge exposed them to an unlimited fine or period of imprisonment.

The three were convicted, fined and received prison sentences of between 9 and 15 months. Neville and Anderson, who were Australians, were also subject to deportation. The convictions were subsequently overturned on appeal.

The Schoolkids edition of *Oz* contained a mix of graphics, cartoons, articles, and reviews, but a great deal of space was devoted to writing by school pupils – on such things as pop music, sexual freedom and hypocrisy, drug use, corporal punishment and examinations.

JUDGES AND JURISPRUDES

Along with many other notables, including the comedian Marty Feldman, Dworkin was called as a witness in the *Oz* trial. He was described as an expert witness in relation to the issues of private and public morality.

At one stage, while trying to explain to the court that the magazine was obscene in neither of the two senses which he had just identified, he was interrupted by the trial judge with the comment, 'This is not a lecture theatre'.

After a pause, Dworkin went on to explain that the *prosecution* was a corruption of public morals, and that it could not have proceeded in the United States (because of the First Amendment).

Where does Dworkin fit?

If you look back at the timeline in Figure 5.1, you will see that between them, positivism and natural law theory dominate the period from way back in the 6th century BC to the present. For much of the time, natural law was the main way in which law was understood, and then for nearly 200 years from the end of the 18th century to the mid-20th century, positivism took over as the dominant explanation of law – at least until the end of World War Two, when there was something of a resurgence of natural law (see Chapter 3).

Dworkin is writing after positivism had demonstrated (at least to some) that it was unable to deal with some of the issues which arose out of the excesses of Nazi law during World War Two. But Dworkin is neither a positivist nor a natural lawyer, fitting into a sort of middle ground between these two major forces in legal theory,[14] guided by *liberal principles*.

Overview

At the heart of Dworkin's theory is the observation that law involves inter-pretation. While we often talk of 'interpreting' when we think about law, we are usually looking to see what a statute means, based on the idea of discovering Parliament's intention when it passed the law. Dworkin's idea of interpretation is not the same thing. What Dworkin suggests is more like literary interpre-tation. You will see this idea emerge in the model which Dworkin uses to explain how judges come (or should come) to their decisions.

CHAPTER 5

---

14 See Davies, p 30.

Judging must be an interpretive activity, argues Dworkin, because law is not, as positivists generally put it, a collection of rules, with judges exercising their discretion to 'fill the gaps' if the rules do not provide a watertight answer to a legal problem. Certainly, judges have to rely on something to act as a game-breaker when cases can't be resolved by a simple application of the rules. Behind the rules lies a network of standards — principles and policies — which can act as arguments in favour of, or against, making a particular decision.

For Dworkin, however, policies and principles are different things, and it is only principles — statements about individuals' rights — which should influence judges when they have to make a decision where the law is uncertain.

To resolve difficult issues, Dworkin suggests that a judge will think about everything he or she knows about the legal environment in which they are operating, as well as the political and social beliefs which are embedded in the community, as part of the process of constructing their decision. Law is, for Dworkin, 'deeply and thoroughly political'[15] — meaning that law is intimately bound up with the political ideals and aspirations which go to make up a society.

Dworkin adds another dimension to this process. Because he is writing within a very strong liberal tradition — remember, the United States was formed as part of the revolutionary movement towards liberal ideals at the end of the 18th century — Dworkin also demands that the legal system embody the very liberal principle of equality. As we will see in Chapter 6, the idea of utilitarianism, which provides for the greatest happiness of the greatest number, also effectively guarantees considerable misery for the rest.[16] This, for Dworkin, meant that rights of individuals in minorities were often sacrificed for the good of the many. This idea did not sit well with the underlying assumptions about individuals and their rights which were built into the American system of government. So Dworkin's theory is, at a fundamental level, liberal — taking the inherently liberal view that government is there to protect the individual, ultimately through the mechanism of rights.

IF DWORKIN THINKS MORALS AND RIGHTS FORM PART OF LAW, DOES THAT MAKE HIM A NATURAL LAWYER?

Not at all. While Dworkin recognises that moral values play a role in the formulation of law, the morals which judges look to are not the 'transcendent and immutable' moral values of natural law theory, written somehow on the fabric of the universe. The values which Dworkin insists form part of the law are those which are very much embedded in the community itself — accepted legal and moral standards of a particular place and a particular time.

---

15 See Bottomley et al, op cit, p 55.
16 See Chapter 6 below, 'Bentham and utility', p 146.

Some detailed aspects of Dworkin's theory

Hard cases

Let's start with the idea of a judge. A judge's role is to dispose of legal disputes. Ultimately, a judge cannot have a bob each way – they must resolve a case in favour of one party or the other.

Many cases present no difficulties at all. Once the facts are discovered, there may well be a rule which determines which of the parties has a legal right to win the case. In Chapter 4, we looked at the case of Tom (who had been charged with exceeding the speed limit). Here, there is a clear rule. Parliament has set a speed limit, and specified that someone who drives at more than 50 kph in a built-up area is guilty of the offence of speeding. Once the facts about the speed Tom was driving are proved, there is no room to doubt how the law applies. Case closed.

But in more difficult circumstances, there may be no clear-cut rule for a judge to fall back on.

RIGGS v PALMER[17]

This an example used by Dworkin of a situation where the accepted rules did not provide a certain answer. The question before the court was: Is a murderer entitled to inherit under a valid will executed by the person they have killed? While inheritance under a will was subject to a number of detailed exceptions in succession law, nothing covered this particular situation, and so the rules appeared to say that the murderer could get their inheritance.

This is an example of a 'hard case' – one where there is a genuine argument as to which of the parties is entitled to win. Hard cases are central to the law, says Dworkin, because they 'test fundamental principles'[18] which give overall shape to the law. And it is the way in which hard cases are resolved which gives us the clearest idea of how Dworkin sees law as operating.

Law as interpretation

Dworkin sees the function of a judge as interpreting. This idea is much more complicated, however, than simply trying to uncover Parliament's intention in enacting a statute. Interpretation in the sense that Dworkin uses it refers to a process of developing a theory which best explains what the law actually is in a particular situation. A judge's task is to interpret all the building blocks which exist within the legal system, and to bring them together to achieve the right outcome in a hard case. To do this, a judge must go through three stages – a pre-interpretive stage, an interpretive stage and a post-interpretive stage.

---

17 (1889) 115 NY 506, 22 NE 188.
18 Dworkin, Ronald, *Law's Empire* (The Belknap Press of Harvard University Press, Cambridge, Mass, 1986), p 43.

CHAPTER 5

The pre-interpretive stage: To begin, a judge has to assemble all the working materials that already exist in the legal system. There may be rules which are established in case law, as well as statutory provisions which are relevant to the case. In the pre-interpretive phase, all of these things are simply accepted as forming part of the underlying ideas from which a decision has to be formed. Dworkin uses the very simple example of peasants doffing their caps to the nobility as a sign of courtesy.[19] The pre-interpretive stage involves nothing more than realising that this rule exists, without having to consider any significance that the rule has beyond just existing.

The interpretive stage: Once these materials have been assembled, it becomes possible to think about them in terms of what they mean. In the simple example of the rule of courtesy, we might imagine that the rule shows respect, and as such, has a value which is significant within that society. Once a meaning has been given to the act (and the rule), there will be situations in which different theories might arise as to how the rule applies, or what it really means. For a judge in a hard case, the interpretation of all the material that emerges at the pre-interpretive stage is a complex issue, and requires the balancing of sometimes conflicting or contradictory ideas, to show the rule in its 'best possible light'.

The post-interpretive stage: The understanding of the meaning of a rule at the interpretive stage will then provide guidance when the rule has to be applied in a hard case. The way in which the rule has been interpreted will determine how it will actually apply in this new situation.

The chain novel

In order to explain how judges behave, Dworkin uses the idea of the chain novel. Chain novels were once a very popular pastime. With the arrival of the Internet, they appear to have made something of a comeback. The idea behind a chain novel is that different people contribute parts of a novel in sequence, with the aim of ending up with a story that looks as if it was written by a single person.

Dworkin assumes that each writer will provide one chapter of a novel. In order for the novel to make sense and to give the appearance of a single author, the writers who supply each new chapter have to stay within certain guidelines. They have to take the story as it reaches them as given — and that means, among other things, that they will have to make themselves thoroughly familiar with the parts of the novel already written. (This corresponds with the pre-interpretive stage.)

Once the novel has been going for some time, certain aspects of the novel are reasonably well set. The type of story is established fairly quickly. If it is a detective story or a science fiction adventure, new writers can't suddenly switch between these types of novels, or move it abruptly to yet another form. The cast of characters, while not fixed in concrete, cannot change abruptly. The setting has to remain consistent. The new characters and aspects of the plot which are introduced by each successive writer have to blend in with 'the story so far' — they have to be plausible developments that are consistent with what

---

19 Ibid, pp 46–86.

has gone before. If the novel is set at the end of the 20th century, the next writer cannot (without a good reason) skip backwards across the centuries and continue the story in the 12th century, or fly into the 25th century for the next sequence of events.

FIGURE 5.7: A CHAIN NOVEL

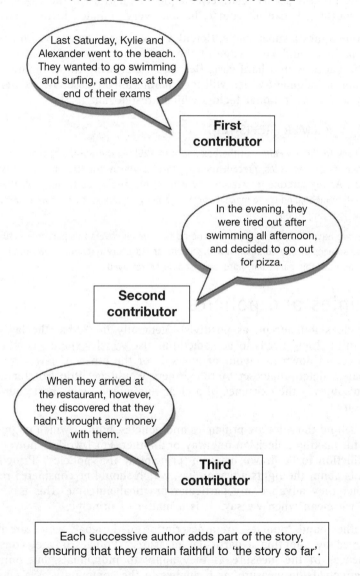

So, too, judges are limited in the way in which they can frame their judgments. 'The story so far' — the accumulated mass of legal rules, principles and approaches which Dworkin calls the 'historical' legal record — has to be respected, and not subject to arbitrary changes. To do this, a judge has to develop an idea as to what the novel so far is about — what its significance is, or what it means. (This corresponds to the interpretive stage.)

Finally, a judge can sit down and write the next chapter — that is, make a decision and write the judgment (in the post-interpretive stage). This, naturally, has to conform to the overall state of the novel as it came to them, and how the story develops will depend on how they have interpreted the mass of materials which are relevant to the case.

While this process seems relatively simple in relation to the example of the rules of courtesy, it can, of course, become very complex in real 'hard cases'.

Dworkin imagines a super-judge, Hercules J, who possesses extraordinary levels of skill, patience and knowledge of the law — not to mention all the time in the world. Faced with a hard case, Hercules J can bring these qualities to bear, and fashion a judgment which will incorporate all the case law, as well as any statutory and constitutional factors which are relevant to the case.

RIGGS v PALMER (REVISITED)

Think back to *Riggs v Palmer* in the box above (p 125). At the pre-interpretive stage, a judge will identify all the rules, precedents and statutes which are relevant to the issue to be decided. At the interpretive stage, they will form a theory as to what all these bits of information mean, and try to make it come together in a coherent whole which explains what the law is trying to do.

But, as we have seen, there appears to be no rule which covers this particular situation. It is not the subject of any common law precedent or statutory regulation. So how is the judge to decide how this particular 'hard case' should be resolved?

Principles and policies

Dworkin does not accept, as positivists generally do,[20] that the law consists only of rules. There needs to be something else which explains why a judicial decision comes down in favour of one side or the other. (If law were nothing more than a determinate set of rules, there would be little call for courts to resolve disputes — the existence of a clear rule would make most court actions unnecessary.)

Lurking behind the rules are principles and policies, both of which might provide reasons for making a decision one way or another. For Dworkin, however, there is a distinction to be drawn between 'principles' and 'policies'. 'Principles' are statements about the rights a person has, which should be considered regardless of whether they advance any particular practical outcome. This is very close to what we mean when we say, 'It is a matter of principle.'

On the other hand, 'policies' are a description of the goals which are hoped to be achieved by adopting a particular measure.[21] Policies do not consider the consequences of the measure as they apply to individuals, but only to the overall effect of the measure, as it applies to the community as a whole.

---

20 See Chapter 6 below.
21 Dworkin, *Taking Rights Seriously* (Duckworth, London, 1978) p 90.

DWORKIN'S EXAMPLES

Dworkin gives an example of a policy in the argument that a subsidy for aircraft manufacturers will serve the community goal of supporting the defence of the nation. By contrast, an argument in favour of anti-discrimination legislation is an argument of principle, because it is concerned to justify such laws by demonstrating that they protects the rights of individuals or groups of individuals.[22]

Unlike rules, principles are not conclusive. They do not provide the answer to a legal problem. Principles perform the function of providing reasons (or justification) why a case *should* be decided in a particular way — notably when a rule, although valid, is not sufficiently clear to provide a simple and obvious answer, or where there is no rule at all. At times there will be conflicting principles.

Policies, on the other hand, are not the province of the courts. Legislatures may enact law in pursuit of specific community goals. The role of courts is to resolve disputes between the individual litigants, on the basis that one of them has a right to win. Courts ought not to use social goals as the basis for choosing between possible outcomes in a court case — to do so would trample on the rights which individuals have in a society.

McLOUGHLIN v O'BRIAN

In this 'nervous shock' case, Lord Scarman said something very similar to this, offering the opinion that 'if principle — requires a decision which entails a degree of policy risk, the court's function is to adjudicate according to principle, leaving policy curtailment to the judgement of parliament.'[23]

That being said, one of the common reasons offered by judges for not taking a certain course of action, like expanding the tort of negligence, is the 'floodgates' argument, which is really based on policy — the goal of not overwhelming courts with cases to be decided — and leaves aside the question of whether, as a matter of principle, people should have a right to bring an action.

So for Dworkin, the superhuman judge, Hercules J, can use arguments derived from principles (though not from policies) as part of the justification for deciding one way or the other.

RIGGS v PALMER — FOR THE LAST TIME

Because the rules of succession did not provide any specific exception which would prevent the murderer from receiving their inheritance, it might appear as if the claim would succeed. But looked at in terms of the whole legal system, there would be some doubt about allowing this to happen. Within the legal system as a whole, there is a *principle* that people should not be allowed to benefit from their own wrongdoing.[24]

Here was a principle — a statement about what rights people had in the legal system. As such, the judge had to take the principle into account (although by giving it 'weight', rather than having it function as a rule, it is by no means certain that the principle will be the determinative factor in the judge's assessment of a proper outcome).

---

22 Ibid, p 82.
23 [1983] 1 AC 410 at 430–431, referred to by Dworkin in *Law's Empire*, op cit, p 28.
24 You may have come across this principle in tort law — under the Latin phrase 'ex turpi causa non oritur actio'.

Why principles and not policies?

We have said that Dworkin's theories embody liberal values. The importance which he attributes to principles (at the expense of policies) in the process of making legal decisions is an indication of one of the most significant values of liberal societies, expressed in the Declaration of Independence — namely, that all men are created equal. (Again, we will leave the gender issue until Chapter 11 on feminism.)

At the centre of Dworkin's ideas about rights (and hence principles), we find the observation that governments must treat people as equals.

DWORKIN'S LIBERAL IDEAS

Dworkin has analysed a number of controversial issues in US culture, and unfailingly comes down on the side of what we might call a 'liberal' interpretation — that is, one which maximises the freedom of the individual. He defends, for example, the right of people to distribute pornography, or live as homosexuals.

His argument in favour of pornography goes like this:

- there is a right to freedom of speech in America;

- while many people think pornography is disgusting, there is no good reason why the social goal of making society 'better' by banning pornography should intrude on the right to distribute pornography;

- therefore, despite the fact that many, or even most, people might want to ban pornography, the individual's right should prevail. As Dworkin says, 'The right of moral independence is part of the same collection of rights as the right of political independence, and it is to be justified as a trump over an unrestricted utilitarian defence of prohibitory laws against pornography, in a community of those who find offence in just the idea that their neighbours are reading dirty books'.[25]

We will see an alternative argument relating to pornography in Chapter 11.

Rights exist to support or maintain the fundamentally egalitarian nature of what Dworkin sees as the most preferable form of social organisation — liberalism. Rights act as a safeguard so that the fundamental equality of individuals is not lost.

If a right exists — say the right to free speech — then it is inconsistent with the existence of that right to say that it can be overturned or ignored just because there is some community benefit to be had by denying a person the right to exercise that freedom. To do so accords individuals the right to 'equal concern and respect'.

'EQUAL CONCERN AND RESPECT' IN COURT?

Recently, the Full Court of the Family Court in Sydney heard an appeal about the right of a person who had undergone a sex change to marry on the basis of their assigned sex.[26] One of the parties to the litigation was the Human Rights and Equal Opportunity Commission (who had been granted leave to intervene on the basis of the implications the case had for international treaties which included the right to marry).

---

25 Dworkin, cited in Lloyd, p 597.
26 *Re Kevin* (2001) 165 FL 404; (2001) 28 Fam LR 158. See p 5 above, notes 5 and 6.

During the course of submissions, counsel for the Commission used the phrase 'equal concern and respect'. There was no reference to Dworkin or his theories, but both counsel and the bench were fully aware of what was being imported into the argument, simply by the use of this highly distinctive phrase associated with Dworkin's theory.

Rights as trumps

The competing weight of social or community goals (policies) and individual rights (expressed as principles) is resolved, for Dworkin, by giving weight (he describes it as 'threshold weight') to principles over policies. If a person has a right, then that right should be protected — it should not be allowed to be ignored or trampled simply because there is a competing community goal which is desirable. This idea — that where individual rights and social goals conflict, rights should win out — is described as rights being a 'trump'.

WHAT ARE TRUMPS?

Some of you may not play card games like bridge or 500. In card games like these, one suit can be chosen as 'trumps' — which means that *any* card of that suit beats *all* cards of any other suit.

So if 'Hearts are trumps', then the 2 of Hearts will beat the King of Spades, or the Queen of Clubs, or the Ace of Diamonds, even though they are 'higher' in the normal hierarchy of a pack of cards.

FIGURE 5.8: RIGHTS AS 'TRUMPS'

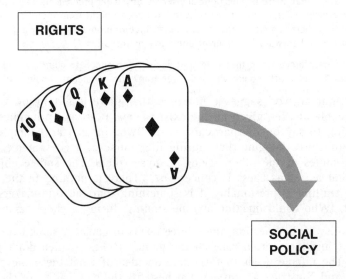

**A right acts as a trump to defeat claims
based on social policy**

Most particularly, rights act as trumps when your opponent plays the 'community goal' card. When the justification for one side winning a court case lies in the wellbeing of the community as a whole — essentially a utilitarian argument —

Dworkin argues that the existence of the right should outweigh policy considerations (regardless of how important the social goal might be). That's where the card-playing analogy comes in. While the right might seem small (like the 2 of Hearts), and the social goal might seem very important (like the Ace of Spades), Dworkin insists that it is the right which should win.

'Rights as trumps' and 'equal concern and respect' do not, however, amount to an overall right to liberty at all costs. Dworkin is not describing a system in which anyone with a right necessarily gets to exercise that right. As we saw in the first part of the chapter, rights can conflict, and there has to be a mechanism for limiting individual rights. What Dworkin is arguing for is that, in the determination of any dispute, individuals and the rights they *do* have should not be left out of the equation, and should not be sacrificed to community welfare. Judges still may need to make value judgments about how conflicting rights of individuals will be resolved.

The end product — 'one right answer'

When these aspects of Dworkin's theory are put together, it becomes evident that law is about finding the best possible answer to a legal problem. Dworkin argues that there is, in fact, just one right answer to even a hard legal problem, and that it is discoverable by the process which he has described.

STUDENTS AND THE 'ONE RIGHT ANSWER'

The observation that there is 'one right answer' to any legal problem usually attracts considerable disbelief from law students, who have been taught from their first day at law school that there is no right answer to an examination problem — simply arguments which you can put forward in favour of one party or the other.

This belief is reinforced when they read split decisions in appellate courts, where four judges think the plaintiff should win, and three think the defendant should win!

Dworkin's 'right answer' suggests, however, that there is a solution which is the best possible answer, given all the existing law, rules and principles which have anything to say on the particular case. Dworkin uses an example based on a game of chess. Imagine that, during the course of a chess game, one of the players smiles at the other, trying to upset them. The smilee objects. Is smiling illegal as far as chess is concerned?[27] There is nothing in the written rules about smiling — presumably it is something that the rule-makers didn't think about. (Who could imagine anyone smiling during a chess game?)

In order to answer the question, the referee needs to consider some background issues — not just the written rules of the game of chess, which don't provide an answer. The referee needs to formulate an idea of what the game of chess is all about and construct an answer that best fits the game as he or she thinks of it. It is not, of course, open to a referee to toss a coin. The chess referee — and the judge in court — both have to come up with an answer.

---

27 Life imitates theory! For a real-life example of the principle, see Wacks, R, *Swot: Jurisprudence*, 5th edition) (Blackstone Press, London, 1999), pp 125–126.

You can probably see now why Dworkin's judge needs to be superhuman. In formulating the 'right answer', Hercules J has to take account of a wide range of ideas which will influence his decision, and most of the time they will not all lead to the same conclusion. Finding the right answer will involve a degree of judgment as to how much weight each of the influences should be given, and how, in the end, all of them should be balanced in order for the decision to slip into the 'seamless web' of the law, fitting as closely as possible in amongst all the other bits and pieces that together constitute the law. So, in *Riggs v Palmer*, the final decision – that the murderer should *not* inherit – is the answer that most makes sense, given everything we know about law and society.

Is Dworkin's world real?

You probably realise now that Dworkin's description of law and the way it operates is not intended as an accurate reflection of what really happens. No judge, for example, has all the characteristics of Hercules J, and even if they did, there wouldn't be enough time for the process to be worked out for each hard case that arises. The 'one right answer' very often turns out, in appellate courts, to be two or even more right answers, according to the various reasons supplied by different, human judges.

Dworkin's picture of a law as a seamless web is an idealisation – how law should work in a perfect world, so that the ideals which were embodied in the political and social system in the United States could be realised. In practice, it doesn't always work out quite like that.

Critical responses to Dworkin

Dworkin's theories have prompted a considerable body of critical responses, including:

- the claim that some of Dworkin's observations about judicial behaviour and the nature of rules simply do not reflect what happens in the real world;
- specific criticisms about Hercules J (primarily that he is mythical and in no way illustrates how judges behave in the real world);[28]
- claims that ideas (like 'hard cases') are inadequately defined;[29]
- the objection that the theory, assuming as it does so much of a liberal democratic viewpoint, does not 'travel well'.[30]

---

28 Ibid at p 131. Wacks lists some more criticisms of Hercules. He gives a brief, but wide-ranging summary of the criticisms which have been levelled at Dworkin.
29 Ibid.
30 Ibid.

QUESTIONS TO THINK ABOUT

1. How many of the characteristics of liberalism can you see in present-day Australia?

2. Can you think of any groups in society whose lives have some of the characteristics of the man in the pit or the woman on the island?

3. We've mentioned 'affirmative action' laws as one form of positive liberty. Can you think of any other ways in which law is used to promote freedom by increasing the range of choices available to individuals?

4. Do the rights which liberalism values operate equally across the community, or are these rights enjoyed by some groups more than others?

5. Do you think that people have rights simply because they are people, or should rights exist only when there are desirable consequences which flow from these rights?

6. Is the 'rule of law' restricted to liberal societies, or could it apply equally in a totalitarian regime?

7. Do you agree with Dworkin that law is 'deeply and thoroughly political'? Can you think of examples where this is evident?

8. Do you agree that there are no individual interests which are harmed by allowing a right to distribute pornography? What argument could you use to counter Dworkin?

9. Is Dworkin's approach to the 'one right answer' any use in terms of removing the problem of retrospectivity from judicial decision-making? Is a plaintiff (or a defendant) any better off if Hercules J (or one of his real-life imitators) discovers the one right answer using Dworkin's method than they were when the judges criticised by Bentham made law according to declaratory theory?

10. Does the fact that judges often come up with different answers in appellate courts make Dworkin's ideas about the 'one right answer' wrong?

FURTHER READING

Barker, E, *Social contract: essays by Locke, Hume and Rousseau* (Greenwood Press, Westport, 1980).

Cohen, M (ed), *Ronald Dworkin and contemporary jurisprudence* (Duckworth, London, 1984).

Dworkin, R, *Taking Rights Seriously* (Duckworth, London, 1978).

Dworkin, R, *The Philosophy of Law* (Oxford University Press, Oxford, 1977).

Dworkin, R, *A Matter of Principle* (Harvard University Press, Cambridge Mass, 1965).

Dworkin, R, *Law's Empire* (The Belknap Press of Harvard University Press, Cambridge, Mass, 1986).

Gaffney, P, *Ronald Dworkin on Law as Integrity: Rights as Principles of Adjudication* (Mallen University Press, Lewiston, 1996).

Gough, JW, *The social contract: a critical study of its development*, 2nd edition (Clarendon Press, Oxford, 1963).

Guest, S, *Ronald Dworkin*, 2nd edition (Edinburgh University Press, Edinburgh, 1992).

Hampton, J, *Hobbes and the Social Contract Tradition* (Cambridge University Press, Cambridge, 1986).

Hunt, A (ed), *Reading Dworkin Critically* (Berg, New York, 1992).

Lessnoff, M (ed), *Social Contract Theory* (Basil Blackwell, Oxford, 1990).

Rousseau, J, *The Social Contract*, translated by Maurice Cranston, (Penguin Books, Harmondsworth, 1968).

Skyrms, B, *Evolution of the Social Contract* (Cambridge University Press, New York, 1996).

Correcting Irrationality: Positivism and Law's Commonsense

Reading. 137
Aim. 138
What is legal positivism? 138
How do the positivist theorists approach
legal analysis? 140
Classical legal positivism –
was Kelsen a positivist? 141
Is and ought. 142
Theories of legal positivism 143
Jeremy Bentham. 143
Bentham's theory. 144
John Austin. 151
Austin's theory 152
Where does this leave us? 164
Critical responses to positivism 164
Questions to think about 165
Further reading. 166

READING

DAVIES, *Asking the Law Question: The Dissolution of Legal Theory*, 2nd edition, Chapter 2 (pp 35-36, 59-63), Chapter 3 (90-94, 102-112) FREEMAN, *Lloyd's Introduction to Jurisprudence*, 7th edition, Chapter 4

AIM

This chapter will introduce you to:

- how the main ideas and themes which emerged at the Enlightenment appear in law in the form of legal positivism;
- the theories of Jeremy Bentham and John Austin;
- the way in which lawyers think about law now, and how this is based in those ideas;
- the methods used by lawyers which are derived from these ideas;
- why the law you learn takes the form it does.

This chapter is set out in two sections. Section A will look at the historical context surrounding the rise of positivism. Section B will look at how these ideas are expressed in law, focusing on the theories of Jeremy Bentham and John Austin, which form the basis of many of our preconceptions of what law is (and what it isn't!).

SECTION A: WHAT IS LEGAL POSITIVISM?

FIGURE 6.1: CLASSICAL ENGLISH POSITIVISM TIMELINE

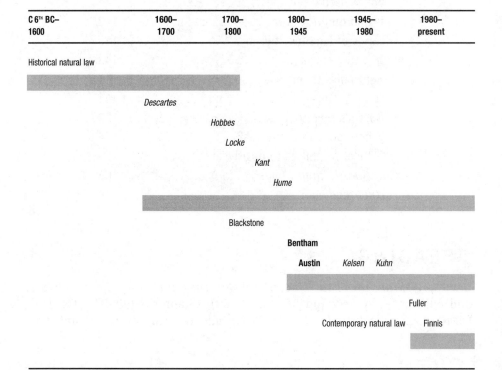

C 6TH BC–1600	1600–1700	1700–1800	1800–1945	1945–1980	1980–present

Historical natural law

Descartes

Hobbes

Locke

Kant

Hume

Blackstone

Bentham

Austin   Kelsen   Kuhn

Fuller

Contemporary natural law   Finnis

This timeline pulls out the modernist components of the detailed timeline in Chapter 1 (Figure 1.2).

We have juxtaposed modernism with positivism and a broad timeframe for historical natural law and marked the classical positivist theories we will consider in detail in this chapter: **Positivism (Classical English positivism)**, *Modernism*, Natural law.

Legal positivism is an approach to legal theory which is concerned with 'posited law' – that is, law which has been laid down, or 'posited', by institutions like Parliament and the courts. This way of looking at law takes law 'as it is' and analyses it within its own terms. One central characteristic of legal positivism is the idea that law is separate from, though not necessarily unrelated to, ideas of morality or other ways of assessing the value of human activities. This is shown in Figure 6.2.

FIGURE 6.2: POSITIVISM'S VIEW OF LAW AND MORALITY

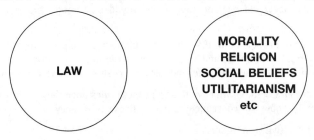

The clearest expression of this idea comes from John Austin, when he draws a distinction between the existence of law, on the one hand, and its 'merit or demerit' – that is, the moral value of the content of the law – on the other.[1] So legal positivists don't care whether law is good or bad.[2]

DO LEGAL POSITIVISTS REALLY NOT CARE ABOUT WHETHER LAW IS GOOD OR NOT?

Just because legal positivists insist on separating law from moral values when they analyse law and legal systems doesn't mean that they have no opinion about which laws are good and which laws are bad. The people themselves might, and usually do, have strongly held beliefs about what laws should do. Bentham, for instance, wrote extensively about utilitarianism as a rational way of ensuring that the content of law was desirable (although this, like much of his work, was not published in his lifetime). Austin, who took much of Bentham's work as the basis for his own, did not write about utilitarianism, but he was also deeply concerned (as an individual) about the social effect that law had.

It's just that, for the purpose of analysing law, legal positivists think it is necessary to keep the content of law separate from the structure of law. Davies calls this the 'separation thesis'.[3]

CHAPTER 6

---

1   Austin, J in *The Province of Jurisprudence Determined* (edited by HLA Hart) p 184, cited in Freeman, *Lloyd's Introduction to Jurisprudence* (7th ed), p 250.
2   Austin, op cit, p 126, cited in Lloyd, p 246.
3   Davies, M, *Asking the Law Question*: The Dissolution of Legal Theory, 2nd edition (Lawbook Co, Sydney, 2002), p 103.

Unlike natural law theory, positivism concerns itself not with whether the content of law can, for example, be derived by a process of reason from what is observable in nature, but rather whether laws could be shown to exist within a definable legal framework — do they have the character of 'law', and *not* do we approve of what they say.

Because it is a close relative of modernism, positivism works from the individual out. It lets people know *what* the law is, sets the boundaries of the law which will apply, and what the consequences will be if they do not obey the law.

ROAD RULES

Imagine what driving would be like if there were no road rules — if we were all free to drive however we liked. Nothing would compel us to drive on the left hand side of the road. Nothing would set any limit on how fast we could drive.

The only way we would ever be caught out would be through the general law of negligence.

Some people do, in fact, think that the road rules are an imposition on their liberty. Society disagrees with them, and through the legislature has said that we will have rules about driving on the road, and that certain penalties will apply if we break them.

Within positivism's method, we have to accept these rules once they are created validly. But they let us know the consequences if we choose to disobey.

This is legal positivism in action.

As we will see in this chapter, the development of legal theory in the 18th and early 19th centuries in the work of Bentham and Austin took a path which eventually rejected any association of law with the values which were embedded in posited law (and focused instead on developing an analytical framework in which to describe the structure of legal systems in general, and laws themselves in particular). In this way, as Davies observes, legal theory (and legal theorists) show their basis in rational thought and analysis and their adherence to the scientific principles which are characteristic of modernist, Enlightenment thinking.[4]

How do the positivist theorists approach legal analysis?

Both Austin and Bentham describe law very much in the terms of the legal systems which they could see around them. As models of legal positivism in its original form, both theories derive their ideas about what a legal system is (and what law is) from an examination of those systems.

---

4 Davies, p 27.

BENTHAM AND AUSTIN'S METHOD – DESCARTES AGAIN?

Descartes set the stage for empiricism as the basis for establishing knowledge. Empiricism is the process of observing, analysing what you see, and coming to a conclusion entirely within the narrow limits of your observations.

You might remember that the first of Descartes' rules for the proper analysis of anything involved the establishment of 'clear ideas' as the basis for inquiry.[5] What better way of clarifying your ideas than setting out, as both Bentham and Austin do, a detailed definition of their subject matter?

Descartes then suggests that a problem should be broken into as many bits as is necessary to solve it. Bentham breaks down human motivation into a series of positive and negative responses – pain and pleasure – which he breaks down further into a large number of types. Austin follows a similar pattern, classifying and breaking down the broad idea behind the word 'law' as it is loosely used into a series of subsets, drawing distinctions between law 'properly so called' and law 'improperly so called' – eventually allowing him to leave out of his analysis of law everything which is not strict black-letter law. These are generally things which, unlike what he calls 'law strictly so called', are not able to be looked at in the appropriate analytical and objective way, and which do not match the model of the independent legal entity of the nation-state.

Classical legal positivism – was Kelsen a positivist?

You will remember that in Chapter 4 we looked at the theories of Hans Kelsen, commenting that his theory was an attempt to exclude subjective material from the scientific analysis of law.[6] As we have seen, one of the characteristics of legal positivism is that it insists on the separation of morality and law. Kelsen certainly falls into the category of legal positivism on that count. But there is a distinct difference between the way that Kelsen approaches law, and the way in which the classical English legal positivists, Bentham and Austin, approach it.

KELSEN v BENTHAM AND AUSTIN

Bentham and Austin both look at law from an empiricist viewpoint. They look at the legal systems, and identify facts about legal systems. So they analyse law – or at least legal systems – from the perspective of the institutions which create and administer law. As we will see, both Bentham and Austin look closely at the notions of *command* and *sovereign*, constructing law as a form of command or series of commands emanating from a sovereign to its subjects, backed up by force in the form of *sanctions*. True, there is a superficial similarity to Kelsen in, for example, the role played by sanctions.

But Kelsen is not concerned with the real-world things, like Acts of Parliament or the person or institution of the sovereign, which figure prominently in Bentham and Austin. When they do get a mention, they are largely incidental to the central idea of the theory, which is the hierarchy of norms with the *Grundnorm* at the apex.

CHAPTER 6

---

5 See 'Descartes and method' in Chapter 4 above (p 88).
6 See 'Kelsen's modernism' in Chapter 4 above (p 98).

Bentham and Austin approach law empirically, while Kelsen approaches it conceptually. For many years, the common law world mistakenly tried to fit Kelsen into the same category as the classical positivists — ignoring this fundamental difference between them.

Is and ought

The source for the analytical method of separating law and morality dates back to the writings of David Hume (1711–1776). Hume drew attention to the lack of logical connection between 'is' and 'ought' — things as they were and things how they ought to be.

THE IS/OUGHT DICHOTOMY

At the centre of positivism is the belief that there is no logical or necessary connection between what can be observed (what 'is') and what we might say about preferred types of behaviour (what 'ought to be').[7]

Hume was concerned that in writings about morality, the argument inevitably jumped from observations 'concerning human affairs' to a series of propositions which set out what the writer thought ought to happen.[8] Hume goes on to argue that this jump could not be in the form of a deduction. He can see no connection between the description of what happens and what someone might think should happen.

In the spirit of the Enlightenment, Hume suggests that all moral systems would break down if people were to reject this irrational leap from the 'is' to the 'ought'.

While we might look at a boiling kettle, analyse what was happening and be certain about our conclusions, we can't follow this empirical process when we think about morality. The 'ought' propositions of morality — you ought not to kill another person — cannot be verified in the same way as observations about a boiling kettle and the scientific explanation of what is happening to the water in it.

Positivism insists that it is irrational to draw conclusions in the absence of solid evidence. So, while empiricism cannot provide us with any certain knowledge of morality, it can tell us something about the *existence* of positive law. Positive law is something which can be ascertained (or its *validity* established as a question of fact). It can be made the subject of analytical observation and enquiry.

WHAT COUNTS AS FACT IN COURT?

You will probably have come across the distinction between questions of fact and questions of law in court cases. Courts are very keen to establish facts according to objective criteria.

---

7   Davies, p 105.
8   Hume, D, *A Treatise on Human Nature* (Penguin, Middlesex, 1969), p 521, cited in Davies, p 105, Lloyd, p 28.

While individuals are not allowed to give their opinions (only their description of observable events), the court often relies on experts in fields which the law recognises (like medicine and engineering) to give their opinions. More often than not, these expert views carry considerable weight, even where an individual's experience is somewhat different. If medical opinion, for example, doesn't support an individual's own perceptions, it is likely that the court will accept the expert view. If it can't be observed and analysed, then it doesn't exist!

SECTION B: THEORIES OF LEGAL POSITIVISM

In this section, we are going to look at two theorists — Jeremy Bentham and John Austin — who together form the basis of classical legal positivist thought. For a long time after his death, Jeremy Bentham's work disappeared from sight. The picture we have of positivism is based very much on John Austin's work (which draws heavily on Bentham). We will look at Bentham first — but remember that much of the subtlety which Bentham brings to his analysis gets lost in the version we get from Austin. Most importantly, the Austinian view leaves out what Bentham had to say about what makes good law.

Jeremy Bentham

Through the 18th and 19th centuries, classical legal positivism began to take hold as the principal way of looking at law. The major ideas of legal positivism first emerged in the works of Jeremy Bentham (1748–1832).

Jeremy Bentham was born in London in 1748 — deep in the heart of the Enlightenment. Both his father and his grandfather were lawyers, and in 1760 Bentham went to Queen's College, Oxford. He graduated in 1764, and went on to study law at Lincoln's Inn.

A NOTE ABOUT DATES

We may not be mathematicians, but in this case, we've worked the sums out correctly!

$$1760 - 1748 = 12$$
$$1764 - 1748 = 16$$

Yes, Bentham went to University when he was 12 years old, and graduated when he was 16! Despite being qualified to practice law, he preferred to write about law and law reform.

Bentham is often thought of as being associated with the founding of University College, London (UCL). As the University's web site records, this is a myth (based on a fanciful mural in the main library which shows the architectural plans for the university being submitted to Bentham for approval).[9] Nevertheless, UCL considers Bentham its 'spiritual father', and its founders thought very highly of Bentham, embodying many of his ideas about education in the university.

---

9 You can read a short description of Bentham's relationship with University College at http://www.ucl.ac.uk/about-ucl/history/bentham/

Bentham, for example, thought education should be made more widely available, and UCL — the first university to be founded in England after Oxford and Cambridge — was open to people (like Catholics and Jews) who were excluded from traditional university education.

Bentham died in 1832, leaving behind tens of thousands of pages in manuscript which had not been published, which are now housed in University College. Indeed, much of Bentham's writing was not published until long after his death, and it was left to John Austin to popularise (or perhaps plagiarise?) many of Bentham's ideas — particular those which go to make up the 'command theory' of law.

THAT'S NOT ALL HE LEFT!

Bentham also left instructions that when he died, his body should be embalmed, dressed in his own clothes, and set on a chair. His 'Auto-Icon' is still there, in a cabinet in the main building of University College.

Bentham's theory

In one sense, it is misleading to talk about Bentham's 'theory' — rather than his 'theories'. Bentham's work represents an attempt to put together a complete theory of law and politics, intertwined with an understanding of psychology and logic. (You should realise that this was a very modernist thing to do. Bentham was trying to explain all the facets of human behaviour, both personal and political, in one, overarching theory!) In this part of the chapter, we will look at aspects of Bentham's theories which relate to both the analysis of law and legal systems (his *expository* jurisprudence) as well as some of his views about what makes law good law (his *censorial* jurisprudence).

We will look at a number of central themes which inform Bentham's view of law — his criticism of the common law as irrational and corrupt, his views about natural rights, his belief that utilitarianism could provide a scientific measure of what was good. These are not, in themselves, positivist in outlook. They do, however, help to explain why Bentham was irritated by the then current thinking about law, and why he formulated a positivist view of law as a better, more rational way of understanding law and legal systems.

Bentham's criticism

A starting point for understanding Bentham's theory is to look at how he viewed law as it was at the time. In the middle of the 18th century, English law was governed very much by the common law tradition described by Blackstone.[10] Bentham, searching for a reasoned basis for law, took aim at the common law, criticising it as being anything but a rational, principled and coherent system.

Instead, he characterised it as nothing more than a hotchpotch of rules which were not based in any series of underlying principles, but merely reflected the prejudices of judges. Judges made decisions according to their personal

10 See Chapter 3 above.

convictions – whether political or moral – and were in this sense corrupt. The decisions were then dressed up as being highly principled by the spurious argument of common law theory, the doctrine of precedent or the use of legal fictions (which Bentham likened to swindling in business dealings!).[11] Bentham was particularly critical of the doctrine of precedent, which perpetuated outmoded rules which had long since stopped serving their original purpose.

RULES WITH A USE-BY DATE?

Think about the rule in *Searle v Wallbank*.[12] The rule, which protected landowners from the consequences when their stock strayed on to the highway, had its roots in 'ancient social conditions' in England, when transport was by horse or horse-drawn vehicles. When the High Court considered the rule in *SGIC v Trigwell*[13] in 1979, highway traffic was much faster, and the potential damage which straying stock could cause was considerably more serious.

The doctrine of precedent is a powerful force for keeping rules like this, even though circumstances have changed significantly since they were first made.

Bentham criticised the common law's lack of clarity and certainty, its lack of accountability, its delays and complexities, the confusing and often incomprehensible language which lawyers used, and even the strange clothes and customs which permeated legal process – describing what he saw as a corrupt and ineffective legal industry dismissively as 'Judge & Co'. Law as Bentham saw it lacked most of the features which had become important in the Enlightenment world-view, and did not meet the needs of the emergent commercial and powerful capital interests of post-Industrial Revolution England.

What was needed was a rationally based system of law which clearly set out the limits of what someone was allowed to do, so that they could order their affairs in advance – not find out later, when they had been sued and a judge made a ruling about what the law was (and supposedly always had been).

LORD MANSFIELD, CHIEF JUSTICE 1756–1788

At the time Bentham was writing, one judge, Lord Mansfield, was in the process of reforming commercial law along systematic and principled lines. The common law was, in Lord Mansfield's time, particularly unable to cope with the rapid development of commerce. Based on his extensive knowledge of Roman law, he created a system of clearly articulated legal principles which had many of the characteristics which Bentham might have admired – they were, in fact, almost a code of commercial law.

Bentham, for some reason, reserved some of his most scathing criticism for this Chief Justice, claiming that Lord Mansfield's system was nothing more than the right for judges to do as they pleased.

CHAPTER 6

Dog law

One of Bentham's main criticisms of the common law was that it created law and applied it retrospectively. Bentham characterised this as 'dog law' – arguing that the way in which common law applied retrospectively was similar to the way in which we train animals.

---

11 See Davies, p 61.
12 (1947) AC 341.
13 (1979) 142 CLR 617.

DOG TRAINING — BENTHAM'S WAY

We do not explain carefully to our dog what behaviour is acceptable (and what is not), and expect them to comply. Obviously, you can't explain to a dog that, say, chewing your shoes is just not on. You have to wait until your dog actually starts to chew the shoes. *Then* you can administer some form of punishment — Bentham says you beat him for doing something that you want to break him of.[14] In this way, the dog learns the limits to its behaviour (based on avoiding the pain which it suffers when it's beaten for going outside those limits).

While this might be all right for a dog, Bentham thought it inappropriate as a way of dealing with human beings. Bentham is, after all, writing within the modernist tradition. Human beings (as individuals) are no longer insignificant, subject to the whims and arbitrary decisions of a divinely authorised ruler who behaves like a dog-trainer. They have the characteristics of the Cartesian subject. They are rational autonomous beings, unlike dogs. So while it may be appropriate to treat dogs like this (though the RPSCA would probably disagree), people deserve something better. And, of course, it *is* possible to explain to a human being in advance what the rules are (like, 'Don't chew my shoes'), and expect them to understand.

Yet the common law was (and remains), in practice, retrospective. The law is determined only after the events which led to the legal action. When a judge lays down a rule, it applies backwards in time to those events, even though the rule had not at the time been articulated. The inappropriateness of retrospective law, when applied to human behaviour, was not cured by the fiction of declaratory theory. What was needed was a system of law which allowed people to know *in advance* what the law was — what they were allowed to do — so that they could arrange their affairs rationally.

Bentham's rational alternative

Bentham's criticism of the common law was a preliminary to his attempt to restructure law along Enlightenment lines — that is, to give it a rational and objective form of support. Bentham saw two ways in which this rational basis could be provided — by being able to work out what the law should be (on the basis of utilitarianism), and by giving it an orderly and accessible form (in the shape of a codified law).

Bentham and utility

Bentham was one of a number of 18th century thinkers, including David Hume and John Stuart Mill, who championed the emerging idea of utilitarianism as the rational basis on which law and morality could be founded. The principle of utility is often encapsulated in the phrase 'the greatest good for the greatest number' — and forms the basis of Bentham's *censorial* jurisprudence, or 'science of legislation'.[15]

---

14 Davies, p 60.
15 Lloyd, p 202.

Bentham starts with the proposition that human behaviour is governed by two motivations – the desire for pleasure and the avoidance of pain.[16] Ideas of right and wrong could be traced to the idea that we are driven to behave in the way that we do in response to the hope of a reward or the threat of a punishment.

Bentham rejects the idea of community which had dominated natural law theory, emphasising the centrality of the individual by describing the community as a 'fictitious body' which is nothing more than the sum of the individuals which go to make it up. The underlying principle of utility, therefore, describes something which tends to increase the total pleasure for the sum of all the *individuals* in the community *more* than it tends to diminish it.

Writing not long after the mathematicians Newton and Leibnitz had independently developed calculus, Bentham tries to apply the same kind of rigorous analytical approach in explaining a rational basis for both morality and law – for private and public acts. He even borrowed the name, styling the analytical study of utility 'felicific calculus' – meaning essentially 'the mathematics of happiness'.[17]

So Bentham identifies 14 pleasures and 12 pains which could be used to work out how much happiness a particular law would create, based on a further six characteristics of pain and pleasure which could be used to arrive at a measurement – intensity, duration, probability, propinquity (speediness), fruitfulness and purity, and extent.

FIGURE 6.3: MEASURING HAPPINESS – BENTHAM'S WAY

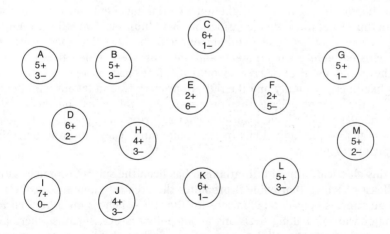

> **62+ 33– = 29+**
> **Proposed measure increases sum of human happiness**

CHAPTER 6

---

16 Bentham, *An Introduction to the Principles of Morals and Legislation*, edited by J Burns & HLA Hart (Athlone Press, London, 1970), cited in Lloyd, p 221.

17 This is perhaps an early example of the tendency which Davies identifies of adopting a scientific name for a branch of study in order to give it a sense of authority – to imbue it with a sense of absolute knowledge (see 'Does modernism have a standpoint?' in Chapter 4 above, p 95, and Davies, p 116.

In Figure 6.3, the pain and pleasure which a proposed measure will cause to each of the members of the community (represented as circles) have been worked out using Bentham's felicific calculus. (Of course, in reality happiness or pleasure can't be measured in this way, with a level of mathematical precision.) They are marked on each of the individuals as a plus figure and a minus figure – the consequences of the measure for most individuals will cause them some pain *and* some pleasure.

THE PAIN AND PLEASURE OF TAXES?

Most laws do not have just good or just bad consequences for individuals. Taxation laws cause us all some pain when we have to pay tax, but we gain some pleasure from the services which are provided by the government out of the funds derived from our tax dollars.

The assessment of whether the proposed measure is 'good' or 'bad' is, from Bentham's utilitarian perspective, just a matter of adding up the pluses and the minuses (calculated using his classification and standards of measurement).

Utilitarianism is concerned only with the consequences of a proposed measure – will it lead to greater happiness? It makes no judgment about the value of a measure in any conventional moral sense, such as whether it is approved by the church, or even by a majority of citizens. In fact, the promotion of greatest happiness is precisely what *creates* any moral value which a course of action has.

Utilitarianism, however, seems to leave no room for the natural rights which were so important a part of Enlightenment thinking. Bentham was scathing in his criticism of natural rights (considering them 'nonsense on stilts'). Rights can only be created by law, and Bentham rejected the idea that there were rights which existed before government and law, or were independent of them. Nevertheless, many of these rights would still form part of a good legal system. Values like liberty, equality and the right to property found favour with Bentham – not on the irrational basis that they were 'natural rights', but because they were principles which would lead to greater security, and hence, greater general happiness for all the individuals in the community. They conform generally to the principle of utility.

While this classical form of utilitarianism has been the subject of much criticism – not least of which that while it promotes the greatest happiness of the many, it also guarantees considerable misery for the rest – it lives on in revised forms as a major way of making decisions about policy issues, such as where public money should be spent. Will a hospital or a school lead to a greater sum of happiness measured across all the individuals in the community? Did the refusal to allow the 'Tampa' refugees into Australia increase the happiness of many individuals more than it will cause pain to a small number?

Bentham and codification

The cure for the ills which Bentham saw in the common law was to codify it. For the laws to be rational, and for people to be able to know in advance what the law was and what was required of them (so that they wouldn't be treated like dogs), it had to be gathered together into a single place, and written in language that was readily understood (rather than the incomprehensible complexity of lawyer-speak). The 'shapeless heap of odds and ends' that for Bentham made up the common law would be replaced by a clear set of rules, knowable in advance by anyone who took the trouble to look. And of course, the content of the codified law would be determined by using felicific calculus.

FIGURE 6.4: COMMON LAW v CODIFICATION

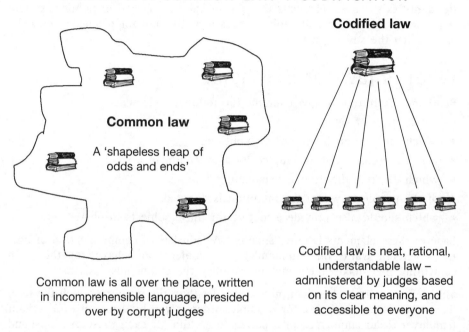

Codified law

Common law

A 'shapeless heap of odds and ends'

Common law is all over the place, written in incomprehensible language, presided over by corrupt judges

Codified law is neat, rational, understandable law – administered by judges based on its clear meaning, and accessible to everyone

A (fortunate) by-product of a sufficiently clear and detailed code is that judges (whose corrupt and whimsical decision-making Bentham despised) would effectively lose any legislative or interpretive function, assuming an administrative role in law.

WOULD CODIFICATION WORK?

Imagine a code which Bentham would approve of. Detailed, clear (and of course, utilitarian). What is likely to happen in the years following its enactment? Will situations arise which don't quite fit within the definitions contained in the code? Can the writers of a code envisage *every* possible situation and define it in advance, so that the code never requires interpretation?

Bentham and the structure of laws and legal systems

We can now look at Bentham's positivist view on what law is – his expository jurisprudence. Bentham's take on law is summed up in a passage from *A Fragment on Government*:

'When a number of persons (whom we may style *subjects*) are supposed to be in a *habit* of paying *obedience* to a person, or an assemblage of persons, of a known and certain description (whom we may call *governor* or *governors*) such persons altogether (*subjects* and *governors*) are said to be in a state of *political* SOCIETY.'[18]

You can see from this passage that Bentham's *expositorial* legal theory is very much a theory of political fact — founded in observation of actual legal systems. He identifies the basic elements that go to make up a legal or political system — a ruler (or *governor*) and subjects, plus a motivation for people to obey the laws which the sovereign makes.

What is law for Bentham?

Bentham's definition of law contains the following elements:

* a collection of signs
* which indicate an intention (or 'volition')
* which are conceived or adopted by a sovereign in a state
* which describe the desired behaviour
* of the people to whom the intention is directed
* which should also provide a motive for those subjects to obey.

Each of these elements is fairly simple. Law consists of communication of how the sovereign wants (or commands) their subjects to behave, together with something that makes them inclined to obey the commands.

This definition is, as Bentham notes, broader than the meaning which the term 'law' often has. It includes, for example, orders given by a master to a servant (employer to an employee), or a parent to a child (or even those of a husband to a wife!). And it includes acts of administrators and judges, even though these two branches of government were then (and still are) thought of as being quite distinct from the legislative (or law-making) functions of government. Bentham argues that these are brought within the definition because they are all traceable in the end to a common source — the sovereign.

Sanctions

Bentham realised that commands which lack any process for enforcement are not real commands (or at least, are not likely to be obeyed). People will not obey laws unless there is something in it for them (and some people, not even then!). His view of the motivating forces which caused people to obey includes what we would call positive *and* negative reinforcement — reward *and* punishment, carrot *and* stick or in Bentham's terms, 'alluring' and 'coercive' motives.[19]

Bentham accepts that the motivating forces may not be legal at all. It is open to the sovereign to rely on 'foreign' motivations (morality and religion), or they might create their own, legal, sanctions to induce people to obey the law. But he concedes that, for the most part, obedience is brought about by legal, rather than non-legal means.

---

18 Bentham, cited in Lloyd, p 221.
19 Bentham, *Of Laws in General*, cited in Lloyd, p 234.

He is, however, realistic enough to recognise that, in practical terms, it is punishment, rather than reward, which formed the basis of enforcement. The practice of government could not be carried on 'for half an hour' if it had to rely solely on reward as a motivating force.[20]

Bentham's sovereign

Bentham's definition of law requires that the signs (orders or commands) should be those of a *sovereign*. A sovereign is further defined as a person, or group of people, whom the people in a society are 'in a disposition to pay obedience'.[21]

FIGURE 6.5: BENTHAM'S SOVEREIGN

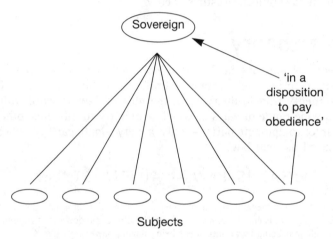

Bentham's sovereign is not complicated by unnecessary limitations (as we will see Austin's is). It is based squarely in the practical and the observable. As a result, it is sufficiently broad to include the different forms which governments in the Western world took at the time he was writing. In its simplest form, it looks something like an absolute monarch (ruling without reference to any institution like Parliament), but because Bentham includes 'an assemblage' of persons, parliamentary systems are clearly possible. Moreover, because Bentham accepts the possibility of divided sovereignty, his definition is quite capable of handling federal systems in which power is shared between different levels of government.

Similarly, Bentham recognises the existence of a class of laws – he calls them 'transcendent', but we know them as 'constitutional' – which constrain the power of the sovereign to use their powers in a certain way.

John Austin

Austin started to study law after a period of five years in the Army, at the age of 22. After qualifying as a barrister, he practiced at the chancery bar, but his

---

20 Bentham, *Of Laws in General*, cited in Lloyd, pp 204, 235.
21 Bentham, *Of Laws in General*, cited in Lloyd, p 227.

career in court is generally described as being 'unsuccessful'. He abandoned chambers after seven years, and took up a position as the first professor of jurisprudence at University College, London — but again, his career as an academic was disappointing.

As we go through the main components of Austin's theoretical approach to law, you will undoubtedly see the similarities (as well as some of the differences) between Austin and Bentham.

Austin has had a vast influence on the way in which we think about law. His theory — very similar to Bentham's expository jurisprudence — was adopted widely in the common law world and was the dominant view of law until Hart showed some of its failings in the 1960s. For many people, the way in which they are taught law reflects Austin's theory.

Austin's theory

Austin's theory is laid out in *The Province of Jurisprudence Determined*[22] — essentially six lectures which he gave as Professor of Jurisprudence at University College. The theory tries to break down the idea of 'law' (a word which is used to describe a wide range of ways in which people try to influence other people's behaviour) into component parts — only a very small part of which is what Austin thinks of as 'real law'.

WHAT IS LAW — AUSTIN STYLE?

'A law in the most general and comprehensive acceptation in which the term, in its literal meaning, is employed, may be said to be a rule laid down for the guidance of an intelligent being by an intelligent being having power over him.'[23]

Austin's commands

Austin's theory is usually described as a 'command theory', and owes much to Bentham's characterisation of law. Austin looks for the basis of law in something very real — commands or orders issued by someone to someone else. These are determinate and intentional human actions (Austin calls them 'wishes') designed to influence or control the way in which the subject of the command behaves.

COMMANDS IN LAW

Think for a moment about the things which you understand by the term 'law'. Most people, even without any legal training at all, might instinctively answer that 'law' was what you found in Acts of Parliament. 'Rules' about what you could or couldn't do. The simplest example is probably a law in the criminal jurisdiction, such as the statutory provisions in the Queensland Criminal Code which create the offence of murder.

---

22 John Austin, *The Province of Jurisprudence Determined* (Noonday Press, New York, 1954). First published in 1832.
23 Austin, op cit, p 10; cited in Lloyd, p 242.

As you started to learn about law, you will have realised that law is not just contained in statutes. The statutory provisions themselves are governed by judicial rules of statutory construction, and some laws do not have a statutory basis at all, but are laid down, in branches of law governed by the common law like torts, by judicial decisions. An example of such a law is found in the idea that someone who breaches a duty of care, and so causes damage to someone, has to pay compensation to the injured party.

Austin creates a definition of a command which owes much to Bentham's. It involves a number of elements:

- *A wish:* Not just any old wish — Austin uses the term to indicate the person giving the command's intention that someone should behave in a particular way — either to do something or to refrain from doing something.

- *Communication of the wish:* Of course, 'wishes' (in the ordinary meaning of the word) need not be communicated to anyone else. The wishes of the lawmakers, in the two examples in the box above, only become commands in Austin's definition when a further criterion — that the wishes should be communicated by words or some other form which is able to be understood — is satisfied.[24]

- *Sanctions:* Unlike Bentham, Austin takes a far simpler view of the sanctions inherent in commands, ignoring the possibility of reward. Sanctions are 'an evil', imposed by the person making the wish on the person who acts contrary to that wish.[25] It is not important *how* the wish is expressed — it may be a rough order or a polite request. Wishes become commands when they carry with them the threat of harm (and so create obligations or duties to obey).[26]

COMMANDS

The first test of whether something is law or not — whether it falls within the province of jurisprudence — is whether it can properly be described as a command. Does it have these essential features of:

- a wish
- given some form of expression
- backed by a sanction?

Look at the examples in the box headed 'Commands in law'. Both these instances of creating law involve these elements of Austin's command. Each involves the 'wish' of one person that another person should do something (like take reasonable care in the example of negligence) or not do something (like kill another person). Each has been communicated. In the case of the crime of murder, it is created by statute, and the wish is embodied in the relevant provisions of an Act of Parliament. For the law about breach of duty of care, the wish appears in the judicial statement by Lord Atkin about what constitutes the tort of negligence in *Donoghue v Stevenson*.[27]

---

24 Austin, op cit, pp 13–14.
25 Austin, op cit, p 14; cited in Lloyd, p 244.
26 Ibid.
27 [1932] AC 562.

Each also involves sanctions — the statute prescribes a punishment for murder, while the common law of negligence provides that people who harm others because of their negligent conduct have to pay compensation.

Generality

A further limitation of commands as they apply to law is that, in order to constitute a law, a command must have the quality of generality. Specific commands, such as might be made by an individual to just one other individual, are not laws. It is only those commands which prescribe behaviour at the general level — which create obligations across the board, either in the population as a whole, or to a class within the whole population — which can fall into the category of law.[28] This is a slightly strange aspect of Austin's theory. There are many examples, even from Austin's time, of laws which were very particular in nature. Divorces, for example, were given effect by private, individual Acts of Parliament (which, among other things, made divorce a very expensive process!).[29]

More than just commands?

Are *all* commands laws? While we have used examples which do, in fact, come from the legal world, it is possible to imagine commands which fit into Austin's description of a command, but which would not ordinarily be thought of as laws. Extortion rackets seem to fit the definition (a wish on the part of the extortionist that you pay up, and the certainty of harm if you don't), but not many people would confuse them with law. Something else appears to be necessary to fill out the idea of command as it applies to law.

If you think back to the two examples, the people who are making the wish, and giving it expression, are not just ordinary people, from a legal perspective. Kings and queens, parliaments and the judiciary have special places in the organisation of legal systems, in that they have the *authority* to issue commands (unlike the promoters of the extortion racket). Implicit in the idea of law is that the wishes (or commands) that go make up the body of law should have as their source some authoritative person or institution. Such a source, for Austin, was termed a *sovereign*.

DOES THIS WORK?

You might, of course, ask whether Austin's idea of law as a sovereign's commands backed by a sanction gives us an accurate picture of what laws are. Can it explain, for example, wills? Rules about the making of wills allow someone to change their legal position, but it is difficult to analyse them from the point of view of sanctions. Many things which we readily accept as law don't appear to have sanctions attached.

---

28 Austin, op cit, p 19.
29 These private Acts of Parliament, relating *only* to the two people who are getting divorced, have the very real legal effect of dissolving the marriage. Yet, the marriage itself was brought into being by processes established in something which Austin would certainly have thought of as law — ie the statute setting out the requirements of marriage.

Austin's sovereign

The word sovereignty, perhaps unfortunately, has a number of meanings. It can include sovereignty as it relates to constitutional law, or even international law. In the real world of 21st century politics, it can take any number of forms, ranging from a single individual who exercises absolute and autocratic power with no apparent basis (much like King Arthur's position in the example from *Monty Python and the Holy Grail* in Chapter 4), through to very complex methods of political organisation involving monarchs, parliaments and a wide range of institutions among which political power is distributed. It is therefore necessary to understand what Austin means when he says that laws are commands issued by a sovereign.

Austin begins his description or definition of sovereignty by distinguishing it from the other forms of superiority in society. It differs from other ways in which people exert influence over others.

A definition of 'sovereign'

Austin observes that, in a given society:

- the *majority* (Austin's term is 'bulk') of people
- are in the *habit of obedience*
- to a *determinate* and *common superior.*[30]

The determinate and common (political) superior is Austin's sovereign. The existence of such a sovereign, together with the people to whom the commands are issued and who are in the habit of obedience, constitute for Austin a 'society political and independent'.[31] You can see the similarity between Austin's concept of a sovereign and Bentham's.[32] The superior can be either an individual (which might accord with the ordinary meaning of a 'sovereign') or a body of individuals (like, for example, a parliament) or some more complex arrangement.

Furthermore, that superior, according to Austin, is not in the habit of obeying any superior.[33] Austin was writing at a time when the idea of the nation-state as a self-contained and independent entity — itself an Enlightenment development — had taken over from feudal conceptions of political organisation (which were often thought of as subject to interference by the Church).[34]

There are, therefore, two aspects to Austin's sovereign. While the sovereign can tell their subjects what to do (and their subjects generally obey the sovereign's wishes), the sovereign itself is not subject to being told what to do by anyone else above it in the social or political hierarchy. In Figure 6.6, obedience flows up from subjects to the sovereign, but not upwards from the sovereign to any higher authority.

CHAPTER 6

---

30 See Austin, op cit, p 194; cited in Lloyd, p 251.
31 Ibid.
32 Compare this description of a sovereign with that of Bentham's, p 151 above.
33 Austin, op cit, p 194; cited in Lloyd, p 251.
34 Lloyd, p 199.

FIGURE 6.6: AN AUSTINIAN SOVEREIGN

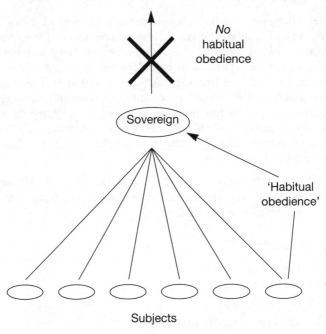

No habitual obedience

Sovereign

'Habitual obedience'

Subjects

WHAT ABOUT JUDGES?

Not sharing Bentham's dislike of common law, Austin is quite prepared to allow for a sovereign to issue commands (or to make law) through a delegate, or a political 'subordinate'.[35] So, a judge makes a law (like that of negligence) on the basis that they do so in the name of the sovereign. Lord Atkin is not simply expressing a private wish on his own behalf that people should take care to avoid foreseeable risk — although, as we have seen, in Bentham's view that might be exactly what is happening!

Both Bentham and Austin, in looking to the idea of habitual obedience to define sovereignty, are showing their Enlightenment roots. Lloyd observes that, as a lawyer, what Austin was looking for was a reliable test (lawyers love tests!) for working out what the source of legal authority was within a legal system.[36] Habitual obedience is, in some ways, like the boiling water in the kettle. It is something which can be demonstrated — it is something which is verifiable factually by observation and analysis.

Some additional characteristics of Austin's sovereign

While Austin's sovereign is defined by the relationship to its subjects and the absence of any superior to the sovereign itself, Austin gives his sovereign some further characteristics. Austin considers that the sovereign is unable to be either subdivided or limited. These two qualities of the sovereign are logical necessities flowing from Austin's definition.

---

35 Austin, op cit, p 226.
36 Lloyd, p 212.

- *The sovereign as illimitable* (ie it cannot be stopped from making any laws it wants to): If law consists of commands issued from a sovereign to people in a state of political inferiority, then no command could be issued *by* the sovereign *to* the sovereign, since it cannot by definition be both a supreme authority *and* in a state of habitual obedience (or inferiority) to itself.[37]

- *The sovereign as indivisible:* Any supposed command issued by the sovereign which had the effect of dividing the supremacy of the sovereign would again be a command of the sovereign issued to itself — and that would involve the same contradiction involved in illimitability.

These characteristics (which are not, you will have noted, part of Bentham's concept of sovereign) have been the source of much criticism of Austin's ideas. They are hard to reconcile even with the legal systems which were in existence in Austin's time.

Austin himself had considerable difficulty, as you might imagine, in trying to apply this part of the theory in the real world, in the form of the sovereign in the United States and the United Kingdom.[38] Any real-world political system which does not match the normal meaning of *a* sovereign — that is, a single entity exercising absolute power very much like King Arthur — is going to present difficulties when you try to describe it in Austinian terms — indivisible and illimitable.

Federal systems like the United States divide power between their Federal institution and their component States. Even the unitary system of the United Kingdom — which has no subsidiary governments which are the equivalent of states and provinces — can be difficult to fit into Austin's scheme of sovereignty. The constitutional arrangements in the UK involve the exercise of legal authority or law-making power through an amalgam of the monarch and the two Houses of Parliament (comprised of hundreds of individuals), as well as the judiciary (who, as we have seen, can make law) and local governments. As Davies observes, Austin's idea of sovereignty appears to depend heavily on an image based in monarchical government.[39]

So what is law, and what is not?

Armed with the central ideas of command and sovereign, we can now look at how Austin goes about the process of drawing the boundary between what is law, and what is some other way of exerting influence on the behaviour of others which does not amount to law.

You will undoubtedly come across a number of diagrams — like that in Lloyd at page 243 — which are associated with Austin's theory. They show the way in which Austin broke up the various types of 'laws' (thought of very broadly)

---

37 Austin, op cit, p 254; cited in Lloyd, p 253. Austin is clearly talking about *legal limitations* by positive law. He clearly recognises that a sovereign power can adopt principles of how it will exercise its supreme power. It may generally act according to those principles, and they may be approved of by the bulk of society. It's just that these laws of limitation — essentially constitutional laws — are not positive law.

38 See Harris, JW, *Legal Philosophies*, 2nd edition (London, Butterworths,1997), p 37 for a brief description of how Austin went about trying to locate sovereign authority in England and the United States.

39 Davies, p 94.

which existed in human society, and how, by a process of exclusion, law as the object of study becomes confined to the very narrow concept of positive law.

> Bearing in mind what we said about different ways of learning in Chapter 2, some of you may want to skip ahead and look at the diagram of how all these bits and pieces fit together before looking at the details.

A process of exclusion

At the very start, Austin draws a distinction between particular commands and general commands. All real laws are commands, but not all commands are laws. Particular commands are not law. Think about the wish Davies describes – that someone should hand in a 3 000 word essay.[40] If that is demanded of just one student, it is a particular command, which is not part of law. On the other hand, if it were an order made as part of a general set of rules about students and what they had to do as part of the assessment for a subject, then it is no longer particular, and will fall within the narrower idea of general commands, or law properly so called.

FIGURE 6.7: THE FIRST BREAKDOWN

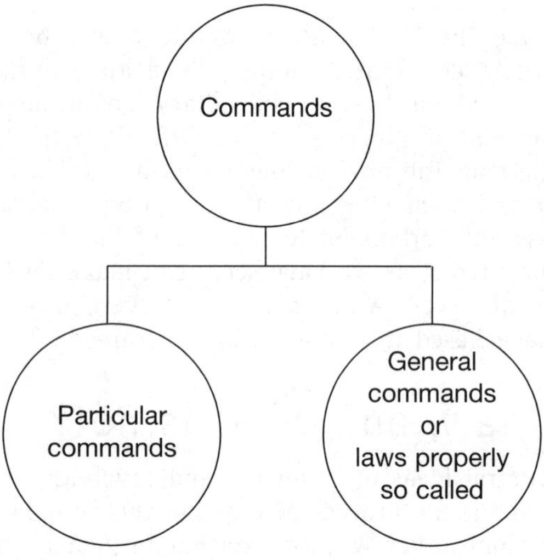

Classifying laws properly so called

Because of the definition of command which Austin adopts, general commands are laws properly so called. These, however, can be broken down further into two categories – divine laws (or the Laws of God), and human laws – laws set by men (as opposed to God). The Laws of God, though commands of a general nature applying apparently to all people, are not issued by a political entity identifiable as a sovereign (and hence are outside the boundary of the self-contained legal system which Austin is describing).

---

40 Davies, p 101.

FIGURE 6.8: THE SECOND BREAKDOWN

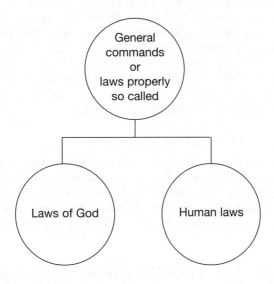

Classifying human law

Human law — a broad description — may or may not be law in Austin's strict sense. What is significant in classifying such human law is its source. The general commands set by humans can be issued by a sovereign, or by a person who issues commands in some other capacity. Laws which have as their source the sovereign are the *positive law*. Laws which are set by human beings, but not by a *sovereign*, do not form part of the positive law, even though they share some of the characteristics of positive law. The positive law is the *sovereign's* wish, expressed in some form of sign, and backed by a sanction.

FIGURE 6.9: THE THIRD BREAKDOWN

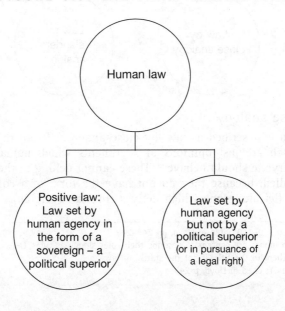

Austin describes laws set by people other than as a sovereign by giving the example of a club, which creates rules for the conduct of its members at meetings, where a breach will lead to expulsion from the meeting.[41] We might think about the rules governing sports in a similar way. The rules of a sporting body have many of the characteristics of law — the game of cricket even styles its rules as 'Laws'[42] — but they are not law strictly so called — positive law. True, they are laws set by humans, and they involve sanctions, but the creators of these rules are not acting in a sovereign capacity, and the rules are not created for the purpose of establishing legal rights.

Classifying laws which are not commands

But to complete the picture of all the ways in which laws (again thought of very broadly) appear in human society, Austin also distinguishes a class described as laws improperly so called. This group contains things which are commonly called laws, but which fell at the first hurdle — they are not even commands. These laws improperly so called are (not surprisingly) further broken down into groups.

FIGURE 6.10: THE BREAKDOWN OF LAWS IMPROPERLY SO CALLED

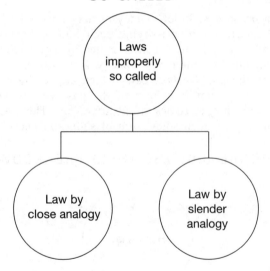

Laws by 'close analogy'

The first group is described as law 'by close analogy'.[43] Into this class, Austin puts laws which are just opinions or sentiments which human beings have about how everyone should behave.[44] These cannot belong in the group of laws properly so called, because they do not have the form of a command backed by a sanction (let alone one which derives from a sovereign).

---

41 Austin, op cit, pp 139–140; cited in Lloyd, pp 248–249.
42 Most sports and games are content to describe their rules simply as rules. Only cricket, as far as we know, elevates them to the title, if not the status, of law.
43 Austin, op cit, p 11; cited in Lloyd, p 243.
44 Ibid.

Examples in this group include what Austin calls the rules of honour (rules set by 'gentlemen', which reflect current opinion about proper behaviour)[45] and the rules of fashion (which, not surprisingly, are current opinions about fashion).[46] We would not have much difficulty in seeing these as being outside law as we know it. But on the basis of the restrictive definitions which he has adopted, Austin places into this category things which we would probably be surprised to find excluded from 'real law'.

International law (or as Austin sometimes describes it, the 'so-called law of nations'[47]) cannot, within this analysis, be positive law. It is, in Austin's view, just opinions and sentiment which happen to be agreed by nations at a particular time. There can be no 'international sovereign' to function as the source of commands in the international sphere, since we have seen that Austin's sovereign is *not* by definition in the habit of obedience to any political superior.[48]

Customary law is similarly barred from law properly so called, since it too is not a command but just opinion – albeit a widely held one – of an indeterminate group of people about the proper conduct of affairs. However, once customary law becomes incorporated into municipal law, taking its authority either directly or indirectly from the sovereign, it then assumes the status of positive law.[49] But it is the act of positing by a legal authority (usually the courts) which gives it this status – not its customary nature – and generates the other requirement of a sanction.

MABO?

In many ways, Austin's analysis of customary law matches our own. Aboriginal customary law – eventually recognised in the series of cases beginning with *Mabo* – gains its status as law *not* as a result of the position it holds in Aboriginal communities, but because it is expressly adopted by *legal* authority in the form of the High Court.

Equally, constitutional law, for Austin, is not positive law for the same reasons that prevent a sovereign being legally limited.[50] Constitutional laws effectively impose limits on the power of the sovereign – and that is something which, by definition, cannot happen. A sovereign is not in subjection to any higher authority, including itself.

Laws by 'slender analogy'

The last class of laws which Austin refers to are those rules which, although termed laws, really have none of the characteristics of law (in a legal sense of the word) – for example, the laws of physics or the rules that govern the behaviour of animals. Austin considers that the use of the word law is based on a 'slender analogy' to law proper – more metaphorical than literal. These so-called laws do not apply to rational beings, but to animals (who lack reason) or to inanimate objects.[51] As such, while they are included for the purpose of

---

45 Austin, op cit, p 140; cited in Lloyd, p 249.
46 Ibid.
47 Ibid.
48 See above, Figure 6.6.
49 Austin, op cit, p 163; cited in Lloyd, p 250.
50 See 'Some characteristics of Austin's sovereign' above, p 155, and footnote 37 above.
51 Austin, op cit, pp 12–13; cited in Lloyd, p 243.

a complete analysis of those things called law, they are not considered in any great detail.

The last piece of the puzzle – positive morality

There is one last piece of the puzzle. Austin writes of a class of rules which he calls positive morality. These rules are not positive law, and in fact are that part of law which Austin is concerned to set apart, as a positivist, from positive law. Positive morality includes rules which are both laws properly so called *and* some laws improperly so called.

Within human law, Austin has excluded from the positive law those rules which are made by people acting other than as a sovereign. These form part of Austin's category of positive morality. The other part of positive morality is the class of law described by Austin as law by close analogy – law deriving from opinion or sentiment, rather than from a determinate sovereign.

So the last breakdown of law unites these two classes together under the heading positive morality.[52]

FIGURE 6.11: SOURCES OF POSITIVE MORALITY

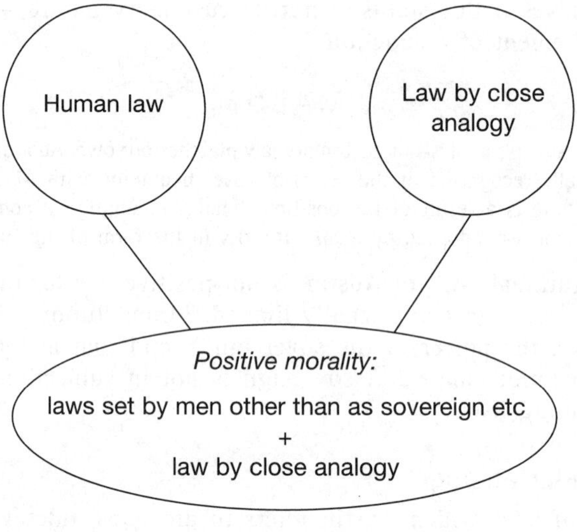

Putting it all together

What Austin's classification does is to exclude from the study of law those types of law which do not match the central idea of commands of a sovereign issued within the legal (or political) structure of an independent nation-state. What's left is described as *law strictly so called*, or the *positive law*. It is only this law which imposes legal constraints on individuals.

The whole collection of broadly termed laws, and Austin's method of breaking them down and analysing them, can now be put together into one (admittedly complex) diagram (Figure 6.12).

52 Austin, op cit, p 12; cited in Lloyd, p 243.

FIGURE 6.12: A MAP OF THE PROVINCE OF JURISPUDENCE

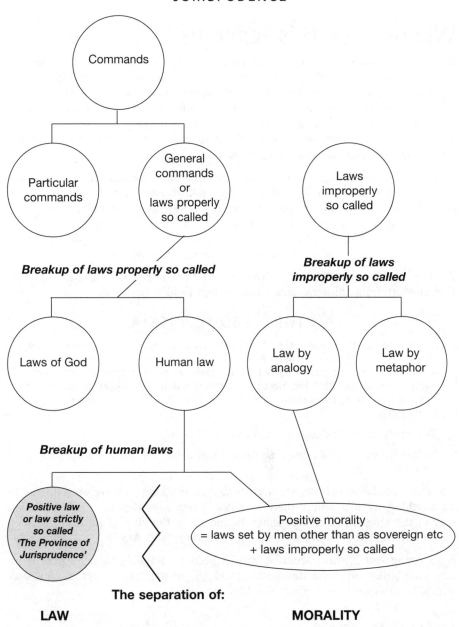

The separation of:

LAW   **MORALITY**

The implications for this classification, of course, are fairly obvious (and they are reflected in the type of law which you will have studied). What is left, after all those things that are like law, but not law according to the definition, have been excluded is the positive law. The proper subject matter of law and legal systems (the province of jurisprudence) is what falls within this idea of laws strictly-so-called — that is, the generalised commands of the sovereign (including commands issued through delegates) which are backed by sanctions. It is to these rules that the term law, 'as used simply and strictly, is exclusively applied'.[53]

Where does this leave us?

We are very much the inheritors of this view of law. The approach of setting law apart from other things — making law a self-contained set of ideas which are explained without looking at anything else but law — has become the 'natural' way to think about law. The idea of law as a command of some sovereign entity, which both Bentham and Austin develop, and the narrow set of laws set out by Austin as law strictly so called, correspond by and large with what we think of, and study, as law.

This view, in trying to provide a stable base for the understanding of law, does tend to fix our understanding of law in the political structures operating at the time that Bentham and Austin were writing — law at a particular time and a particular place. Part of our inheritance from positivist theory is that we sometimes have trouble changing law — we are, for example, suspicious of the High Court when it takes an activist role in shaping the law.

But the liberal ideas of freedom from government intrusion into our lives also find support from thinking about law in this rigid way.

A STORY ABOUT RUSSIA

At a seminar on the human genome project a few years ago, a senior counsel began his paper by telling a story about a recent visit he had made to Russia. While walking in the park with some friends, he had left the path to look at something more closely. But he soon realised that his friends were calling out to him, signalling for him to come back. When he got back to them, they explained that he wasn't allowed to walk on the grass.

'But there's no sign,' he complained, 'which says I can't.'

'In this country,' they said, 'there would be a sign which said that you *could* walk on the grass.'

The point of the story? We are accustomed to thinking that we are allowed to do anything we like *unless* there is a law which says that we can't. This is a way of thinking which is very much bound up in the kind of positivism which developed from the groundwork laid by Bentham and Austin.

By defining law in this particular way, it becomes possible to say 'There is no law prohibiting me from doing this', and so we are free to act in any way which is not specifically constrained by law.

Critical responses to positivism

We have already seen in Chapter 3 that the horrors of World War Two, and the use of valid law to justify terrible invasions of human rights, in part heralded a revival in natural law thinking. We will see in the later chapters of this book (on non-conventional theory) a range of detailed criticisms of positivist thought.

53 Austin, op cit, p 11; in Lloyd, p 242.

Some of the major criticisms of positivist thought include:

- that by detaching values from law, it is unable to provide a positive force for the promotion of values which we believe are important. Certainly in its classical form, positivism makes no attempt to comment on the merit of law's content; and

- that by fixing our view of law and legal systems very much in particular forms which were in place at the time positivism evolved, positivism has tended to impose a 'law-centred' view of law, which has not been open to the observations and insights which other disciplines can bring to the discussion of law.

QUESTIONS TO THINK ABOUT

1. Do you think it is a good idea (or even possible) to separate out what law is from what the content of law should or could be?

2. How does Kelsen's form of positivism differ from that of the classical English positivists, Bentham and Austin?

3. Do you think that the common law still has the characteristics which Bentham thought it had? If not, how has it changed?

4. If you had been sitting on the bench in *SGIC v Trigwell*, would you have supported the majority view (that changing or overturning the rule was a matter for Parliament), or would you have wanted to abolish the rule?

5. Can you think of any instances in which utilitarian thinking has played a part in the development of law?

6. Does Austin's definition of a sovereign adequately explain the ultimate source of authority in the Australian legal system?

7. Can you see how Austin's view of law — characterised as legal positivism — underlies many of the assumptions we make in Australia about what law is, and how you have been taught law?

8. In the recent controversy about the treatment of refugees (the 'Tampa' crisis), what aspects of Austin's theory were used to support the government's approach?

9. Can you see how the nature of the sovereign which Austin describes requires, as a logical necessity, that the sovereign be indivisible and not subject to limitations? We know, by looking at real-life situations, that this is not the case. Is this a weak point in Austin's argument?

10. Has international law changed since Austin's time? Would Austin be more likely to think that it was 'real law' now? And would this mean that Austin would have to revise other parts of his theory (like the nature of the sovereign) to accommodate these developments?

FURTHER READING

Austin, J, *The Province of Jurisprudence Determined and the Uses of the Study of Jurisprudence* (Noonday Press, New York, 1954).

Bentham, J, *Of Laws in General*, edited by HLA Hart (Athlone Press, London, 1970).

Bowring, J (ed), *The Works of Jeremy Bentham* (Russell and Russell, New York, 1962).

Campbell, T (ed), *Legal Positivism* (Ashgate/Dartmouth, Aldershot, 1999).

Detmold, M, *The Unity of Law and Morality: A Refutation of Legal Positivism* (Routledge Kegan Paul, London, 1984).

George, R (ed), *The Autonomy of Law: Essays on Legal Positivism* (Oxford University Press, Oxford, 1996).

Guest, S (ed), *Positivism today* (Dartmouth, Aldershot, 1996).

Hart, HLA, *Essays on Bentham: Studies on Jurisprudence and Political Theory* (Clarendon Press, Oxford, 1982).

Kramer, M, *In Defence of Legal Positivism: Law without Trimmings* (Oxford University Press, Oxford, 1999).

Lee, K, *The Legal-Rational State: A Comparison of Hobbes, Bentham and Kelsen* (Avebury, Aldershot, 1990).

Lyons, D, *In the Interest of the Governed: A Study in Bentham's Philosophy of Utility and Law* (Clarendon Press, Oxford, 1991).

Morison, WL, *John Austin* (Edward Arnold, London, 1982).

Postema, GJ, *Bentham and the Common Law Tradition* (Clarendon, Oxford, 1986).

Rumble, W, *The Thought of John Austin: Jurisprudence, Colonial Reform, and the British Constitution* (Athlone Press, London, 1985).

Waldron, J (ed), *Nonsense upon stilts: Bentham, Burke and Marx on the rights of man* (Methuen, London, 1987).

CHAPTER 7

Doing Common Sense: Positivism in Action

Reading. 167
Aim. 167
Principles 168
HLA Hart — who is he?. 168
Hart's view of law: law as rules. 169
The 'internal aspect': habit vs critical reflection. . 170
Obligation rules and non-obligation rules 171
Law and meaning — law as 'open textured'. 179
Some critical responses to Hart. 181
Questions to think about 182
Further reading. 182

READING

DAVIES, *Asking the Law Question: The Dissolution of Legal Theory*, 2nd edition, Chapter 3 (pp 94–96)
FREEMAN, *Lloyd's Introduction to Jurisprudence*, 7th edition, Chapter 6 (pp 331–350; 367–374)

AIM

This chapter will:

• introduce you to the positivist aspects of the theory of HLA Hart;

• look at how Hart's form of positivism differs from the classical positivist theories of Bentham and Austin.

WHAT'S IN THIS CHAPTER?

Neither Davies nor Lloyd give a complete coverage of the theory of Hart — Lloyd, for example, doesn't use any extracts from *The Concept of Law*, except a short extract about the separation of law and morality (pp 367–370). What we will do in this chapter, therefore, is to give an outline of the major components of Hart's approach to law as a positivist, looking at the system of rules which he describes as the basis for the ordering of society (both in a legal and a non-legal sense), as well as looking at what happens when, as Hart suggests, the nature of language means that the rules do not provide an answer.

HLA Hart — who is he?

HLA Hart (the initials stand for Herbert Lionel Adolphus) was born in 1907, the son of a Jewish tailor of German and Polish origin. He practised at the chancery bar from 1932 to 1940, but unlike Austin, his eight years in practice are not generally considered to have been a failure. During World War Two, he was unfit for active service, but he worked for British military intelligence (MI5).

After the war, he took up a tutoring position in philosophy at New College, Oxford, and in 1952 was appointed to the chair of jurisprudence at Oxford. He held that position until his resignation in 1969 — to be succeeded by Ronald Dworkin. His major work on jurisprudence, *The Concept of Law*, was based on lectures which he gave at Oxford.

FIGURE 7.1: HART TIMELINE

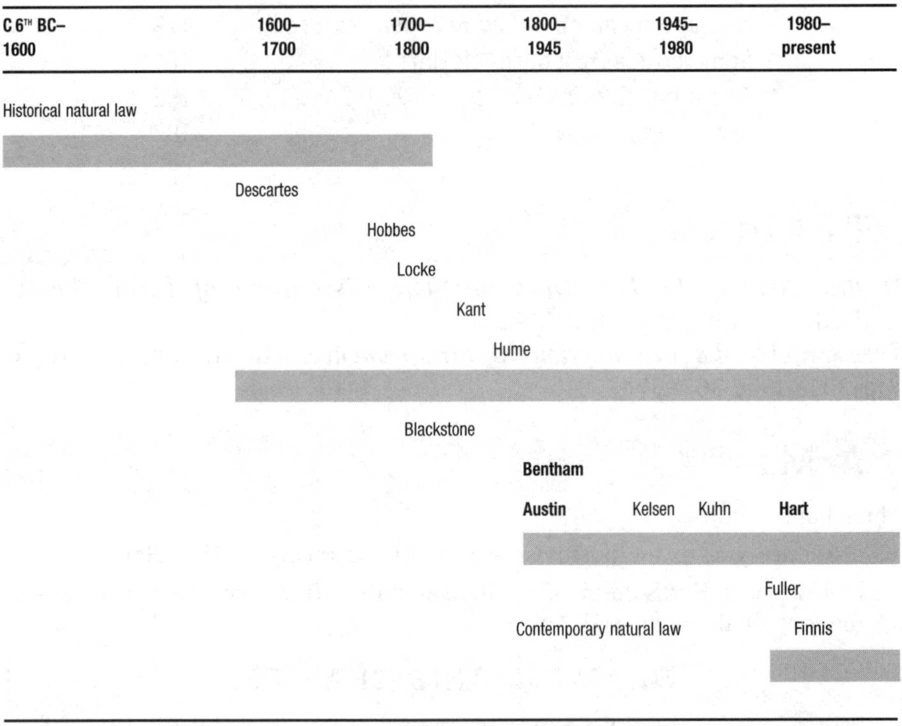

C 6TH BC– 1600	1600– 1700	1700– 1800	1800– 1945	1945– 1980	1980– present

Historical natural law

Descartes

Hobbes

Locke

Kant

Hume

Blackstone

Bentham

Austin   Kelsen   Kuhn   **Hart**

Fuller

Contemporary natural law   Finnis

This timeline shows where Hart fits into the history of legal thought. We have marked Hart and the related classical English positivists: **Positivism**.

Positivism revisited

The classical theory of positivism – in the form in which it was passed down from the 18th and 19th centuries in the work of Jeremy Bentham and John Austin – focused, as we saw in Chapter 6, on the idea of the commands made by a sovereign to govern the conduct of individuals in the community.

For Hart, the reduction of law to a single formula – the command of a sovereign – does not adequately explain law. Some laws, like the law which proscribes murder, may impose duties, and such duty-imposing laws share many of the characteristics of a command. But there are many rules within a legal system which do not impose duties. Some rules confer power on individuals – for example, the power to make decisions about legal issues is conferred on judges, and the power to make wills or to enter contracts is conferred on private individuals.

Rules which impose duties and rules which confer powers perform different functions in the legal system, and are framed in different language.[1] The language in which laws are framed is very often 'remote' from the language of orders or commands (except where, as in the case of criminal laws, the rule is closely analogous to a command).[2] But to conceive of legal systems as being made up solely of commands in this classical positivist sense, and trying to analyse rules using the command as a model, distorts the different social functions that are performed by these different types of rules.

Hart's view of law: law as rules

Like Bentham and Austin, Hart considers that rules in one form or another are a significant part of law. Hart, however, looks at rules in a very different way from these earlier, classical positivists.

Hart is not concerned with rules in the sense that they are the commands of a sovereign. Rather, their significance arises because of the way in which rules operate in society. Rules act as regulators of human conduct, but they also have a social quality, which is tied up with the way people respond to rules and the attitudes they have to them.[3]

Hart was critical of classical positivism in the form which it had emerged from the 18th and 19th centuries. The Austinian model had some very obvious flaws – particularly in the difficulty which Austin had in fitting some laws, like constitutional or international law, into the rigid classification of commands issued by a sovereign. This form of positivism was unable to cope with all the different types of rules which were clearly law, like international law, but which had to be excluded from law strictly so called. However, it was not these failures which were at the centre of Hart's rejection of Austinian positivism. Rather, it was the failure of Austin's theory to accommodate some very familiar laws *within* domestic legal systems – laws which conferred powers, rather than

---

1 Hart, HLA, *The Concept of Law*, 2nd edition (Oxford University Press, Oxford, 1994), p 38.
2 Hart, p 29, but note that even criminal laws do not use language which directly prohibits certain conduct, but rather specify sanctions for certain conduct (see Hart, pp 35–36).
3 Hart, p 56.

demanding particular forms of conduct — which indicated its inability to describe law without distortion.[4]

As we did with Austin, we will be looking at the different distinctions which Hart draws in his scheme of rules in a legal system. Some of you may want to look ahead to the complete structure at Figure 7.8 to get an idea of the overall shape of the system before looking at the details.

Hart sets out to identify the types of rules which operate within the practices of a society, and to see how they are put together into something that can be called a 'system'.

The 'internal aspect': habit vs critical reflection

Hart observes that there is a distinction between habits and rules, using as an illustration the difference between a *habit* of going to the cinema on Saturday nights with a *rule* (albeit not a law) that men should take off their hats when entering a church.[5] At the level of external behaviour, it may not be possible to see the difference — in the case of both habits and rules, people's behaviour will generally show a degree of consistency, as they conform to either the habit or the rule.

There are, however, a number of ways in which habits and rules can be distinguished. Deviating from a habit will not generally produce criticism by other members of the community. Where there is a rule, however, it will usually produce criticism from other members of the community if it is not followed, and these people will consider that such criticism is legitimate simply because of the existence of the rule.[6]

Rules, therefore, have what Hart calls both an external and an internal aspect. The *external* aspect of a rule is the observable action which a person takes in complying with the rule. It says nothing about what the person thinks about the rule. Using chess moves as an example, Hart observes that someone who moves a chess piece in the prescribed way not only demonstrates an observable behaviour, but also usually has a specific attitude to the proposition that, for example, queens move diagonally or in straight lines across the board.

Without such an *internal* aspect or attitude to the rule, moving the queen in a particular way might be nothing more than a reflex or habit. A chess player, however, accepts that this proposition is a standard which applies to the game of chess. This understanding of the conventions as rules, rather than mere habits, adds a further dimension to the rule in that the existence of the rule now incorporates expectations about other players' behaviour as well as their own.

It is much the same with what we ordinarily think of as laws. Most people recognise that rules represent standards of behaviour, and are more than just

---

4   Hart, p 79.
5   Hart, p 55.
6   Hart, pp 55–56.

habits.[7] However, it is not necessary for everyone to accept laws as a standard of behaviour. Any society may have a number of hardened offenders who do not accept the rules in this way, but that is not inconsistent with the existence of the rule itself.[8] What matters is that the existence of the rule should 'generally' be accepted, and form the basis for demands for conformity and criticism when the rule is not obeyed.[9]

FIGURE 7.2: AN INTERNAL REFLECTIVE ATTITUDE

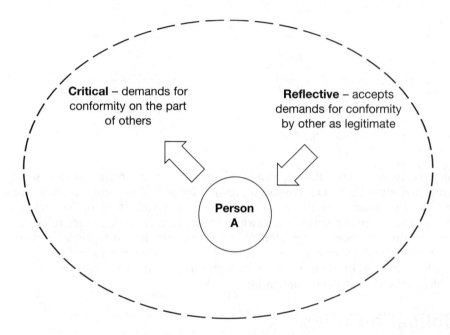

Hart describes this internal aspect as a 'critical' and 'reflective' attitude to the rules.[10] It is 'critical', because the rule acts as a basis for the criticism of non-conforming conduct. It is 'reflective' because it refers not only to an individual's demand for compliance with the standard in others, but also to the standard's role as a basis for their own conduct.[11]

Obligation rules and non-obligation rules

Once rules are distinguished from mere habits, Hart sets about analysing the types of rules which are found in society The first distinction Hart draws is between rules which produce obligations, and other social rules, such as those which provide guidance on etiquette, or which provide a framework for playing games or sports.

---

7   Hart is not specific about what proportion of the community needs to exhibit this internal aspect of a rule in order for it to be a rule — see p 56.
8   Ibid.
9   Hart, pp 55–56.
10 Ibid.
11 Hart, 'Postscript', op cit, p 255.

FIGURE 7.3: SOCIAL RULES — OBLIGATIONS OR NO OBLIGATION

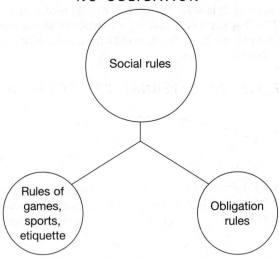

Some rules in society relate to things which are seen as important in a social sense, and attract considerable social pressure for people to conform. Such rules are said to impose a 'duty' or an 'obligation' on members of the community to conform to the standards laid down in these rules. However, other rules (like those relating to sports, for example) do not generate the strong social pressure to conform, and operate in areas which do not involve the important values which Hart associates with laws.[12] Although these are rules (as opposed to mere habits), they do not create obligations.

Obligation rules

The category of rules which create obligations includes rules associated with both law and morality.

FIGURE 7.4: RULES CREATING OBLIGATIONS

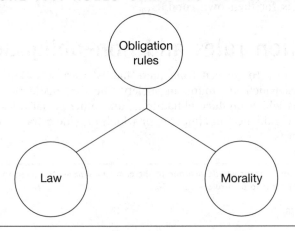

---

12 Hart, p 86.

Rules associated with morality are most often supported by social pressure based on inducing feelings of shame on the part of someone who breaks these rules. Other rules in a society, however, are met with another form of disapproval – often in the form of physical sanctions imposed by the community. Such rules are, for Hart, set apart from the rules which create moral obligations. In a primitive society, as we shall see, there may be no central institution or official whose function is to administer such sanctions. Nevertheless, these rules form, for Hart, a rudimentary form of law.[13]

Given Hart's views in relation to the minimum content of law, it is not surprising that he recognises that it is possible that both forms of pressure – the legal and moral – may be associated with one rule of conduct.[14]

Primary and secondary rules

Hart suggests that the obligation rules which are legal in nature can be further subdivided. All forms of social order must have laws which apply generally to all members of the society, setting out what legal obligations they are under. Hart calls these *primary rules*.

FIGURE 7.5: PRIMARY AND SECONDARY RULES

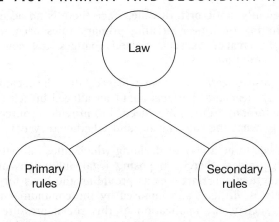

These rules, for example, forbid certain forms of conduct, described by Hart as 'violence, theft and deception'.[15] At a minimum, for a community to survive, as we saw in Chapter 3 (pp 71–72), there must be rules which protect individuals' physical existence (their person), the things that they acquire (their property) and which enforce their promises.

But any rule which is of general application, and which regulates the conduct of the members of the community to which it applies, is, in this scheme, a primary rule. Davies, for example, equates primary rules with rules of substantive law, citing road rules and the law of negligence as examples of laws which 'generally regulate behaviour in a social context'.[16]

---

13 Ibid.
14 Hart, pp 86–87.
15 Hart, p 89.
16 Davies, *Asking the Law Question: The Dissolution of Legal Theory*, 2nd edition (Lawbook Co, Sydney, 2002), p 94.

CHAPTER 7

A PRIMARY RULE

Section 300 of the Queensland Criminal Code (or its equivalent in other jurisdictions) represents a perfect illustration of one of Hart's primary rules. It is a general rule regarding conduct — it makes killing another person a criminal offence — which also happens to fall within the basic set of primary rules that Hart thinks all societies need to have to survive — it protects 'persons'.

However, primary rules extend beyond the protection of 'persons, property and promises', and may regulate conduct in any field.

Simple societies, Hart suggests, can get by with just these primary rules, although as Davies points out, he provides no evidence, in the form of anthropological studies of simple societies, to support this idea.[17]

PRIMITIVE SOCIETIES? AN EXERCISE IN IMAGINATION

Try to imagine how such a primitive society might look. How would rules arise in a society which has no established rules about what makes a rule? How would anyone know that there were rules, or what they were? What would happen to people who broke the rules?

Such a simple arrangement of rules suffers, however, from a number of defects.[18]

First, it is inherently static or inflexible, since there is no accepted method for deliberately altering the rules. Existing primary rules need to adapt, or new rules need to be created, as society itself changes and new situations arise which require regulation.

Secondly, it is also uncertain. As we will see later, the meaning of rules can never be entirely clear and the facts about an alleged breach may well also be disputed. Some form of arbitration is needed to provide a source of authoritative statements as to what the rules mean, and whether they have been broken.

Lastly, there needs to be a way of deciding which rules fall within the category of 'law' or 'legal rules', thereby imposing legal obligations and enforcement. The social pressure which Hart sees as providing the basis for conformity in a primitive society is 'diffuse', and imposed by the community as a whole. In a more complex society, the application of this social pressure will usually be carried out on behalf of the community by specific institutions or individuals.

In order to manage the primary rules, more advanced societies create what Hart calls *secondary* rules, corresponding to the three ways in which primary rules need to be managed.

The three types of secondary rules that Hart describes are: rules of *change*, rules of *adjudication*, and the rule of *recognition*. They are easy to remember by thinking of the initial letters of each — they spell C-A-R.

Rules of change are those rules which control change within the legal system. These include a very obvious public dimension, in the form of rules about who has the power to make or amend the rules which are in operation in the society, and how that process should be done. These rules of change often have a constitutional quality.

---

17 Ibid.
18 Hart, pp 89–90.

FIGURE 7.6: HART'S SECONDARY RULES — THE CAR

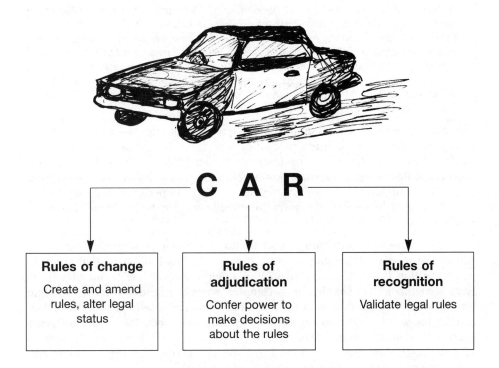

C A R

Rules of change	Rules of adjudication	Rules of recognition
Create and amend rules, alter legal status	Confer power to make decisions about the rules	Validate legal rules

But rules of change also include rules which create changes in the private domain — laws which allow individuals to change their legal status or the nature of their legal relationships. These include rules about making wills, forming contracts, getting married (or divorced) — rules which Austin had difficulty with.

RULES OF CHANGE

Section 1 of the Queensland *Constitution Act* 1867, provides for a Legislative Assembly in Queensland, and under s 2, the Crown has the power to 'make laws for the peace welfare and good government ... in all cases whatsoever' with the advice and consent of the Legislative Assembly. This is a very broad conferral of power, but nevertheless functions as a basic rule of change within the legal system of Queensland. Similar provisions exist in the constitutions of other States and the Commonwealth.

However, not all rules of change are associated with parliaments and the power to enact or amend legislation. Section 9 of the Queensland *Succession Act* 1981 specifies the formal requirements for making a valid will. By making a will, the nature of the testator's legal relationships (with the beneficiaries, for example) is altered.

Rules of adjudication are those rules which determine who in the society has the power to make decisions about when laws have been broken, and what the legal consequences of the breach are — whether it be to award damages for a breach of the rule about duty of care in negligence, or to sentence a criminal who has broken a provision of the criminal law.

RULES OF ADJUDICATION

Section 11 of the *Supreme Court of Queensland Act* 1991 defines the composition of the Supreme Court, and provides that the Governor in Council appoints judges to the Court. The judges who are appointed under the Act have the power to decide the outcome of criminal trials and civil actions within their jurisdiction (which is itself created by s 58 of the *Constitution of Queensland Act* 2001). Together with other rules, which specify *how* judicial decisions are to be made (such as the rules of precedent or statutory interpretation), these are rules of adjudication in the Queensland legal system.

The rule of recognition is somewhat different from the other two types of secondary rules. Both the rules of change and those of adjudication effectively confer power on individuals or institutions. The rule of recognition is not, however, a device for conferring power.[19] Rather, it is a device for determining what the valid law of a legal system is. As such, it performs the last of the three functions which are necessary to manage more complex legal systems — validating the rules.

The name 'rule of recognition' seems to suggest that it is a single rule which can be invoked to determine validity. It might be (as Hart says) that the rule of recognition is 'what the Queen in Parliament enacts is law'.[20] But that is, as Hart recognises, too simple. In a complex society where there are multiple sources of law, it may be necessary to specify a way in which sources of law can be ranked, in order to resolve any conflicts between laws from different sources.[21] A more sophisticated version might involve a hierarchy of sources of law, describing these different legal sources within the legal system and (more importantly) the way in which they interact.

Imagine a legal system governed by a constitution. The simplest view of the rule of recognition will be that it is the constitution itself. But underneath this will be the rules enacted by Parliament in accordance with the constitution. Below this will be legislation delegated according to the constitution or legislation. Below this, rules made by judges which are within their jurisdiction. Below this, there may be further sources of law, depending on the way in which the legal system is organised.

A FULLER DESCRIPTION?

You can read a full description of this sort of hierarchy, based on a hypothetical state, in Sir Neil MacCormick's book, *HLA Hart*.[22]

After looking at MacCormick's hypothetical hierarchy, try to put together a similar description of the rule of recognition for the Australian legal system.

But if either of these two ways of looking at the rule of recognition were all there were to it, then it would be nothing more than a statement about where law comes from in a particular legal system. We said at the beginning of this chapter that Hart's conception of law involved the attitudes which people had

---

19 See Lloyd, p 343.
20 Davies, p 95.
21 Hart, pp 100–101.
22 MacCormick, N, *HLA Hart* (Stanford University Press, Stanford, CA, 1981) p 110.

to law, over and above the mere existence of a rule. It is *this* aspect of the rule of recognition – the nature of the attitude which legal officials have to the rule – that makes Hart's form of positivism significantly different from its earlier, classical form.

In Bentham and Austin's version of positivism, laws are commands issued by sovereigns to a citizenry who are in a habit of obedience. Hart's rule of recognition requires something more.

In a primitive legal system, the absence of secondary rules means that there are no 'legal' institutions which perform the functions of making and changing law, or adjudicating on disputes about law. In order for the system to work, every member (or at least the vast majority) of the community has to accept rules as a common standard – to adopt the internal point of view. If a large number of people do not accept the rules in this 'internal' way, then the social pressure, which Hart sees as the basis for conformity to the rules, will be insufficient to control their behaviour.[23]

In a complex society where there are secondary rules, there must also be institutions or individuals who have had powers conferred by rules of change and rules of adjudication. A legal system in such a complex society requires only that officials show this internal point of view. Officials *must* accept that the rules are, indeed, valid rules within the system, but there is no reason why every member of the society must have an internal point of view.

FIGURE 7.7: A CIRCULAR RULE OF RECOGNITION? WHICH CAME FIRST, THE OFFICIAL OR THE RULE?

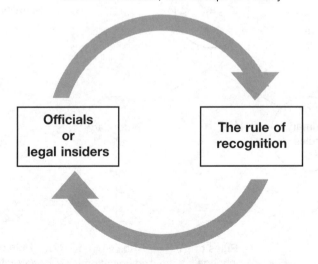

The rule of recognition depends on the attitude of officials, who accept its validity

Officials or legal insiders

The rule of recognition

The officials are officials ultimately because their status is confirmed by the rule of recognition

---

23 Hart, p 89.

This aspect of the rule of recognition, however, has been the subject of much criticism — primarily because it appears to be a circular argument.[24]

The rule of recognition depends for its existence on its acceptance by officials within the system. Yet the officials themselves owe their existence (as officials) to the rule of recognition.

FIGURE 7.8: THE WHOLE SYSTEM OF RULES

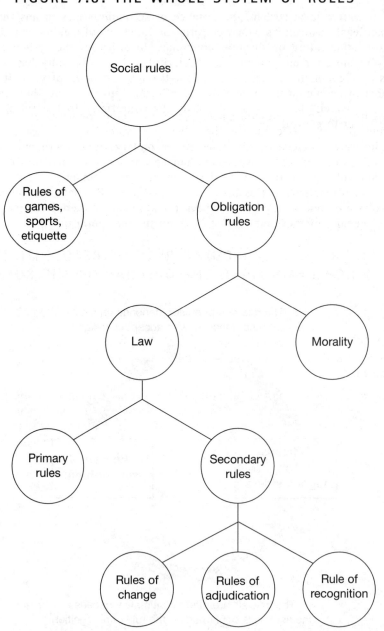

---

24 Davies, p 95, where she identifies a number of writers who have made this observation (footnote 84).

A legal system

Hart describes the process of establishing rules in each of the three categories of secondary rules as taking a step 'from the pre-legal into the legal world'.[25] By establishing all three forms of secondary rules – whereby the primary rules can be changed, decisions can be made about when the primary rules have been broken, and rules can themselves be validated – the structure becomes a fully fledged legal *system*. The whole scheme of rules in Hart's system is shown in Figure 7.8 (opposite).

Law and meaning – law as 'open textured'

As we have seen, Hart describes legal systems as being composed of a framework of rules. But Hart is conscious that all law is framed in terms of words, and that in order to be practicable, rules must refer to *classes* of people and *classes* of acts.[26] But however precise we might try to be in describing or defining these classes, language cannot always be relied on to convey the precise scope of such a classification.[27] Language simply lacks mathematical precision.[28] Hart calls this characteristic of language (and as a consequence, of rules) 'open texture'.

When you read a statutory definition, you might get the impression that the drafters had tried to think of every situation which might arise – making the language of statutes difficult to read. In reality, however, no-one can anticipate every possible situation that could arise which might fall under the rule which is being drafted.

Hart's description is that language has a 'core of certainty', surrounded by a 'penumbra' of doubt or uncertainty: see Figure 7.9. ('Penumbra' is a technical word in astronomy for describing an area of partial shadow around the full shadow cast during an eclipse – it comes from the Latin meaning 'almost a shadow').

When a rule uses a particular word, there will be a number of things which quite clearly fall within the meaning of the word. There will be no doubt as to whether these are included within the meaning of the word. For example, Hart uses the example of a rule that forbids the taking of vehicles into a park. In order for the rule to have meaning, we have to know what is included within the term 'vehicle'. Now there are a number of things that do obviously come within the meaning of the word 'vehicle'. A car obviously does. So does a bus or a motorbike.

Similarly, there is a vast range of things which clearly fall *outside* the meaning of the word used. 'Vehicle' obviously does not include a book or a packet of potato chips.[29]

---

25 Hart, p 94.
26 Hart, p 124.
27 Hart, p 126.
28 Freeman, MDA, *Introduction to Jurisprudence*, 7th edition (Sweet & Maxwell, London, 2001), pp 346–347.
29 As Fuller suggests, a ten-tonne truck would be clearly not be allowed into the park, but a pram would
   – see Lon Fuller, *Anatomy of the Law* (Penguin, Harmondsworth, 1971), p 82.

FIGURE 7.9: THE CORE AND THE PENUMBRA

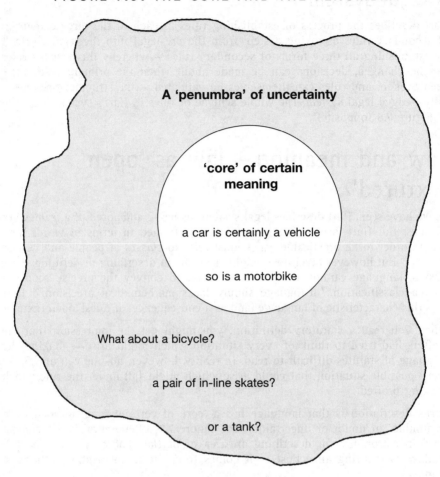

A 'penumbra' of uncertainty

'core' of certain meaning

a car is certainly a vehicle

so is a motorbike

What about a bicycle?

a pair of in-line skates?

or a tank?

But beyond these obvious members and non-members of the category 'vehicle', there are a number of other things that are not as clearly inside or outside the definition. What about bicycles? Roller skates? What if someone wanted to put an Army tank in the park to commemorate a battle?[30]

Each of these uncertainties could, of course, be resolved by making the definition tighter. If it were 'motor vehicle', bicycles and roller skates wouldn't be included in the prohibition. Yet the principle remains — that language cannot be tied down to a complete, hard-edged meaning. There will always be situations which defy the legislator's attempts to remove all uncertainty about what is covered.

The consequence of this innate uncertainty at the margins of language is that, when faced with a situation which is not within the core of certainty, judges must exercise a discretion as to what the law applies to — and hence, they engage in law-making when deciding on which side of the line a particular

30 See Lloyd, p 346.

situation falls.[31] Unlike Dworkin's view that the legal system already contains the 'one right answer' to a difficult legal problem, Hart sees the legal system as incomplete in the sense that the indeterminacy of language provides no answer in such cases.[32] Hart sees nothing wrong with allowing judges discretion to make law to 'fill up the gaps' in legal rules which arose when language proved imprecise, or that in doing so, they balance competing interests of varying weight and incorporate their own moral judgments.[33]

GAPS – DWORKIN AND HART

In Chapter 5, we saw that Dworkin's view of law was that it was a 'seamless web' – there were no gaps. Judges dealt with situations where the rules were not conclusive or clear by looking to principles already within the legal system which determined how a case should be resolved. For Dworkin, the 'one right answer' was already there in the legal system – needing only the superhuman skills of Hercules J to draw it out. For Hart, it is not only the case that judges made law where there was none, it is a desirable characteristic which gives flexibility to the system.[34]

Some critical responses to Hart

We have already mentioned some of the points in Hart's theory which have attracted criticism. The main criticisms which have been levelled at Hart's approach include claims that:

- Hart offers no specific evidence of the existence of 'primitive' societies which lack secondary rules;
- the rule of recognition is vaguely defined (at some times a single rule, at other times, 'rules' of recognition);
- the rule of recognition is circular (see pp 177–178 above);
- the theory adds little to Austin's view of legal systems, still accepting that obedience by the 'bulk' of the population is sufficient to validate a legal system;[35]
- the characterisation of law as rules oversimplifies the situation – Dworkin, for example, argues that as well as rules, legal systems operate by reference to principles and standards.[36]

Some of these criticisms are addressed by Hart in his 'Postscript' to the 1994 edition of *The Concept of Law*.

---

31 Hart, p 127.
32 Hart, 'Postscript', op cit, p 252.
33 Hart, 'Postscript', p 254.
34 See Lloyd, p 346.
35 Ibid.
36 See Lloyd, p 347.

QUESTIONS TO THINK ABOUT

1. Can you imagine a society which demonstrates the characteristics that Hart attributes to a 'primitive' culture? How would it operate? Can you find any examples where such a society has been described?

2. Given that Hart sets no specific limit for the proportion of a community that needs to adopt the 'critical reflective attitude', what do you think would be the status of a society in which *only* the officials (or legal insiders) adopted this position, while private individuals didn't accept the rules as being legitimate guides to conduct?

3. What is the significance of Hart's inclusion of a social dimension to the concept of a rule?

4. Does Hart provide any basis for distinguishing between law (as we understand it) and a complex set of rules such as those governing a sport?

5. Are there similarities between Kelsen's *Grundnorm* and Hart's rule of recognition? What about differences?

6. Can you find any examples of what Hart calls the 'open texture' of language in substantive law?

7. Are the rules of statutory interpretation themselves subject to a degree of open texture? If so, would any rules which were devised to govern how these were interpreted *also* be subject to some uncertainty? Does this go on forever?

8. Does Hart provide any guidance as to how judges should exercise their discretion when faced with a 'gap' on the law?

9. Do you think it is desirable that a judge's sense of morality should be used in interpreting law where its meaning is not clear?

10. Does Hart's rule-based description of legal systems provide a more accurate picture of law than Austin's command theory?

FURTHER READING

Campbell, T & Goldsworthy, J (eds), *Judicial power, democracy and legal positivism* (Ashgate/Dartmouth, Aldershot, 2000).

Detmold, M, *The unity of law and morality: a refutation of legal positivism* (Routledge & Kegan Paul, London, 1984).

Gavison, R (ed), *Issues in contemporary legal philosophy: the influence of HLA Hart* (Clarendon Press, Oxford, 1987).

Hart, HLA, *The Concept of Law*, 2nd edition (Clarendon Press, Oxford, 1994).

Hart, HLA, *Law, liberty and morality* (Oxford University Press, Oxford, 1963).

Jori, M, *Legal Positivism* (Dartmouth, Aldershot, 1992).

Skubik, D, *At the intersection of law and morality: Hartian law as natural law*, (P Lang, New York, 1990).

Martin, M, *The legal philosophy of HLA Hart: a critical appraisal* (Temple University Press, Philadelphia, 1986).

MacCormick, N & Weinberger, O, *An institutional theory of law: new approaches to legal positivism* (Reidel, Dordrecht, 1986).

Moles, R, *Definition and rule in legal theory: a reassessment of HLA Hart and the positivist tradition* (Blackwell, Oxford, 1987).

Waluchow, W, *Inclusive legal positivism* (Clarendon Press, Oxford, 1994).

CHAPTER 8

Marx and Law: Breaking Down the System

Reading. 185
Aim 185
Principles 186
Who is Marx and what is his influence on
legal theory?. 186
Encountering non-conventional legal theory. . . . 186
Marx's social theory 190
Analysing law using Marx 198
Marx as the springboard 199
Critical responses to Marx's theories 200
Questions to think about 200
Further reading. 201

READING

FREEMAN, *Lloyd's Introduction to Jurisprudence*, 7th edition, Chapter 12
DAVIES does not deal with Marx

AIM

This chapter will:

- introduce you to Marx and his influence on law and legal theory;
- explain Marx's theoretical methods;
- provide a foundation for how later legal theorists developed Marx's ideas and theories;
- show you how Marx's ideas provide insights into the effects of the substance and practices of law.

PRINCIPLES

Who is Marx and what is his influence on legal theory?

Karl Marx (1818–1883), along with his collaborator, Friedrich Engels (1820–1895), is popularly known as the architect of the political concepts of communism and socialism. Some of you may hold strong views about Marx, on the basis of these political outcomes of his ideas, but this is only one aspect of the range of ideas attributed to or derived from Marx. Of far more significance, for our purposes, are his observations and theories about the *relationships* between individuals and groups in society, all of which he saw as based in the economic forces that drove society. Marx provides us with a means to assess and analyse the effects of law on different sectors of society.[1] However, Marx did not provide a coherent or structured legal theory himself, though he did write on the topic.[2] Instead, the most interesting 'Marxist' legal theories are those developed by later legal theorists who used Marx's theories to reveal inequalities and assumptions about the law. This work shows how the substance, practices and methods of law privilege, or more actively accept as valid, views of some groups in society over others. The influences of his work can be found in the non-conventional legal theories we shall be looking at in the rest of this book.[3]

The scope of Marx's writings is immense. This short chapter will introduce you to a tiny portion only of Marx's work and ideas. His theories are also complex, relying on, and arguing against, the theoretical and philosophical inclinations of his time. He sometimes changed or altered his position, so it is not always possible to say what Marx 'said'. What we seek to do in this chapter is to draw out some of Marx's ideas at a very basic level of complexity. If you have already studied politics, philosophy, sociology, history, or economics, you will have encountered other aspects of Marx in more detail than we will cover in this chapter.

Encountering non-conventional legal theory

Changing places

This chapter will mark a turning point in the story of legal theory we have told you so far in this book. This means that we will start looking at law from

---

1   Marx originally studied law in Germany; he changed his course of study to philosophy.
2   We will be leaving out some of Marx's own theories about law and justice, and its relationship to the state. You will find that Lloyd deals with this aspect of Marx and law very fully. A number of general jurisprudence texts deal with Marx and Marxism. In some cases, their focus is on Soviet or Communist law. If you need to consider the practical uses of Marx in Communist legal systems, you might wish to look at McCoubrey and White, *Textbook on Jurisprudence*, 2nd edition (Blackstone Press, London, 1993), Chapter 6.
3   See Chapter 1 overview, p 3 above.

the 'outside in', and you will find yourself 'changing places' from a legal insider to an outsider in the legal process. If you find this difficult to do, then place yourself in the position of a barrister bound by the 'cab rank' rule: you neither have to like or believe your client or their position, but you are duty bound to represent them to the best of your ability, as required by law.

WHAT DO WE MEAN BY CHANGING PLACES?

In the previous chapter, we saw how HLA Hart conceived of law operating 'internally', from the standpoint of accepted mores. What would he have thought of the anti-Establishment counter-culture that produced magazines like *Oz*?[4] The method by which he allowed for legal change, particularly the idea of the 'critical reflective' attitude, assumed conformity to the established society and legal system. His method did not look at law from the outside in, but from a legal insider's point of view.

An outsider will not necessarily be someone who wants to break the law or start revolutions. An outsider may simply ask questions about the norms, assumptions and practices of law that we may otherwise accept unquestioningly.

To be able to ask these sorts of questions, different types of theories from those we have used so far will have to be employed.

A little bit of history from the 1960s and 1970s

What is the anti-Establishment? And what is counter-culture? And why does it matter for this topic? Before we find out what the *anti-Establishment* is, we need to know what 'The Establishment' is. The Establishment as a term emerged in the 1950s, and is still used to refer to the, usually conservative, social and political groups that exercise power in all aspects of society. Anti-Establishment groups opposed these values, and anti-establishment activities were a hallmark of the 1960s and 1970s: men began wearing their hair long and growing beards, people participated in anti-Vietnam war protests, and some rejected conventional living arrangements by developing collective and communal living. For those who rejected the dominant culture, a new 'counter-culture' was created, which adopted its own social values and practices. The counter-culture was treated as odd and 'alternative' because it was a lifestyle opposed to the conventional or dominant groups in society.

The anti-Establishment and counter-culture saw law, lawyers, and the legal process as part of the 'Establishment', and as the chief form of support for conventional forces in society. They would see Hart's views as those of a legal insider, whose theory would not accommodate radical change. The anti-Establishment wanted this sort of radical change, though its lawyers, like the Australian Geoffrey Robertson (now an eminent silk in the UK) worked within 'the system'.[5] In the 1960s, a number of lawyers, including Geoffrey Robertson, sought justice for people unfairly treated by the legal system. But as well as working *within* the system, some radical legal theories emerged out of this era, which sought to change 'the system'. This social and political change did not just 'happen': it developed off the back of the ideas of Karl Marx.

---

4   See Chapter 5 above, pp 122–123, and also Chapter 12, pp 281–282.
5   Robertson, G, *The Justice Game* (Vintage, London, 1999). He describes the role of the 'alternative' bar. As a Rhodes scholar at Oxford, Robertson also researched the law for the *Oz* trial.

RADICAL

These groups sought a *radical* overhaul of the conventional norms of society. In this sense, 'radical' means going back to the origins of something, such as the way people live, or political or social change. It looks afresh at conventional approaches by going back to the origins of accepted thought and standpoints.

Marx's theories are radical because they go back to the origins of a way of thinking, and argue for fundamental change.

Looking at society

Most of the conventional legal theories we have encountered so far distance themselves from the *real* effects that law has on people or groups of people in society. For instance, liberal political philosophy assumes that all people are treated by law the same. By treating everyone as equal, it does not need to ask if a law will adversely affect some people more than others, or benefit some more than others (see Chapter 4, pp 112–122). Legal positivism's abstract methods and interests are unconcerned about the effects of law − if a law has the correct pedigree or follows the correct structure, its effects can be disregarded (see Chapters 6 and 7). Even natural law theories can disregard the unfair or oppressive nature of laws, in favour of the common good.[6]

On the other hand, *non-conventional* legal theories look at law and its practices from the outside in. Some take an external approach to radically reconceive the law, such as the legal theories which developed out of the techniques of postmodernism, or the radical counter-cultural anti-Establishment legal theories that developed out of the 1960s (Chapters 10–13). Others barely shift outside the internal method of legal theory, like Roscoe Pound's 'sociological juris-prudence', which uses techniques derived from sociology to better manage the development of doctrine.[7] It may surprise you to find that whatever their differences, these non-conventional legal theories which look outside the law are indebted to the Marx's social theories: see Figure 8.1, opposite.

How can such vastly different theories derive from Marx?

Marx's ideas and methods have been picked up by other thinkers, who then develop their own theories. These theories might be directed related to Marx's own ideas, or take a small part of Marx's theories and take them into another area of thought completely. Marx has been adapted to the needs of such diverse areas of thought as economics, politics, sociology, cultural studies, literature, and, of course, law.

The method that the later theorists use can be likened to a technique you are familiar with − the doctrine of precedent. The core idea of a theory will be pulled out and adapted to new circumstances or for different purposes.

This process is known as 'extrapolation'. We will take this topic up in Chapter 12.

---

6   See Chapter 3's criticism section, pp 79–80 above.
7   See Chapter 9. You may be wondering how his method differs from Hart and Finnis' anthropological and sociological approaches − the difference is that neither of these theorists used these techniques as the central plank of their theories. Instead, they used them to support their arguments for their core theory, whether it be natural law or positivism.

FIGURE 8.1: MARX TIMELINE

1600–1700	1700–1800	1800–1900	1900–1945	1945–1960	1960–1970	1970–1980	1980–1990	1990–present

Hobbes

Locke

    Kant

       Hegel

    Rousseau

    Blackstone

      Industrial Revolution

       Laissez-faire capitalism

         Marx

        Durkheim

         Weber

           World War One

           Russian Revolution

             Development of the welfare state (UK and Australia)

        Holmes

         Pound

          Legal Realism

           Rise of Nazism

           World War Two

          Kelsen

             Hart

             Fuller

               Marxist legal theories

               Sociological influences

                 Contemporary critical legal theories

                   Finnis

                     Fall of communist states

                     Dismantling of the welfare state (UK and Australia)

This timeline shows where Marx fits into the history of legal thought, and some related social, economic, and historical events.

Marx's social theory

Labour, economics, and social change: a snapshot

We are familiar with the changes brought about by revolutions in technology. Only 20 years ago, we would have written this book long-hand, and it would have been typed on a typewriter by a secretary or a member of the typing pool. Most of you will find this description of work quaint, odd, or may not even know what a typing pool was. But we know, because we used to work like this. We now work on computers, communicate by email, use the web to research, and have forgotten how long research and writing used to take (see Chapter 10, p 237). Business and labour now operate differently than they did 20 years ago. Globalisation, free markets, and casualisation of the workforce are the norm. Our work has changed dramatically because of this revolution, and our society has changed also in response to the changes in the way we work. Law and the legal process have had to respond to the challenges of technological change, from electronic contracts to computers in court.

In a number of years, we will be able to look back and ask how whether a simple change in the *mode of production* – the means by which work is carried out – triggered a revolutionary change in all facets of society. At present, we are living in a period of uncertainty – the old stable society is gone, challenged by technology. Eventually, we will be able to see a stable outcome – until the next challenge. See Figure 8.2, opposite.

Congratulations! You have just worked your way through the process of historical change that Marx called *dialectical materialism*. Again, look at Figure 8.2. The dialectic, developed by the philosopher Hegel, is like a work in progress. For Hegel, a stable situation (a *thesis*) will be destabilised (by an *antithesis*) to be replaced by an improved, or better outcome (the *synthesis*). Hegel's dialectic sought to find the Absolute, or the perfect State,[8] based on a philosophy called 'idealism'.[9] We are only interested in the technique of the dialectic for the purpose of considering Marx's theories.

THE ESTABLISHMENT AND ANTI-ESTABLISHMENT

The tension and struggle between these groups can be liked to a mini-dialectic. The Establishment is not so 'establishment' now, the anti-Establishment is only a small part of society, and the society we live in now is a blend of both (a synthesis).

In Marx's adaptation of Hegel, the dialectic was also a work in progress, but one which explained historical change out the realities of human existence. This type of reality (the opposite of idealism), was known as 'materialism'. The *materialism* that mattered, for Marx, was based in the changes to economic

---

8   You will remember this concept from natural law with Aristotle – Marx considered Hegel to be a German Aristotle, and he wasn't being complimentary.

9   Extract of Hegel, 'Philosophy of Right' in Lloyd pp 990–991; cf Marx, 'Critique of Hegel's Philosophy of Right' in Lloyd pp 991–992.

conditions of life, through changes in the *mode of production*.[10] Marx's dialectical materialism sought to show how change happened in societies, through some kind of movement or struggle.

FIGURE 8.2: ADDING MATERIALISM TO THE DIALECTIC — DIALECTICAL MATERIALISM IN ACTION

	Thesis	Antithesis	Synthesis
Era	1970s–1980s	1990s–now	?
Change in mode of production	Working with a typewriter	Working with a computer	?
Effect of change on work	Stable full-time employment	Casualised workforce	?
Role of law in employment	Arbitration and conciliation, centralised bargaining	Individual contracts, minimal centralised bargaining	?
Effect of change on social circumstances	8 hour day	12 hour shifts as required	?
Income earning	Wage and Salary Sick leave, holidays	Casual rates	?
Ability to access loans from financial institutions	Wage and salary acceptable. Can be used to buy cars, houses	Casual rates unacceptable. Impacts on ability to buy cars, houses	?
Living arrangements	Home ownership	Rental only	?
Balance of work and other facets of life	8 hours of work, 8 hours of sleep, 8 hours of recreation/household duties = 24 hours	Inability to plan or balance work and other aspects of life	?
Child care	Commonwealth funded child care	Reduction in Commonwealth funded child care	?
Health care	Medibank and Medicare – bulk billing predominates	Reduction in bulk billing	?

Economic change leads to massive social upheaval

Marx constructed a colossal portrayal of human progress through history, in which all changes were attributable to and pivoted on the changes in the *economic forces* that drove that society, which Marx called the *base* or *infrastructure*. All other aspects of society changed off the back of the base, which

---

10 He drew on the changes that occurred when humans altered their interaction with nature, from the primitive stage of human history, where man was dominated *by* nature, through to man's domination *of* nature.

were known as the *superstructure*.[11] He identified five epochs, where change was driven by alterations in the mode of production, and the consequences for social practice and organisation: see Figure 8.3.

FIGURE 8.3: MARX'S FIVE EPOCHS

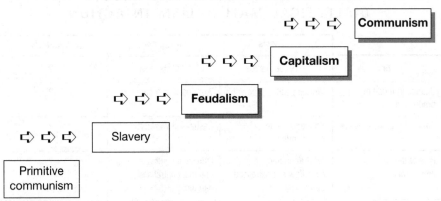

Marx did not have anything to say about the technological revolution in which we now live. He did not have a crystal ball. We have extrapolated.

Let's look at some aspects of the process of change through the shift from *feudalism* to *capitalism* in England. See Figure 8.4, opposite. The shift did not happen quickly. You will see how a series of events based in changes in the base resulted in changes to the superstructure. You will see that *law is part of the superstructure* — we will explain why this is the case shortly.[12]

You may remember Dennis the Peasant's arguments for political change in Chapter Four — re-read them and see if you can locate where they may belong in our description of the changes that occurred from feudalism to capitalism.

The class struggle

One of the facets of Marx's theory that we haven't yet referred to is the effect of the changes for different groups or 'classes' in society.[13] Marx saw an economic basis for class structures, which was based on the ability of the class to control and exploit their *property*. During capitalism, the classes that were able to exploit property were the landowners, who had always controlled property, and the merchant class (which he called the *bourgeoisie*), who only gained access to this sort of power through the period between feudalism and capitalism. On the other hand, the ordinary working class, (the *proletariat*), were left behind, having only their labour to sell, and Marx argued that they were

---

11 See Lloyd pp 958–963. In the 'Preface to The Critique of Political Economy' set out in Lloyd at p 1005, you will see that Marx includes law, politics, religion, aesthetics and philosophy in the superstructure. Marx suggests that the base could be determined with precision, while the superstructure appears to be less capable of quantification.

12 Marx, 'Preface to Contribution to Critique of Political Economy' in Lloyd, pp 992–993; Marx and Engels, 'The German Ideology' in Lloyd, p 993; Engels, 'The Housing Question' in Lloyd, pp 994–995.

13 See Lloyd, pp 964–965.

kept out of the system which benefited the other classes in society. Marx also recognised the existence of a number of other classes, but focused his attention on the bourgeoisie and the proletariat. He argued that a *class struggle* between the bourgeoisie and the proletariat would ensue, when the proletariat realised how they were being used by the capitalist system, to make money for others, and how they were *alienated* (see p 194) from their true nature — the freedoms held out by the assumptions of equality were not for them.[14]

FIGURE 8.4: THE SHIFT FROM FEUDALISM TO CAPITALISM[15]

		Feudalism (thesis)	300–400 years (antithesis)	Capitalism (synthesis)
BASE or INFRASTRUCTURE	Work (mode of production)	Ordinary people worked in small groups under the protection of a feudal lord	Ordinary people worked as sole tradespeople and organised into guilds in towns, or worked on small farms	Ordinary people now worked in large towns or cities for an employer, or worked in support services to maintain the towns
	Land (mode of production)	Land was owned by the feudal lord, though the commons and waste land were available for ordinary people	In the lead up to the 18th century, ownership of land was centralised through the process of enclosure, enlarging landholdings of the landowners	Farms were now large, with no place for the spare farm workers. Ordinary people lost their means of survival and had to move to the cities
SUPERSTRUCTURE	Religion	Catholicism	Church of England	Church of England and non-conformists
	Philosophy	Church teachings	Rise of modernism and liberalism; autonomy of the propertied (male) citizen emerges	Modernism and liberalism predominate; autonomy of more classes of (male) citizen
	Politics	Absolute monarchy People accepted their status	Divine right of kings gives way to constitutional monarchy	Expansion of the franchise (the right to vote) to include some working men
	Law	**Local institutions and king's courts**	**Independence of the courts and judiciary from Crown**	**Formalised legal system to maintain and support commerce**
	Communication	Oral traditions	The printing press	Books and newspapers
	Entertainment	Religious miracle plays	Monarchical control of theatres	Commercial theatre

14 We wish to acknowledge our student Scott Edwards for reminding us of the role of alienation in Marx's theory. This aspect of Marx's theory was taken up by the Critical Legal Studies movement, which we will look at in Chapter 12.
15 Marx, 'Preface to Contribution to Critique of Political Economy' in Lloyd, p 1005.

ALIENATION

For Marx, alienation is the condition in which the proletariat is unable to or is powerless to fully realise their own lives. You may be alienated because there is no direct connection between the work you produce and the income you receive from it. As a worker, you become a commodity to be bought or sold on the market. Alienation is not confined to the effects of work. The consequence of alienation, for Marx, is 'self-alienation' from your true nature. This means you are unable to reach your full potential as a human being.

You may not know that you are alienated; you may think that you are fulfilled, but you are actually denied from really fulfilling your life potential.

Once the proletariat realised the true nature of their condition under capitalism, then they would overthrow the other groups. Capitalism would be replaced by communism, where all people would be fulfilled. The class system would be abolished, private ownership of property would not exist, and political structures, religion and the law would no longer be needed. Nor would the *state*, an institution whose role was designed to maintain the system of capital.[16]

This revolutionary facet of Marx's theory, when put into practice in Communist states like Soviet Russia, failed to match up to Marx's predictions. Communism, as Marx meant it, has never happened.

We are still in the period of capitalism.

Capitalism and law

Marx's theories fundamentally criticised capitalism and the *laissez-faire liberalism* (meaning a free market unfettered by any constraints) that supported it. We need to briefly look at what it was about capitalism that led Marx to construct his theory of alienation, the notion of a world driven by economic imperatives, and the desire for the revolution that would overthrow this system. For this aspect of his work, Marx collaborated closely with Engels,[17] who provided him with empirical data (observations) of the lives of the working poor in the new, grim cities which fed Britain's prosperity in the 18th and 19th centuries off the back of the 18th century's Industrial Revolution.

The Industrial Revolution is famous because of its technological innovations, like the steam engine, which helped the rapid rise of British power and influence, particularly in the 19th century. But life and social forces were also dramatically affected by this revolution that fed what Marx saw as the grasping capitalism of this era. If you look at the next box, you will be able to see a snapshot of work, life and the law during this period.[18]

THE INDUSTRIAL REVOLUTION

You may have lived in a small rural community in England. Through the passage of an enclosure act for the benefit of the local landowner sometime in the 1760s (enclosure acts were private acts of parliament, through which the common lands became the property of the landowner), you were now displaced. You could not live on the land any more, and you could not use the commons to produce food or goods for survival.

---

16 Marx and Engels, 'The German Ideology' in Lloyd, pp 1004–1005.
17 Engels' work on the social conditions of workers in the new cities profoundly influenced Marx.

You had no choice but to migrate to a new industrial city like Manchester, where you would work in the cotton or woollen mills. The work was dangerous, you were expected to work 12 or 13 hours a day, and the pay was poor. There was no sick leave or holidays, and your employer was not liable for any injuries you suffered. If you stayed in your employment knowing your employer engaged in negligent conduct, it was inferred that you had consented to whatever dangers you faced, through the voluntary assumption of risk, volenti non fit injuria (though the doctrine was read down by the end of the 19th century).[19] The courts assumed that you *chose* to work there, knowing the risks you faced. The doctrine meant that employers were not liable for any injuries you received.

Your housing might have been a small room in a crowded tenement with no running water, with a common toilet (and electricity had not been invented). You had no rights to vote.[20] Things were not so bad if you were a skilled tradesman, or if you worked for industrialists who created new communities of labourers.

**But if you were a member of the propertied upper and middle classes,
your world was far more comfortable.[21]**

From his observations of society, Marx concluded that the values of liberalism – including freedom, rights, equality – were the tools of oppression and exploitation of the workers. Laissez-faire liberalism assumed that everyone had *freedom,* but the reality was that freedom would not benefit those who could not participate fully in the system of capital – the workers. Looking at the example of *volenti,* we can now see, in hindsight, that it would have been virtually impossible for a worker without social security to refuse to work in a job, however dangerous it was. But the laissez-faire liberalism of the 19th century, expressed through this doctrine, would reconstruct the worker's decision to remain in that workplace as a true expression of their freedom of choice.[22]

Law falls into the superstructure

If we follow through Marx's argument that the base drives all other forces in society, where do we position law's role in this process?

Before we go on, remember:

CONVENTIONAL **legal theory assumes that law is not influenced by or
subservient to external factors.**

But Marx placed law within the superstructure.[23] What this means is that law is not seen as the separate or distinct entity that conventional legal theory assumes. Placing law within the superstructure *subverts* the assumption of conventional legal thought, that law is independent of external pressures, Marx instead sees law as having a role in *maintaining and facilitating* the economic interests of the system in which it functions.

18 Marx, 'Capital Vol 1' in Lloyd, pp 1005–1013.
19 *Smith v Baker* [1891] AC 325.
20 Chapter 3 above, p 65.
21 If you are interested in following these ideas further, you might like to look at Roy Porter's *English Society in the Eighteenth Century,* revised edition (Penguin, London, 1990).
22 See Marx, 'Critique of the Gotha Programme' in Lloyd, pp 1020–1021.
23 There is some possibility that he may have meant it to be included in the infrastructure: see GA Cohen 'Karl Marx's Theory of History' in Lloyd, pp 995–999; S Lukes 'Can the Base be distinguished from the Superstructure?' in Lloyd, pp 999–1004.

FOLLOWING THE ECONOMIC LOGIC THROUGH ...

This means law would accept arguments to create, and to then maintain, doctrines like *volenti*, because it suited the needs of capital. To provide a safe workplace costs money; such costs eat into the profits that the employer would receive from the *surplus value* produced by the workers. Reduction in profits reduces the ability of capital to receive investment from shareholders, and the law should not impede economic prosperity.

Marx argues that any laws designed to improve the lot of the workers were subverted by employers; and any that did have a good effect simply hoodwinked the workers into a false sense of protection, and were designed to delay or forestall the revolution.[24]

You may want to compare this argument with a reading of volenti from the standpoint of conventional legal theory.

A less subtle reading of the law can be found in the penalties and sentences imposed by the criminal law in this period. The criminal law was also used to harshly punish the actions of people, usually the poor or workers, who interfered with the property rights of others. The First Fleet to the colony of Australia was filled with convicts who had stolen objects of relatively low monetary value, some of whom had escaped the gallows for the price of a loaf of bread. Within this reading of Marx, the law is clearly designed to support a system which will protect property at all costs.[25]

But the superstructure works in more complex and subtle ways as well.

Let's look again at Figure 8.4, which shows some of the shifts that occurred in the movement between feudalism and capitalism.

You will see under the category of *politics* that the assumption about the divine right of kings gave way to the development of constitutional monarchy, in which all (propertied) citizens now had a role in deciding the actions of government. If we stay within superstructural thinking, this process of shifting from *autocracy* to *democracy* can be seen as absolutely necessary to the developing economy, which had moved away from being land-based into commerce. The political process shifted in line with the needs of the economic base. You might like to look at Dennis' views again: pp 90–91.

Such an analysis differs markedly from the political ideas which feed into conventional legal thought: that the ability of the autonomous subject to directly participate in the process of government was a triumph of liberalism.

Legal consequences flow from these types of political changes as well. In particular, *interference by the state or government* was now an unacceptable intrusion on people's lives. It was not uncommon for the king's agents to enter property and arrest people without a search warrant. The law's assumptions of the relationship between us and those who rule us changed dramatically in this period, and insisted (if we were propertied) that no-one interfere with our private

---

24 Marx, 'Capital Vol 1' in Lloyd, pp 1005–1013, sets out Marx's views on the approaches of capital towards the workers when reforms were attempted.

25 Cf EP Thompson 'Whigs and Hunters' in Lloyd, pp 1013–1019. We will consider EP Thompson's version of Marxism in Chapter 12 below.

world. This mistrust extended to any activity that intruded on business or commerce, as well as the need to protect ourselves from unwarranted police intrusions in our lives. Look back at Chapter 5 on liberalism, and consider this change in action, through the principles expressed in the case of *Entick v Carrington* (p 121).

While protecting the individual from unwarranted government and State intrusion, the law in this period was now used by individuals to assert their rights against each other. To facilitate the needs of commerce, the law developed principles that now underpin commercial law, particularly through the judgments of Lord Mansfield.[26] Company law assisted the needs of commerce. The legal profession established a commercial focus, in addition to the conveyancing practices needed to support land transactions.[27]

Law, in effect, began to speak the mind of capital ...

Ideology

We have inherited a belief that law's real role is as an adjunct of the commercial world, and that law should resist state intrusion in business, in particular. Other forms of law, like consumer law, family law, criminal law and social security law are somehow less like 'real law'.

What we have described here is what Marx would call our 'legal consciousness'. We have somehow acquired an idea about what law is, and Marx tells us that these ideas are not just 'out there', but instead reflect the interests and needs of the (economically) dominant groups in society. He calls this 'social consciousness' or 'ruling ideas'.[28] What this means is that all of us accept these *ruling ideas* as normal, without being aware that we have accepted the *ideology* that suits the dominant group's agenda.[29]

Law takes on a key role in reproducing social consciousness, at both a popular level and at a more conceptual level. At a popular level, the law tells us how to behave in acceptable ways, through notions like 'law and order'.

> ## REMEMBER THE ANTI-ESTABLISHMENT?
>
> People engaging in new and different ways of living and behaving will often attract the attention of the 'law'. If you were a member of the Establishment or acted in ways that conformed to acceptable social behaviour, then the law would be less likely to be used against you.
>
> **At the time leading up to the Oz trial,**
> **the Establishment's ideology was more acceptable.**

At a more conceptual level, we can find ruling ideas expressed in our assumptions about liberty or freedom of speech. Law is given a role to tell us how to behave, but also privileges some ideas over others, which have a broader

---

26 See Chapter 6 above, p 145.
27 Renner, K, 'The Institutions of Private Law and their Social Function' in Lloyd pp 1023–1031.
28 Marx and Engels, 'The German Ideology' in Lloyd p 1013.
29 Lloyd, pp 965–969.

impact on society. We do not always know that we are taking these views and accepting their normality. The way these ideas are reproduced is called hegemony.[30]

> We will look at the way more recent legal theorists have used Marx to critically consider law and legal practice in Chapter 12.
> These later interpretations or extrapolations are often known as Marxist or Marxian legal theory.

Analysing law using Marx

Classical Marxist analysis

The version of Marx we have set out in this chapter is called 'classical' Marxism. A classical Marxist analysis of law may differ from later interpretations of Marx.

> ### THIS IS NOT AN EXAMPLE OF CLASSICAL MARXISM
>
> EP Thompson suggested that magistrates in the 18th century would act independently from the wishes of landowners, and treat criminal offenders more leniently, because of an abiding commitment to the rule of law.[31]
>
> EP Thompson leaves the way open to argue that law was more autonomous than Marx had suggested.

Ansett

Let's analyse a recent example from Australia, which lends itself to a classical Marxist legal analysis.

Despite their emotional connection and devotion to 'the company', employees of the now defunct Australian airline, Ansett, found that their loyalty was not repaid when the company ceased trading in 2001. The employees were not paid their separation entitlements by their employer, including various forms of leave, as well as redundancy payments. Many of the employees were unable to see themselves as different from the company, and did not know that, in law, they were simply unsecured creditors.

To be able to claim their entitlements, the employees were left in line with other unsecured creditors, at the bottom of the chain. Their union found that the best way to get the employee's entitlements was to operate within the system. The government imposed a levy on air travellers to assist with paying their entitlement. The funds acquired by the levy will not be used solely for this purpose.

---

30 In Chapter 12, we will look at the concept of hegemony, developed by the Italian Marxist theorist, Gramsci (pp 281–282).
31 Thompson, EP, 'Whigs and Hunters', extracted in Lloyd, pp 1013–1019. We will come back to this in Chapter 12 below, p 275.

This example illustrates the following:

- An unfettered market allowed Ansett to be run down and become unviable
  - The law will not (generally) intrude in the internal workings of companies except at the time of insolvency
- Employees assumed that they would be treated fairly by the company and by the law — they had to bring on expensive legal action instead
  - This is an example of the difference between social consciousness and legal consciousness
- Law will adopt methods to best facilitate capital
  - The difficulty facing the workers was compounded by their status as employees. Their lack of capital is something they were unaware of, as emotional attachment and devotion to a company is not recognised as a legal category
  - As individuals, they would have been unable to afford to bring actions themselves
  - Their union had to rely on corporations law, rather than employment law, to get any relief for the ex-employees
  - Employment law gave them rights to redundancy pay which were hollow in this case.

Taking this kind of external view of law suggests that law is never abstract, or divorced from wider political or social issues.

> You may wish to compare this analysis with the approach which would be taken by a conventional legal theory.

Marx as the springboard

Marx critiquing modernity

We will conclude this chapter by considering a set of deeper questions that Marx leaves us with. If you think about his methods, you will know that he was, largely, a modern thinker.[32] He was interested in big ideas, and big epochs. These big pictures are known as *metanarratives*. But there was another side to the insights he came up with; if you demonstrate that big changes can be made to societies, including changes to the superstructure, then the basic methods of modernity hit a snag. Why? Because the moment you suggest that ways of thinking can be changed by, for example, different ruling ideas, then ideas that are central to modernism, like *objectivity*, come into question. Marx inadvertently opened the door to the ideas of postmodernism, which fundamentally questioned the assumptions of modernity. We will take up that story in Chapter 10.

Building on Marx

Marx also influenced a direct line of critical thinkers who adopted his ideas or picked up aspects of his theory. In Chapter 12, we will build on the Marx we

---

32 See Chapter 4 above.

have met in this chapter, and look at a range of contemporary readings of Marx. We will look at the Critical Legal Studies movement, whose ideas were inspired, in part, by Marx, and also by the theorists we will meet in Chapter 9.

Critical responses to Marx's theories

Lloyd sets out a series of arguments that have been made in response to Marx's theories. As we have done previously, we have tried to leave questions and criticisms of Marx until the end of this chapter so that you will have had an opportunity to read, digest, and think about his underlying theories.[33]

Here are some of the arguments against Marx's theories:

- Criticisms are directed at Marx for his placement of law in the superstructure, not the base. These criticisms are founded on the notion that no economic activity can be carried out without law.

- Arguments are mounted on the basis that because Marx's political arguments have failed in a practical sense, his entire theory should be disregarded. Similar arguments are based on Marx's use of the epochs, which can be seen as historically flawed.

- The special nature of law, as a unified, logical and rational system is disregarded by Marx, and it is wrong to suggest that law will privilege economic values for the benefit of capital.

- Marx failed to effectively theorise law, which means his ideas are irrelevant for law.

- Marx mistakenly conceived of ruling ideas when many ideas driving social values came from the workers themselves, who were inherently conservative.

- Marx did not foresee the changes that would be wrought in the 20th and 21st centuries, where capital would be shared between more individuals, and welfare initiatives would be dropped in favour of the re-emergence of a new kind of laissez-faire liberalism. Law would no longer be used to redress imbalances in society.

QUESTIONS TO THINK ABOUT

These are not questions to which we will provide you with answers, but are questions designed to start you thinking about Marx's ideas, in comparison with other theories you have seen so far:

1. What is the difference between an insider's and an outsider's views of law?

2. Can you explain the relationship between the mode of production and law in Marx's theory?

3. Why would conventional legal theory dislike Marx's analysis of law as being part of the superstructure?

---

33 Lloyd, pp 986–990.

4. Can any links or comparisons be made between Marx and natural law theory?

5. Liberalism and Marxism take vastly different views of liberty. What are they? How might they differ when considering a basic legal right we have in Western society: free speech?

6. Why does law, from Marx's viewpoint, adversely affect workers and their rights?

7. Why do business and commerce dislike government intrusion into their operations? What role does law play in denying this kind of government intrusion?

8. How has Marx influenced law and legal practices?

9. Were the Ansett workers aware that Marx would suggest they were alienated? Did law contribute to their alienation?

10. How valid are the criticisms of classical Marxism?

FURTHER READING

Beirne, Piers & Quinney, Richard (eds) *Marxism and law* (Wiley, New York, c1982)

Cain, Maureen & Hunt, Alan (eds), *Marx and Engels on law* (Academic Press, London, 1979).

Collins, Hugh, *Marxism and law* (Oxford University Press, Oxford, 1982).

Douzinas, Costas & Ronnie Warrington, with Shaun McVeigh, *Postmodern jurisprudence: the law of text in the texts of law* (Routledge, London, 1991).

Fitzpatrick, Peter (ed), *Dangerous supplements: resistance and renewal in jurisprudence* (Pluto Press, London, 1991).

Harris, JW, *Legal Philosophies*, 2nd edition (Butterworths, London, 1997).

Hunt, Alan, *Explorations in law and society: towards a constitutive theory of law* (Routledge, New York, 1993).

McCoubrey, M & White, N, *Textbook on Jurisprudence*, 2nd edition (Blackstone Press, London, 1993).

Morrison, Wayne, *Jurisprudence: from the Greeks to post-modernism* (Cavendish Press, London, 1997).

Phillips, Paul, *Marx and Engels on law and laws* (Barnes & Noble, Totowa, NJ, 1980).

Sugarman, D (ed), *Legality, Ideology and the State* (Academic Press, London, 1983).

Varga, Csaba (ed), *Marxian legal theory* (Aldershot, Dartmouth, 1993).

Ward, Ian, *An introduction to critical legal theory* (Cavendish Publishing, London, 1998).

CHAPTER 8

CHAPTER 9

Law Meets Society

Reading 203
Aim. 203
Principles 204
Influencing law. 204
Foundational sociological theories and law 206
Sociological jurisprudence: Pound 212
The American legal realists. 216
Critical responses 222
Questions to think about 225
Further reading. 225

READING

DAVIES, *Asking the Law Question: the Dissolution of Legal Theory*, 2nd edition, Chapter 4 (pp 142–151), Chapter 1 (pp 26–31)
FREEMAN, *Lloyd's Introduction to Jurisprudence*, 7th edition, Chapter 8 (pp 659–691, 703–766), Chapter 9

AIM

This chapter will introduce you to:
- sociology and its methods;
- how sociology and its methods have influenced law and legal theory;
- the foundational sociologists of law;
- some of the key ideas of Roscoe Pound's 'sociological jurisprudence';
- the American Legal Realists.

Influencing law

What does sociology have to do with law?

Understanding how a society works, the relationship between individuals in that society, and the institutions of that society, is the task undertaken by sociology and associated areas of study. It is perhaps not surprising that law, because of its effects on individuals and communities, its professional practices, its processes and methods, and its status as one of the core institutions of society, is a fertile area of interest for sociology.

THE ESTABLISHMENT

When we introduced you to the Establishment in the previous chapter, you might have wondered how you could find out what it is, what its influence is, and whether it actually exerted an influence over the rest of society. And is the legal profession part of the Establishment? Some sociologists try to answer these questions by undertaking rigorous, empirical, systematic research. Others will critically analyse the reasons why the Establishment came to exert influence over society, by using critical forms of social theory.[1]

As well as looking at big questions about institutions like law, smaller studies will look at matters like the effectiveness of sentencing practices, and the role of the legal profession. Legal sociologists will use these methods to investigate the 'reality' behind the assumptions made by law.

UNCOVERING AN ASSUMPTION THROUGH SOCIOLOGICAL RESEARCH

Up until the latter part of the 20th century, lawyers assumed that the comment made by Hale LJ in the 17th century that rape 'is an accusation easily to be made and hard to be proved, and harder to be defended by the party accused',[2] was correct. The assumption that women lie about being raped was embedded in the common law.

But was this assumption correct? Sociologists and some lawyers wanted to find out, and from research that began in the 1970s, it was found that women were actually reluctant to complain about rape, and that police prosecutions were low.[3] This sociological research provided information which showed that this axiom was not based in fact, but was an assumption only.

Sociology and its methods can therefore have broad and far-reaching consequences for law and its practices, and is a useful, practical tool to help develop policy; it may also lead to legislative reform.

---

1 See Chapter 12 below.
2 cited in G Geis, "Revisiting Lord Hale, Misogyny, Witchcraft and Rape" (1986) 10 *Criminal Law Journal* 319.
3 Edwards, Susan, *Sex and Gender in the Legal Process* (Blackstone, London, 1996) refers to a number of different studies, pp 330–335.

FIGURE 9.1: LAW MEETS SOCIETY TIMELINE

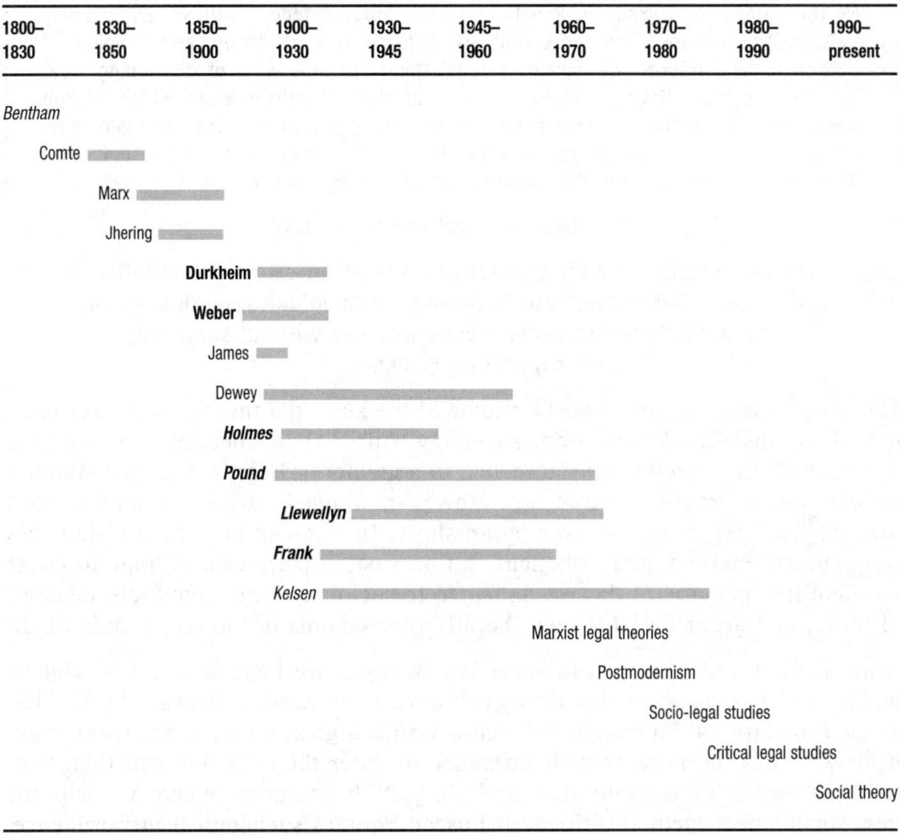

1800–1830	1830–1850	1850–1900	1900–1930	1930–1945	1945–1960	1960–1970	1970–1980	1980–1990	1990–present

Bentham

Comte ▨

Marx ▨

Jhering ▨

Durkheim ▨

Weber ▨

James ▨

Dewey ▨

Holmes ▨

Pound ▨

Llewellyn ▨

Frank ▨

Kelsen ▨

Marxist legal theories

Postmodernism

Socio-legal studies

Critical legal studies

Social theory

Sociology and legal theory

As well as this very *practical* influence on law, sociology, its methods, and its underlying philosophical foundations have informed a number of different legal theories. The way that different legal theories have used sociological insights varies widely, with a range of positions in between:

1. Legal theories which use information obtained from sociological studies *to inform a theoretical position.*

2. Legal theories which explicitly adopt and use sociological methods to create a specific *sociological legal theory*

INFORMING A THEORETICAL POSITION

Sociological studies have resulted from, or been used to inform, the research of *non-conventional legal theories*, such as feminist legal theories (Chapter 11), some critical legal theory (Chapter 12) and many of the American Legal Realists, whose work we will look at later in this chapter. But none of these theories can or should be called sociological legal theories — they just use sociology to inform their own theoretical suppositions, which often seek to expose how law fails to meet up to its rhetoric, its claims and assumptions.

SOCIOLOGICAL LEGAL THEORY

We think *sociological legal theories* fall into two broad categories: those relying solely on *sociological theory*, and those that use *both* sociological theory and sociological method to help inform and develop a legal theory or new ways of developing legal doctrine. The first category includes Pound's sociological jurisprudence, which we will look at in this chapter. The second includes *aspects* of the work of the American Legal Realist, Karl Llewellyn; and Roger Cotterrell, who uses sociology to provide insights into doctrine, but based in an explicit understanding that law has a social function.[4]

Why have you left out HLA Hart?

Didn't he claim that THE CONCEPT OF LAW was an essay in descriptive sociology?[5] Hart did not use 'sociology' or sociological method at all, and actually makes claims about societies without supplying supporting evidence.

This chapter will therefore consider some of the key legal theories that developed out of the insights derived from sociology. All of these theories challenge the approaches of conventional legal theory, to a greater or lesser extent, by adopting an *external* approach towards law. However, it needs to be emphasised that they do not 'sing from the same hymn sheet'. On the contrary, their differences in approach, method, and argument can be vast, and we cannot hope to cover all the different types of theories indebted to sociology, or the conflicts, debates, disputes, and arguments between the different schools of thought in this field.[6]

Instead, by introducing you to some key theories, we hope you will be able to make your own way unaided through this vast topic. We will begin by looking at the foundational European 19th century sociological theories that specifically dealt with law, because of their influence on later theorists. We will then look to the America of the late 19th and early 20th centuries, where we will see how sociological method influenced Roscoe Pound's sociological jurisprudence. Staying in America, we will then step back into the 19th century to explore the influence of the 'do it' philosophies of pragmatism. This philosophical turn influenced the American Legal Realists, whose work spanned from the 1930s through to the middle of the 20th century.

Foundational sociological theories and law

A thumbnail sketch of sociology and its developments

Sociology, as an area of study in its own right, began in the 19th century. Key among its founders were Auguste Comte, Herbert Spencer, *Emile Durkheim*, *Max Weber*, Georg Simmel, Ferdinand Tönnies and *Karl Marx*. Sociology, in its early form, relied upon a range of disciplines to inform it, including history, philosophy and economics, and, of course, law. Others specifically considered

---

4   Lloyd, pp 684–686, 744–758.
5   See Lloyd, p 336.
6   Extracts in Lloyd: Selznick, pp 727–732; Hunt, pp 737–739; Cotterrell, pp 744–758; Nelken, pp 759–766.

law in sociological terms, including von Jhering[7] and Ehrlich.[8] The methods of the founders of sociology were broadly based, and as we saw with Marx, guided by a strong vision of what constituted society: Figure 9.2.

By the middle of the 20th century, sociology took a decidedly 'scientific' turn, through the work of the American sociologist Talcott Parsons.[9] Parsons assumed that sociology could be used to remove conflict from society. For instance, his sociology separated law and politics into different spheres of study. But his use of empirical research, including statistical data analysis, became the norm, even amongst sociologists who questioned Parson's underlying assumptions. Of course, these methods are central to sociology, but Parson's comfortable view of societies was called into question by the conflicts that emerged in the 1960s and 1970s, including the counter-culture we talked about in the previous chapter. Interest was again sparked in the founding theorists, especially Marx, Weber and Durkheim, with a new attention paid to the critical versions of these theories, like Gramsci's hegemony, and the Frankfurt School. Now, some strands of sociology have again changed into a broader 'social theory' and critical theory that we will look at in Chapter 12.

The founding fathers of the sociology of law

As well as having had a major influence on sociology itself, Marx, Durkheim and Weber[10] specifically engaged with the question of the role of law in society, and its effects on the individuals in that society. We have already seen what Marx had to say about the law; we will now look at Durkheim and Weber's approaches. We will see that while these early theorists used data and information to support their position, they were more interested in providing *explanations* for their understanding of societies and their functions. Durkheim and Weber's theories operate as a platform or wallpaper for both *theories which are informed by sociology* and *sociological legal theories*.

FIGURE 9.2: COMPARING THE FOUNDERS –
SOCIAL FORMS AND LAW

	Marx	Durkheim	Weber
View of society	Social conflict	Social cohesion	Individualism and capitalism
Role of law	Superstructure maintaining base	External index symbolising social solidarity	Law assists capitalism, especially rational legal systems

The French sociologist **Emile Durkheim** (1858–1917) was, among other things, concerned with explaining the changing nature of societies, and the place of individuals in society.[11] Durkheim worked from the principle that societies were

---

7   Lloyd, p 662.
8   Lloyd, pp 670–667.
9   Lloyd, pp 681–682.
10 Lloyd, p 660.
11 Lloyd, pp 666–670, 714–717.

stable and cohesive entities, which were dependent on the social solidarity or cohesion that formed the glue to keep the society functioning. Like Marx, Durkheim proposed an evolutionary approach towards social development: a more cohesive primitive society had a *mechanical solidarity* between its members. As societies modernise, a new type of social cohesion is needed to bring together the more fragmented, individualistic needs of the society. Durkheim called this *organic solidarity*.

FIGURE 9.3: DURKHEIM'S SOCIAL COHESION AND LAW

Mechanical	Repressive law	Organic	Restitutive law
Primitive • Prehistoric and pre-agricultural	*Change in law reproduces essential aspects of social solidarity* • Criminal behaviour repressed brutally • Law's role is repressive – Injury – Deprivation of possessions or liberty	*Modern* • Organic because of reliance on the other organs or individuals of that society	*Change in law reproduces essential aspects of social solidarity* • Civil law, commercial law, constitutional law, administrative law • Law's role is to restore the balance between interdependent interests • Criminal law would be restitutive rather than repressive
Integrated • similarities among individuals • all members performed the same tasks – no division of labour • few specialised institutions • common rituals, assumptions, morality • religion		*Disintegrated* • individualistic • secular • division of labour between different tasks • different values and beliefs • stable institutions needed to balance out the wants of individuals • social controls needed to limits wants • contractual solidarity	
Stable society • society unchanged by change in its members • collective consciousness from society		*Consensus* • individuals had to rely on each other • collective consciousness now abstract	
Collective		*Interdependent individuals*	

The role of law was central to the development of society, and it operated as the 'external index' symbolising the moral needs of that society. Law, therefore, reflected or tracked the essential characteristics of the society in question. Why external? Law, for Durkheim, was made up of sanctions, rules and institutions. Law was a 'social fact'. We can see from Figure 9.3 how law related to the forms of society in which it existed. The nature of law differed according to the needs of that society. Durkheim's ideas about law have been subjected to considerable criticism because of his failure to properly examine law and its processes. Lloyd sets out a number of these criticisms, some of which adopt the position of *sociological legal theory*, or sociological jurisprudence, that we described above. The criticisms are based in the lack of evidence in Durkheim's schema of law. However, interest in his sociology about law persists because of its identification of the interconnectedness between law and social forms.

The German lawyer and sociologist **Max Weber** (1864–1920)[12] is often described as a 'bourgeois Marx' because of his attempts to free social thought from the influence of economic imperatives, and to place the individual at the centre of society. He took the view that social function was to be determined by the needs of individuals. He was also the first sociologist to construct a specific *sociology of law*, and to not treat it as peripheral to sociological method. His work also emphasised the role that institutions, such as the legal profession and bureaucracies, play in modern societies.

Having said this, Weber's sociology provides insights into the role of law as a facilitator of capitalism. What did Weber mean by law? He adopted a definition that is very familiar to us because it sounds like Bentham and Austin's definitions, which we saw in Chapter 6. Law:

- is externally guaranteed by the probability that it will be supported by physical or psychological coercion

- will bring about conformity or avenge violation

- will be applied by a staff of people holding themselves specially ready for that purpose.

Having established this definition of law, Weber then sought to work out the best way for law to facilitate capitalism. He assumed (and concluded) that *rational* legal systems, processes and practices could ensure the development of capitalism. On the other hand, *irrational* legal systems, processes and practices, would not allow this development.

HOW ARE FORMALLY IRRATIONAL DECISIONS MADE?

In one scene of *Monty Python and the Holy Grail*, the community has to decide whether a woman is a witch. The test they use is to throw her into the pond: but it first has to be determined if she weighs the same as a duck. If she does, she is made of wood and is a witch.

This scene is based on a test used in the middle ages to decide if someone was guilty or innocent of criminal behaviour. If you sank, you were innocent; if you floated, you were guilty.

Weber undertook historical and comparative studies to describe and explain the different types, or *typologies*, of law, legal thought, and legal systems, in order to show why rational legal systems were best for capitalism. The ideal types he described were based around the different methods used by legal systems to achieve justice: see Figure 9.4 (overleaf).

12 Lloyd, pp 662–666, 705–713.

FIGURE 9.4: WEBER'S TYPOLOGY OF LAW — INTERNAL MODES OF THINKING

HOW LEGAL RULES DEVELOP	SUBSTANTIVE	FORMAL
	External criteria • politics, ethics, religion • individual cases • emotion or faith	*Internal criteria* • rules and procedures for all decision-making exist in the system
Rules and procedures used to decide cases	*Irrational*	*Rational*
	Rational	*Irrational*

Legal systems develop and unfold so that the legal form most suited to capitalism would result through the adoption of formal rationality: see Figure 9.5.

FIGURE 9.5: THE CHARACTERISTICS AND ELEMENTS OF WEBER'S TYPOLOGIES OF LAW

		Characteristics	Who	Legal systems
4th stage	FORMALLY *rational* law	• Systematised elaboration of law • Abstract principles • Integration of all legal propositions	Professionalised administration of justice	European codes *Best for capitalism*
3rd stage	SUBSTANTIVELY *rational* law	• Imposed justice through religion or justice • Non-legal principles used • Lacks consistency	Secular or theocratic powers	Theocracy or justice-based system
2nd stage	SUBSTANTIVELY *irrational* law	• Case by case, ad hoc • Merits without reference to general principles	Legal *honoratiores* Expert knowledge Social prestige	English common law *How could capitalism develop in this type of system?*
1st stage	FORMALLY *irrational* law	• Emotional, charismatic • Trial by ordeal, oracle • Tests beyond human control	Law prophets	Primitive

But an additional factor was needed to make sure that rational systems were put in place to facilitate the formally rational system. He claimed that *bureaucracies* would produce the most rational means to administer the law, for the needs of society. Administration could only work if rational law was in place. To support the rational system, a formally trained legal profession was needed, with legal eduction based in legal theory and science. However, he argued that 'natural law' was necessary to legitimate legal change, and to support the rationalisation of positive law.

THE ENGLAND PROBLEM

How could the most advanced Western capitalist system fall into the second bottom stage of legal development? Because the common law used precedent, legal fictions, and methods of analogy, rather than structured, systematic, rational principles, it was a *substantively irrational legal system*. It adopted and maintained archaic procedures. It was 'craft' and apprentice based, beholden to the bar, and judges were not trained in formally scientific legal methods.

Weber therefore was able to argue that law is not bound to economic forms, contrary to Marx. This conclusion supported his wider view that social thought was not beholden to economics.

Weber sought to also explain the way legal power is exercised and accepted in society, through his theory of *legitimate domination*. Weber follows his typologies to demonstrate how the rational form of domination coincides with the rational legal order needed to support the development of capital: see Figure 9.6.

FIGURE 9.6: WEBER'S THEORY OF LEGITIMATE DOMINATION

Legitimate Domination	Traditional	Charismatic	Legal rational
Characteristic	Age old rules and powers	Devotion to a person	Legality of enacted rules Right of those in authority to issue commands
Method	Substantive, personal	Revelation, empirical	Impartial, impersonal Without hatred or passion
Who	Hereditary	Judging in a common law system	Bureaucracy professional
Related Typology	**Formally irrational** (1st stage)	**Formally irrational** (1st stage)	**Formally rational** (4th stage)
	Substantively rational (3rd stage)	**Substantively irrational** (2nd stage)	

We have traced a core aspect of Weber's sociology of law here, but you should be aware that he undertook a broader set of studies of the relationship between particular forms of law, like contract law, in which he acknowledged the economic structures which supported certain groups in the community. These studies provided a basis for later legal theorists or legal sociologists to make their own studies into these aspects of law. But Weber's observations about legal systems and the structures that support those systems appear to support a particular model of law based around capitalism. Like other theories of this type, you will find a range of criticisms of his method, his assumptions, his ideal types, and his views of economics, history and law.

Sociological jurisprudence: Pound

Taking it to the law: sociological legal theory

Roscoe Pound (1870–1964),[13] Dean of Harvard Law School from 1916 to 1936, relied on the insights derived from sociology to create a *legal theory* that sought to bring the 'law in books' into direct contact with the 'law in action'. He wanted to draw law out of isolation from the society around it. His *sociological jurisprudence* challenged the legal positivism and common law methods prevalent in the early 20th century – closed, unresponsive to social change, and unable to adapt to the needs of a booming American economy. From the standpoint of the early 20th century, Pound's sociological jurisprudence was revolutionary, but from the standpoint of the early 21st century, it did not shift far beyond the methods and approaches of the internal legal theory of which he was so critical at the time. Later in his life, Pound returned to the common law methods, and sought to retreat from the dynamic approaches he championed earlier in his theoretical life.

WHY CAN POUND'S LEGAL THEORY BE CALLED A SOCIOLOGICAL LEGAL THEORY?

Pound developed his theory in an attempt to make law as effective as possible as a facilitator of the social needs it regulated. By recognising this relationship, Pound adopted the language and ideas of sociology to inform his legal theory. But his theory, which *he* called 'sociological jurisprudence', is sociological because it recognises law's social function, rather than being based solely on the adoption of the techniques and methods of sociological research in its later 20th century form.

What is sociological jurisprudence?

Sociological jurisprudence can be portrayed by what it challenges: as a technique to keep law from being stifled by a formalistic, mechanistic, analytic legal method that fails to accommodate the change needed to keep law relevant for society. But what does it propose? It seeks to provide an effective, programmed and systematic way to keep the law moving in step with the needs of society, through the inter-connected actions of legal academics, the courts, and the profession itself,[14] which Pound called *social engineering*.

Pound's sociological jurisprudence is therefore LAW–centred,
but the techniques he used to develop his theory were based in
TECHNOLOGY and SCIENCE.

13 Lloyd, pp 672–679.
14 Lloyd, pp 721–723.

Pound's method: the theory of interests

Pound argued that law's role was to facilitate social cohesion, through the use of techniques to enable all the claims that could be made on law to go around as far as possible, with the 'minimum of friction and waste'. He adopted a multi-faceted and multi-staged technique called the *theory of interests* to achieve the goal of social engineering by the legal system.[15] You need to be patient with his method, so let's map out the stages which need to be followed, starting with Figure 9.7.[16]

FIGURE 9.7: MAPPING OUT POUND'S THEORY OF INTERESTS

Stage One	Stage Two	Stage Three	Stage Four
Finding out what an interest is	List and classify interests	If there is a conflict: weigh and balance interests	New interests: apply jural postulates

The first thing that needs to be done is to find out what is meant by an interest. Let's look at Figure 9.8.

FIGURE 9.8: STAGE ONE: FINDING OUT WHAT AN INTEREST IS

What did Pound mean by interests?	How did he identify these interests?	Is an interest the same as a legal right?
Interests are: • claims • demands • expectations which people (individually or collectively) want the law to recognise	He looked to the law only, by: • identifying the claims brought to court • lobbying the legislature	• Interests are only *potentially recognisable* by law • An interest will only become a right once adjudicated or legislation is brought into effect

Criticisms can be made of Pound's program of identifying interests

• Interests are assumed by Pound to form the data warehouse of society's needs and wants, but only once they are brought to law's attention • Interests do not come from society as a whole	• This is a very narrow sphere from which interests can be drawn • It disregards the ability of sociological or other research tools to provide data • It disregards 'interests' which have no 'voice' and which have never attempted to access the legal arena	• Interests are a small pool and cannot adequately inform the legal rights of society or the community • The legal rights that will be derived do not deviate far from the common law method which he criticised

We can see that the process by which interests are identified is *law-centred* and not society-centred.

---

15 See extract in Lloyd, pp 726–727.
16 Lloyd, pp 724–727.

Pound sifted through the range of interests that he found contained in the law, or in claims for changes to the law. You will find what Pound has to say about the interests in the extract in Lloyd (pp 724–726). You may want to undertake a matching exercise to see which interests can be equated to known areas of law. Pound classified interests into three types, detailed in Figure 9.9:

- Individual interests (which equate to private law)
- Public interests (which equate to public law)
- Social interests (the most generalised form of all the other interests)

FIGURE 9.9: STAGE TWO: LISTING AND CLASSIFYING INTERESTS

Individual interests	Public interests	Social interests in …
Personality	The interests of the State in its own security, honour, and integrity and ability to hold property	*General security*
• The physical person		• Safety
• Freedom of will		• Health
• Honour and reputation		• Peace and order
• Privacy		• Security of acquisitions
• Belief and opinion		• Security of transactions
Domestic relations		*Security of social institutions*
• Interests of individuals and community, both personally and in the institutions of family and marriage		• Domestic
		• Religious
		• Political
		• Economic
Interests of substance		
• Property		*General morals*
• Freedom of industry and contract		*Conservation of social resources*
• Promised advantages		• Natural resources
• Advantageous relations with others		• Children and defectives
• Freedom of association		*General progress*
• Continuity of employment		• Economic
		– Freedom of use and sale of property
		– Free trade and industry
		– Inventions
		• Political
		– Free speech and association
		• Cultural
		– Free science, letters, arts
		– Promotion of education and learning
		– Aesthetics
		Individual Life
		– Self-assertion
		– Opportunity
		– Conditions of life

In a society, Pound recognises that the claims made by people will conflict. Pound says that it is necessary to balance out the conflict by *weighing and balancing* their claims on what he calls *the same plane*, or within the same classification of interests. What he means by this is that it is wrong to balance individual interests against social interests, or public interests against individual interests: see Figure 9.10.[17]

FIGURE 9.10: STAGE THREE: WEIGHING AND BALANCING INTERESTS TO OVERCOME CONFLICT

Individual interests	have to be balanced against	Individual interests
Public interests	have to be balanced against	Public interests
Social interests	have to be balanced against	Social interests

The final step Pound put in place was to test if a new interest should be recognised by law. This test is the measure of values called a *jural postulate*.[18] These are set out in Figure 9.11 overleaf. Jural postulates are found within the law itself, and will be used to test these new claims. A jural postulate will be used as a method of reasoning. Pound said jural postulates are generalised principles of the law at a given place and time: they are not closed, and will continue to develop and change as the new claims are brought into law. So, Pound changed his own original list of postulates over time, and proposed additions to the list.[19]

Pound's legacy

Pound has been subjected to a series of critical observations of his method, his process and his assumptions.[20] At the heart of the complaints made about his sociological jurisprudence is his insistence that social values are expressed within the law itself. Despite his desire to break down the narrow, mechanistic, and infertile approach of positivism, his own method was hampered by its internalised method of social engineering. This is why, in the previous chapter, we suggest that Pound barely shifted outside the internal method of legal theory.[21]

> The balancing method found in sociological jurisprudence is still used by some policy makers in an attempt to reconcile claims between competing interest groups in areas of law, like environmental and cultural law.

---

17 See Lloyd, p 675.
18 Pound adopted the conception of jural postulates from the German jurist Josef Kohler (1849–1919).
19 A list of the jural postulates, and Pound's explanation of their creation, is set out in Lloyd, 6th edition, pp 578–579. The 7th edition does not include this material.
20 A number of criticisms are set out in the commentary in Lloyd, pp 672–679. See R Wacks, *SWOT: Jurisprudence*, 5th edition (Blackstone Press, London, 1999), pp 162–163 for others.
21 See Chapter 8 above, p 188.

FIGURE 9.11: STAGE FOUR: TESTING NEW INTERESTS – USING JURAL POSTULATES

Jural postulates are values applicable to that society at the time	They are discovered within law and form broad general abstract principles	They are subjected to continual revision

Jural postulates assume certain forms of behaviour in a civilised society:

No intentional aggression will be committed
People will be able to control for beneficial purposes what they have discovered and appropriated to their own use, by their own labour, and acquired under the existing economic and social order
There will be good faith in dealings such as contracts
Due care is taken not to unreasonably injure others
Should a new postulate be recognised? • Job security • Collective bargaining • Workers compensation

The American Legal Realists

Just do it!

At the same time that Roscoe Pound was developing his sociological juris-prudence, other American legal theorists (or were they stirrers, as they considered themselves a movement, or 'fermenters' not part of any movement?)[22] were also reacting to the strictures of legal formalism and positivism: the American Legal Realists.[23] Though in general terms they were not *sociological legal theorists*, the 'realists' were mindful to a greater or lesser extent of the social effects and consequences of law and the legal process. As you will have realised, the realists were not a unified or uniform group, but individual legal thinkers whose ideas, for the most part, were shaped out of the American philosophy known as *pragmatism*.

---

22 See Llewellyn in Lloyd, pp 830–831.
23 Another form of realism exists: the Scandinavian realists who are discussed in Chapter 10 of Lloyd. We won't be considering the Scandinavian realists in this book.

DOES IT WORK?

A very basic way to explain *pragmatism* is to say that it requires ideas to 'pay up' with results or observable practical outcomes. Pragmatism says that ideas have to be proved *empirically*,[24] and it requires the adoption of an outward-looking approach.[25] The truth of a philosophical claim can only be supported using these sorts of approaches.

Pragmatism was impatient with legal methods divorced from the experience of those who *just do it!* It disliked abstract mechanically applied formalism which uses the technique of logic known as a 'syllogism', on which formalist legal reasoning is based:

The syllogism, which Aristotle created, adopts this logical pattern:
'all dogs are green, Rex is a dog, and therefore Rex is green'.

The logic is perfect, but the outcome fails to accord with 'experience' (and is in any case a very odd conclusion).[26]

The philosopher, John Dewey, argued that real logic occurred out of testing against experience. So, legal principles would be logically valid when tested against experience. This meant law was a 'work in progress', not a set of unchanging, preformed rules.[27]

Pragmatism influenced the American Legal Realists.

And so did Justice Oliver Wendell Holmes (whose work also influenced Dewey).[28]

Justice Oliver Wendell **Holmes** (1841–1935) famously contended that 'the actual life of the law has not been logic: it has been experience'.[29] Influenced by philosophical pragmatism, he claimed that law needed to be seen in the here and now, and not based in the experience of a past world. As well, people's understanding of their legal obligations would also need to be tested against experience. Holmes' creation, 'the bad man' (not, note, the abstract or imaginary *reasonable* man), will test his behaviour or obligations, not against logic, morals, or old rules, but against what the courts *will actually do*.[30]

What was American Legal Realism?

Realism began to emerge in America in 1920s and 1930s, a period characterised by the optimism of the brave new world of the American Dream, which was then dashed by the economic and social consequences of the Great Depression.[31]

---

24 See Chapter 4 above.
25 William James (1842–1910) was a key pragmatist: an extract setting out what he means by pragmatism is available in Davies, pp 143–144.
26 An invalid syllogism, using the same technique, was used in *Monty Python and the Holy Grail* by the community to decide that a woman was a witch: see the box 'How are formally irrational decisions made?' above, p 209.
27 John Dewey (1859–1952): see Davies, pp 144–145.
28 Lloyd, pp 802–803.
29 See Davies, pp 143–145 and Lloyd, pp 800–802, 821 for a more detailed discussion of Holmes.
30 See Twining, 'The Bad Man Revisited' in Lloyd, pp 821–827, for an evaluation of the uses of the bad man concept as a legal theory.
31 Cotterrell examines 'The Political Context of American Legal Realism' in Chapter 7 of *The politics of jurisprudence: a critical introduction to legal philosophy* (Butterworths, London, 1989), pp 202–206.

HOW DO THE REALISTS USE SOCIOLOGY AND ITS METHODS?

For the most part, the American Legal Realists used sociology to *inform their own theoretical suppositions*; to find data to prove or disprove the claims of law. Some of the realists, like Llewellyn, partly relied on the second category of *sociological legal theory*. Some realists, perhaps 'unquestioningly', used empirical research, based in sociological methods, without looking to see what lay under the 'facts' they used. They used the research to support the reality they described, against which law had to 'pay up'.

In a broad sense, realism wanted law to respond to the needs of society, from seeking to use empirical research to test doctrine, to overtly acknowledging the role of legal personnel and legal practice in the development of law, and the social effects of judicial decision-making.[32] Closest to the approach of *sociological legal theory*, Llewellyn proposed that the law needs to take into account the insights and information provided by *sociology*,[33] but he also used anthropological insights to inform his theories. But realism was also a movement indebted to pragmatism. Felix **Cohen** (1907–1953), for instance, argued that if a doctrine or rule did not 'pay up' in fact (or experience), the doctrine was 'bankrupt', meaning it failed to accord to a legal truth (he was closely following Dewey).[34] We can see Oliver Wendell Holmes' influence in this form of American Legal Realism.

Realism had a profoundly practical impact on American law. Llewellyn, a commercial lawyer as well as a key realist, brought the influence of realism into the development of the Uniform Commercial Code, and influenced American restatements of law. Cohen wrote *The Handbook of Federal Indian Law*, which reflected his realist methods and his commitment to 'New Deal policies' (the New Deal was President Roosevelt's policies designed to overcome the effects of the Great Depression in the 1930s, based in collectivism, social security, and public works, and a number of realists supported this policy). Law teaching and textbooks reflected the approaches of the realists, so much so that its methods became part and parcel of the American legal landscape, as a number of leading realists were also law academics, including Llewellyn and Cohen.[35]

American Legal Realism fizzled out by the 1960s. Two narrow offshoots of realism continued to have influence: the 'science' of jurimetrics, and judicial behaviourism, which focused on judicial attitudes.[36] The more radical and revolutionary aspects of realism were revived in the 1970s and developed into a more critical form by another American movement − the Critical Legal Studies movement, which we will return to in Chapter 12.

---

32 See the extract from Llewellyn 'Some Realism about Realism − Responding to Dean Pound' in Davies, pp 146–147.
33 Llewellyn, op cit, p 840.
34 See Davies, pp 149–151.
35 See Lloyd, pp 811–813.
36 See Lloyd, pp 813–817.

The influence of realism on American law can be contrasted to the rest of the common law world between the 1920s and late 1950s, where the narrow internalised positivism, which HLA Hart reacted to, held sway.

Realism's practices and approaches were sceptically and sometimes incorrectly understood outside America.[37]

What did the realists propose?

As we observed earlier, the realists were not a uniform group, and had diverse interests and different viewpoints. In 1931, Karl **Llewellyn** (1893–1962) produced a 'realist manifesto',[38] which mapped the different activities that realists carried out. Here is a 21st century translation of what he said (we have used Llewellyn's numbering so that when you look at the original you will be able to see what he actually said):[39]

As you go through this list, remind yourself of the influence of pragmatism on the realists.

Remember that not all realists think the same way — don't try to 'reconcile' all the items on this list.

1. Law is the subject of ongoing development, and realists recognise that judges do make law.

2. Law has to be considered in terms of its 'social outcome' and not on its own terms. Law has to be re-examined and re-appraised to see that it does what it says it is doing.

3. Society changes rapidly and social change will outpace law. Law has to be re-evaluated regularly to ensure that it meets it social purpose and effect.

4. *We need to separate 'is' and 'ought', on a temporary basis. The data obtained can then be analysed cleanly, and the law evaluated on an 'ought' basis, using this data, rather than speculating about the situation being considered. This will allow realists who seek to critique the assumptions of a rule or practice to have an objective basis on which to base their political or social criticisms of the rule or practice.[40]

5. Realists don't accept, or are sceptical, that conventional approaches to rules and doctrine describe what actually happens in practice.

6. *Realists are also sceptical of legal theories (such as positivism), which assume that legal decisions are primarily derived from abstract rules.

7. *Realists think that law is better conceived of by connecting law to its social or factual situation. Broad general principles should be replaced by law which understands the field in which it is operating: should the same general approach to sale of goods apply to both potatoes and works of art?

8. *Law has to be evaluated on the basis of the effects it has, and these effects need to be studied and assessed.

9. *Law needs to be subjected to an *ongoing* program of re-evaluation and re-appraisal, using combinations of the ideas and approaches set out in this list.

   * Llewellyn tells us that the items with an asterisk are activities undertaken or accepted by realists only; while the others items are also used by realists, others also hold those views.

---

37 See Twining in Lloyd, pp 848–853.
38 See the extract from Llewellyn, 'Some Realism about Realism' in Lloyd pp 830–834.
39 Llewellyn liked to wax lyrical (he was also a poet).
40 See also Lloyd, p 832, footnote 69, which sets out a dispute amongst realists about this proposition.

A tale of two realists

There were a great many realists – Gray, Cohen, Oliphant, Underhill Moore, Corbin, and Clark, among others. We will look briefly at the ideas of two of the more famous and infamous of the realists: Llewellyn as a *functionalist*, and the *radical skeptic*, Jerome Frank (1889–1957), or as Frank calls them, 'rule skeptics' (Llewellyn) and 'fact skeptics' (Frank).[41]

Llewellyn

None of us may find it odd to suggest that law is an important 'institution' in society. We may find it easy to see the courts, the judiciary, the legislature and the like as law's 'institutions', but would we also include precedents, values, and ideals, and law's practices as being part of the 'institution'? And do we see the institution called 'law' as responding to the needs of the community, and being integral to the maintenance and survival of society?[42]

> Llewellyn did. For him, the INSTITUTION of law was not just the bricks and mortar, but included rules, principles, and values and had an integral role in the survival of the community.

Law has the *function* (this is why Llewellyn is a functionalist) of ensuring that the society it belongs to will survive and it has to carry out its tasks, or *law-jobs* (what follows adapts and paraphrases what Llewellyn said):[43]

LAW-JOBS: KEEPING SOCIETY GOING

1. *Disposing of 'the trouble-case'.* He called this law-job the 'garage-repair' work of society, because it involves a continual process of remaking and reordering society. We can see this process occurring through case law.
2. *Preventive channelling.* This law-job works towards changing conduct and expectations with the aim of avoiding trouble. It includes, but is not limited to, legislative corrections of behaviour and people's activities.
3. *Allocating authority.* This law-job ensures that legal authority and procedures have a real and authoritative basis, through constitutions. The law also needs to contain other ways of determining authority.

Ideal aspects

4. The role of law as providing integration, direction and incentive to the society as a whole.
5. The aspiration of those doing law-jobs to do them better, which he called 'juristic method', ie lawyers and judges need to aspire to excellence.

How do law-jobs happen? Those people responsible for carrying out the law-jobs (those people referred to in point 5), need to be trained in the *craft* of law. The major crafts of law are advocacy, judging, counselling, administering and law-making, while other crafts of law include mediation, organisation, policing, teaching and scholarship. The role of the different crafts is to contribute to the ongoing improvement of the institution of law through the development of *rules*. Llewellyn does not mean rules in their narrow, black-letter sense.

41 See Frank, 'Law and the Modern Mind' in Lloyd pp 827–830.
42 See Lloyd, pp 805–806; Llewellyn, 'My Philosophy of Law' in Lloyd, pp 834–836.
43 Llewellyn, ibid.

Rules are derived from all the skills of the different crafts of law, whether it be judging or policing.[44]

Chief among the law crafts was judging, and Llewellyn proposed that the *outcome of cases could be predicted*, if enough were know about the judge and their judging style. Llewellyn identified two styles – the formal style and the grand style. The *formal style*, as you may have already guessed, adopts the method of abstraction, logic, and narrow legal method disliked by the realists. The *grand style*, as we would now see it, adopts a much broader set of techniques, designed to take into account policy and social research, and to openly acknowledge the role of the decision-maker in the decision itself. Armed with knowledge of the different styles, a litigant would be able to predict the outcome of a case, though the use of the grand style will lead to far greater *certainty* than will the use of the formal style.[45]

Frank

Frank, who was to sit on the US Court of Appeals 2nd Circuit from 1941–1957, was unimpressed by Llewellyn's version of realism.[46] Frank considered that Llewellyn's emphasis on prediction was a 'childish' desire for certainty, and that his emphasis on 'real rules'* and upper courts missed the real problem of law: the uncertainty and unpredictability of *facts* at trial level. In a sense, the rule skeptics disregarded or ignored the factual basis on which the 'real rules'* applied. (* By 'real rules', you will have realised that Frank was talking about something like Llewellyn's *institutions*.)

BUT WHAT MADE FACTS UNPREDICTABLE AT TRIAL LEVEL, ACCORDING TO FRANK?

Witnesses who make mistakes
The unconscious, hidden and unhidden biases and prejudices of judges and juries

Some prejudices and biases are obvious:
Racial
Religious
Political
Economic

Some are hidden, and may lead to a positive or negative response to
a witness and their evidence:
Women
Unmarried women
Red-haired women
Brunettes
Men with deep or high voices
Fidgety men
Men who wear thick eyeglasses
Men with pronounced gestures or nervous tics

So the main obstacle to predicting the outcome of a trial is the inability to work out what the judge or jury will decide the facts are.

---

44 Ibid pp 836–840.
45 See Lloyd, pp 806–810; Llewellyn, 'The Common Law Tradition' in Lloyd pp 840–847.
46 Frank, op cit.

But there is more. The conventional approach towards judging and legal problem-solving is to apply facts to law. But Frank says that facts and law may actually be intertwined or decisions made that do not accord with the reasoning of the judge.[47]

WHAT DOES THIS MEAN?

Have you ever suspected that judges work backwards from the outcome they may want to achieve in a case and make the facts and law work to achieve that result? This is what Frank was suggesting, which, of course, undermines the fundamental basis on which we assume legal reasoning occurs.

You may not be surprised that there was some surprise when Frank was appointed a judge.

All of these factors made it impossible to know with any certainty how a case would proceed (and, in any case, why would anyone litigate if they knew with certainty what the outcome would be?).

Realism's legacy

The social aspects and influences of American Legal Realism have sometimes been hidden from view, in favour of some of its more 'technical' and practice-oriented features: pragmatics, certainty, prediction, and judicial bias. It is not surprising that these aspects of realism would be emphasised when encountered outside America, where positivism was the dominant influence. The legacy of jurimetrics and judicial behaviourism contributed to this narrow view of the realists. Though important to their work, these features of realism have been disconnected from the social role of law, which perhaps does a disservice to (many but not all) realists. Some radically sceptical realists were also overtly political, such as Frank and Cohen, but it may be argued that the rest of the realist enterprise could not help but be political through its recognition of the relationship between law and society. We will see how these traces of the social and political were picked up by the 'crits' — the Critical Legal Studies movement — in Chapter 12.

Critical responses
Developing your critical abilities

The critical responses to this diverse range of theories are vast and diffuse. Rather than list critical responses, as we have done up until now, we will instead pose generic criticisms that can be directed towards any theory or theorist, whether we have looked at them in this book or not. We have positioned this exercise at this stage because it sits roughly 'half-way', and you will have acquired some 'theoretical confidence' to start questioning criticisms made of theories by other theorists or critics. You will be able to use the same tools to

---

47 The 6th edition of Lloyd includes an extract from Frank, 'Courts on Trial', which deals with these issues in more depth, and which contains prescriptions for change and techniques to make lawyers and law students aware of bias: Lloyd, 6th edition, pp 683–686. This material is not included in the 7th edition.

evaluate criticisms levelled at the other theories in this book and you may want to re-evaluate your response to the criticisms you have already seen.

START ASKING QUESTIONS[48]

One of your starting points is to ask why 'the critic' is proposing their criticism of the theory or theorist.

- Is there a fundamental flaw in the position, method or approach of the theorist, which the critic is seeking to uncover?
- Is the criticism designed to make room, or provide a platform, for the critic's own theoretical position?
- Does the critic simply dislike the standpoint of the theorist, or disagree with them from a political, philosophical or theoretical viewpoint?
- Does the critic compare 'apples' with 'pears', or attempt to criticise a theory from a different theoretical approach?

Not all criticism is valid criticism:

- A critic has to have some knowledge and understanding of the source material used by the theorist.
- A critic has to understand or appreciate the arguments and methods of the theory they are criticising.
- Before you can decide whether or not the criticism is valid, *you* need to have acquired a full understanding of theory being criticised.

The same applies to your own writing.

Don't accept that the criticism you read in a book is 'gospel'.

Don't copy other people's criticism unthinkingly.

Don't criticise a theory without demonstrating that you understand it yourself.

Some examples

We have set out some broad criticisms that can apply to a range of theories. We have illustrated them with a few examples from this chapter, and have then asked whether the criticism is valid. You can try this technique with other theories from this chapter, and then try it out on other chapters:

Criticism	Illustration	Is it valid: why?
The theorist has failed to fully consider, misunderstood, or misread the data on which they rely.	Durkheim did not have a full grasp of the societies on which he based his ideas of mechanical law.	Lenman and Parker have studied the operation of the law in Europe at various stages of history to show that it was wrong to suggest repressive sanctions were replaced by restitutive law.[49] This looks like a valid set of questions to be raised about a core aspect of Durkheim's theory.

---

48 Also refer to Chapter 3, above (pp 51–52) for some other ways of thinking about these issues.
49 Lloyd, 7th edition, pp 667–669.

Criticism	Illustration	Is it valid: why?
The theorist has little under-standing of the system they are talking about.	Durkheim is a legal sociologist and he does not appear to understand how law is made or applied.[50]	It seems a bit tough for Durkheim to be classed a 'legal sociologist' — law is tangential to his real interest, so it perhaps not surprising that he does not deal with it fully. Having said that, his disregard of these questions gives scope for others to springboard into their own study of these kinds of issues.
The theory does not match up to its name, but simply uses words rather than concepts.	By ignoring sociology, psychology and other ways of obtaining data, Pound's classification of interests is a rationalisation of the actual, and simply reflects the political aims of a liberal capitalist society.[51]	Pound's method of using only resources accessible within law is extremely narrow and leaves his work open to these types of criticisms. Pound was making claims for a practical program, but was he actually following the conceptual way of thinking that we have seen with the founding fathers of sociology?
The theory is misguided.	Realists like Cohen wanted concepts to 'pay up' in fact, and considered that without being verifiable or provable, concepts and metaphysics were to be disregarded. His approach can be seen to be very close to Dewey's pragmatism.[52]	An over-reliance on the ability of facts to tell the 'truth' fails to accommodate the aspect of reality that is imposed through concepts, and that facts themselves have origins which are themselves capable of being reconceived or re-examined. By adopting Dewey's pragmatism, Cohen has taken on board a theoretical framework and stayed within its parameters. While it is not wrong in itself, a theory needs to be aware of the consequences of sticking closely to another theory. Cohen's own practical work appears to soften his theoretical stridency. The theory forms a useful basis for reappraisal of how law is done. While not misguided, if taken literally it would make it difficult for the law to function.

50 Lloyd, p 670.
51 Lloyd, pp 674–675.
52 See Davies, pp 149–151.

QUESTIONS TO THINK ABOUT

1. How can a sociological approach to law be used to inform the approaches of conventional legal theory, like legal positivism? Should conventional legal theories consider these theories in the development of law, or should law be isolated from society – why?

2. How have foundational sociological ideas (Marx, Weber and Durkheim) influenced our understanding of the role and function of law in our society?

3. How can Weber's sociology of law be used to improve law, legal systems, and legal professional practice?

4. How is Roscoe Pound's sociological jurisprudence influenced by sociology and its methods?

5. Is 'sociological jurisprudence' very different from conventional legal theory? You will need to explain why you adopt the viewpoint you hold, using an understanding of Pound's methods, and the criticisms made of his method.

6. How and from where does Pound derive his 'jural postulates'?

7. Why is the 'bad man' the benchmark for the operation of law and the legal system?

8. How can Llewellyn's notion of law-jobs be used to understand and make law function for the benefit of society?

9. What does Frank mean by fact skepticism?

10. Using examples from your own study of law, what influences has American Legal Realism, in all its forms, had on the way law is studied, practiced, and thought about in Australia?

FURTHER READING

Banakar, Reza & Travers, Max (eds), *An introduction to law and social theory* (Hart, Oxford, 2002).

Cotterrell, Roger (ed), *Law and Society* (Aldershot, Dartmouth, c1994).

Cotterrell, Roger, *The politics of jurisprudence: a critical introduction to legal philosophy* (Butterworths, London, 1989).

Fisher, W, Horwitz, M, & Reed, T (eds), *American legal realism* (Oxford University Press, New York, 1993).

Harris, JW, *Legal Philosophies*, 2nd edition (Butterworths, London, 1997).

Hunt, Alan, *The sociological movement in law* (Macmillan, London, 1978).

McCoubrey, M & White, N, *Textbook on Jurisprudence*, 2nd edition (Blackstone Press, London, 1993).

Morrison, Wayne, *Jurisprudence: from the Greeks to post-modernism* (Cavendish Press, London, 1997).

Ross, Hamish, *Law as a social institution* (Hart, Oxford, 2001).

Wacks, R, *Swot: Jurisprudence*, 5th edition (Blackstone Press, London, 1999).

CHAPTER 10

Reconceptualising the Practical: Postmodernism

Reading 227
Aim. 227
Principles 228
What is postmodernism and
how is it relevant to law? 228
A short exercise in difference 230
Some basic concepts 231
Deconstruction. 241
Deconstruction as a legal method 244
Power/knowledge 246
Why deconstruct?. 248
Critical responses to postmodernism 249
Questions to think about 250
Further reading. 250

READING

DAVIES, *Asking the Law Question: The Dissolution of Legal Theory*, 2nd edition, Chapter 8
FREEMAN, *Lloyd's Introduction to Jurisprudence*, 7th edition, Chapter 15

AIM

This chapter will:

- introduce you to the underlying ideas of postmodernism;
- consider the impact these ideas have when they are applied to law.

What is postmodernism and how is it relevant to law?

Like many non-conventional theories, postmodernism was not originally and is not primarily a theory of law. Rather, it has developed from theories about language, and began life as an approach to art and literary criticism.

FIGURE 10.1: POSTMODERNISM TIMELINE

1945–1960	1960–1970	1970–1980	1980–1990	1990–present
Hart				
Fuller				
		Marxist legal theories		
		Sociological influences		
			CLS and contemporary critical legal theories	
			Finnis	
		Fall of communist states		
	Foucault			
	Madness & Civilisation (1961)			
	The Archaeology of Knowledge (1969)			
		Discipline and Punish (1975)		
			The History of Sexuality (unfinished – 1984)	
	Derrida			
	Of Grammatology (1967 – French)			
		Of Grammatology (1976 – English)		
	Lyotard			
		The Postmodern Condition (1979)		
	Andy Warhol – Pop Art			
			Madonna – postmodern icon	

This timeline shows where postmodernism fits into the history of legal thought, and some related social, economic and historical events.

Let's start with a definition. In doing so, we are conscious of the difficulty (if not the impossibility) of reducing postmodernism to something that can be contained within a formula.[1] Trying to define postmodernism will, at best, only

---

1 Lloyd cites Jennifer Wicke's ironic observation that there are 'more than 31 flavours of postmodernism' to illustrate the variety of approaches which fall within the broad description 'postmodern' — see *Lloyd's Introduction to Jurisprudence*, 7th edition (Sweet & Maxwell, London, 2001), p 1254.

touch on the core ideas which unite all of the varying ways in which post-modernism is thought of and used.

WHAT IS POSTMODERNISM?

Postmodernism is a broad term which encompasses an approach to analysis which rejects (or at least critiques) Enlightenment values and the belief in absolute values which had characterised modern philosophy, including legal theory. Postmodernism is suspicious of authority, received wisdom and values, and does not accept that rationalism represents an unbiased, neutral and independent tool for seeking truth.

Postmodern attitudes are sceptical of so-called metanarratives – universal theories which claim to provide a single, overarching explanation for things – and focus on local and particular explanations which are accepted as being 'true' only in that they represent the best explanation in the particular context. 'Truth', in a postmodern context, is always contingent, and conceals and suppresses other truths.

From its beginnings in art and literature, postmodern thought has expanded across a bewildering variety of subjects – architecture, music, film, anthropology and psychoanalysis, as well as providing a critical commentary on social organisation generally, and eventually migrating into legal theory.

For this reason, we can only hope to scratch the surface of postmodernism and to introduce you to some basic ideas which are relevant to postmodernism as it applies to law.

Some stars of postmodernism

To give you *some* idea of the breadth and variety of postmodern thought, here are some of the fields and major figures associated with postmodernism and postmodern thought: philosophy (Jacques Derrida,[2] Jean Francois Lyotard and Giles Deleuze), history and cultural criticism (Michel Foucault[3] and Roland Barthes[4]), sociology and aesthetics (Jean Baudrillard), anthropology (Claude Levi-Strauss[5]), psychiatry (Jacques Lacan[6]), art (Jeff Koons and Andy Warhol) and cinema (David Lynch and Peter Greenaway).

Modernism and postmodernism

One of the primary characteristics of Modernism is, as we have seen, the belief that there is an overarching 'Truth' which can be discovered about the world.

POSTMODERNISM AND 'TRUTH'

The belief in an underlying unity has led natural law theorists to try and explain law by reference to universal principles which hold true regardless of where or when you are. A similar belief saw positivists try to close off the analysis of law from things which are not law, and to describe an idealised structure of 'the legal system'. In both cases, such theorists are attempting to provide 'one right answer', independent of its context.

---

2   See M Davies, *Asking the Law Question: the Dissolution of Legal Theory*, 2nd edition (Lawbook Co, Sydney, 2002), p 332ff. Derrida and deconstruction are discussed below, p 241ff.
3   See Davies, pp 327–332. Foucault's concept of power/knowledge is discussed below at p 246ff.
4   See Davies, pp 323–324. Barthes' 'death of the author' is discussed below at p 234ff.
5   See Davies, p 314.
6   Davies gives a brief description of Lacan's approach to the subject, p 314.

As we will see later in the chapter, postmodernism is a way of looking at the world which *rejects* the underlying unity which drives modernist approaches to law. For postmodernists, there can be no absolute or universal principles which are true in all circumstances – or at least, if there are, then we cannot fully know them. 'Truth', from a postmodern perspective, is always contingent, and as such, loses its capital 'T' and becomes plural – there is not one 'Truth' but many localised 'truths', which change according to where and when they relate to, and who is claiming them as truth.

So, from a postmodern perspective, natural law theory does *not* provide an accurate reflection of what law is or does. The principles which it claims lie at the heart of law are not accepted as universal within the postmodern view, but simply as expressions of dominant values in a particular time and place.[7] Equally, the positivist view of law considered separately from the society and the social beliefs or the systems which give rise to it and maintain it, cannot be justified from a postmodern perspective. The attempt to analyse law as a discrete subject matter disconnected from, for example, politics, is contrived and flawed, because law exerts a coercive force (or violence) on individuals. As such, it is inherently political.

POSTMODERNISM AS CRITICAL

Postmodernism is, by definition, anti-conventional and destabilising. By rejecting the core assumptions of modernism, postmodernism seeks to expose the assumptions and the implications which are contained in them to scrutiny and criticism.

Postmodernism regards *everything* as fair game. A constant theme of postmodern legal inquiry is 'Who gains from looking at law this way? Who loses?'

A short exercise in difference

But before we head too far into a more detailed look at postmodernism, we want you to take part in a simple exercise, comparing your experience of the world with Marett's and mine. To do this, we would like you to fill in some details about yourself opposite the significant events from our lives which we have set out in the boxes in Figure 10.2 (p 232). We have put what we think are some of the important events and influences in our lives into a timeline. You can see from the events that appear in the box that we have chosen quite different things, even though we were born at roughly the same time.

The purpose of this short exercise is to illustrate what we probably all know instinctively – that each of us is the product of a unique set of influences, operating on a uniquely constituted mind. Is it any wonder, then, that we will often disagree about things? For example, would you find it surprising if someone whose parents remained married will think about family law differently from someone whose parents divorced? Or that someone whose family was involved in business might think about contract law differently from someone who, like me, grew up with a priest for a father?

---

7   See Davies, pp 85–86.

If you have read Borges' fictional Chinese taxonomy of animals,[8] you may have been struck by how strange the way it classifies animals is. It seems to defy (what is for us) the rational groupings of animals with similar characteristics. While the way each of us sees the world may not differ as dramatically or radically as the example in Borges' taxonomy, postmodernism recognises that the structure which governs the way we understand the world — our individual 'schemes of interpretation' — is nevertheless a unique response which can never exactly match any other.

While certain ways of categorising the world around us become accepted as the 'right' or 'natural' way of thinking, Borges' story reminds us that there are always different ways of looking at something, and that our conventional view can never exhaust the possibilities.

Conventional legal theories generally describe a legal system whose characteristics are determined by insiders. Insiders tend to think about law in similar ways. This is not particularly surprising, given that insiders have generally been exposed to law through an education system which promotes uniform approaches to law, and breeds a degree of conformity.[9] Postmodernism seeks to break down that conformity, and provide new insights into how law operates.

Some basic concepts

In the rest of this chapter, we will be looking at some of the basic ideas and concepts which emerge as part of a postmodern view of the world. These will include:

- the concept of 'text' (which in postmodern thought is much broader than what we mean when we use the word in its everyday meaning);
- the relationship between text and its author (which breaks down the conventional view of the author as the ultimate source of a text's meaning);
- the legal subject (highly individualised and related to its context);
- the nature of language and its impact on legal interpretation through the technique of deconstruction; and
- the relationship between power and knowledge.

We will also look at how postmodernism can offer something more than negatives, by utilising the insights of postmodern analysis to suggest positive alternatives to the prevailing or dominant viewpoint.

Like Borges' taxonomy of animals, much of this may appear quite strange when compared with the conventional ways that law has been presented to you.

---

8 Michel Foucalt, extracted in Davies, p 9.
9 See, for example, Duncan Kennedy, 'Legal Education as Training for Hierarchy' in D Kairys (ed), *The Politics of Law* and extracted in Lloyd, p 1104.

FIGURE 10.2: AN EXERCISE IN DIFFERENCE

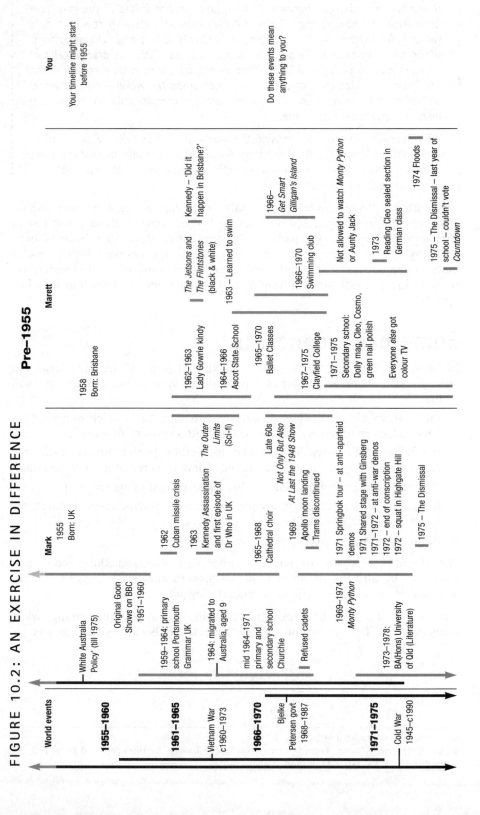

World events

1955–1960

White Australia Policy' (till 1975)

Original Goon Shows on BBC 1951–1960

1961–1965

Vietnam War c1960–1973

1959–1964: primary school Portsmouth Grammar UK

1964: migrated to Australia, aged 9

1966–1970

Bjelke Petersen govt 1968–1987

mid 1964–1971 primary and secondary school Churchie

Refused cadets

1969–1974 Monty Python

1971–1975

Cold War 1945–c1990

1973–1978: BA(Hons) University of Qld (Literature)

Mark

1955 Born: UK

1962 Cuban missile crisis

1963 Kennedy Assassination and first episode of Dr Who in UK

The Outer Limits (Sci-fi)

1965–1968 Cathedral choir

Late 60s Not Only But Also At Last the 1948 Show

1969 Apollo moon landing Trams discontinued

1971 Springbok tour – at anti-aparteid demos

1971 Shared stage with Ginsberg

1971–1972 – at anti-war demos

1972 – end of conscription

1972 – squat in Highgate Hill

1975 – The Dismissal

Pre–1955

Marett

1958 Born: Brisbane

1962–1963 Lady Gowrie kindy

The Jetsons and The Flintstones (black & white)

1963 – Learned to swim

1964–1966 Ascot State School

1965–1970 Ballet Classes

1966– Get Smart Gilligan's Island

1966–1970 Swimming club

1967–1975 Clayfield College

Not allowed to watch Monty Python or Aunty Jack

1971–1975 Secondary school: Dolly mag, Cleo, Cosmo, green nail polish

1973 Reading Cleo sealed section in German class

Everyone else got colour TV

1974 Floods

1975 – The Dismissal – last year of school – couldn't vote Countdown

You

Your timeline might start before 1955

Kennedy – 'Did it happen in Brisbane?'

Do these events mean anything to you?

You

What would you
put here?

Marett

The Saints
The Go-Betweens
Ray Hughes Gallery

1976–1978
BA (UQ)
Refec honours

1979 Grad Dip T (KGCAE)
First ever year of drama teachers
Performance at KGCAE
(but didn't know Mark)

1981–1982
performance with New
Theatre, Sydney

1981–1986
Cth govt

Mid 80s
MA
Theatre
Studies

Bicentennial

1987–1992
Australian
Broadcasting Tribunal

1990–92
LLB (Hons)
QUT

Mid-93
Left ABT
(now ABA)

1995
Casual academic
GU/QUT

Full-time
Academic
QUT

Moved to Sydney
– arrived the day
John Lennon shot

Bands – lots of
bands – parties

Returned to QLD

Sept 1993
Admitted as barrister

1993–94
LLM – London

1993–1994
Living in London

1995 – Litigation
Reform Commission

'There's a lot of other things happening you
don't need to know about …'

Rugby World Cup
– supporting the Wallabies

Mark

1977 – Right to march demos

1979
Bellevue demolition

1976 Honours year
1977–1978
Postgrad study
+ journalism major

1978–1980
Work
Photography
in theatre including KGCAE

1981 – bought first house for $9,000
First space shuttle
The 'underarm incident'

Commercial release of CD players
1983–84
Bought first CD player – 1984

1980–1996
Work CPS Economic
analysis of labour markets –
econometric modelling

1986
Challenger disaster

1989
Fitzgerald Report

1992 – Footpath dining
Mabo – allowed in Brisbane

P/T student

1992–1998
Law degree

F/T student

(*Marett lectured Mark*)

Caxton Legal Centre volunteer

Casual academic and
postgrad student

Full-time academic

2000
Admitted as barrister

Caxton management

Rugby World Cup
– supporting Wales, England,
France, Ireland, Scotland …

World events

1976–1980
Cold War
1945–c1990

Bjelke Petersen
govt
1968–1987

1981–1985
1981– AIDS

1986–1990
1991 Desert
Storm

1991–1995

1996 on
2001
Sept 11

2003
Gulf War (II)

Text

As we have said, postmodernism has very close connections with language and literary criticism. For that reason, it often focuses closely on the idea of text. 'Text' from a postmodern perspective, however, means something different from how we ordinarily think about texts.

A FEW WORDS ABOUT TEXTS

When lawyers think about 'text', they usually think of words collected together into the 'text' of either a statute or a judgment — words on a page. 'Text' as it is used by postmodern writers has a far broader connotation, referring not just to the written word, but to any form of representation. It includes, for example, paintings and sculpture, architecture and the outpourings of mass media both as words and as visual images.

Indeed, it has been suggested that for a postmodernist, the *whole world* is 'text' — that is, everything in the world is to be taken as a representation, susceptible to interpretation (and, as we will see later, deconstruction).

To use Davies' example, a judge's robes are not text in the ordinary meaning of the word, but within postmodern writing, they do constitute text. They represent the relationships which exist between people who wear them, people who wear other, but different robes, and people who wear ordinary street clothing in court.[10]

WHAT HAPPENS TO TEXT?

Texts, in their conventional legal forms of statutes and judgments, are approached by lawyers as something from which a 'correct' meaning can be extracted. In the case of a statute, the words of a legislative provision are analysed to try and uncover, for example, what it was that Parliament meant when it enacted the words. When we read Lord Atkin's judgment in *Donoghue v Stevenson*, we are trying to discover what his Lordship meant when he chose the words he used to define duty of care, and what this means for the law of negligence.

Reading legal texts in this way seeks to discover a single, clear idea or set of ideas. Postmodern approaches to the interpretation of text, whether in the broad use of the word referred to in the box above, or in the narrower sense of a legal text, reject the idea that there is a single, determinate meaning which can be discovered in the text. Moreover, conventional views of reading text often assume that this meaning is in some way related to the intention of the author — that the 'proper' meaning of the text is what the author meant it to mean.

From a postmodern perspective, however, the author, having created the text, casts it adrift, and the 'meaning' (or meanings!) of text are *created* by the process of interpretation. In this context, the idea of a single, correct and authoritative meaning for a piece of legal text is an impossibility.

DEATH OF THE AUTHOR

We probably do not have a great deal of difficulty with the idea of 'the author'. The author is the person who wrote the text that we are reading. In this very simple sense, I can say that 'I' am the author of the words in this box. From a postmodern perspective, however, the idea of authorship is not so simple.

---

10 Davies, pp 313–14.

In a 1968 essay, Roland Barthes wrote of the 'death of the author'. The author was, for Barthes, a construct of the social, cultural and historical forces which had gone into producing the person who wrote the text.[11] Barthes' idea is that once written, text exists in itself, and the meaning of text is not constrained simply to what the author meant (or thought they meant) when they wrote the text. The author does not have a privileged or authoritative view of what the text means.

Texts are a 'fabric' woven out of ideas and sources from within the culture, creating an 'interplay' of signs which generate a multitude of layered meaning, which are resolved, if at all, by the process of *reading*, not writing.[12] This may, in part, explain why seven judges sitting in the High Court can produce seven different sets of reasons for their decision.

FIGURE 10.3: INTERPRETATION OF TEXT

Conventional view of interpretation

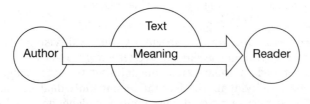

The author's intended and authoritative
meaning is extracted by the reader

'Death of the Author'

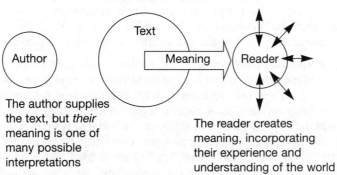

The author supplies
the text, but *their*
meaning is one of
many possible
interpretations

The reader creates
meaning, incorporating
their experience and
understanding of the world

Of course, interpreting a legal text like a statute and interpreting a novel are quite different things. We might accept that a novel or a film can function on different levels, and produce a number of overlapping, complementary and even conflicting meanings which cannot be reconciled. We would be disappointed if it didn't. Interpreting legal texts in this way, however, would be a recipe for confusion.

---

11 You will already have come across a version of this idea in the chapter on Marx — that the individual is constructed by their relationships within a society. (See also Chapter 1 above, pp 7–8.)

12 See the extract from Barthes, and Davies' commentary, p 323ff.

Nevertheless, legal interpretation does, at times, cut the text adrift from its author, and see legal meaning as something which arises from the interpretation of the text in its social context, rather than as something that was set in concrete at the time the words were drafted. Davies, for example, considers that in practice, the meaning of Constitutional text is not governed solely by recourse to the intention of those who framed the document, the 'founding fathers', but is derived from an interpretive processes which locates the text not at the time of its drafting, but in the particular historical and social context at the time it falls to be interpreted.[13]

The significance of postmodernism for law is probably not that this view of a text's meaning will supplant the 'ordinary' process of legal interpretation, but rather that such a revised view of interpretation (coupled with the postmodern technique of *deconstruction*) may throw new light on the ideas which go to make up law, and allow these ideas to be subjected to continuing scrutiny.

The legal subject

Conventional legal theories — particularly the positivist brands which have dominated thinking about law in the Western world over the last two hundred years — have relied to some extent on defining the legal subject as a stable and determinate individual. The Enlightenment individual or Cartesian subject we saw in Chapter 4 is a rational, autonomous, independent and unified whole. To take an obvious example, the legal subject of Austin's theory is the habitually obedient political subject (whose significance lies in the fact of obedience). This legal subject is a 'passive component' of legal analysis whose individual characteristics are downplayed or ignored entirely in favour of a set of assumed characteristics. Law proceeds *as if* the people who come into the legal system actually possessed these characteristics. Their behaviour, for example, is often tested against the hypothetical 'reasonable man' without any regard to the specific characteristics that the individual concerned really has.

Legal analysis in its conventional form does not step outside these assumptions, nor does it generally seek to incorporate understandings from outside the legal world.[14] Even when law appears not to be sufficient (as in Hart's judicial discretion, or Dworkin's 'hard cases'), legal decision-making will be guided by judges who have been trained to think in particular ways either as legal insiders or as members of the (legal) interpretive community. Conventional legal frameworks are inherently conservative. While Hart talks about a 'critical' reflective attitude, the term is, in some ways misleading. Such an attitude is not one which looks critically at the law or the way in which it is being applied. The criticism implied by Hart's use of the word 'critical' is directed to non-conforming conduct, not to the law itself. Legal insiders — the people who create, define and apply law — are required, through the rule of recognition, to accept law as it is (even though they may personally not approve of it).

---

13 Ibid.
14 Courts do, admittedly, admit expert evidence which relies on knowledge other than legal knowledge, but the range of areas in which such evidence is accepted is limited, and shows a very clear preference for expert opinions which are founded in accepted scientific disciplines (preferably from the 'hard' sciences, like engineering, rather than 'soft' sciences like sociology).

The postmodern legal subject

Go back for a moment to the exercise you did at the start of this chapter. You can see from the outline of our histories that major influences on the way I think about the world include the Vietnam War (roughly 1960 to 1973) and the dismissal of the Whitlam government in 1975. I have lived most of my life has against the background of the Cold War, with the accompanying tensions and, at times, the very real threat of nuclear war. The Cold War was at its least cold during the Cuban Missile crisis of 1962.

My sense of humour is largely formed from the school of irreverent British comedy of the Goons through to Monty Python. When I was young, radios had only just become portable, and television was a small and somewhat blurry image in the front of a large wooden box in the corner of the living room (and it was black and white!). I played records — round black vinyl discs which were easily scratched — rather than listening to CDs or MP3s/WMAs. When I left England, the number of computers in the world could probably have been counted using your fingers (and maybe toes). There weren't many more in 1972, and all the assignments for my Arts degree in the 70s were either handwritten or (inexpertly and very slowly) typed. When I got my first 'real job' (with a desk) in 1980, there were no desktop computers, and it wasn't until 1982, I think, that I first had to deal with a PC. (See Chapter 8, p 190.)

Marett was born only three years after me, but you can see from the events which she has included in her timeline that her experience of the world has been shaped by quite different forces. I won't attempt to describe the aspects of her life which are included in the timeline, or to imagine the reasons why she has chosen these particular things.

What is significant is that although we were born only three years apart, the range of political events, TV programs and personal memories we have chosen to 'illustrate' our lives are markedly different; and to imagine that we can both be adequately described by an idealised abstraction seems rather strange.

We can compare the highly idealised conventional legal subject with the subject as constructed in postmodern thought: see Figure 10.4.

FIGURE 10.4: LEGAL SUBJECTS – MODERN AND POSTMODERN

Modernist legal subjects	**Postmodern legal subjects**
The conventional legal subject is:	Postmodern legal subjects are:
• atomistic	• not disconnected from their context
• disconnected from context	• unique and highly individualised products of the experiences which have gone into their formation
• assumed to be the same as each other	

Unlike the Cartesian subject, there is no hard boundary between the subject and the surrounding world. It is embedded in its social and historical context, and is uniquely created by the range of its experiences, so that its outline is a dotted line which allows influences in the surroundings to flow into the subject. Its outline in the diagram is also grey (rather than black), because the individual subject is often invisible to law.

While the conventional legal subject does form relationships, it retains a constant, self-contained nature throughout these relationships. The postmodern subject, however, is in one sense created *by* its relationships:[15] see Figure 10.5.

FIGURE 10.5: MODERN AND POSTMODERN LEGAL SUBJECTS FORMING RELATIONSHIPS

The subject and its relationships

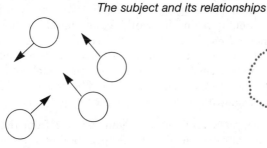
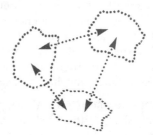

The conventional legal subject:

- forms temporary connections with others in pursuit of their objectives
- but retains its atomistic nature

Postmodern legal subjects:

- form relationships (both with other individuals and with their context)
- which alter their nature

We are at once individuals *and* members of a disparate range of social groupings. In different situations, my dress, my behaviour or the type of language I use might differ according to how I am arranged within my social context.

When I am in court, I may have to wear barrister's robes (and I certainly have to behave according to the rules associated with appearing in court). When I go for a motorbike ride through the mountains, I obviously dress differently (and the conversations I have seem to require a different type of language from the formal language of advocacy). As I move through a series of interactions with the various groups which I, as an individual, am associated with, many of the aspects of my self adjust accordingly.

So, unlike the stable model of the modernist legal subject, the postmodern subject is affected by its relationships. At any given time, it is a matrix of all of the influences which have gone into its creation, but as these influences and its immediate context change, so too will the subject.

---

15 This is similar to the way in which Saussure describes meaning in language as being created by the relations between signs — see Davies, pp 309-311.

FIGURE 10.6: INDIVIDUALS AND GROUPS

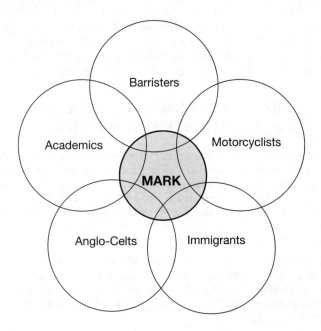

FIGURE 10.7: MODERN AND POSTMODERN LEGAL SUBJECTS OVER TIME

The subject over time

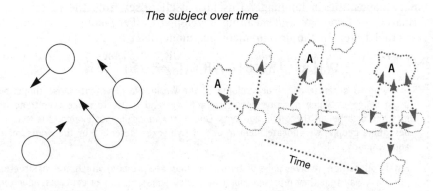

The conventional legal subject:

- does not change as a result of its relationships
- is an idealisation used to explain law from a conventional viewpoint

Postmodern subjects:

- constantly redefine themselves by reference to these relationships
- have a view of the world, including law, which is a product of their interaction with it
- and the view changes as their interconnections change

Be cautious, however: there is no single postmodern approach to the nature of the unstable subject. Lloyd emphasises that the instability of the subject can take two forms – one focusing on the failure of traditional groupings (based on gender, sexuality, race or even economic and legal status) to capture the subject sufficiently, while the other focuses on the fragmented nature of the individual within themselves as they absorb and respond to their social context.[16]

BACK TO MONTY PYTHON – A FRAGMENTED INDIVIDUAL

In Chapter 4, we looked at two characters in *Monty Python and the Holy Grail*. King Arthur and Dennis the Peasant were cast as representing the conflict between the 'old' way of looking at the world, including the world of law and power, and a modern (or modernist) way, based on a reformulated version of the individual. Dennis, as a modern individual, displayed many characteristics of the Cartesian individual – autonomous, independent and rational. The modernist view of the legal subject reflected this idea of a unified, rational person, personified in the 'reasonable man'.

Later in the film, we meet a completely different character who more closely resembles the fragmented aspects of the postmodern individual – the three-headed knight. Each of his heads is constantly arguing with the others, unable to agree which course of action to take, and driven by different imperatives, like whether to kill brave Sir Robin, or be nice to him.

Postmodernism and language – binary opposition

One of the more important insights arising from postmodernism is the idea of binary opposition in language. This idea itself arises from the theories of the formation of language and meaning developed by Ferdinand de Saussure, and is a crucial step in the development postmodernism itself.[17]

WHAT IS 'BINARY OPPOSITION'?

In trying to organise our understanding of the world, we often categorise things by using concepts which describe opposites, and we tend to try to make everything fit into one or other of these two concepts. One of the most obvious examples is that, in describing people, we allocate them to one of two sexes, described by the words 'man' and 'woman'.[18]

Binary opposition involves pairs of terms (like man and woman) which are constructed in such a way that they represent opposites. Such pairs of terms or concepts, however, are not simply a neutral way of dividing up the world, but carry with them a marked preference for one of the terms – usually the first term in the pair. Derrida argues that there is a superior or dominant term in the pair, and that the secondary term is

---

16 See Lloyd, p 1254.
17 Davies provides a description of the relevant aspects of this theory in Chapter 8 of *Asking the Law Question*, particularly at pp 307–313.
18 This, of course, ignores the small percentage of people who do not fit perfectly into this classification. Law nonetheless often requires that an individual be classified as *either* a man *or* a woman for some purposes, like marriage – see *Attorney-General for the Commonwealth v Kevin and Jennifer* (2003) 172 FLR 300.

devalued or inferior. So, for example, in each of the pairs, 'good/evil', 'light/dark', 'life/death', it is the first term that we think of as being 'better' than the second. Good is preferable to evil, light is preferable to darkness, life preferable to death.

Binary oppositions abound in legal thinking. Guilty/innocent, express term/implied term, admissible/inadmissible ...

Looking at the world wearing 'binary opposition' glasses can reveal some strange things. Think about the binary opposition inherent in the concept of man/woman. Postmodern interpretation of the idea of man suggest that the paired concepts of man and woman contain a presupposition that one of these — 'man' as it happens — is pre-eminent, and that the other, 'woman', is a lesser concept.

A STORY ABOUT DOCTORS

A young boy and his father are involved in a car accident. The boy is seriously injured, but his father is killed. When the boy arrives at casualty, the surgeon is distressed, and cries 'I can't operate on this patient. He is my son.'

There is really no riddle — the surgeon who is shocked to find *her* son seriously injured and who cannot, for ethical reasons, operate on the injured boy is, of course, his *mother*. While this story is now a very familiar one, often used to expose the unstated assumptions we often make in deciphering the stories that we hear, many people still have to think quite hard before resolving the apparent contradiction the story presents.

Occupations are a fruitful source of these unstated assumptions. Most of the professions are dominated by male practitioners, and when we hear a reference to one of these — doctor, engineer, judge — the picture that often springs to mind is of a male. There are examples of occupations where we tend to think first of a female, and have to mark out the 'unusual' example of a male by specifying gender — such as 'male nurse'. But these tend to be associated with occupations which have traditionally been thought of as having less status.

SPORTING BODIES AND BINARY OPPOSITION

Think about the naming of these sporting bodies — the PGA and the LPGA, the NBL and the WNBL. Only the female equivalents are identified by a term denoting gender — it is the Professional Golfers' Association, but the *Ladies* Professional Golfers' Association, the National Basketball League but the *Women's* National Basketball League. Behind these naming conventions lies the presumption that, unless otherwise indicated, a sporting body will refer to the male.

We will look at gender-based assumptions and the way in which they impact on law in Chapter 11, on feminism.

Such lesser halves of a binary opposition are often marginalised in legal discourse, and it is a major part of postmodern jurisprudence to bring out these silenced values and views.

Deconstruction

Deconstruction is often associated with negative or nihilistic interpretations of texts — with the idea that any reading of text or any interpretation is as good as any other.[19] This is not an accurate picture of what deconstruction is about.

---

19 See Davies, p 304.

Nor, as Balkin suggests, is it just a fancy way of sticking out your tongue at, or 'trashing', liberal ideas.[20] Deconstruction represents a particular way of analysing concepts to uncover what is lost or pushed into the background.

If you think back to Jeremy Bentham, and his preference for codification, you will see that it assumes that it is possible to define words in such a way as to give a complete understanding of what a word or a concept means, so that the judicial role of interpretation is rendered unnecessary. Bentham's 'code' would provide an exhaustive and comprehensive description of what the law *is*. Legal concepts, like murder, for example, would be defined in such detail that no further elaboration of what murder was would be needed. Such a code could be said to be 'unmediated' — that is, there would be no need for anyone to act as an intermediary between the words of the code and the ideas which they are intended to cover.

LOOK BACK TO CODES

Remember that in Chapter 6 we asked you to think about whether a legal code really could provide such definitive meanings for legal concepts. What did you conclude? Can any set of words ever fully describe a legal idea in such a way as to make interpretation unnecessary?

The later version of positivism suggested by Hart[21] recognised explicitly that language was not always a precise mechanism for communicating ideas. In a legal context, the words used to make a legal statement (such as 'No vehicles can be brought into the park') were always subject to the possibility that there were situations which could not be resolved simply by looking at the words of a statutory provision or common law definition. While some situations would fall inside or outside a legal definition without any real possibility of argument, Hart argued that language retained a penumbra of uncertainty about its meaning.

Such views about legal language imply that there is a meaning which is built into the words, and that this meaning is fixed (usually by reference to the intention of the person who wrote the words).[22] Even for Hart, who recognised that language is imperfect and leaves an area of uncertainty around meaning, language was nonetheless basically stable.

Postmodern approaches to language differ radically from this model of language as being about the direct transmission of ideas from a writer to a reader. All texts are, from a postmodernist perspective, mediated — they are mediated by language, they are mediated by the cultural systems and assumptions of the person who writes them *and* the person who reads them. They are mediated even by the assumptions we make about, and the way we go about, the process of reading itself. Do you read, for example, the newspaper or a novel in quite the same way that you read a judgment?

---

20 Balkin, JM, "Deconstructive Practice and Legal Theory" (1987) 96 Yale LJ 743, p 744, also available at http://www.yale.edu/lawweb/jbalkin/articles/decprac1.htm

21 See Chapter 7 above.

22 See 'Death of the author' above, p 234ff. In reality, of course, the intention which is significant from the point of view of legal interpretation is often *not* the intention of the people who actually wrote the words, Parliamentary drafters, but the legislators whose ideas the drafters are trying to reduce to words.

WAYS OF READING

In many law courses, you will have been introduced to the skill of reading a legal judgment. When you read a new case which has recently been handed down, for example, you do not (or at least, as a law student, you should not) approach it as if it were a novel. You are reading it for a specific purpose — the analytical purpose of trying to distil from it, in as clear a fashion as you can, the ratio decidendi of the case. Your expectation is that, often buried somewhere within the words of the judgment, there will be a proposition of law.

When you read postmodern theorists, it is unlikely that you will find anything like a ratio embedded in the words.[23]

The task of deconstruction is to strip away the layers of meaning which are associated with words, to arrive at a 'new' understanding of what the words mean and the (often unstated) assumptions that are embedded within them. Of course, this new meaning is *not* the final or definitive meaning, and may itself be the subject of deconstruction.

FIGURE 10.8: DECONSTRUCTION

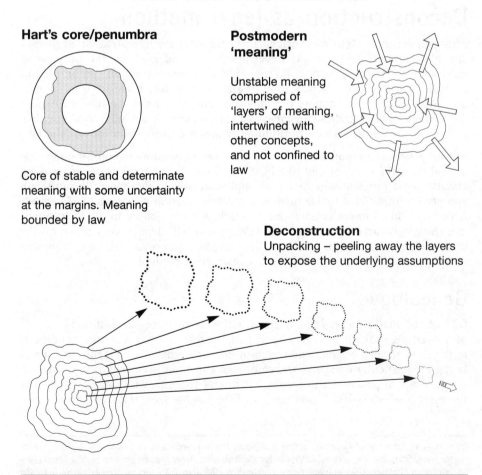

Hart's core/penumbra

Core of stable and determinate meaning with some uncertainty at the margins. Meaning bounded by law

Postmodern 'meaning'

Unstable meaning comprised of 'layers' of meaning, intertwined with other concepts, and not confined to law

Deconstruction
Unpacking – peeling away the layers to expose the underlying assumptions

---

23 See Davies, p 295.

When an idea or view becomes widely accepted or dominant and is generally regarded as speaking the truth about its subject matter, it has, by necessity, excluded alternative views about the same subject matter. When the law of contract was being formulated, it gave expression to one particular view of how the law should operate, closely associated with the beliefs of the mercantile class, for whom meaningful contractual negotiations were a real possibility. In framing the law of contract on this basis, there was a clear advantage given to those people who fitted the underlying image of a free and independent competitive agent, capable of making bargains for their own benefit. But there were entire classes of people — ordinary consumers for example — who did not fit the mould, and whose interests and concerns were suppressed in the formulation of contract law principles. A deconstructive analysis may expose an 'after-image' of these aspects which got lost in defining contract law from one particular point of view.

In applying a postmodern critique to contract law, then, we seek to expose the voices which were silenced while the dominant group's views found expression in legal doctrine.

Deconstruction as legal method

Although deconstruction was born as a technique for the interpretation of literary and philosophical texts, it has nevertheless been adapted for the purpose of legal analysis. Balkin suggests, for example, that deconstruction can be used to critique legal doctrine, showing how the arguments which are used to support a doctrine might also support the opposite rule. It can also be used to expose the ideological basis and the unstated assumptions that lie behind a legal doctrine, as well as providing a way of critiquing mainstream interpretations of the law.

During your studies, you will probably have been taught a method for analysing a legal scenario — something like IRAC or ISAAC.[24] These are ways of thinking about a legal problem which can be applied relatively mechanically (although you need to think hard to use them well). Deconstruction as a method of analysis is not like this — there is no *formula* which you can follow in every instance, and the way you go about deconstructing a text will depend very much on the nature of the issue and its context. There are, however, some relatively common techniques which form part of the deconstructive method.

Genealogy

One of the major *methods* of deconstruction is to trace the historical origins of a doctrine, looking for clues as to *how* it arose — what were the conditions at the time an idea became embedded in law, and what was 'left out' in formulating the particular doctrine? Genealogy as a method is closely associated with a forerunner of postmodern thought, Friedrich Nietzsche, who sought to uncover the origins of ideas like 'good' and 'evil' in *On the Genealogy of Morality*.[25]

---

24 IRAC is an acronym for Issue; Recite the law; Apply the law; and come to a Conclusion. ISAAC stands for Issue; State the law; give an Authority for the legal rule; Apply the rule; and come to a Conclusion.
25 Friedreich Nietzsche, *On the genealogy of morality*, edited by KA Pearson, translated by C Diethe (Cambridge University Press, Cambridge, 1994).

Differance

Differance is a term coined by Derrida – it is actually a pun in French on the two ideas of difference and deferral. *Differance* implies, first, that there is a difference between the two terms of a binary opposition, secondly that meaning is never entirely complete within the text, but is in some way deferred, and finally that the meaning of each of the terms in the opposition defers to the other because although they are opposites – each requires the other in order to have any meaning at all.[26]

Trace

Trace refers to the marks left by the half of the binary opposition which is not explicitly present. By looking back to the time when an idea became the accepted view – and so left out the alternative possibilities – we can see the traces of those alternative views. Deconstruction allows us to bring out those traces.

Deconstruction of a legal doctrine

If deconstruction were nothing more than a philosophical method, its relevance to law would be minimal. However, it is possible to look at legal concepts using deconstructive techniques, and to reveal some of the meanings which are glossed over in the legal text. While we may never go into court and argue that a piece of legislation has no stable meaning, we may nevertheless learn a lot about why law is the way it is by deconstructing it (and even use that as a basis for improving it).[27]

RAPE AS A LEGAL CONCEPT

Not all that long ago (in 1988), the definition of rape in the Queensland *Criminal Code* began like this:

> '347. **Definition of rape.** Any person who has carnal knowledge of a woman, or girl, not his wife, without her consent ...' [28]

Carnal knowledge was defined (in s 6) and the offence of rape was one which, at the time, could only be committed by a male on a female.

You probably won't be surprised that a postmodern analysis of this definition would latch on to the term 'wife', constructing it as one half of a binary opposition 'husband/wife'.

The process of peeling away the layers of the definition of rape might begin by placing the offence within the context of relationships between males and females. But the inclusion of the phrase 'not his wife' has the effect of making the offence of rape impossible in the context of marriage. In order for there to be a rape by this definition, the complainant cannot be the accused's wife.

---

26 This idea flows from Saussure's observation that words acquire meaning by reference to their relationship with other words and ideas which are contrasted with them. We cannot understand 'good' without having a concept of 'evil' – see Davies, p 310.

27 If you want to read a detailed account of a deconstructive analysis (complete with Derridean terminology) in the context of a legal doctrine, see JM Balkin, "Deconstructive Practice and Legal Theory" (1987) 96 Yale LJ 743, under the heading 'An Example of a Legal Deconstruction', p 767.

28 See *Carter's Criminal Law of Queensland*, 7th edition (Butterworths, Sydney, 1988).

Tracing the historical origins of this idea — searching for the genealogy of this aspect of the law of rape — would uncover firstly the idea of perpetual and irrevocable consent. When a woman married, society (and law) saw this as her giving her consent to intercourse with her husband at any time. This itself is an extension of the old idea that, at law, the 'very being or legal existence' of a woman was suspended during marriage, as husband and wife become one person in law.[29] Even more deeply embedded is the idea that a wife was the property — a chattel — of the husband (and there could be no offence in a husband dealing with property as he wished).[30]

A deconstructive reading of the law as at 1988 exposes the inequalities and hierarchies which were present at the time of the law's formulation, but which are effectively de-emphasised or glossed over in the text. Since 1988, the law of rape in Queensland has, on the basis of analyses like this, undergone considerable change, and now includes no presuppositions about the sex of the offender or the victim, and certainly provides no immunity for a husband or exclusion of rape in marriage.

Power/knowledge

Conventional ideas of power in legal theory centre on a single, monolithic structure which 'has power', and exercises that power in the form of government or the making and enforcing of laws. Bentham and Austin's sovereigns, for example, hold power because of their position within a political or legal structure — their institutional power is demonstrated by the fact that most of the people within the structure habitually obey the sovereign's commands.

For Michel Foucault, a major figure in postmodernism, power does not work like this. Power is intertwined with knowledge, and constructed within a network of constantly shifting social relations.[31]

THE INNER RING

In 1944, CS Lewis, professor of medieval and Renaissance English at Cambridge University gave the Memorial Lecture at King's College, University of London, entitled 'The Inner Ring'.[32]

Lewis distinguishes between the stable, formal and institutional structures of power within a hierarchical organisation (the Russian Army) and the informal and constantly rearranging, circle of officers who, contrary to the apparent order imposed by the formal structures, actually exercised power within the regiment.

While Lewis was anything but a postmodernist — the lecture was trying to make a point about morality from a very conventional perspective — the description of the institutional power structures, and the circulation of power in an informal structure based on social interactions, illustrates Foucault's point.

---

29 Blackstone, *Commentaries on the Laws of England*, Vol 3 (1830), cited in Ngaire Naffine, "The Legal Structure of Self-Ownership: or the Self Possessed Man and the Woman Possessed" (1998) *Journal of Law and Society* 25:2, 193, p 208.
30 See eg M Wilson and M Daly, 'The Man Who Mistook His Wife for a Chattel' in, JH Barkow, L Cosmides, J Tooby (eds), *The Adapted Mind: Evolutionary psychology and the generation of culture* (Oxford University Press, New York, 1992). See also above, Chapter 4, p 116.
31 See Davies, p 329.
32 Subsequently published in CS Lewis, *The Weight of Glory and Other Addresses* (Macmillan, New York, 1980), p 100.

Foucault's idea of power/knowledge draws attention to the fact that truth and power are mutually dependent. Within the world of science, what is accepted as scientific orthodoxy — 'truth' — is determined by the scientific community itself, which has the power to determine what will be accepted as true or valid because it sets up the rules which are used to assess scientific theories. A similar process takes place in law. The doctrine of precedent, for example, describes a system in which those with power (appellate courts) set the rules which determine what is true and how something which claims to be true should be tested.

FIGURE 10.9: POWER/KNOWLEDGE

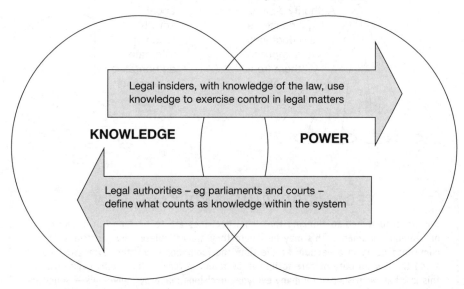

KNOWLEDGE

Legal insiders, with knowledge of the law, use knowledge to exercise control in legal matters

POWER

Legal authorities – eg parliaments and courts – define what counts as knowledge within the system

But in describing power, Foucault concentrates on the local, or small-scale, relationships which cumulatively create ideas of what is acceptable or true within the particular system, rather than the monolithic structures described by conventional legal theory (which are not the *source* of dominant views, but promulgate the results of accumulated power/knowledge).

Law, then, is not described by reference to institutions or institutional forces ('the uniform edifice of sovereignty'[33]), but by the myriad local and particular interactions which constitute society ('the multiple forms of subjugation that have a place and function within the social organism'[34]).

The focus of this type of analysis of legal systems moves away from the top-down view of power exercised by a central authority, and towards a bottom-up analysis, which takes account of the individuals involved in the legal system on a day-to-day basis. Pierre Schlag gives a more detailed version of the informal networks which actually exercise power in 'LA Law's Empire'[35] — a

33 Foucault, *Power/Knowledge*, cited in Davies, p 329.
34 Ibid.
35 Extracted from "Normativity and Politics of Form" (1991) 139 Univ of Pennsylvania L Rev 801 in Lloyd, pp 1283–1292.

world in which the legal truth of a lawyer's guilt or innocence of a charge of drink-driving is determined not by the world of rational analysis carried out in a courtroom, but by a series of manipulations by the lawyers involved – the 'shadow law' which operates in the background, behind the monolithic legal structures which modernist views of law claim constitute the legal system.

FIGURE 10.10: TOP-DOWN AND BOTTOM-UP VIEWS OF LAW

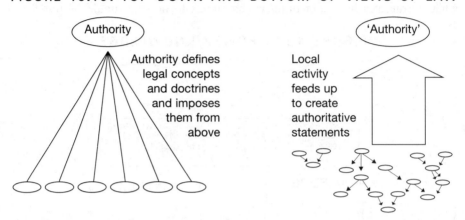

Authority

Authority defines
legal concepts
and doctrines
and imposes
them from
above

'Authority'

Local
activity
feeds up
to create
authoritative
statements

LEGAL DOCTRINE AND CASE LAW

We are accustomed to thinking that legal doctrines are to be found in authoritative or 'leading' judgments. This may be where they are articulated, but doctrines do not come into being in a vacuum at the time the judgment is written. What we under- stand the law on duty of care to be can be found in recent High Court decisions, but this law has been shaped by many everyday decisions made by individuals — solicitors who interview clients, and advise as to whether or not a particular set of circumstances is likely to be viewed by the court as giving rise to liability in negligence. Since courts can only work with the cases that come before them, these localised decisions have the effect of determining what issues will be made the subject of court decisions, and therefore, how the law actually develops.

Why deconstruct?

We said earlier that postmodernism, and the technique of deconstruction, were not to be confused with destruction, anarchy or nihilism. Nevertheless, postmodern approaches to law and jurisprudence are inherently critical.

Underlying postmodern and deconstructive approaches to law is the realisation that law is inherently political – that the positing and enforcing of laws is a political act which affects individuals, and that underlying the laws which are chosen is a preference, not necessarily conscious or intended, for a particular dominant position.

Why deconstruct? Chapter 8, on Marx, marked the turning point in this book. There we moved away from conventional legal theories which were developed specifically as theories of law, into theories or approaches which were often not principally about law, but which could throw new light on legal concepts.

Postmodernism (and deconstruction) are like this. By recognising and highlighting the existence of a dominant position which finds expression in law, and bringing to the surface the other views which get lost or drowned out by that dominant view, postmodernism exercises a subversive role in legal analysis,[36] but also opens the way to new possibilities of achieving just outcomes. As Derrida suggested, if we had no sense of justice, we would not be interested in deconstructing.

However, postmodern analysis does not necessarily throw out the rules. It is entirely conceivable that the process of deconstruction might conclude that a given rule is the most appropriate rule (although this will only ever be an assessment of the rule in a particular time and place, subject itself to another deconstruction). One of the hallmarks of postmodern legal analysis is that it demands a constant re-assessment of law as the circumstances in which it operates change.

The main way in which postmodernism feeds into the analysis of law is through its preparedness to challenge *any* doctrine or legal concept, using its own methods to open up legal ideas to scrutiny. What postmodernism cannot provide is a neat methodological technique or answer to a problem, much less a complete and final explanation of what law is.

Critical responses to postmodernism

We have mentioned a number of criticisms of postmodernism in passing already – notably that postmodernism is often thought of as being inherently negative, and provides no secure benchmark against which legal ideas or concepts can be measured. Deconstruction may pull ideas apart, but there is no real guidance as to how to put them back together.

The main criticisms that are levelled at postmodernism include:

- the postmodernist rejection of metanarratives is *itself* a metanarrative (which involves postmodernism in an internal contradiction);

- postmodern approaches to meaning are not appropriate to law, which relies on a secure and stable meaning. If we can't know what legal texts mean (in the sense of the ratio decidendi of a judgment), then we can't base our actions on any clear idea of what is lawful;

- important concepts for law, like objectivity and neutrality, are broken down by postmodern analysis. What it seems to offer in return is indeterminacy, uncertainty and confusion;

- it is far harder to fix responsibility – a cornerstone of law – on an unstable postmodern subject than on the rational autonomous agent of modernism;

- the rejection of rationalism as a fundamental basis for understanding is, paradoxically, usually undertaken by the development of a rational argument … against rationality!

---

36 Lloyd, p 1257.

QUESTIONS TO THINK ABOUT

1. If postmodernism is not a theory about law, can it be relevant to the practice of law?

2. What use can be made of Barthes' idea of the death of the author in legal analysis?

3. Pick a legal doctrine (such as terra nullius) and use a deconstructive approach to uncovering the fundamental assumptions which lie behind it.

4. We've already given you some examples of binary oppositions. Can you think of some more examples within legal terminology? Is one of the pair dominant?

5. The doctrine of precedent is one example of the interrelationship of power and knowledge within law. What are some other features of the legal system which demonstrate this relationship?

6. Would you rather be dealt with by the courts on the basis of an 'objective' view, or as a postmodern subject?

7. Can you think of some more examples of 'text' made of things other than words?

8. Can you see some of the influences which might lie behind your adopting a particular stance on a legal issue?

9. Why do you think postmodernism arose at the time that it did?

10. What purpose is served by deconstructing legal doctrines?

FURTHER READING

Balkin, JM, "Deconstructive Practice and Legal Theory" (1987) 96 Yale LJ 743.

Carty, A (ed), *Post-modern Law: Enlightenment, Revolution and the Death of Man* (Edinburgh University Press, Edinburgh, 1990).

Davies, M, *Delimiting the Law: "Postmodernism" and the Politics of Law* (Pluto Press, London, 1996).

Douzinas, C & Warrington, R, *Postmodern Jurisprudence: the Law of Text in the Texts of Law* (Routledge, London, 1991).

Nicholson, LJ (ed), *Feminism/Postmodernism* (Routledge, New York, 1990).

Litowitz, D, *Postmodern Philosophy and Law* (University Press of Kansas, Lawrence, 1997).

Minda, G, *Postmodern Legal movements: Law and Jurisprudence at Century's End* (New York University Press, New York, 1995).

Stacey, H, *Postmodernism and Law: Jurisprudence in a Fragmenting World* (Ashgate, Aldershot, 2001).

Ward, I, *Kantianism, Postmodernism, and Critical Legal Thought* (Kluwer Academic Publishers, Dordrecht, 1997).

CHAPTER 11

Feminist Legal Theory

Reading. 251
Aim. 251
Principles 251
What is feminism? 252
Feminism in history 253
The range of feminisms 255
Anti-feminism 267
Critical responses to feminism. 268
Questions to think about 268
Further reading. 269

READING

DAVIES, *Asking the Law Question: The Dissolution of Legal Theory*, 2nd edition, Chapter 6

FREEMAN, *Lloyd's Introduction to Jurisprudence*, 7th edition, Chapter 14

AIM

This chapter will:

- introduce you to the underlying ideas of the major forms of feminist legal theory;

- consider the impact these ideas have when they are applied to law.

PRINCIPLES

Before we start, I have a confession to make. This chapter is being written by the male author in 'Leiboff and Thomas'. As such, I am conscious of the criticism which is sometimes levelled at male writers dealing with feminist issues that they are unable to *know* what it is like to be a woman, and hence to be the subject of systematic and systemic discrimination – or worse.

A STORY ABOUT 'KNOWING'

I play squash regularly. One evening, I was sitting with my (male) squash partner after playing for an hour, having a drink before heading home. Across from where we were sitting was a room with about 20 electric treadmills, arranged in rows and all pointing towards a large TV screen. They were all in use. Without exception, the people walking and watching the TV were women.

It seemed strange that anyone would join a gym and spend hours walking on a treadmill, when all they really had to do was to go for a walk. If I'd wanted to, I could have left the bike at home, walked the mile or so to the squash courts and got all the exercise I needed.

Then it struck me. While it was easy enough for me to walk home through the quiet suburban streets at nine o'clock at night, there were obvious problems for a woman who wanted to do it. So I tried to imagine an experiment which would allow me to experience what walking home in the dark might be like for a woman.[1] I could *dress* as a woman, or go a bit further and shave off my beard and wear a wig. If it were dark enough, I might be taken for a woman. So if I were to encounter three males (let's say they're a bit drunk and loud) on a walk through the suburban streets at night, I might alter *their* perception of me to the extent that they thought I was female.

But what I can't really alter (and can only ever change imaginatively) is my own set of responses to a threat. Despite the change in my outward appearance and the altered perceptions (and assumptions) of others, I would retain all the internal feelings about an imminent threat and violent confrontation that have been conditioned by forty-eight years as a male. I can't really experience the subjective feelings which a woman would have in this situation — all I can do is think about them intellectually and try to imagine, both intellectually and emotionally, how it might feel to be *the other*.

Can you imagine a situation which I could be placed in which might come closer to simulating the experience of a woman walking through suburban streets at might?

So I accept that I can't ever personally experience being a woman. But I can still appreciate intellectually and explore imaginatively the issues that feminist thought raises.

What is feminism?

It is widely recognised that there are a range of theoretical positions and approaches described as 'feminist', and that the use of the word 'feminism' in the singular creates the (wrong) impression that feminism is a unified theoretical stance.[2] Davies, for example, identifies at least five 'strands of feminism — liberal, radical, cultural, Black, lesbian and postmodern' — as being more or less standard categories (although she also points out that the boundaries between some of these categories are unclear, and becoming more so).[3] Wacks lists another eight![4] Nevertheless, it is possible to see a core proposition which is common to *all* strands of feminism.

---

1   I might add that this was by way of what Einstein called a *Gedenkexperiment* (or 'thought experiment'). I had no intention of actually carrying out this particular piece of empirical research.

2   See M Davies, *Asking the Law Question: The Dissolution of Legal Theory*, 2nd edition (Lawbook Co, Sydney, 2002), p 203.

3   Davies, pp 205, 230.

4   Wacks, R, *Swot: Jurisprudence* (Blackstone Press, London, 1999), p 230 — Marxist, socialist, existentialist, structuralist, post-structuralist, deconstructionist, linguistic and psychoanalytical.

A DEFINITION OF 'FEMINISM' (IN THE SINGULAR)

Despite the variety of ways in which feminist thinkers approach their work, feminism is united by the central proposition that society is organised by men in a way which privileges men, and operates to disadvantage women. The feminist project is to expose and bring about the end of sexism by exploring the ways in which the subordination of women is manifested, and considering how and why this occurs.[5]

In the later parts of this chapter, we will look at some of the major categories of feminism, and identify what the underlying theoretical position is for each. You should, however, remember that while there are substantial (and sometimes irreconcilable) differences between the categories, they are not *entirely* separate. Some feminist writing, written primarily from one stance, may nevertheless incorporate ideas from more than one category, or use techniques which are usually associated with another type of feminism.

Feminism in history

In the overall timeline (Figure 11.1), we've placed feminist legal *theory* as beginning around 1980. The first use of the word 'feminism' dates from the second half of the 19th century, when it was used in the context of the struggle for equal legal and political rights for women. But feminism itself (rather than its direct application as a legal theory) has a much longer history than that.

FIGURE 11.1: FEMINIST LEGAL THEORY TIMELINE

1700–1800	1800–1900	1900–1945	1945–1960	1960–1990	1990–present
	Anti-slavery campaigns (US)				
	Seneca Falls (US) First women's rights convention				
	Married Women's Property Act (UK)				
	Women's right to vote (NZ)				
		WSPU – Emmeline Pankhurst			
		Women's right to vote (Australia) Women (over 30) given right to vote (UK) Women (over 21) given right to vote (UK)			
				Women's Liberation Liberal feminism Radical feminism Cultural feminism	
				Postmodern, black lesbian etc feminism	

---

5 See Clare Dalton, cited in Lloyd, p 1124. See also the catalogue of questions suggested by Heather Wishik as forming the basis for feminist inquiry at pp 1124–1125.

In the major timeline covering all the theories (Figure 1.2), we have identified feminist legal theory as beginning around 1980. Figure 11.1, however, goes further back and shows some of the major figures and events in more general feminist thought. While feminist legal theory is a relatively recent development, feminist ideas have been around a long time.

Long before anything now identified as feminism emerged, there were concerted efforts made to draw attention to the inferior status of women in society, and to correct the inequalities.

SOME EARLY MANIFESTATIONS OF FEMINIST THOUGHT AND ACTION

1791   Olympe de Gouges' *Declaration of the Rights of Woman and Citizen*, paralleling the *Declaration of the Rights of Man and Citizen* of the French Revolution.[6]

1792   Mary Wollstonecraft's *Vindication of the Rights of Women*.

1833   Sarah Mapp Douglass and others establish the Philadelphia Female Anti-Slavery Society, serving as inspiration for the American women's rights movement.

1848   First women's rights convention, Seneca Falls, New York — identified the 'injuries and usurpations' inflicted by men on women.[7] 'All men and women are created equal.'[8]

1856   Launch of the *Englishwoman's Journal* for the debate of issues such as women and work, education and suffrage.

1860   By the end of this year, 14 of the US States had passed reforming legislation allowing women to own property.

1869   John Stuart Mill's *The Subjection of Women* argues that men and women are fundamentally equal, but that differences in upbringing and education accounted for any differences.

1879   Belva Ann Lockwood is the first woman lawyer to practise before the US Supreme Court.

1882   *Married Women's Property Act* passed in the UK — married women given legal control of property which they owned at marriage or which they acquired after marriage either by inheritance or by their own earnings.

1893   New Zealand is the first country to give women the right to vote.

1903   The WSPU (Women's Social and Political Union) is established by Emmeline Pankhurst.

1909   Women win the right to vote in Australia.[9]

1918   Women aged over 30 given the right to vote in the UK.

1928   Women over 21 given the right to vote in the UK.

1949   Simone de Beauvoir's *The Second Sex* published.

1960s   Women's liberation movement — re-emergent recognition of inequality and discrimination in society, again inspired by Afro-American struggle — this time for civil rights.

1968   Strike for equal pay at Ford plant in Dagenham (London).

---

6 See Davies, p 214.
7 See 'Declaration of Sentiments' in *The Seneca Falls Declaration* of 1848, available at http://www.ku.edu/carrie/docs/texts/seneca.htm
8 Ibid.
9 Note that *indigenous* women were not entitled to vote until 1967.

1970   First Women's Liberation conference (UK) at Ruskin College, Oxford.

1973   *Roe v Wade* establishes right to choose an abortion in US.

1980s   Early 1980s — development of three major schools of feminist scholarship and jurisprudence: liberal, cultural and radical.

Late 1980s — 'Third wave' feminism — recognises the non-essentialist nature of women's experience, and analyses differences based on, eg, age, race and sexuality. Emergence of postmodern feminism, black feminist criticism and other forms of feminism.

The range of feminisms

We have already said that feminism takes many forms. The women's movement had generated three major strands of theory by the late 1980s — liberal feminism, radical feminism and cultural feminism. Since then, there has been a proliferation of theoretical approaches which fall under the umbrella of feminist thought.

FIGURE 11.2: THE RANGE OF FEMINISMS

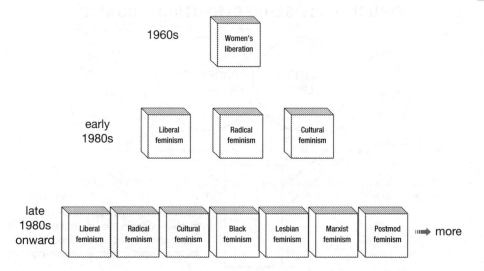

In this chapter, we will be looking at these three major branches or strands of feminist thought, as well as making a some observations about some other, more recent, ways in which feminist thought has developed in response to specific aspects of society, or to perceived flaws in the main branches of feminism.

Liberal feminism

Liberal feminism is an outgrowth of the original Women's Liberation movement of the late 1960s and focuses on the establishment of rights which parallel the rights enjoyed by men in liberal societies.

LIBERATION

At the start, the voices of protest were not intent on establishing a theory, but responding to the (re-emerging) recognition that women enjoyed fewer rights than men in society, and were subordinated to a male model of 'femininity'. Employment and educational opportunities were limited. Women were paid less than men for doing the same work, and were virtually unrepresented in senior positions.

Liberal feminism, as we now look back on its origins and impose a theoretical perspective, assumes that the underlying principles of liberal theory are essentially correct. The liberal subject is affirmed – that is, the model of the atomistic, autonomous, rational and independent person is accepted as the basis for social organisation. The rights which are accorded to individuals – the right to own property, to participate in political affairs (including voting), to work, to be educated – are therefore valued by liberal feminism. In order to be fulfilled, therefore, women should aspire to (and the system should allow them the same possibility of achieving) these liberal goals. As such, liberal feminism is often referred to as a 'partial' critique (as opposed to 'total' critiques like radical feminism).

FIGURE 11.3: GENDER–NEUTRAL EQUALITY

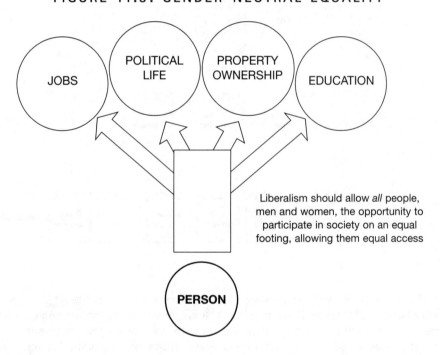

Liberalism should allow *all* people, men and women, the opportunity to participate in society on an equal footing, allowing them equal access

The problem, seen through liberal feminist eyes, is that in putting the ideas of liberalism into practice, something has gone wrong, and the equality which *should* be guaranteed by those liberal principles doesn't actually apply to women.[10] Everyone is created equal, but some (men) are *more* equal than others.

---

10 See Davies, pp 210–211.

While men are treated according to the ideal of the atomistic, rational, autonomous and independent subject, women have been consistently relegated to a lesser position and assumed (as a class) to have different aspirations.[11] In practice, then, society is ordered in such a way as to make the achievement of core liberal rights, such as the right to vote or to work, more difficult (or in some cases, impossible) for women.[12]

FIGURE 11.4: INEQUALITY

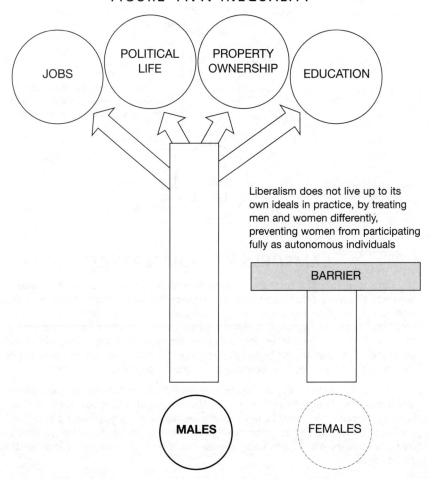

Liberalism does not live up to its own ideals in practice, by treating men and women differently, preventing women from participating fully as autonomous individuals

JOBS

POLITICAL LIFE

PROPERTY OWNERSHIP

EDUCATION

BARRIER

MALES

FEMALES

Liberal feminism is, therefore, a conservative position. It recognises that society is organised along patriarchal lines, but it does not constitute a revolutionary attack on the institutions of liberal society.[13] Above all, it is a practical stream of feminist thought. It is primarily concerned with reform and the correction of the perceived inequalities in the everyday world, rather than the creation of any abstract theory.[14]

---

11 See Davies, p 211.
12 Ibid.
13 See Davies, p 217.
14 See Lloyd, p 1124 — citing M Fineman's the 'desirability of the concrete'.

FIGURE 11.5: LIBERAL FEMINISM — REFORM

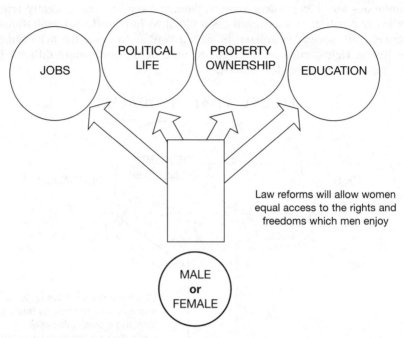

SAMENESS AND DIFFERENCE

The ways in which reform can be effected depend on the approach to the so-called sameness/difference debate. One approach stresses the similarities between men and women, and suggests that women are not really different from men in any significant way. Equality can be therefore be brought about through ensuring *equal* treatment. If equality of opportunity can be achieved, then economic and social inequalities will disappear.[15] This approach has historically been used to rectify some obvious inequalities, such as the right to vote and the removal of formal barriers to employment.[16]

The alternative approach is to look at the inherent differences between men and women (often, but not by any means exclusively, those imposed by biology, such as child-bearing). Identical treatment is, in these circumstances, not a possibility, and requires laws to acknowledge and accommodate the differences. This approach has resulted in laws and policies which specifically address the differences and try to level up the playing field.[17]

As we will see below, both these approaches have been the subject of criticism by writers who see them as doing little more than making women imitations of men, expected to live 'up' to male-based standards and measured against male-oriented benchmarks.

---

15 See eg Elizabeth Sheehy, *Personal Autonomy and the Criminal Law: Emerging Issues for Women*, background paper for the Canadian Advisory Council on the Status of Women, September 1987, and the Australian Law Reform Commission report which draws on Sheehy's analysis, *Equality Before the Law* (ALRC Report No 69, Part II, 1994) extracted in R Graycar & J Morgan, *The Hidden Gender of the Law* (Federation Press, Annandale, 2002), p 28ff.

16 See Graycar & Morgan, op cit, p 28.

17 See Graycar & Morgan, op cit, p 29.

Radical feminism

Radical feminism does not simply mean 'extreme' feminism or feminism exhibiting a highly militant nature. 'Radical' is derived from the Latin *radix* meaning *root* and *radicitus* meaning *by the roots*. To approach something from a *radical* perspective is to pull it up *by the roots*, and critically examine the very foundations of what it is you are dealing with.[18] (See also Chapter 8, p 188.)

Radical feminism, therefore, is a version of feminism which engages with the very foundations of social organisation. Unlike liberal feminism, it is not content to accept the underlying assumptions of liberal society, or that the liberal view can provide a neutral standpoint, but seeks to expose a fundamental flaw in those assumptions.

RADICAL FEMINISM — A DEFINITION

The core proposition of radical feminism is that oppression on the basis of sex (that is, *of* women *by* men) is the most fundamental source of inequality in society. This oppression manifests itself in the systematic subordination of women through the existence and maintenance of patriarchal structures. Political structures, industrial organisations, religious establishments, indeed all the institutions of society, are dominated by males and operate to benefit men and oppress women. The world is created in the image of *man*.[19] Such oppression is not confined to the public sphere, but exists in the private sphere as well, where individual males oppress women through rape or domestic violence.

A radical view of the nature of society as sex-based oppression cannot be content to resolve the inequalities by simple legislative reform, leaving the underlying oppressive relationship untouched, but seeks a *radical* transformation of the relationship between the sexes.

Radical feminism and Marxism

There are some underlying similarities between Marxist views of social organisation and radical feminism's stance. Marx describes society as an economically-based struggle between the oppressor (the bourgeoisie) and the oppressed (the proletariat). Parallelling this struggle in the social field is the struggle between sex-based 'classes', male and female. Both Marxism and radical feminism are descriptions of how power arises, how it operates in society and how it is distributed unequally between the relevant groups.[20]

---

18 See Davies, pp 220–221.
19 See eg Catharine MacKinnon, 'Feminism, Marxism, Method and the State: Towards Feminist Jurisprudence', in *Feminist Legal Theory: Readings in Law and Gender*, edited by K Bartlett and R Kennedy (Westview Press, Boulder, Colorado, 1991), extracted in Davies, pp 222–223.
20 See, for example, Catharine MacKinnon, *Towards a Feminist Theory of the State* (Harvard University Press, Cambridge, Mass, 1989), pp 3–4.

FIGURE 11.6: RADICAL FEMINISM AND MARXISM

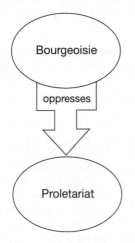

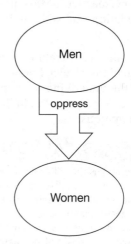

| Economic oppression – class (Marx) | Sexual oppression – gender (Radical feminism) |

Bourgeoisie — oppresses → Proletariat

Men — oppress → Women

FALSE CONSCIOUSNESS

Another Marxist idea which sometimes arises in feminist thought (although there is no uniform view) is that of *false consciousness*.[21] We referred in Chapter 8 to the ideas of 'legal consciousness' and 'social consciousness'.[22]

The ideas which support the preferences of the dominant group (its *ideology*) are often accepted unquestioningly as normal and natural — the way things are.

It has been argued that women suffer from *false consciousness* in the sense that the messages which dominate society blind them to the reality of their oppression. Ideas which support and reinforce a male perspective are so pervasive within social institutions that women are simply unable to recognise that they are constantly subject to, for example, objectification. False consciousness has been proposed as a reason why some women deny that they are, in fact, oppressed.

One of the projects of radical feminism, therefore, is 'consciousness raising' — the removal of the veil of false consciousness through a process of making oppression evident to women, so that they come to understand the way in which they are subordinated to male views and standards and subjected to the dominance of male-oriented society.[23]

These (and other) parallels between radical feminism and Marxism, however, do not mean that radical feminism is, itself, a form of Marxist thought — quite the opposite, in fact. Marxists, for example, often claim that feminism works to the advantage of the ruling class, in that it undermines the need to create changes by deflecting effort away from the important (economic and class)

---

21 See, for example, MacKinnon, 'Feminism, Marxism, Method, and the State', op cit.
22 See Chapter 8 above, p 197, 'Ideology'.
23 See Davies, pp 253–254.

aspects which Marxism identifies as crucial. Feminism counterclaims that Marxism is a male-defined theory which addresses issues of gender, as Catharine MacKinnon suggests, 'only in passing',[24] and that the changes which Marxism seeks could be achieved without any material alteration to the oppression of women.[25]

MacKinnon therefore defines feminism as 'post-Marxian', identifying sex-based oppression as the core oppression. Radical feminism has 'gone beyond' Marxism, having recognised the failure of Marxism to address the problems of male-dominated social structures.

Radical feminism and pornography

DWORKIN AND PORNOGRAPHY

We looked briefly at Ronald Dworkin's argument in favour of pornography in Chapter 5. Dworkin argued that the *right* of an individual to distribute pornography, tied up in the right to free speech, should be supported, even if it were thought that society as a whole would be better off if the distribution of pornography were stopped. The individual *right* trumps the utilitarian goal of improving society in aggregate by banning pornography.

Feminist writing takes a variety of positions on pornography, including calls for censorship, pragmatic concerns that censorship would drive pornography underground and into the hands of organised crime, the classification of pornography with other, less overt, images (such as advertising) which nonetheless degrade women, and even support for alternative forms of pornography which promote positive images of women and female sexuality.

Radical feminism, however, sees pornography as a *prime* example of the mechanisms within society which perpetuate patriarchal values and male dominance. Male power creates a way of treating women which is accepted and forms the basis of the way in which society is organised. It is the inequality of power within society — the powerlessness of women — which constitutes the discrimination in pornography. Pornography institutionalises inequality, creating bigotry and aggression and desensitising men to sexual violence.

RADICAL FEMINISM IN PRACTICE — THE PORNOGRAPHY DEBATE

For MacKinnon, pornography is not speech (thereby attracting the Constitutional protections of free speech), but an *act*. Furthermore, it is an act which discriminates against women, and is as such a violation of their civil rights.[26] Pornography is representative of the male view of women, and embodies the idea of male access to women as defining women's inferiority.[27] Pornography (and how it is conceived in law)

CHAPTER 11

---

24 See MacKinnon, 'Feminism, Marxism, Method, and the State', op cit, p 19.
25 See MacKinnon, 'Feminism, Marxism, Method, and the State', p 5, and generally Chapter 1 of *Towards a Feminist Theory of the State*, 'The Problem of Marxism and Feminism'.
26 See the *Model Antipornography Civil Rights Ordinance* by Andrea Dworkin and Catharine MacKinnon in *Pornography and Civil Rights: A New Day for Women's Equality* (Organizing Against Pornography, Minneapolis, 1988), pp 138–142.
27 See Catharine MacKinnon, *Towards a Feminist Theory of the State*, (Harvard University Press, Cambridge, Mass, 1991), p 195.

takes a male viewpoint.[28] The pornography industry functions by exploiting women as sex objects for profit. Pornography is, therefore, a political practice which arises from the exercise of power by those with power against the powerless.

The effect of pornography is to present sexuality from the dominant male perspective, distorting or misrepresenting eroticism, and defining women in a way which fulfils male fantasies. It objectifies women, and promulgates attitudes which are ultimately expressed in violence against women. Women are forced to live in the world 'created by pornography'.[29] Harm is not limited to overt acts of violence, and the boundary between 'speech' and 'act' is not clear-cut. (MacKinnon asks whether saying 'Kill' to a guard dog is a word or an act.[30]) Pornography harms women by dehumanising them, constructing them as a means to the end of male pleasure.

MacKinnon, therefore, rejects the appeal to Constitutional protection of pornography as free speech. That liberal view of the Constitutional protection assumes that free speech leads to truth by exposing all ideas to scrutiny. Radical feminism argues that pornography simply impresses ruling male ideology on society, and in doing so conceals the voice of protest and dissent. There is no 'freedom' in freedom of speech when women's free speech is systematically silenced.

Radical feminism's analysis of pornography comes to a different conclusion from Ronald Dworkin because it views pornography as an act which affects lives, rather than thinking of a world without pornography as an abstract, utilitarian vision of a 'better world' which is trumped, in Dworkin's view, by the individual's *right* to pornography. For radical feminism, pornography is *not* an abstract phenomenon divorced from actual behaviour, but a *real threat* to women's safety. As such, it is a clear violation of the civil rights of women (or anyone who is harmed by pornography on the basis of their sexuality).

FIGURE 11.7: TWO VIEWS OF PORNOGRAPHY

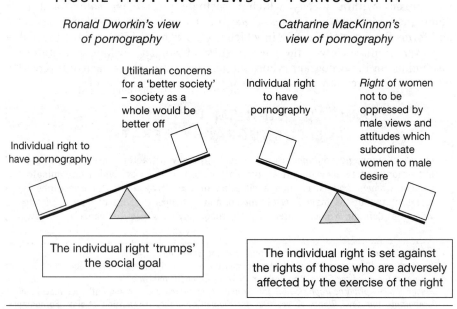

Ronald Dworkin's view of pornography

Catharine MacKinnon's view of pornography

Utilitarian concerns for a 'better society' – society as a whole would be better off

Individual right to have pornography

Individual right to have pornography

Right of women not to be oppressed by male views and attitudes which subordinate women to male desire

The individual right 'trumps' the social goal

The individual right is set against the rights of those who are adversely affected by the exercise of the right

---

28 Ibid, p 197.
29 Ibid, p 205.
30 Ibid, p 207.

RADICAL FEMINISM ON THE BENCH?

For an example of radical feminism articulated from the bench, look at Pat O'Shane's comments on dismissing charges against four women, quoted at page 110 of Davies.

Can you see the ideas of radical feminism as the basis for O'Shane's characterisation of society as dominated by males, with laws designed to protect the property interests of a male-dominated society, backed by huge financial resources?

Cultural feminism

The third major strand of feminist thought, cultural feminism, draws heavily on the work of psychologist Carol Gilligan. Cultural feminism argues that there is a distinctively 'feminine' way of approaching moral and legal dilemmas that is quite different from the way in which established legal theory and practice approaches them.

Gilligan was a student of the developmental psychologist, Lawrence Kohlberg. In devising his theory of moral development, Kohlberg had proposed a series of moral dilemmas – we'll look at one, the 'Heinz problem', below – using them as the basis for researching the way in which people thought about the ethical issues raised by the problem.

CHAPTER 11

THE HEINZ PROBLEM

This was one of the ethical dilemmas devised by Kohlberg in his research into moral development. Research subjects were presented with the following scenario, which has been paraphrased:[31]

> A woman is dying of cancer. Doctors think that a drug, recently discovered by a local druggist, might save her life. While the drug is expensive to make, the druggist is selling it for 10 times its cost of manufacture. The woman's husband, Heinz, does not have the money to buy it, but manages to borrow about half the price. He goes to the druggist, and asks if he will sell it to him at a reduced price, or if he can get the drug now and pay the full amount later. The druggist refuses, saying that he discovered the drug, and that he was going to make money from his discovery.

> The dying woman's husband, in desperation, breaks into the druggist's shop and steals the drug.

Subjects were asked whether Heinz should have broken into the shop and stolen the drug, and *why* they answered that way.

Kohlberg thought that the more a person valued the *rights* of the people in the scenario, the more advanced their moral thinking was. The Heinz scenario seemed to present a conflict between the right of the drug's inventor to exploit his invention, and the *right* of the dying woman to life (or a chance at life).

Gilligan was struck by the fact that in many of Kohlberg's studies, women scored lower in terms of moral development than men. She argued that women were not stunted in their moral growth[32] (as these results were used to claim),

---

31 Lawrence Kohlberg, *The Psychology of Moral Development: The Nature and Validity of Moral Stages* (Harper and Row, San Francisco, 1984), p 640.

32 This was a conventional interpretation of women's psychological development by a number of major theorists, including Freud.

but that the test itself was skewed towards those who adopted what she eventually described as a male way of thinking about ethical problems. If you thought about the problems in this particular way, you tended to score higher.

Gilligan argued that *male* moral reasoning focuses on abstract questions of rights and justice (an 'ethic of justice'), while women's approach to moral problems tends to focus more on issues of responsibility and seeing a moral dilemma in its context (an 'ethic of care').[33]

The male way of thinking privileges a way of looking at situations based on competing rights 'owned' by autonomous and independent individuals, and relies on the ability to take them out of their context (that is, to think about them as abstract ideas) and to apply universal principles about rights to come up with an answer. People are 'decontextualised' – that is, taken out of their social and relational context and thought about as abstract entities. The underlying imperative is to protect these rights against interference.[34]

FIGURE 11.8: GILLIGAN'S MALE AND FEMALE PERSPECTIVES

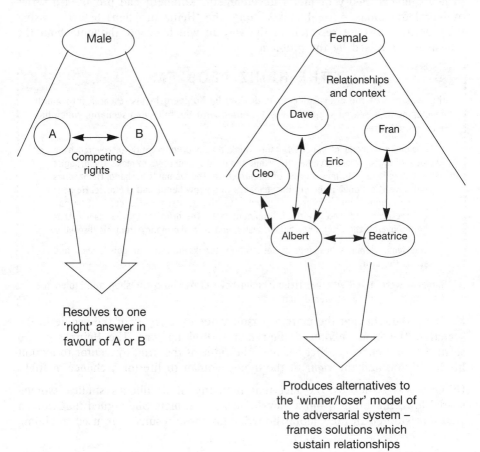

---

33 See Davies, p 230.
34 Carol Gilligan, *In a Different Voice: Psychological Theory and Women's Development* (Harvard University Press, Cambridge, Mass, 1982), pp 159–160.

The 'female' way of thinking about such problems tends to orient towards the relationships involved and how they might be sustained, rather than on any abstract idea of who might be entitled to what. Such a view stresses the connectedness of people (through their relationships), rather than the independent and autonomous view of the individual. Behind this approach is the desire to recognise and alleviate the trouble of the world.[35]

Just why men and women should think differently about these issues presents something of an unresolved problem. One view argues that the different way in which men and women think is a conditioned response – women are *taught* to think in terms of relationships – to care and to nurture. The alternative proposition, which has received considerable support from recent discoveries in neuroscience (which shows that the male and female brains are *structured* or *wired* differently), is that these different ways of thinking are the product of anatomical differences which occur in the development of the brain under the influence of sex-linked hormones.[36]

SOLVING LEGAL PROBLEMS

In learning how to solve legal problems, you may have been encouraged to use the initials of people in a legal scenario, and to think about the problem in terms of the legal status of these people, classifying them as specific types of legal actors. Examiners often give the people in their scenarios names (like Albert, Beatrice and Cleo) which make this easier. A and B enter into a contract, for example, or C is a fiduciary and D is a beneficiary.[37]

While using the initials certainly saves time in exams, it also has the effect of depersonalising the individuals involved in the scenario, and allowing them to be thought of more easily as abstract legal actors (rather than actual human beings, who will be dramatically affected by law's 'solution' to their problem).

**Which of the two forms of reasoning (rights or responsibilities)
do you think this represents?**

The 'different voice' associated with women's moral reasoning would emphasise the context in which events were occurring and the relationships which were formed, and import values such as compassion and empathy in framing a solution to the problem.

SAMENESS AND DIFFERENCE – AGAIN

Cultural feminism certainly emphasises the differences between men and women. Where it differs from, for example, liberal feminism in its assertion of difference is that it does not stress difference as the basis for law reform with a view to making women 'like men' – that is, using the male standard as the basis for everyone. Difference, to cultural feminists, is positive rather than a negative. It asserts that, while there are indeed differences between men and women in the way in which they think about legal and ethical issues, they are just that – differences. It is not that one, the male, is necessarily any better or should form the benchmark against which everything else is measured.

What impact would this have on law?

---

35 Ibid.
36 See eg Zhou et al, "A Sex Difference in the human brain and its relation to transsexuality" (1995) *Nature*, vol 378, pp 68–70, which was considered in the transsexual marriage case, *Re Kevin (validity of marriage of transsexual)* (2001) 165 FLR 404.
37 See Chapter 4 above, Part B, p 96.

Feminist arguments based on Gilligan's work suggest that the way in which law works (and the type of reasoning which is taught in law schools as being appropriate to legal analysis) reflects very much the male view — that the *rational* and *objective* view dominates the way that law and legal reasoning is structured. This represents only *one* way in which such issues could be approached. However, it is a way of thinking which has been privileged in legal institutions.

Cultural feminists argue that law's institutions and methods would be improved if the 'different voice' of half of the population were to be included. Such an approach to law would favour the use of mediation to resolve disputes, rather than the traditional adversarial mode assumed in litigation. It would focus on communal values over the primacy of individual rights.

An important aspect of this change would be increasing the representation of women on the bench. This is not significant simply as a question of equal opportunity or access for women, but would bring a different form of reasoning which would become part of the act of judging. The 'different voice' which female judges would bring to their function would incorporate into the judicial function the values which lie behind the different way in which cultural feminists see women approaching moral, ethical and legal problems.

Some other feminisms

As we have said, there are many other forms of feminism which have developed out of the initial position that women are discriminated against and occupy an inferior position in society (and legal thinking).

Postmodern feminism

We have already touched on some of the core issues raised in postmodern feminist thought by using the binary opposition of man/woman to illustrate postmodernism in Chapter 10. In keeping with its postmodern character, this form of feminism considers the way in which legal language and reasoning creates law's understanding of what gender and sexual equality mean, using techniques like deconstruction.[38] Postmodern feminism sees a basic flaw in the way in which traditional forms of feminism, particularly radical and cultural feminism, *essentialise* women — that is, they work from the assumption that the nature of women can be represented by a common experience which captures the 'essence' of what it is to be a woman in society.[39] Postmodern feminism focuses rather on the diversity and individual nature of women's experiences, emphasising the myriad different experiences which women have.

Black feminism

Black feminist thought takes issue with what it sees as the tendency of feminist writers to see race and gender as separate and mutually exclusive forms of experience. Its critique of feminism generally is that is based on the experiences

---

38 See Chapter 10 above, on postmodernism.
39 Note that Davies argues that radical feminism and postmodern feminism are not necessarily 'mutually exclusive' but can operate in parallel — see Davies, p 249ff.

and insights of privileged white females, and is in many cases not relevant to the experience of other groups of women. Feminist analyses often proceed from assumptions that the experience of discrimination by women in Western (white-dominated) cultures is in some way expressive of all women's experience.

This practice has the effect of marginalising the experience of women of colour, since feminism (particularly radical feminism) treats oppression on the basis of gender as the fundamental or most important form of oppression.[40] Analysing legal issues by concentrating on one form of inequality (either gender or race) without incorporating a critique of the other characteristic simplifies and distorts the picture which is created. Davies gives the example of rape, which from a radical feminist perspective is seen as an expression of male domination. This analysis, however, excludes the racial aspects which may be found by looking from other perspectives.[41]

Pragmatic feminism

As its name implies, pragmatic feminism is concerned with how discrimination and oppression actually occur in social and institutional practices, often from a historical perspective, rather than adopting any single theoretical position. Pragmatic feminism is geared to intervention and the removal of systemic oppression, and favours using any form of analysis which contributes to 'fixing things'. Pragmatic feminism has its roots in a range of other theoretical approaches, but draws heavily on Dewey's form of pragmatism.[42]

Anti-feminism

The beginning of the 21st century has heralded a negative reaction to feminist theories and feminism in some quarters. Young women now often do not see any problem with pornography (or many of the other issues which have been the subject of feminist critique). While this attitude may be seen to be politically driven, it sees a desirable outcome in women staying at home and looking after children, and sees judging as a neutral enterprise best carried out through the male eye – 'male' in this sense meaning neutral.

Recent research shows that there has been backsliding in female access to senior levels in the workforce in general.[43] The recent appointment of Australia's first female Chief Justice in Victoria has prompted conservative complaints that there are other, more deserving (male) candidates.

As with all forms of legal theory, the feminist legal project has not stopped, and will be the subject of ongoing change and development.

---

40 See Deborah King, "Multiple Jeopardy, Multiple Consciousness: The Context of Black Feminist Ideology" (1988) 14 *Signs* 42, extracted in Davies, p 237ff.
41 See Davies, p 238.
42 See Chapter 9 above, p 216, 'Just do it!'
43 See E Symons, "Back to the Ironing Board" in *The Weekend Australian*, "Review", pp 6–7.

Critical responses to feminism

Because of the different forms which feminism can take, there is no common ground which can function as a general critical response to feminism in itself. As Wacks observes, we can no more criticise feminism as a whole than we could be critical of an anti-racist stance[44] (although there have been criticisms that the exclusive concern of feminism for women's issues denies the 'universality' of law and legal institutions).

Critical responses to feminism need to be directed to the actual theoretical position or analysis being used, rather than to any underlying dispute with the starting point of inequality.

Most of the criticisms – many of which derive from *within* feminist thought and have been the basis for newer forms of feminist critique – are therefore directed at specific forms of feminism, and illustrate weaknesses or flaws which that particular form is claimed to demonstrate. Some of these include:

- radical feminism's argument that women are the subject of false consciousness (and necessarily unaware of it) seems to contradict the emphasis which is placed on women's own experience, suggesting that feminists 'know better';

- some forms of feminism, particularly radical and cultural feminism, are seen as *essentialising* woman – that is, they assume that there is a single or uniform female nature, and thus perpetuate stereotypes;

- some forms of feminism work from white middle class assumptions about gender in society, and ignore or marginalise the experience of women from other groups;

- liberal feminism 'buys into' the system, and uses a male standard as the benchmark for women.

QUESTIONS TO THINK ABOUT

1. Is the fact that I am male something which disentitles me to write about feminism?

2. Can you think of any areas of law where there is an underlying but unexpressed bias against women?

3. Do you think that legislative reform can correct the inequalities in society which disadvantage women?

4. Is every woman who does not see herself as oppressed necessarily suffering from false consciousness? What does this imply about radical feminism's view of the world?

5. Which of the arguments about pornography do you find more convincing (and why?). Does your answer depend on any fundamental assumptions about what law is and what it should be doing?

---

44 Wacks, R, *Swot: Jurisprudence*, 5th edition (Blackstone Press, London, 1999), p 230.

6. You are walking down a city street early in the morning and come across an injured child sheltering in a shop doorway. How would you respond? Does your response match up with Gilligan's finding about male and female responses?

7. Is it really the case that all women think about issues from an ethic of care?

8. How would it be possible to use feminist theory in the presentation of a case to the courts?

9. Can you find any examples where a feminist perspective has been accepted by the courts, and the law changed as a result?

10. If the position of women in society is attributable to their innate qualities and differences, or to the oppressive nature of male power, is significant change possible?

FURTHER READING

Barnett, Hilaire, *Introduction to Feminist Jurisprudence* (Cavendish Publishing, London, 1998).

Barnett, Hilaire, *Sourcebook on Feminist Jurisprudence* (Cavendish Publishing, London, 1997).

Bartlett, Katharine & Kennedy, Rosanne, *Feminist Legal Theory: Readings in Law and Gender* (Westview Press, Boulder, 1991).

Berns, Sandra, *To Speak as a Judge: Difference, Voice and Power* (Ashgate, Aldershot, 1999).

Bottomley, Anne (ed), *Feminist Perspectives on the Foundational Subjects of Law* (Cavendish Publishing, London, 1996).

Graycar, Regina & Morgan, Jenny, *The Hidden Gender of Law*, 2nd edition (Federation Press, Annandale, 2002).

hooks, bell, *Feminism is for Everybody: Passionate Politics* (Pluto Press, London, 2000).

James, Susan & Palmer, Stephanie (eds), *Visible Women: Essays on Feminist Legal Theory and Political Philosophy* (Hart Publishing, Oxford, 2002).

Lacey, Nicola, *Unspeakable Subjects: Feminist Essays in Legal and Social Theory* (Hart Publishing, Oxford, 1998).

McGlynn, Clare (ed), *Legal Feminisms: Theory and Practice* (Ashgate, Aldershot, 1998).

Naffine, Ngaire (ed), *Gender and Justice* (Ashgate, Aldershot, 2002).

Olsen, Frances (ed), *Feminist Legal Theory* (Ashgate, Aldershot, 1995).

Scutt, Jocelynne, *Women and the law: commentary and materials* (Law Book Company, Sydney, 1990).

Showalter, Elaine (ed), *The new feminist criticism* (Virago, London, 1986).

Smart, Carol, *Law Crime and Sexuality: Essays in Feminism* (Sage Publishing, London, 1995).

Thornton, Margaret, *Public and Private: Feminist Legal Debates* (Oxford University Press, Melbourne, 1995).

Critical Legal Theories

Reading. 271
Aim. 271
Principles 272
Being critical 272
Marxist legal theories. 274
CLS. 282
CST and law 287
Critical responses to these theories 290
Questions to think about 290
Further reading. 291

READING

DAVIES, *Asking the Law Question: the Dissolution of Legal Theory*, 2nd edition, Chapter 5, Chapter 3 (pp 102–112)
FREEMAN, *Lloyd's Introduction to Jurisprudence*, 7th edition, Chapter 8 (pp 683–703, 759–798), Chapter 12 (pp 965–969, 979–990, 1013–1019, 1031–1039), Chapter 13, Chapter 6 (pp 441–451, 481–497)

AIM

This chapter will introduce you to:

• the ideas and methods used by critical legal theory;
• the ways that critical legal theories change and develop as part of an ongoing critical project;
• what Marxist legal theories are, and how they have influenced critical legal theory;
• the Critical Legal Studies movement;
• the emerging legal theory based in contemporary social theory.

PRINCIPLES

Being critical

Multi-critical legal theories

How much critical legal theory can there be? Quite clearly, lots.[1] Critical legal theory can include all the non-conventional legal theories we have looked at in this book, and then some, as critical thought, by its own definition, is constantly open to change.[2] Being critical is not the sole preserve of non-conventional legal theory — even conventional legal theory will be critical of itself, its methods and its approaches.[3]

It seems that 'critical', 'critique', and 'criticism' are everywhere in this book and they are used differently from their ordinary meanings.

In this chapter, we will look at the Critical Legal Studies (CLS) movement, which was indebted to a form of theory called critical theory (as well as Marxism and American Legal Realism). See Figure 12.1, opposite.

We will look at critical theory shortly.

We will look at CLS a little later.

Back to the future

As we will see, CLS has discontinued as group, and its members and adherents are now taking different theoretical paths including postmodernism, psycho-analytical legal theory, law and aesthetics, and law and literature. But some remnants of the *ideas and methods* used by some members of CLS have morphed into an *emerging legal theory* that we will also look at in this chapter. We will briefly look at what we will call *contemporary social theory* (CST) to illustrate how ideas and methods can spin out of one theoretical orbit into another. CST, as a variant of sociology, is indebted to critical theory, Marxism in a variety of forms, history, poststructuralism, postmodernism and more. But please keep in mind that we are not saying that CLS became CST!

You will have guessed that non-conventional legal theories do not stand still, nor do they remain isolated from each other. As well, they are interdisciplinary, using the knowledge, methods and ideas of other non-legal disciplines to illuminate law's assumptions.[4] This chapter will give you an insight into the relationships, influences and connections that occur in an *ongoing critical project* that Margaret Davies talks about:[5] see the box 'Illustrating Connections', opposite.

---

1 Davies, pp 26–31, 167–169.
2 Critical legal theory can also describe theories that are 'critical' in a general sense. In Chapter 10 of R Wacks *Swot: Jurisprudence*, 5th edition (Blackstone Press, London, 1999), critical legal theory is used as an umbrella term, covering Critical Legal Studies, postmodernism, feminism and critical race theory. Wacks does not use the term 'critical' in the same way that we are using it here.
3 Davies, p 168. See Schauer in Lloyd, pp 441–451 for a critical form of positivism, and 'Positivisms of the 1990s' in Davies, pp 102–104.
4 We have seen this at work when we looked at aspects of sociological theory, postmodernism and feminist legal theories, and we will see it again with critical race theory and postcolonial legal theory.
5 See Davies, pp 167–169.

FIGURE 12.1: CRITICAL THEORIES TIMELINE

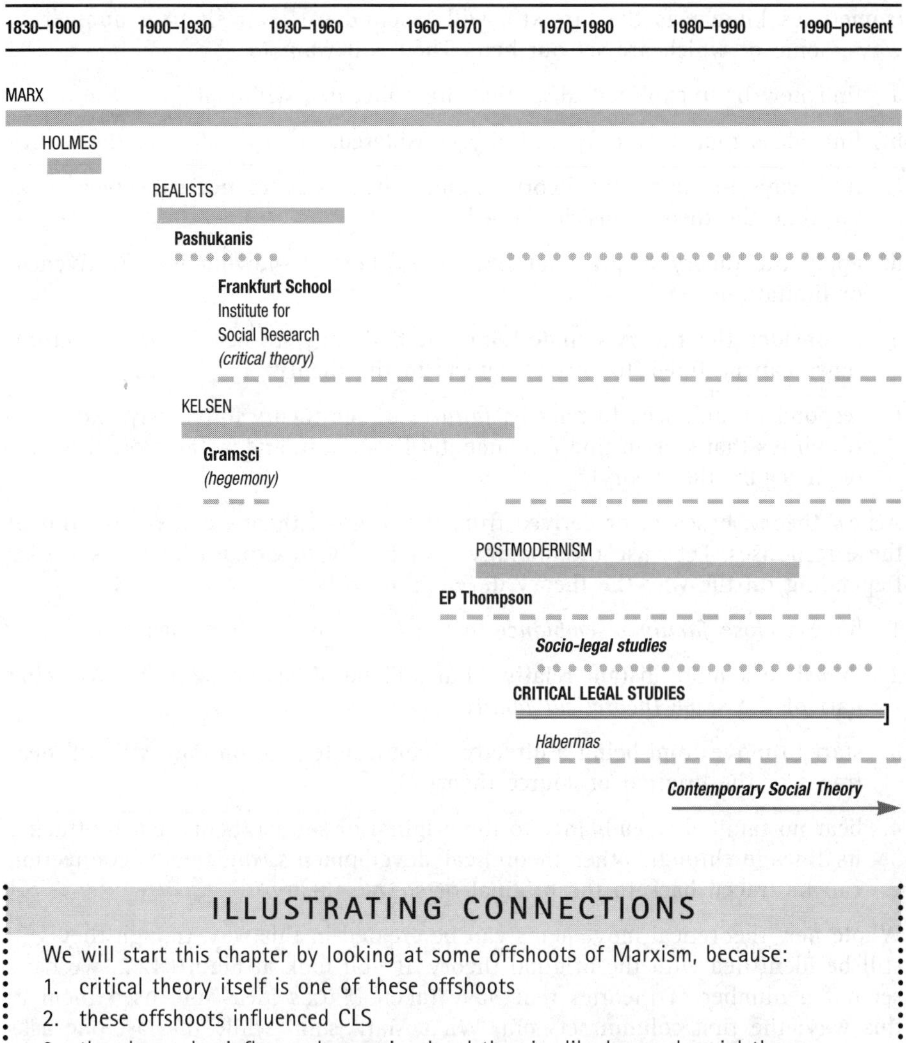

1830–1900	1900–1930	1930–1960	1960–1970	1970–1980	1980–1990	1990–present

MARX

HOLMES

REALISTS

Pashukanis

Frankfurt School
Institute for
Social Research
(critical theory)

KELSEN

Gramsci
(hegemony)

POSTMODERNISM

EP Thompson

Socio-legal studies

CRITICAL LEGAL STUDIES

Habermas

Contemporary Social Theory

ILLUSTRATING CONNECTIONS

We will start this chapter by looking at some offshoots of Marxism, because:

1. critical theory itself is one of these offshoots
2. these offshoots influenced CLS
3. they have also influenced emerging legal theories like law and social theory.

If you look ahead at Figures 12.3 and 12.4, you will see how complex these relationships and developments can be. We will return to these figures later in this chapter, so don't worry about the detail.

How are these offshoots and new theories created?

In Chapter 2, you will remember that we showed how basic knowledge will be transformed by being applied, analysed, synthesised and evaluated.[6] In the same way, a source or original theory will be analysed, examined, and criticised to

---

6   See pp 33–37 above.

expose its deficiencies and weaknesses, or applauded for bringing to light new insights.[7] Other theorists who *like and accept* the *source or original theory* (sometimes known as the 'urtext'), will respond to it afresh in a number of ways, some of which are set out here. They will want to:

a. find new or unexplored ideas that are concealed within it

b. find ideas that were only partially considered, or explicated, in the theory

c. find ways to adapt the theory to new circumstances not conceived of at the time the theory was developed

d. apply the theory to practical situations, thereby showing its effectiveness or limitations

e. reconsider the theory's underlying methodology, to see if any structural flaws can be fixed, to correct defects in the theory

f. respond to, and seek to remedy, *failures* of the theory (obviously excluding responses that seek to find fundamental flaws in it, and to therefore discount or disregard the theory).

A new theory, based in or derived from the original theory, can emerge out of these responses. Let's use the analogy of a family to explain how this works. Depending on the way the theory develops it will:

1. have a *close family resemblance* to the source or original theory

2. look like a more distant relative, but still be highly recognisable as being part of the *same theoretical family*

3. start to move from being a directly recognisable relation, but will still bear traces of the original or source theory

4. bear no familial resemblance to the original or source theory, but by tracing its lineage through other theoretical developments, the family connection can be traced back to the original or source theory.

Whole new theoretical movements can be created in this way, though they will still be identified with the original theory. If you look at Figure 12.2, we have set out a number of theories that have taken Marx's ideas and used them in this way: the first column sets out 'What Marx said', while the last one asks 'Is this new Marxist theory close to Marx's ideas?' Don't worry about the detail yet, but you might want to think about how closely or distantly related the theory is to Marx.

The same techniques can be used for any theory, not just for Marx.

Marxist legal theories

Haven't we already 'done' Marx?

In Chapter 8, we looked at Marx's social theories, but we have not spent any time considering the offshoots of Marx's theories, called Marxist or Marxian

---

7 We saw some of the ways that theories are criticised in Chapter 9, pp 222–224 above.

legal theories (MLT).[8] Most MLTs are interested in questions of ideology, the role of institutions (not just government), and the liberal ideal in law in maintaining inequalities in society. They have shifted away from Marx's emphasis on class structure, the demise of capitalism, and revolution. Along with Marx's own ideas, the MLTs have influenced CLS and CLT (critical legal theory), as well as postmodernism, poststructuralism, some feminist thought and some critical race and postcolonial theory. We will look at two of these – critical theory and hegemony – in a little more detail later in this section because of their influence on critical legal theories. We have set out a number of key MLTs in Figure 12.2.

We will pull out two MLTs to show you how you can use Figure 12.2. Of course, the table is not a substitute for reading the theories or descriptions of them in your texts. The first MLT we will look at is (1) *The blunt instrument approach*, which is a very close family member of Marx's original theory. It wanted to show how law was used to coerce the working class and to support the dominant class's own interests, including its moral interests. Why is it an MLT if it is so close to Marx's own ideas? Simply because it is not Marx's own theory, and because it is an example of how a theory can be applied to practical situations to show its effectiveness.[9]

DO YOU REMEMBER THE 'OZ' CASE?

In Chapter 5, we talked about the *Oz* trial in the context of liberal ideals of freedom of expression. A blunt instrument analysis of the prosecution of the publishers and their original conviction would say that the law was used to repress non-ruling views and morals.

The second MLT we will look at is a more distant relative, (2) *EP Thompson's relative autonomy model*. This MLT *disputes* some of the fundamental ideas of Marx: that law is part of the base or infrastructure, and that law will always be used to deny the interests of ordinary people. EP Thompson did not accept Marx's assumption of stable class structures,[10] so he took issue with Marx's underlying methodology. Thompson used a new methodology, which saw class formation as an ongoing process. He was able to show how the law would not be used against ordinary people in all cases, but not just to assert that the law was always just and fair. He also sought to remedy a *failure* of the theory,[11] to ensure that the subtleties of ideological domination, which a fair legal system would hide, were made apparent.[12]

---

8 The range and types of Marxist legal theories is set out in Alan Hunt 'Marxism, Legal Theory and Jurisprudence' in Fitzpatrick, Peter (ed) *Dangerous supplements: resistance and renewal in jurisprudence* (Pluto Press, London, 1991), p 102.
9 See point d above, p 274.
10 See point e above, p 274.
11 See point f above, p 274.
12 Cf Lloyd, pp 986–987, which suggests that EP Thompson wholeheartedly accepted the rule of law. A different reading of Thompson suggests that he maintained a scepticism not indicated in Lloyd's commentary.

FIGURE 12.2: MARXIST LEGAL THEORIES — EXTRAPOLATING FROM MARX

What Marx said	What question follows?	How is this played out?	Coming up with a new theory	Is this new Marxist theory close to Marx's ideas?
1 **Marx says law is part of the super-structure maintaining the base**	Does law maintain the economic interests of the dominant class?	• Law emphasises property and commercial interests • Law cannot help but support the interests of capital over other interests • Law discriminates against the working classes • Lawyers have a natural tendency to support the existing practices of law • Law supports the moral values of the dominant class • Property offences harshly treat workers, while white collar crime is treated leniently[A]	1960s–1970s (still has some influence) **The blunt instrument approach:**[B] Law is used as an instrument of social control and to maintain class power	• The social control reading of Marx is very close to Marx's base/superstructure model • This type of interpretation is sometimes referred to as 'vulgar' or 'crude' Marxism because of its relative lack of sophistication
2 **Marx established a clear separation and structure of class interests, divided between bourgeoisie and proletariat**	Does law more subtly work to support the system of capital than a simple class-based explanation would suggest? Is the law such a blunt instrument?	• The Marxist historian **EP Thompson** saw class as contingent and as a process, not a fixed structure • He wanted to find out what *happened historically*[C] • Did the legal profession act in the interests of the dominant class? • In 18th century England repressive legislation was read down by judges and magistrates contrary to the desire of the ruling classes	1960s–1990s (considerable interest maintained) **Law had to abide by its own rhetoric** *But this meant:* Law was *more subtly* used to maintain power than the blunt instrument model would suggest	• This **relative autonomy model** moves considerably from Marx's class-based methods • Thompson's *anti-structuralist* reading of Marx led to a freeing up of the understanding of the relationships in society • Ruling classes would abide by the law because it gave their dominance legitimacy – to do otherwise would leave the law open to the claim that it did not abide by its own rhetoric
3 **Marx claimed that law was part of the superstructure**	Does all law exist to support the economic?	• EP Thompson found that existing practices or immemorial usage would be converted into law, and these conversions could not be explained in economic terms	1960s–1990s (considerable interest maintained) **Law is not simply part of the super-structure**	• Law operates within the infra-structure, which contradicts (most of) Marx's claims

A See Lloyd, pp 965–969.
B See EP Thompson's description of this instrumental reading of Marx in Lloyd, p 1013, p 1017.
C See p 198 above; Lloyd, pp 986–987; EP Thompson 'Whigs and Hunters', pp 1013–1019.

What Marx said	What question follows?	How is this played out?	Coming up with a new theory	Is this new Marxist theory close to Marx's ideas?
4 **Marx assumed that law, as part of the superstructure, supports the economic form, the base**	But is the economic form instead *embedded* within law itself?	• **Pashukanis** argues that all forms of behaviour are commodified, and turned into a *contract* model • Individuals are treated as objects of exchange • This includes social relations as well as economic relations • All forms of social behaviour are given an equivalent exchange value • The commodity form assumes formal equality on the part of its 'owners' • An abstract relationship created through the commodity form is based in appropriation and alienation[D]	**1920s–1930s** (popularised by Isaac Balbus in the 1970s and remains influential) **Commodity-form theory** There is no need for law and its personnel to reflect or impose class-based differences because the law itself embeds the needs of capital in its very form	• As well as base/superstructure theory, Pashukanis relies upon Marx's construction of use and exchange value, and alienation • It takes these aspects of Marx's theory and connects it to one of law's fundamental forms – contract – to reconsider the relations between individuals and groups in the system of capital • Pashukanis suggest that law contributes to the process of alienation by turning individuals into an abstract commodity form that disregards their personal and social differences
5 **Marx identified that ruling ideas, found in the superstructure, supported the interests of the dominant class.** **The state coerced people to behave according to its wishes, and therefore those of the dominant class**	Could *ruling ideas* – culture, law, values and beliefs – be the basis for class domination, and not economics? Did the state impose these beliefs?	• **Gramsci** argued that dissent is minimised in capitalist societies through an acceptance of ruling ideas by everyone in society • These ideas are not *directly* imposed from above by the state through coercion or repression • Society's 'educators' include the law, media, mass culture and education • Ruling ideas are accepted by persuasion and negotiation[E]	**1920s–1930s** (considerable ongoing influence since it became available in the 1970s) Gramsci called this **hegemony** – dominant classes direct and organise society through their cultural and ideological power; other classes consent to those views, beliefs and values Law hides its capitalist leanings or moral values. We adopt the values of the dominant class through ideals of justice, neutrality and the rule of law	• This theory shifts away from Marx's theory in a dramatic fashion because it disconnects base from superstructure, and the economic fundamentals of Marx's theory • It adopts a process model (adopted by EP Thompson) and treats the hegemonic process as ongoing

---

D   Pashukanis, 'Law and Marxism' in Lloyd, pp 1031–1039, commentary pp 982–986.
E   Lloyd, p 981.

What Marx said	What question follows?	How is this played out?	Coming up with a new theory	Is this new Marxist theory close to Marx's ideas?
6 **Marx assumed the inevitability of the revolution**	How did capitalism survive? Why did authoritarian states prevail in the 1920s and 1930s? What were the effects of mass communication?	• The problem Marx identified needed to be realigned in the face of the world order of the 1920s and mass society • Citizens had lost their capacity to fully participate in society • Rampantly developing technology threatens humanity • Reason could be used as a repressive tool against humanity	**1920s–present** (currently Habermas) **Frankfurt School** or **Critical Theory** New forms of critical analysis were adopted through Kant, Hegel and Marx, and psychoanalysis. Habermas has now revitalised enlightenment ideals through the idea of uncoerced participation in the public sphere	It shifted beyond Marx to the extent that its origins are now virtually unrecognisable, especially in its current forms It retains some underlying methodological connection to Marx in relation to critique
7 **The dominant class maintains ideology for its own purposes**	How is this ideology transmitted?	• **Althusser** argues that ideology drives the conditions that enable capitalism to occur, not the other way around • The State maintains the desired ideology needed to repress groups in society • The dominant class can get the State to carry out its requests and wants, so the state is used to coercively achieve outcomes • Law is a prime site of coercion and manufactures the ideas needed for capitalism to function	**1960s–1970s** (interest has waned at present) **Ideological State Apparatuses** (ISAs) are used to maintain the ruling or dominant class' interests ISAs extend to 'non-state' forms of control, like family and communication The state sanctions acceptable modes of conduct and behaviour at all levels of society	Althusser turns Marx around by placing ideology first and capital second Althusser is indebted to Gramsci's insights, but this theory stays rigidly within a class-based system The structural foundation of Althusser's position runs contrary to EP Thompson's approach

WHY BOTHER WITH METHODS?

Using different methods leads to different results. If you understand the basis underlying a theory, you will better understand the theorist's intention than if you simply look at the information the theorist will use to support their argument. It is possible to misunderstand their argument if their method is disregarded or misunderstood.

Think of it like cooking. If you follow the method of putting an unshelled raw egg into a pan of boiling water, you will get a boiled egg. If you want to get a boiled egg but you crack the egg open and fry it, you have followed the wrong method, and will get something else. You might like the result, but you have misunderstood the process.

This does not stop a theorist (like EP Thompson) using a new method to see if this will achieve a better result: like adopting the correct method to get fried eggs.

Critical theory

One of the reasons why a new theory will develop is the need to adapt the theory to new circumstances. By the 1920s it had become apparent that capitalism, despite Marx's revolutionary prediction, was going to survive. Not only that, but totalitarianism (a dictatorial government that required people to be totally subservient to the state) had overtaken the purportedly communist Russia, while in Germany and Italy the seeds of totalitarianism — Nazism and Fascism — were starting to bear fruit amongst the disaffected working class. The USA, capitalism's shining star, was characterised by a new technologically-driven, impersonal mass society.

In 1924, the Institute for Social Research,[13] or *Frankfurt School*, began a form of multidisciplinary critical social theorising to pick up Marx's social idealism and humanism. They reinvigorated Hegel's idealism[14] in an attempt to prevent ordinary people being seduced into totalitarianism. Their ideas were based, in part, on the notion that the ideals of the Enlightenment had been betrayed. The modern world created unbridled materialism. Instead of emancipating ordinary people, it led to their exploitation, and resulted in their dehumanisation.

The Frankfurt School's members included Horkheimer, Adorno and Marcuse, all of whom had different intellectual and disciplinary interests, including sociology, philosophy, linguistics and art. Their work was grounded in modernism.[15] Seeing a failure in Marx's emphasis on economics, their work focused on the role of culture and aesthetics and human interaction. As well as Marx, Hegel and Kant, they were also influenced by Freudian psychoanalysis, in part to uncover the influence of desire on humanity. By 1934, as Nazism took hold, the Institute closed and its members moved to the USA, where it was re-established. In the 1950s some of the members of the Frankfurt School

---

13 Frankfurt University, Germany.
14 See Chapter 8 above.
15 See Chapter 4 above.

returned to Germany, and in its current form, it operates well beyond its origins, through the work of Jürgen Habermas.[16]

While critical theory has been through a number of phases, some of its key theoretical structures were formed during its earliest years. The reason why we have plotted out a brief history of critical theory is to fulfil an aspect of its theoretical mission, which is to *make explicit* the basis on which observations of the theorist are made. We have also told the Frankfurt school's story to situate and explain aspects of their critical project that are relevant for our purposes:

- Knowledge: critical theory denies that it is possible for 'facts' to be pre-formed, able to be objectively determined and value-free. *Critical theory seeks to trace the origins of those facts.*

- Society: critical theory sees individuals as *enmeshed* within the social and historical web in which they are situated and connected. *Critical theory wants these inter-subjective relationships and connections to be made explicit.*

- '(Con)fessing up': critical theory wants to practice what it preaches. It is impossible for a theorist to be able to 'stand outside themselves' to impartially and objectively see the world, and 'describe' what they see out there. Everyone observing the world is the product of their history, society, and other contexts, so supposedly 'objective' observations will be affected by these factors. Critical theory says that theory itself is influenced by and embeds these factors. *Critical theorists are therefore required to identify and establish their own theoretical position.*[17]

> **You might think that this looks the same as postmodernism.**
>
> Critical theory is not the same as postmodernism. It is a modernist theory, but its critique-oriented techniques were adopted by some postmodern and poststructural theorists.

Why is critical theory relevant for law? The techniques of critical theory provide a useful tool by which accepted theoretical positions can be uncovered, and then challenged. If modernism and liberalism claim that their position is uncontaminated by social and historical factors, then critical theory will seek to uncover why they make this claim.[18] These techniques open the way towards asking whether key assumptions of modernism and liberalism, such as *reason* and *objectivity*, are socially and historically constructed, and not naturally

---

16 Critical theory has not remained in any one form. By the 1980s, it had moved well away from its origins into the current work of Jürgen Habermas. His focus on inter-subjectivity (the relationships between people), among other things, influenced his theory of communicative action. In part, this theory seeks to give individuals a valued place in the public arena. Habermas' theoretical premise is highly complex and difficult to do justice to in this context, and is beyond the scope of this book. You may want to look at some of the ways his theory is played out in connection with law in the extract in Lloyd: Habermas 'Between Facts and Norms: An Author's Reflections' pp 794–798. Habermas' ideas about law fit into his wider theoretical premise. The commentary in Lloyd, pp 693–697, takes him to task for his failure at developing a sociological legal theory without necessarily considering the underlying influence of his theory of communicative action. You may want to think about all these observations for yourselves.

17 We have relied on Davies' account of their project here: see Davies, pp 167–168.

18 See Chapters 4–6 above.

ordained. They challenge the empiricist and positivist sociologies of Talcott Parsons that have influenced sociological theories of law[19] (which disregard the social formations of knowledge) and have influenced the CST we will look at later in this chapter.

As you will have realised, critical theory has shifted well beyond its origins in Marx. Its emergence in CLS and its transmission to CLT have ensured its place as an 'urtext' in its own right, albeit one which is also going through a process of continual change and adaptation. Which version of critical theory is being used is something you will need to keep your eye on, and you will also have to be aware that other theories which are critical generally, though not part of Frankfurt School critical theory, will also be called 'critical theory'. You will need to be alert to these variations and the looseness of terminology.

Hegemony

Another reason why new theories develop is to consider ideas that were only partially considered, or explicated, in the original theory. **Antonio Gramsci** (1891–1937), wanted to understand why working people would act against their own (class) interests without being forced to do so. Gramsci was a Marxist philosopher, Italian Communist Party founder, and member of parliament, who was arrested and imprisoned by the Fascist Government in 1926, and remained imprisoned until he died at the age of 46. His works were virtually unknown until the 1960s and only generally accessible after 1975.

Relying on the political philosopher Machiavelli and the sociologist, Pareto, as well as Marx, Gramsci argued that people *consented* to the interests of the dominant class, but not because they were told to. The dominant classes instead organise society using their *cultural power* to achieve dominance through a subtle *negotiation* process. Gramsci called this process 'hegemony', through which dissent is minimised. Rather than have the state impose its views, the more effective way for the values of the ruling or dominant classes to be made apparent was through cultural power: law, the media, social values and beliefs.

PROSECUTION FOR CORRUPTING PUBLIC MORALS

Oz magazine, London, May 1970 edition (Number 28)

Imagine living in 1970s England. What would you have thought of the long-haired radical anti-Establishment editors allowing schoolkids to edit their magazine, *Oz*, using sexually explicit material, and containing revolutionary Marxist material? Were you an ordinary reasonable person who considered such behaviour anathema to the moral fabric of society? Or would you have been keen to break the shackles of a narrow regimented society and set swinging London alight?

CHAPTER 12

---

19 See Chapter 9 above.

It was only a few years after the Hart–Devlin morals debate,[20] so how would the law deal with the moral outrage that accompanied the case? Ruling views were in a state of flux, ranging from Hart's permissiveness to Lord Devlin's moral outrage. Reflecting the approach of ordinary people, the judge at first instance instructed the jury on the basis of a moral panic. The editors were found guilty, imprisoned, and were forced to have their hair cut. Public outrage followed, and on appeal, their convictions were overturned.[21] Thirty years on, one of the schoolkid editors called the prosecution a cultural war.[22] Law perhaps carried out its hegemonic role by ensuring justice, but in this instance, law, society, morals, and the media were on the edge of a cultural change.

At the beginning of the 21st century, the pendulum has swung back the other way in Australia – wearing the wrong T shirt will lead to arrest and conviction for obscenity – the current hegemony refects a conservative return to moral behaviour.

CLS

What is CLS?

The rebelliousness that gripped England in the 1960s was a polite version of the revolutionary movements that emerged in 1960s USA: Vietnam demonstrations, the Woodstock rock festival, and the practical effects of the liberation movements – gay, black and women's. Lawyers were in the thick of the social change of the 1960s, helping out in civil liberties cases, staffing 'shopfront' law centres which provided free legal advice for people in need. At the same time, radical law academics were sacked from Yale, an 'Ivy League' law school, and student radicalism infected the atmosphere at other law schools. The American version of CLS appeared to be most fundamentally disenchanted because they saw the reality of law to be at odds with the values of liberalism and freedom that permeated American legal thinking.[23]

A deep dissatisfaction with what law stood for led to questioning its very fabric. Now everything was up for grabs – law's underlying political values, its supposed neutrality, objectivity and fairness, its methods of legal reasoning, the origins of its doctrines, law teaching, law's procedures and practices. At the end of the 1960s and in the early 1970s, individual CLS scholars were starting to undertake research and scholarship into these topics,[24] before a (now) famous first CLS conference held at Madison, Wisconsin in 1977, which gave a greater focus to the work of these scholars, who were also called 'the crits'. But like the American Legal Realists, the crits also adopted different approaches and interests. Here are some of the strands of CLS thought:[25]

---

20 This debate, which occurred during the latter part of the 1950s and 1960s between HLA Hart and Lord Devlin, originally formed one of the key disputes in jurisprudence. Its influence is now historical: Lloyd, pp 362–367.
21 See Geoffrey Robertson, *The Justice Game* (Vintage, London, 1999), Chapter One, for a full account.
22 Charles Shaar Murray, 'I was an Oz schoolkid' *The Guardian*, Thursday 2 August 2001
    http://www.guardian.co.uk/g2/story/0,3604,530949,00.html
23 Versions of CLS took hold in the UK and Australia.
24 See Davies, p 174, for some of the key early CLS thinkers. We will talk generally about the movement and some of its main ideas rather than look at the work of individual CLS scholars.
25 We won't pretend that we have covered all the variations and permutations of the CLS project. Davies' account of CLS looks at the themes of CLS: Davies pp 170–175. Lloyd includes a good selection of 'crit-lit' that illustrates the CLS strands we set out here. We have left out the way the crits sought to revise legal eduction, which now forms the way many law schools teach law: see Duncan Kennedy, 'The ideological content of legal education' in Lloyd, pp 1104–1108.

1. Conventional approaches claim that law contains neutral, abstract principles uninfected by politics, society, and personal viewpoint. CLS argues that not only is it impossible to keep these factors out of legal reasoning and decision-making, but by hiding behind its cloak, these legal catchcries will obscure the way that law can be used to obtain whatever result it wants.

2. Law claims to be a complete system of rules, norms and doctrines, but CLS says that law is open to be played with, and that rather than being determinate (or certain), it is instead indeterminate (or uncertain). What this means is that legal decision-makers will 'pick and choose' doctrine to fit the desired result.

3. We assume that legal principles, legal categories are not simply organisational categories, but 'the real thing'. We talk about contract, for instance, as if it was part of the fabric of the universe, but this is a 'false necessity'. Instead, CLS says that it is not that these principles and categories are not real, but that we could actually organise social relations differently, to not favour the sectors of society who can use law to their advantage.

4. Law operates as an alienating force in society,[26] by turning people against each other. Every time you assert a right against someone else, you are alienating yourself from society, which hardens existing social structures, disadvantage or advantage, into a permanent form. Look back at Figure 10.5 in Chapter 10 (p 238), which illustrates the difference between the relationships of individuals in modernism and postmodernism. The image also illustrates the difference between alienated individuals in (liberal, modern) society, and the webs of interconnection that would exist in a non-alienated society.

5. We assume that we all have unassailable rights that the law will protect, but CLS says that rights are a furphy. Because rights are abstract (they are not grounded in the specific forms of human life), they can be manipulated. One person's right to free speech will be destroyed if it clashes with a more acceptable right to liberal society, such as protecting property. Rights will be empty of meaning if they cannot be given effect.

6. CLS confronts the idea of liberal legalism as an unqualified 'good thing'. The crits tackle the idea that law expresses liberal values, as well as taking issue with the society that gives law its validity and form.[27] Law reflects an alienated society, so law alienates through its doctrines and practices. Law privileges objectivity and reason as being value-free rather than recognising the way these notions deeply embed political or social choices, while dismissing 'subjectivity' and individual circumstances as unstable and wrong-headed.

CHAPTER 12

---

26 See Chapter 8 above, p 194.
27 See Chapters 4–7 above.

FOR THE CRITS, CONTRACT LAW STANDS FOR EVERYTHING WRONG WITH LAW:

- It represents the type of legal action needed in an alienated society, where individuals must assert formal rights against each other.
- Through its formal structures, it masks inequality that became embedded in contract doctrines during the 19th century's laissez-faire period.
- It assumes that parties are formally equal and disregards individual circumstances as subjective and unstable.
- It favours of objective tests, but can choose the 'right' rule to get the 'best' outcome in the case.
- We cannot imagine a world without contract law.

It is liberal legalism in action![28]

FIGURE 12.3: MORPHING THEORY — THE RISE AND DEMISE OF CLS AND ITS TRANSFORMATION AND REDIRECTIONS

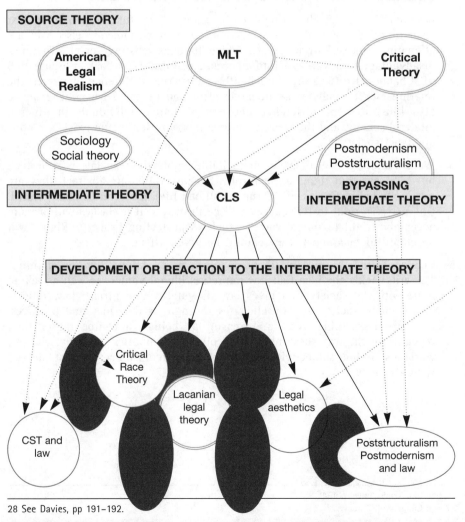

28 See Davies, pp 191–192.

FIGURE 12.4: CONNECTING THE THEORETICAL METHODS: INFLUENCING CLS TO CST

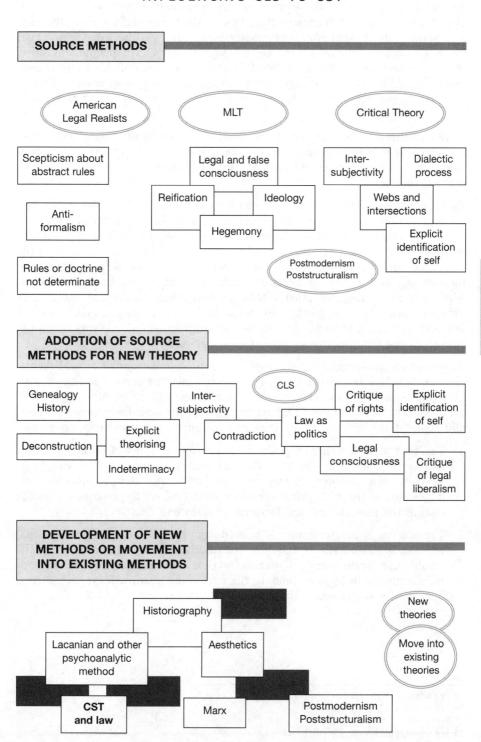

Finding where the crits got their ideas

You might find some of the strands of CLS very familiar to you – a little bit of postmodernism and deconstruction, lots of MLTs (especially critical theory,[29] hegemony, and Pashukanis' commodity-form theory), the American Legal Realists, and some sociology. We are not saying that CLS is plagiarising other theories; rather, as we saw with the MLTs at the beginning of this chapter, each theory builds on another theory, and comes up with a new approach. We can trace the influences of other theories on CLS in the top part of the diagram in Figure 12.3 (p 284).

If we take this one step further, we can start to find those theoretical techniques and methods that inform or influence a theory. Figure 12.4 (p 285) shows how *new techniques* were used and adapted by CLS from the source methods of the original theories.

Knowing where the ideas come from can help us understand why the crits adopt their particular political or other standpoint, why they use certain ways of writing or other forms of language, and where their method came from. We won't be able to walk you through all the theories or methods included in the diagrams, but you will be able to use them when you are working your way through any reading by or about the crits to check if you have worked out what they are saying. In other words, knowing their theoretical pedigree or influence can tell us so much more about their ideas. This can help if we get lost amongst trashing, nihilism, deconstruction, contradiction, demystification, delegitimating, marginality, or other CLS buzz words.

Of course, by knowing about the psychoanalytic foundations of critical theory, through which a theorist will need to situate their own standpoint, we may now understand why the crits spend so much time talking about themselves.[30] Let's return to the strands of CLS thought and identify some theoretical pedigrees, and some of the techniques the crits used to uncover the problems they saw:

1. The idea that law has a political dimension is derived from the *blunt instrument* approaches of MLT, the *fact skeptic* strands of American Legal Realism, and sociology.[31] One way the crits will seek to uncover this dimension is by examining the foundations of legal principles, through tracing the genealogies and histories of rules and doctrines.

2. The concept of indeterminacy is derived from critical theory, American Legal Realism, postmodernism and poststructuralism. Language-based, the crits would use techniques of deconstruction to uncover incoherence or indeterminacy in legal method, or the crits could also *trash* (or deconstruct) doctrines, assumptions and methods.[32]

---

29 See Lloyd, pp 1051–1052.
30 See Davies, p 177.
31 See Chapter 9 above.
32 See Davies, pp 180–186.

3. When we assume legal principles are real, we *reify* them.[33] We forget that they were made up in the first place, and cannot imagine functioning without them. The crits would expose reification through deconstructive historical and genealogical techniques, and this reflects the concern of critical theory to source the origins of 'facts'.

4. Imagining an alienated society returns us to Marx's original concept of alienation.[34] It also takes us to critical theory's concerns about inter-subjectivity and the historical relationships and connections between people in society. The crits would undertake all the forms of critical scholarship that we have discussed to demonstrate how law alienated.

5. A critique of rights invokes reification, commodity-form theory, hegemony, and the psychoanalytic concept of 'denial', inherited from critical theory. We engage in denial because we *want to believe* that we have rights, but our own experience belies the promise of those rights. The contradiction between hope and reality is too great to cope with, and we hide behind what we want to believe – in other words, we are in denial. The crits would again adopt all forms of critical scholarship to expose this situation.

6. We will leave liberal legalism for you to work out!

What happened to CLS?

By the mid-1990s the American version of CLS, as a defined movement, was over,[35] with considerable speculation as to the reasons *why* it ended. While other theories have come and gone,[36] our interest in the end of CLS (though not of the people themselves, it should be pointed out) is perhaps linked to our own *denial* about the end of a once flourishing movement. We shan't speculate ourselves, but thought we would point out some of the theoretical homes where ex-crits now reside. If we go back to Figures 12.3 and 12.4, we will see that some crits now work within postmodernism, or a form of psychoanalytic technique derived from the work of Lacan. Some have simply developed the theoretical approach, or moved out into other theories like feminist legal theory or the race and Lat-crits.[37]

The end of CLS is not the end of critical forms of thinking about law.

CST and law

So what is CST?

'Social theory' can have many meanings. Marxism is a 'social theory', as is sociology (you will often see the term 'sociology' used interchangeably with 'social theory', though this excludes exclusively scientific types of sociology).

33 Reification is a concept derived from Marx and developed by the Hungarian Marxist thinker Lukacs.
34 See Chapter 8 above, p 194.
35 Davies, pp 168–169, 193–195; Lloyd, pp 1055–1056.
36 See Chapter 9 above, on the realists.
37 See Chapter 13 below, pp 299–303; Lloyd, p 1055.

The social theory with which we associate CST (contemporary social theory) investigates the assumptions made about individuals in society, including questions of identity. Social theory examines the composition, structure, and development of social phenomena and knowledge – including culture, economics, law and politics – in both contemporary and historical contexts. It looks at the function of the public 'space', including the role of institutions like law, and the influence of civil society, including the nature of power in a society, and the forms of agency and rationality. It will also engage in critical assessments of social science literature to investigate existing descriptions, analyses and critiques of social forms. An explicitly *critical* social theory fashions another dimension to social theory, by overtly engaging with its own presuppositions and role in the social world. It will establish its own foundations to explain its reasons for supporting or criticising the institutions, practices and thought processes that inform the social world, and will encourage overlaps between the practices of disciplines to assist in explaining social phenomena.

You may have recognised some concepts here – some from Habermas and critical theory, variations of Marxist thought, classical forms of sociology, postmodernism, poststructuralism, feminist theories, political theory and cultural studies, among others. Social theory is an interdisciplinary and multidisciplinary form of study, which emerged in the 1960s as a reaction to the types of objectivist social science research associated with Talcott Parsons.[38]

A little genealogy

One of the reasons why the American crits set up their own conference was because they were dissatisfied with the Law and Society Association,[39] with which a number of them had been associated.[40] Instead of adopting a form of critical inquiry into law and its social forms, the law and society movement had become associated with the narrow forms of social research based in behaviourism and empiricism.[41] This type of research disregarded the types of questions the crits were engaging with, in favour of looking at the institutions and practices of law in an unquestioning way.[42]

The crits' dissatisfaction with law and society paved the way for the emergence of CLS in its own right. But by the 1980s, a critical form of law and society was emerging in the USA which relied on some of the ideas of *social theory* to supplement the sociological methods used by law and society.[43] In the UK, *critical legal theory* (CLT) emerged out of Critical Lawyers Groups, which by

---

38 See Chapter 9 above.

39 See Lloyd, p 1040.

40 David Trubeck, one of the original crits, sets out a history of the law and society movement, which explains the basis of the problems of the law and society movement at that time. He also charts some of the changes that we can see as a nascent contemporary social theory: Trubeck, 'Back to the Future: The Short and Happy Life of the Law and Society Movement' in Lloyd, pp 766–774.

41 Cf Silbey and Sarat, 'Critical Traditions in Law and Society Research' in Lloyd, pp 774–779.

42 Lloyd, pp 684–687. Lloyd called this research 'socio-legal studies'. It is perhaps misleading, as contemporary socio-legal research does not adopt these characteristics. Lloyd calls the contemporary form 'critical empiricisms', pp 697–700. Also see Nelken 'Blinding Insights? The Limits of a Reflexive Sociology of Law' in Lloyd, pp 759–766.

43 Silbey and Sarat, op cit, p 774.

the early 1990s had grown more along the lines of *social theory* than CLS in its American form. CLT relied upon critical theory, postmodernism and post-structuralism and feminist thought to uncover the role of law within social structures.[44] But the American crits were also dipping into *social theory* (in a loose sense) through critical theory and hegemony, to consider the contingency of social relations and their effect and relationship with law.

What is the relationship between law and CST?

Lloyd makes the point that CLS showed the importance of integrating legal theory with social theory.[45] Social theory is now taught in law schools, though often contained to classic sociology and postmodernism, but the type of integrative social theory we described earlier has been adopted in some courses. At the London School of Economics, topics in the Law and Social Theory course look at 'Law, Modernity and Society, Rules and the Boundaries of the Social' and 'The Human and the Social Subject'.[46] Texts such as Banakar and Travers' *An introduction to law and social theory* show the way that social theory has recently made a foray into law. A range of social theories are discussed in their book, reflecting the broad and interdisciplinary interests of social theory,[47] and the insights they provide into law.

Social theory provides a way of engaging with the social constructs that characterise the legal project. But is it a viable project? Law appears to have an affinity with the objectivist sociology that has tended to characterise the sociological project in law: it is 'real', which makes sense to law's empiricist tendencies. Social theory, on the other hand, as a form of critical legal theory, takes a far broader interest in social questions beyond knowledge and data.[48] Will an emerging legal theory, such as CST, encounter the kinds of territorial disputes over the proper role of legal theory that we have traced throughout this chapter?

---

44 Grigg-Spall, Ian & Ireland, Paddy (eds) *The critical lawyers' handbook* (Pluto Press, London, 1992) which was published as part of the Law and Social Theory Series.

45 See Lloyd, pp 1051–1052.

46 http://www.lse.ac.uk/resources/calendar/courseGuides/2003-LL465.htm

47 Banakar, Reza & Travers, Max (eds) *An introduction to law and social theory* (Hart, Oxford, 2002).It is set out in six sections:

1. *Classical Sociology and Law:* The Problematisation of Law in Classical Social Theory. Sociological Jurisprudence.

2. *Systems Theory:* The Thick Description of Law: An Introduction to Niklas Luhmann's Theory. Jurgen Habermas and the Sociology of Law.

3. *Critical Approaches:* Marxism and the Social Theory of Law. Sharing the Paradigms? Critical Legal Studies and the Sociology of Law. Feminist Legal Theory. A Raced and Gendered Organisational Logic in Law Firms. Putting Gender and Sexuality on the Agenda. The Power of the Legal Field.

4. *Interpretive Approaches:* Symbolic Interactionism and Law. Ethnomethodology and Law.

5. *Postmodernism:* Foucault and Law. Postmodernism and Common Law.

6. *Pluralism and Globalisation:* Legal Pluralism. Globalisation and Law. Comparative Sociology of Law. Law and Sociology.

48 Lloyd, p 686.

Critical responses to these theories

This chapter has been written to illustrate the ways in which legal theory develops, changes, and morphs into and out of different theoretical homes. As well as showing the process of change that legal theories go through, it has necessarily engaged with the types of critical responses that mark the ongoing nature of the legal project. We will leave you to think about your own critical responses. We will pose one for you, though, to start the ball rolling:

> Are we better off not worrying about what law actually does in reality,
> and adopting the internalised methods of conventional legal theory?
> (You may want to look at the ideas of contemporary positivism,
> to inform your responses.)[49]

QUESTIONS TO THINK ABOUT

Just as we have left it to you to start developing your own critical responses to these theories, you should have acquired sufficient confidence to know what questions you would like to ask about the theories, movements, and developments we have covered in this chapter. We will pose a few questions to start you off:

1. What insights can be drawn from observing the changing nature of legal theory?

2. Is conventional legal theory right after all — is justice best served by law divorced from social and other externalised influences which are constantly changing?[50]

3. What is the point of being critical about law?

Over to you:

4. _____

5. _____

6. _____

7. _____

8. _____

9. _____

10. _____

---

49 Schauer, 'Positivism as Pariah' in Lloyd, pp 441–451; Kramer, 'How Moral Principles can Enter the Law' in Lloyd, pp 481–497; see also Davies, pp 102–104.
50 See Davies, pp 104–112.

FURTHER READING

Banakar, Reza & Travers, Max (eds), *An introduction to law and social theory* (Hart, Oxford, 2002).

Boyle, James, *Critical legal studies* (Aldershot, Dartmouth, 1992).

Caudill, David S, *Lacan and the subject of law: toward a psychoanalytic critical legal theory* (Humanities Press, Atlantic Highlands, New Jersey, 1997).

Ewick, Patricia; Kagan, Robert, & Sarat, Austin (eds), *Social science, social policy, and the law* (Russell Sage Foundation, New York, 1999).

Fitzpatrick, Peter (ed), *Dangerous supplements: resistance and renewal in jurisprudence* (Pluto Press, London, 1991).

Fitzpatrick, Peter & Hunt, Alan (eds), *Critical legal studies* (Basil Blackwell, Oxford, 1987).

Grigg-Spall, Ian & Ireland, Paddy (eds), *The critical lawyers' handbook* (Pluto Press, London, 1992).

Hunt, Alan, *Explorations in law and society: towards a constitutive theory of law* (Routledge, New York, 1993).

Thomas, Philip A, *Socio-legal studies* (Aldershot, Dartmouth, 1997).

Ross, Hamish, *Law as a social institution* (Hart, Oxford, 2001).

Ward, Ian, *An introduction to critical legal theory* (Cavendish Publishing, London, 1998).

CHAPTER 12

CHAPTER 13

Critical Race Theory and Postcolonialism

Reading 293
Aim. 293
Principles 294
The liberal subject — again?. 294
What is 'race'? 296
Civil rights 297
Critical Race Theory (CRT) 299
Postcolonialism and postmodernism 303
Critical responses to Critical Race Theory
and postcolonialism 307
Questions to think about 307
Further reading. 308

READING

DAVIES, *Asking the Law Question: The Dissolution of Legal Theory*, 2nd edition, Chapter 7
FREEMAN, *Lloyd's Introduction to Jurisprudence*, 7th edition, Chapter 16

AIM

This chapter will:

• introduce you to the major influences in the development of Critical Race Theory and postcolonialism; and

• consider the major ideas and themes which emerge in these theories.

FIGURE 13.1: CRITICAL RACE THEORY AND POSTCOLONIALISM TIMELINE

1600–1900	1950–1960	1960–1970	1970–1980	1980–1990	1990–present
	Civil Rights Movement (US) Segregation declared unconstitutional *Brown v Board of Education* (US)				
		Montgomery bus boycott			
		Freedom rides March on Washington			
			Bloody Sunday (Selma, Alabama)		
					Critical Race Theory Madison CRT Conference
					Australian scholarship – race conscious narrative
					Postcolonialism
1776 Loss of the American colonies (War of Independence)					
		Late 19th–early 20th century – independence of the British dominions (Canada, Australia, NZ and South Africa)			
			Post World War Two–1970s Decolonisation of much of the remaining colonial empires		
				Said's *Orientalism*	

As with the chapter on feminist legal theories (Chapter 11), this timeline looks back before the time when the legal theories (CRT and postcolonialism) arise (identified in Figures 1.1 and 1.2, in Chapter 1) to some of the significant historical events which were in some way responsible for the development of the theories.

PRINCIPLES

The liberal subject — again?

Let's go back for a moment to the liberal legal subject. It claims to have no distinctly personal characteristics, but is rather assumed to be a 'featureless' individual — autonomous, independent and atomistic. The legal subject is neither male nor female, is not characterised by reference to its economic circumstances or class, and is neither 'white' nor 'black'.

FIGURE 13.2: THE LIBERAL LEGAL SUBJECT

The liberal subject is 'blank' – that is, it has no personal characteristics, but is assumed to represent everyone as an autonomous, free and independent subject

Based on this lack of identifiable features in the legal subject, conventional forms of legal theory have presented law as neutral, operating on everyone equally and without distinction. With specific reference to issues of race, law is presented as 'colour blind'.

However, the liberal subject reflects very much the characteristics of the people who were creating law – it assumes that the subject has many of the characteristics of the white propertied males who effectively defined law, disguising these assumptions behind a veil of supposed neutrality. The 'position-lessness' of liberalism and the legal subject is, as later, non-conventional theories show, very much a position (although it often does not itself recognise this).

Because the legal subject, however, has been conceived in terms of only one particular and dominant section of the community, individuals and groups who do not possess these assumed characteristics are not 'seen' by law, in the sense that law is made for the benefit of the subject as law conceives it. 'Other' groups – outsiders, like races other than the dominant one – are invisible, subject to the burdens, but not the benefits, of law.

FIGURE 13.3: OTHER SUBJECTS

The liberal legal subject 'seen' by law

Other subjects – not 'seen' by law

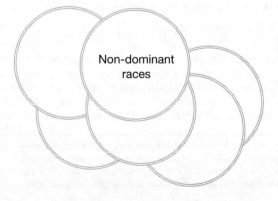

Non-dominant races

Paradoxically, while law in this sense does not 'see' these other subjects, they are often very clearly in law's sights. On the settlement of Australia and the imposition of English law in the colony, the rights and status which the indigenous inhabitants had under their own system of law evaporated, to be replaced by liabilities and obligations to which they were subject, despite knowing nothing of the content of the imported law, or even that they were subject to it.

WITH THE ARRIVAL OF EUROPEANS, INDIGENOUS AUSTRALIAN PEOPLE:

- lost their land on colonisation, with the planting of the British flag
- became subject to a law that they had never known about or accepted
- became objects of study, with their bodies taken by Australian and overseas museums
- were removed, from the time of settlement to within living memory, from their land so that it could be given to white settlers
- were not paid for work they did, but had to ask for their money, which was controlled by other people
- had their children forcibly removed; and
- were denied the ability to participate as members of society, through such measures as not being allowed to marry without permission.

Ordinary white Australians did not have to live like this.

The liberal ideal of equality is focused on the idea of the legal subject, assuming that this represents *all* people. So, the story that law tells often does not protect the interest of groups other than the dominant (and is often an active force in discriminating against these groups which, by focusing on the idealised legal subject, it cannot see).

The two theories which we will look at in this chapter, Critical Race Theory and postcolonialism, are approaches to law which engage directly with questions of race — questions which are, for the most part, either glossed over or entirely ignored by other forms of legal theory.

What is 'race'?

Before looking at the two theoretical perspectives in this chapter, we should first clarify what we mean when we use the word 'race'.

SCIENCE AND RACE

The origins of racial classification as we understand it lie in the 18th century, with the publication by Johann Blumenbach of *On the Natural Variety of Mankind*. Building on earlier work by Linnaeus, Blumenbach established the racial classifications which persist today. Blumenbach himself thought that racial diversity was superficial.[1] He nevertheless constructed a chart of human racial variation which was based on subjective

---

1   See M Davies, *Asking the Law Question: The Dissolution of Legal Theory*, 2nd edition (Lawbook Co, Sydney, 2002), p 262. The original classification by Linnaeus was also devoid of any reference to the superiority of any of its racial groups, although the descriptions used to mark out the groups certainly carry subjective judgments about characteristics which are more (or less) desirable.

characteristics — notably aesthetic considerations of physical beauty — in which the Caucasian form (the term was coined by Blumenbach to describe the white European race) stood at the pinnacle, and the remaining forms represented varying degrees of 'degeneration' from this ideal.[2]

Later, scientists sought to establish a *hierarchy* of the races based on sound scientific principles. In the second half of the 19th century, for example, anthropologists sought to demonstrate the smaller brain size (and thus, lesser intelligence) of the 'inferior races'.[3]

As a way of classifying people, the concept of race was well adapted to the underlying political system, particularly in the period of colonialism, by providing an ideological justification for and rationalisation of the inequality inherent in slavery and colonisation.[4] Proponents of slavery in the 18th and 19th centuries, for example, used the supposed inferiority of African Americans to justify its retention.

WHERE IS 'RACE' NOW?

With the unravelling of the human genetic code, it has become clear that 'race' has no meaning in terms of human genetics — indeed the differences *within* the so-called races are considerably greater than the differences *between* them.[5]

So, if race as a *biological* construct is dead, does that mean that it has no relevance to law? Not at all. As the struggle to overturn the idea of *terra nullius* and recognise native title shows, issues of race remain deeply embedded in law. The concept of race may have no biological foundation, but race and racism remain significant forces in Western society (and for this reason, we can still make reference to race as a concept — referring now to the awareness of distinct and identifiable communities within society whose experience of law, for example, is markedly different from the dominant white community). The disproportionate rates of imprisonment of indigenous Australians, for example, show that the liberal ideal of a colour-blind law has not been realised. While the concept of race does not correspond to any real distinction within the human species, it has nevertheless a very real presence in social practice as the basis for oppression by dominant social groups.[6]

Civil rights

In the late 1950s and 1960s, left-wing liberals in the United States became conscious of the different treatment which people of other races experienced at the hands of the law, notwithstanding its allegedly colour-blind nature. The supposedly neutral operation of law was shown to impact differently on these groups. A similar movement followed in Australia, often modelling its tactics on those used in the United States.

CHAPTER 13

---

2   Gould, SJ, "The Geometer of Race" in *Discovery*, November 1994, pp 65–69. See also the descriptors used by Linnaeus for his classification, extracted in Davies, p 262.
3   See, for example, SJ Gould, 'Wide Hats and Narrow Minds' in *The Panda's Thumb* (Penguin, Harmondsworth, 1980), p 124. The same line of scientific enquiry also showed that women's brains were far smaller than men's — see Gould, pp 128–129.
4   Defined below at p 304.
5   Davies, p 264.
6   See Colette Guillaumin, *Racism, Sexism, Power and Ideology* (Routledge, London, 1995), pp 106–107, extracted in Davies, p 266.

SOME SIGNIFICANT MOMENTS IN THE CIVIL RIGHTS MOVEMENTS

United States

1954 *Brown v Board of Education*. Racial segregation in schools, widely practised in the US till the 1950s, was held by the Supreme Court to be unconstitutional.

1955 *Montgomery Bus Boycott*. A 43-year-old black woman was arrested for refusing to give up her seat on a bus to a white. The Supreme Court eventually declared that segregation on buses also violated the Constitution.

1961 *Freedom Rides*. A campaign of non-violent protest, aimed at ending segregation in bus terminals, the Freedom Rides met violent opposition in the South.

1962 *Mississippi Riot*. The first black student to enrol at the University of Mississippi required an escort to attend the University. A riot broke out in which two students were killed before reinforcements could arrive.

1963 250 000 people assembled in Washington to protest against racism, demanding the passage of civil rights legislation. Martin Luther King delivered the 'I have a dream' speech.

1965 *Bloody Sunday*. Martin Luther King Jr agreed to lead a march to Montgomery, the capital of Alabama, to protest the killing of a demonstrator. Refused permission, protesters nevertheless marched on Montgomery, to be met at the city limits by State troopers, who attacked the crowd with tear gas and batons.

Australia

1965 *Freedom Rides*. Inspired by the US Freedom Rides, a group of students travelled by bus through western NSW to test community attitudes towards Aboriginal Australians. Events came to a head over the issue of Aboriginal admission to the Moree swimming pool, with violent confrontation between the students and townspeople.[7]

1966 Wave Hill walk-off in protest against working conditions and inadequate wages, and demanding the return of traditional lands. This began a seven-year fight by the Gurindji people to obtain title to their land.

1966 The South Australian *Prohibition of Discrimination Act*, the first of its kind in Australia, outlawed race discrimination in employment, accommodation, legal contracts and public facilities.

1967 Referendum passed ending Constitutional discrimination against Aborigines, granting them the vote in Federal elections and referendums and including them in the census.

1972 Establishment of Aboriginal tent embassy in front of Parliament House.

2000 Bridge walks across Australia in support of reconciliation.

---

7   Among the organisers of these rides were Charles Perkins (Aboriginal activist) and Jim Spigelman (later to be Chief Justice of NSW) — both then students.

The civil rights movement in both the United States and Australia was dedicated to the removal of racism, and the creation of racial equality. Anti-discrimination laws outlawing overt racism were eventually passed in both countries, seeking to 'equalise' these differences. Yet, while these changes instituted formal equality, it is doubtful to what extent they actually translated into any substantial changes at a fundamental level. Most indicators show that these groups still suffer considerable political, social and economic disadvantage, and are still the subject of systemic discrimination *despite* the existence of anti-discrimination laws. The experience of non-white people within Western democracies remains one of substantial disadvantage.

Critical Race Theory (CRT)

The roots of Critical Race Theory lie in the United States in the mid 1970s, and the writings of Derrick Bell (a black civil rights activist and lawyer) and Alan Freeman. Both had realised that the movement towards equality promised in the civil rights movement had slowed, if not stopped, and that many of the hard-won gains of the 1960s were being eroded. A small group of lawyers and legal scholars recognised the need for a new form of legal analysis which could address this failure, and set out to create a body of scholarship that was racially distinctive and geared to challenging and overcoming the problems and limitations which were identified with traditional civil rights theory and scholarship. Bell, for example, thought that the strategies of civil rights discourse needed to be revised, incorporating the challenge to legal formalism embodied in the legal realism movement.

Where does CRT 'come from'?

CRT 'formally' came into existence when it held its first conference at a convent outside Madison, Wisconsin, in 1989. CRT theorists were intent on exploring the relationships involved in race and power (which had been themes of the civil rights movement), but introduced into the equation other disciplines such as economics, history and literature.

CRT has used the insights of a wide range of other theoretical approaches. Its primary sources lie in CLS[8] (with which it was originally associated before splitting off), radical feminism[9] and the civil rights movement,[10] although it is critical of all of these as failing to adequately address issues of race and law.

CHAPTER 13

---

8   See Chapter 12 above.
9   See Chapter 11 above.
10 See above.

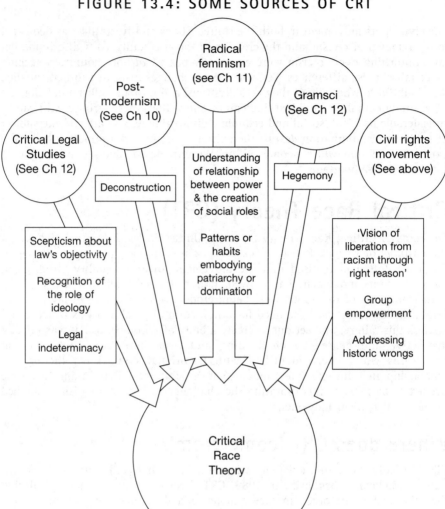

FIGURE 13.4: SOME SOURCES OF CRT

Themes of CRT

The central aim of CRT is the establishment and development of a racially distinctive body of scholarship which seeks to overcome the limitations in existing scholarship within the white-dominated academy.[11] While the movement is not homogenous, it nevertheless centres on a range of common themes, united by the conviction that race remains a significant source of inequality in social institutions, including the law. Delgado and Stefancic identify a number of themes which effectively define and characterise Critical Race Theory.[12] These themes include:

---

11 See K Crenshaw, N Gotanda, G Peller & K Thomas (eds), *Critical Race Theory: The Key Writings that Formed the Movement* (The New Press, New York, 1996).

12 R Delgado & J Stefancic, "Critical Race Theory: An Annotated Bibliography" (1993) 79 *Virginia Law Review* 461, extracted in Lloyd, p 1342.

- *Critique of liberalism:* Liberalism fails to address the issue of race. Traditional liberal approaches to race and the law suggested that the establishment of colour-blind law would eradicate discrimination by ensuring equal treatment for everyone under the law. The establishment of anti-discrimination laws, which create *formal* equality, did not however alter the underlying nature of US society. The concept of race remains a potent force within society, serving as the basis for both differing treatment of people of colour by individuals and institutions, and the continuing difference between the experience of members of the dominant culture and that of other racial groups.

- *Narrative method:* Narrative — the telling of one's personal story — is an important technique in Critical Race Theory. Narrative is used to bring out the reality of racism in society, as experienced by the people against whom it is directed and to counter the dominant story told by law (which supports liberalism's claims to equality). Narrative jurisprudence seeks to capture and identify the race consciousness which is missing from 'colour-blind' legal and social analysis, with the aim of ultimately embodying it in legal thinking and method. CRT argues that people of colour experience the world (and law) from a fundamentally different perspective. Reliance on narrative, therefore, has close associations with postmodernism, which also seeks to have voices heard which have previously been silenced.

- *Critique of the civil rights movement:* The civil rights movement in the United States sought to eradicate racial discrimination through law reform. But as the early writers within CRT observed, the political aims of the civil rights movement were not achieved in practice, despite the creation of statutory protections and formal equal rights. The victories won by the movement in the form of anti-discrimination legislation masked the fact that racist ideology, deeply embedded in American culture, remained fundamentally intact. CRT scholars seek to explain *why* the civil rights movement has proven ineffective in addressing inequality.

- *Multidisciplinary approaches:* Some CRT writers utilise research from other disciplines to explore the nature of race and racism, and how they impact on the lives of individuals in minority communities. CRT looks to social science, for example, to see how particular strategies, designed to combat racism, actually work in practice.

- *The intersection of race, sex and class:* CRT considers whether race and class or race and sex are *independent* sources of disadvantage. Individuals, for example, do not have a single and determinate identity based on solely on race, class or sex, but are a combination of different social identities which often overlap or conflict. While Marxist and feminist theories of law consider issues of class and sex-based disadvantage within legal systems, CRT scholars are concerned with whether these forms of analysis are sufficient to deal not just with issues of race, but also with the way in which issues of race, class and sex combine to form more complex problems than each of the issues individually.

- *Race and essentialism:*[13] CRT scholarship is concerned with the question of how issues of race should be analysed. It is, for example, not clear whether the issue of race should be explored on the basis of a common experience of oppression, or whether analysis should be adapted to the particular community under consideration, accommodating the different *experiences* which a community has, the diverse *needs* of different communities, and the search for solutions which address these differences in a specific way.

- *Race and legal institutions:* CRT engages with issues of representation in law schools and in practice. The relationship between race and legal education is a theme which gained momentum in the 1990s. CRT scholars identify continuing racism in the US educational system, drawing analogies between sexual and racial harassment, and characterising US colleges as a hostile educational environment which militates against the pursuit of increased representation of racial minorities in legal education and in practice.

Critical Race Theory considers that racism — the differential treatment of social groups on the basis of their race — is not an *exception*, but rather the normal state of affairs as experienced by people of colour.[14] As we have seen, race has no basis in biology, but represents categories which society *invents* and *maintains* in order to justify discriminatory practices which further the interests of the dominant (white) class.

CRT and rights

CLS's rejection of rights[15] is rejected within CRT scholarship. Rights have been characterised by CLS scholars like Gabel from their own, privileged, perspective, ignoring the role which rights might have for other groups.

A STORY ABOUT RACE AND RIGHTS

Look at the story about Peter Gabel and Patricia Williams in Chapter 5 of Davies.[16] Both are looking to rent property in New York, but they take very different attitudes to the legal processes involved. Gabel is blasé about the formalities. Williams, on the other hand, wants to tie the legal relationship down with all of the formalities of contract law.

As Delgado points out, the critics of rights live in a world where their rights are generally respected.[17] Gabel can *afford* to be blasé because rights form part of the *background* of his world. They do not need to be brought to the forefront. Williams, on the other hand, uses the formalities of legal relationships, and the rights embedded in them, to protect herself. The 'automatic' respect which Gabel can take for granted is *not* part of Williams' experience.

---

13 We considered the problem of *essentialism* briefly in Chapter 11 in relation to feminism. In the context of race, essentialism refers to the idea that there is a true essence, or a set of invariable and fixed properties, which defines race and the experience of racial groups.

14 See Lloyd, p 1335.

15 See Chapter 12 above.

16 Davies, pp 190–191.

17 See Davies, p 188.

While formal rights do not guarantee substantive equality, they can nevertheless play an important role in bringing about improvements in social practice through political action.[18]

SOME GOOD THINGS ABOUT RIGHTS

Rights can serve as a mechanism for governing the behaviour of individuals who would otherwise discriminate (which has practical benefits for those discriminated against).

Rights might not be the answer to all the problems of discrimination, but critics of rights do not offer any alternative forms of protection for minorities.

The distancing from the community which crits attribute to rights can help to unite minority communities.

For CRT, rights function as a significant mechanism by which oppressed racial groups can secure equality.

Other contexts

While Critical Race Theory focuses primarily on the experience of African Americans in the United States context, its approach and themes translate readily across racial boundaries, and CRT has spawned a range of related movements such as Lat-Crit — a project similar to CRT based on the experience of Latino/Latina people in the United States.

In Australia, Larissa Behrendt (among others) has advocated the use of narrative in pursuing radical change, arguing that indigenous women are empowered by being able to tell their stories after being silenced for so long.[19]

Postcolonialism and postmodernism

Closely associated with postmodern analysis, postcolonialism first emerged as an identifiable movement in the late 1970s. Its roots are generally seen to lie in the publication of Edward Said's *Orientalism* in 1978. This book set out a critique of the way in which the Orient (that is, parts of the world other than the West, but particularly, in Said's case, the Islamic world) had been, and continued to be, represented in the West.

WAS SAID THE FIRST TO LOOK AT IT THIS WAY?

A number of other scholars, including the Syrian scholar Abdul Lafit Tibawi (in 1965), the Tunisian historian Hichem Djait (in 1977) and the Malaysian sociologist Syd Hussain Alatas (also in 1977), mounted similar arguments to Said. However, Said was writing in New York, and adopted 'fashionable' postmodern concepts as the basis for his work, so it achieved considerable prominence, while others' remained in relative obscurity.

---

18 See K Crenshaw, "Race, Reform and Retrenchment: Transformation and Legitimation in Anti Discrimination Law" (1988) *Harvard Law Review* 1331, extracted in Lloyd, p 1352ff — specifically at p 1365.

19 See L Behrendt, "Aboriginal Woman and the White Lies of the Feminist Movement: Implications for Aboriginal Women in Rights Discourse", extracted in the *first* edition of M Davies, *Asking the Law Question* (Lawbook Co, Sydney, 1994), pp 208–210.

Said highlighted the inaccuracy of the assumptions which formed the basis of Western images and understanding of Oriental culture, many of which were derived from very particular observations and then became amplified into essential truths. A single line from the Koran, for example, might be used as evidence of a general truth about all Islamic people. The result was the depiction of non-Westerners in essentialist terms which stressed their supposed undesirable characteristics — the Western academic tradition characterised 'the Oriental' as inferior, irrational, depraved and primitive.[20]

FOUCAULT AND POWER/KNOWLEDGE — REVISITED

This description of the way in which the ideas of non-Westerners and non-Western culture were defined and analysed within the Western academy is based on Foucault's idea of power/knowledge.[21] Said describes the creation of a body of *knowledge* within European institutions about the West's 'other' (or binary opposite) which sought to make 'authoritative' or 'true' statements about non-Western culture, characterising it as everything the West was not (or at least, thought it wasn't). Conversely, the West conceived *itself* as a contrast to the image of this 'other', non-Western, culture.[22]

These images are made within a mutually supporting relationship between power and knowledge — Western institutions had the *power* to create the *knowledge* about non-Europeans, and the knowledge which they created justified European domination.

The nature of non-Western people and culture is set in opposition to the characteristics which Europeans attributed to themselves. Reflecting the postmodern flavour of his analysis, Said characterised the Western view of the Orient as being among the deepest and most persistent images of the 'Other'. The images with which non-Westerners were constructed were so deeply embedded and so authoritative that it became impossible to think about the Orient without incorporating these ideas.

Such characterisations suited the ideology of the West — particularly during the colonial period. They reinforced notions of European superiority and served to justify the political, military and economic domination of the colonised people.[23] At the same time, the process of colonisation spread these ideas to the colonised world, and became part of the *colonised* people's understanding of themselves.

So what is postcolonialism?

Some basic definitions

IMPERIALISM AND COLONIALISM

Imperialism refers to the influence, particularly in terms of commercial exploitation, by one nation over other parts of the world using political, legal and military power as the means of control. *Colonialism* and *colonisation* refer to one specific way in which imperialism worked — the *settlement* of one group of people in a new territory, accompanied by exploitation of resources and the governance of the indigenous occupants of the settled land.[24]

---

20 This process parallels the development of scientific theories of racial inferiority — see pp 296–297 above.
21 Davies, p 279–280.
22 See Davies, p 279.
23 See Davies, p 279.
24 See, for example, J McLeod, *Beginning Postcolonialism* (Manchester University Press, Manchester, 2000), pp 7–8.

While colonialism in this sense is now largely a thing of the past, imperialism is still well and truly alive, in the form of globalisation.

DECOLONISATION

Decolonisation is the process by which former colonies become autonomous political entities. As an example, the British Empire decolonised in three stages:

• the loss of the American colonies in the War of Independence (1776);

• the ceding of political autonomy to the 'dominions' — Australia, Canada, New Zealand and South Africa — which took place in the latter half of the 19th and the beginning of the 20th century; and

• the move to independence by colonised countries in Asia, Africa and the Caribbean, dating principally from the end of World War Two until the 1970s.

The 'post' in 'postcolonialism' does not refer to what happens *after* decolonisation.[25] Postcolonial analysis looks instead at the impact which European colonialism has had on the shaping of the relationship between the colonial powers and the non-Western colonised people. It describes the formerly-colonised people's continuing engagement with, resistance against and reconstruction of, the ideas embedded during colonisation. Postcolonial theory, therefore, considers the experience of oppression and resistance in relation to the dominant narrative created by the colonial presence, and the process of establishing post-colonial institutions and culture which nevertheless retain some traces of the now-departed coloniser.[26]

HYBRIDITY

While colonisation involves a clash of cultures,[27] the political and social structures which develop after decolonisation are neither an imprint left by the departed colonial power, nor a resurrected form of the pre-colonial culture. The process of colonisation and decolonisation does not leave the colonised peoples unchanged — when the coloniser departs, the colonised do not return to their pre-colonised institutions or social organisation.

What emerges, either from the anti-colonial struggle or successful decolonisation, is a new political object which is neither of its political or social precursors, but formed out of their interaction and conflict.[28] Homi Bhabha[29] describes postcolonial culture as a hybrid, in which colonial history is displaced, and replaced with a new and different process of negotiating meaning for the emergent culture, generating new institutions and political structures.

Where does Australia fit in?

The most common sequence of events for countries which are the subject of postcolonial critique involves settlement or colonisation by Europeans, who then exercise political authority over the indigenous, non-European inhabitants. After this period of colonisation, during which the colonising power establishes

---

25 See Davies, p 278.
26 Ibid.
27 See, for example, the description of the colonial state by Franz Fanon in *The Wretched of the Earth* (McGibbon and Kee, London, 1965), extracted in Davies, p 273.
28 See L Ghandi, *Postcolonial Theory: An Introduction* (Allen & Unwin, Sydney, 1998), p 130; Davies, p 280.
29 See Homi K Bhabha, *The Location of Culture* (Routledge, London, 1994).

institutions of government and social organisation which dominate the landscape, there is a period of decolonisation — usually in response to resistance and agitation for independence by the original inhabitants — in which control is returned.

DECOLONISATION IN AUSTRALIA?

The first and second of these stages certainly took place in Australia's post-settlement history. However, *decolonisation* for Australia did not involve the return of power and the grant of political autonomy to the indigenous inhabitants. The imperial government merely relinquished power in favour of the predominantly European population which had grown up under colonial rule, but which never left.[30]

Given that the final stage — the return of political power to the colonised people — did not occur in Australia, does this preclude the use of a postcolonial analysis? Or does the 'non-linear' definition of POSTCOLONIALISM allow this approach, because the period of colonial rule has impacted on both the colonisers and the colonised?

This characteristic of the process by which Australia became independent of British rule produces a particular effect when the law tries to take account of indigenous law and legal institutions — although Australian law may try to incorporate, for example, indigenous customary law or indigenous concepts of land title, it does not confer any authority or legitimacy on such law in its own right, but subsumes it within the dominant legal system, altering it in the process so that it becomes consistent with the dominant conceptual structures of law.[31] Any authority which such law might have derives not from its original significance or status within the indigenous culture, but from its being part of *Australian* law.

Some postcolonial themes

Although writers in the area of postcolonialism address a wide range of issues related to colonial experience, some of the recurrent themes addressed by postcolonial writers include:

- The effects which colonisation and decolonisation have had on *both* the colonisers and the people who were colonised.

- The exploration of ideas which have been left behind by retreating colonial powers within the institutions of education, government and law (among others) in decolonised societies, and how these impact on the development of those societies after the colonisers have left.

- The question of whether decolonisation should take the form of a radical re-establishment of pre-colonial culture and institutions.

- The nature of the national identities which emerge after the colonisers leave.

- The extent to which the military/political domination which characterised the colonial period has been replaced by new forms of domination in the form of economic imperialism or globalisation.

---

30 Davies, pp 277–278. Watson argues that Australia remains colonial, to which Davies adds the caution that use of the term postcolonial in the Australian context could be misleading and obscure the continuing domination of indigenous people and culture by a 'continuing colonialism'.
31 Davies, p 275.

Critical responses to Critical Race Theory and postcolonialism

Critical Race Theory

- The highly individualised treatment by the law which CRT seems to suggest is necessary to eradicate discrimination presents a practical problem for law. Law cannot generally work with highly personalised stories, but has to operate on the basis of categories.

- One of the key features of CRT scholarship, the use of narrative, is a major source of criticism of the movement, relying as it does on a subjective perspective.

- It has been argued that race-conscious writing is detrimental to scholars from racial minorities, in that it subordinates intellectual criteria ('is the scholarship "good"?') to race-based criteria ('is it written from a "good" perspective?').

Postcolonialism

- Postcolonialism can have the effect of essentialising colonial and postcolonial experience, assuming that there is a single set of characteristics which defines the intersection of colonising and colonised cultures.

- Postcolonialism masks the continuing oppression of people, through the continuing reliance on Western theory — it is said that this constitutes a new colonisation of the intellectual life of these peoples, with Western academia remaining the primary site of postcolonial theorising.

- Some critics have argued that Postcolonialism perpetuates the mistakes of Orientalism, even when carried out by people from formerly colonised countries.

CHAPTER 13

QUESTIONS TO THINK ABOUT

1. Look at the black-letter law which you have studied. Does it present itself (or has it been presented to you) as 'colour-blind'?

2. Can you see examples of where law, despite this apparent colour-blindness, nevertheless operates to the disadvantage of racial minorities? Can you think of any legislation which appears neutral, but which has a differential impact on Indigenous Australians?

3. To what extent does the Australian experience of civil rights match CRT critiques of the civil rights movement in the United States?

4. Have anti-discrimination laws substantially altered the Indigenous experience of law in Australia?

5. Does your experience of legal education match CRT's observation that tertiary institutions teaching lawyers are a hostile environment for Indigenous Australians?

6. What other groups can you identify who are not 'seen' by law?

7. Does the history of European treatment of Indigenous Australians conform to Said's description of the European construction of non-Western culture?

8. Do you think that the experience of countries which have had political autonomy transferred to the former colonised people is similar to that of Australia?

9. Has *Mabo* and subsequent native title law eradicated the effects of *terra nullius* for indigenous Australians?

10. Do you agree that thinking about Australia as a postcolonial country could obscure the 'continuing colonialism' experienced by Indigenous Australians?

FURTHER READING

Ashcroft, W, Griffiths, G & Tiffin, H (eds), *The Postcolonial Studies Reader* (Routledge, London, 1995).

Barker, F, Hulme, P & Iversen, M (eds), *Colonial discourse/Postcolonial theory* (Manchester University Press, Manchester, 1994).

Crenshaw, K, Gotanda, N, Peller, G & Thomas, K, *Critical Race Theory: The Key Writings That Formed the Movement* (The New Press, New York, 1996).

Darian-Smith, E & Fitzpatrick, P, *Laws of the Postcolonial* (University of Michigan Press, Ann Arbor, 1999).

Delgado, R & Stefancic, J, *Critical Race Theory: An* Introduction (New York University Press, New York, 2001).

Gandhi, L, *Postcolonial Theory: A Critical Introduction* (Allen & Unwin, Sydney, 1998).

McLeod, J, *Beginning Postcolonialism* (Manchester University Press, Manchester, 2000).

Mills, CW, *The Racial Contract* (Cornell University Press, Ithaca, 1997).

Quayson, A, *Postcolonialism: Theory, Practise or Process* (Polity Press, Cambridge, 2000).

Saltman, M, *The Demise of the Reasonable Man: A Cross-Cultural Study of a Legal Concept* (Transaction Books, New Brunswick, 1991).

Spivak, GC, *The Postcolonial Critic: Interviews, Strategies, Dialogues* (Routledge, New York, 1990).

Spivak, GC, *Critique of Postcolonial Reason: Towards a History of the Vanishing Present* (Harvard University Press, Cambridge Mass, 1999).

CHAPTER 14

Case Studies: Theories in Action

Aim. 309
Principles 309
Do the courts tell us when they're using
theory?. 309
How do we know how legal theory is used? 310
Case study: Yorta Yorta 310
Case study: Re Kevin. 317
Where to from here? 321

AIM

This chapter will show you how theories find their way into judicial reasoning and the kinds of critiques which can be made of the decisions of the courts, by looking at two recent cases which have been decided by Australian courts – *Members of the Yorta Yorta Aboriginal Community v Victoria* (2002) 194 ALR 538; and *Re Kevin (validity of transsexual marriage)* (2001) 28 Fam LR 158. Both of these cases involve untested areas of law and are cases which deal with the kind of social and moral questions legal theory engages itself with.

PRINCIPLES

Do the courts tell us when they're using theory?

How do we know when courts (or counsel) are using theory? Sometimes they tell us. Sometimes they don't, as we saw in Chapter 1 (pp 4–5). As we will see in *Yorta Yorta*, the majority judgment makes some specific and explicit references to legal theory. The judges refer to a number of writers by name, but they also use law's 'secret language' – the phrase 'rule of recognition'. Can you remember where this phrase comes from? If you can't, we'll see shortly.

In the other case, the judge doesn't tell us at all. The ideas which flow into the decision from theory are not explicitly sourced, and we have to work them out for ourselves.

We will show you some of the ways theory and practice come together in the forming of the judgment.

How do we know how legal theory is used?

As you know, it's a very good idea to start at the beginning. After a brief description of the subject matter of each case and some specific observations made by the some members of the court during the course of their judgment, we have listed some starting points for an exploration of the use of theory in the judgments. We haven't covered all of the possible theories which can be found in the decisions or which lie behind them. Neither will we give you a final answer about how specific theories might 'deal with' the issues. No such animal exists! One of the important things about theory is that it is a guide. What we might think forms a base of theoretical analysis may differ from what you think (see Chapter 2, pp 33–37). What we are doing is leaving gaps for you to work out your own ideas about the theory in the cases:

- In some instances, we've gone into some detail about how the theory and the cases intersect, posing some questions to prompt you as to how the analysis might develop.

- In others, we've simply made the most basic connection, and directed you back to the part of the book that will help you come to your own conclusions.

- We have also left out many of the theories we've looked at in this book, and, of course, theories we haven't looked at. We will leave it up to you to make some connections with these.

Case study: MEMBERS OF THE YORTA YORTA ABORIGINAL COMMUNITY V VICTORIA (2002) 194 ALR 538

The Yorta Yorta people had claimed native title to an oval-shaped area of public lands and waters in northern Victoria and southern New South Wales, bisected by the Murray River. The claim failed. In their original application the claimants provided some anthropological material setting out what had happened to the Yorta Yorta people since European settlement in the area 155 years before. There had been massive alterations in technical, environmental and economic circumstances; depopulation from disease and conflict; separation of children from their parents; ceremonies and other traditional customs and practices had been forbidden; the use of traditional languages had been inhibited; and where they lived was controlled. At various times, different policies − absorption, segregation, integration − had their effect.

Among the range of issues Gleeson CJ, and Gummow and Hayne JJ had to consider the continuing connection of the Yorta Yorta people to their land and social customs. They decided that they had to find out if the traditional laws and customs of the Yorta Yorta people, concerning their rights to lands and waters, was a 'body of norms (that) has a continuous existence and vitality' (para 48). As part of addressing this issue, their Honours considered the 'inextricable link between a society and its laws and customs' to find that the Yorta Yorta people did not have this necessary link.

Here are some of the observations that the court made in the course of their judgment (see paras 49–54):

- Gleeson CJ and Gummow and Hayne JJ decided to be guided in their decision-making by wanting to understand whether or not a valid legal system still existed for the Yorta Yorta people. As part of the starting point, they decided to ascertain what happens with deciding whether a legal system exists. They found that laws and customs don't exist in a vacuum, but that they are, in Professor Julius Stone's words, 'socially derivative and non-autonomous' (Julius Stone was an Australian adherent of the American legal realist movement). They also quoted the view of the Oxford jurisprude, Professor Honoré, that it was axiomatic that 'all laws are laws of a society or group', adding a comment from Paton's *Jurisprudence*[1] that 'law is but a result of all the forces that go to make society'.

- Their Honours observed that law and custom arise out of a society and also *define* a particular society in important ways. If the society which gave rise to a body of laws and customs ceased to exist and no longer acknowledged or observed those laws and customs, then such laws and customs ceased to have a continued existence and vitality. It is still possible to know their content, but in the absence of any society acknowledging and observing them, it was no longer useful, or even meaningful, to talk about them as a body of laws and customs, or of their producing rights or interests in relation to land or waters.

- They concluded that if the content of laws and customs were later adopted by another society, then they would owe their existence and validity to that later society. They would become laws acknowledged by that later society, and no longer laws or customs which could be described as the existing laws and customs of the earlier society.

- Their Honours concluded that, so far as it was useful to analyse the problem before the court in the terms of legal positivism, the relevant rule of recognition of a traditional law or custom was a rule of recognition found in the social structures of the relevant Indigenous society, as those structures existed at sovereignty. It was not some later created rule of recognition rooted in the social structures of a society, even an Indigenous society, if those structures were structures newly created after, or even because of, the change in sovereignty.

---

1 Paton, G, *Textbook of Jurisprudence*, 4th edition (Oxford University Press, London, 1972).

What legal theories emerge from this case?

Classical positivism[2]

We know that positivism is still the major conventional legal theory, so it is not surprising that this decision (and this part of the reasoning) is based in a positivist view. Both Bentham and Austin locate the source of law in a *single* sovereign. (The native title cases in Australia have consistently refused to consider the issue of Indigenous sovereignty justiciable. It is simply not on the agenda.)

- Their Honours' approach to establishing the current validity (if any) of traditional customs and laws is not to search for any intrinsic validity within the Indigenous society which gave rise to them. On the basis of the break in connection with the land, the court validates traditional custom and law, if at all, in the body politic which *now* recognises them. This takes other sources of validity out of play.

- Does this approach affect the likely outcome? If traditional law and custom were able to be validated by reference to Yorta Yorta social practice, would the same problems with native title still emerge?

HLA Hart[3]

Did you recognise the reference to the 'rule of recognition' and remember where it came from?

- Their Honours locate the rule of recognition in the 'social structures' of an Indigenous community. Hart's rule of recognition is something which *insiders* use, and is generally associated with the attitude of legal officials.

- Hart thought that in primitive societies, *all* the members of a community had to recognise and abide by the primary rules because of the absence of specific legal institutions or officials. Does this suggest that their Honours are thinking of the Indigenous society in this way, or can 'social structures' be read to include specifically legal structures?

Natural law[4]

When we think about natural law, two key factors need to be considered. One is community; the other is the role of reason. We get our idea of community in part from Aristotle's conception of teleology – that the law should be designed to promote the good of the 'community'. The Yorta Yorta people can't compete with the wider community, because they are merely one element within it. What counts as community is the wider Australian community as a whole.

Can Finnis' theory provide any insights into the situation in this case?

It is tempting when looking at Finnis to try to 'apply' his *goods*. Is this a good idea?

---

2   See Chapter 6 above.
3   See Chapter 7 above.
4   See Chapter 3 above.

A WORD OF CAUTION ABOUT FINNIS' GOODS

For the purposes of working out how natural law provides for good law, we can't simply use Finnis' goods. They don't determine what is good law. Where they fit in Finnis' theory is that they inform the *reasoning* which fashions appropriate law. They are a resource, not the answer, so just because something seems to promote one, or even a number, of these goods, that doesn't mean it is necessarily a good law.

You have to keep going. As you can see from Figures 3.6 and 3.7, we need to take the next step.

With that in mind, some relevant goods are:

- *Life:* The good of life relates to the living of a 'good and fruitful life', so the nature of the relationship between Indigenous people and the land is particularly significant here. But the type of life that would be good for them would conflict with the rest of the community.[5]

- *Religion:* The social systems of Indigenous Australians involve their relationship with the land as a significant aspect of their religious life. Again, the nature of Yorta Yorta beliefs about the land suggest that Finnis' good, religion, is a relevant starting point.[6] (You will see that we didn't discuss this good, religion, in Chapter 3. You will need to go back to the relevant extract in Lloyd.)

- *Sociability or friendship:* How do you think this fits?

Remember that Finnis tells us that everything we need for a good society comes from a mix of these things.

- *Practical reasonableness*: How does practical reasonableness then operate to turn these relevant goods into appropriate law? Go back to Figure 3.7 and look at the list of the requirements of practical reasonableness. Are we dealing with a coherent life plan? Are we dealing with the efficient pursuit of goals? Remember, the purpose is to foster 'a good and harmoniously ordered community'.[7]

SOMETHING FOR YOU TO THINK ABOUT

Finnis observes that a regime of private property is a fundamental aspect of society.[8] How does the Yorta Yorta claim sit against this virtual presupposition in Finnis' image of society?

How does this fit into the 'big picture' of Finnis' theory?

Pound[9]

This case is very much about balancing the interests of the Yorta Yorta people with other interests in the community, and could be analysed using the structure developed by Pound.[10]

---

5 See Chapter 3 above, pp 75 and 77; Freeman, *Lloyd's Introduction to Jurisprudence*, 7th edition (London, Sweet and Maxwell, 2001), pp 133, 173–174.
6 See Chapter 3 above, p 77; Lloyd, pp 133, 175–176.
7 See Chapter 3 above, pp 75, 77.
8 See Chapter 3 above, p 78; Lloyd, p 182.
9 See Chapter 9 above.
10 See Chapter 9 above, pp 212–216.

Here are some points for you to think about:

- How would you classify the Yorta Yorta people's interest according to Pound's scheme?
- What other interests need to be taken into consideration?
- Are these interests on the same plane — individual against individual; social against social? How do we balance the interests of the Yorta Yorta people against those of the wider Australian community?
- Does Pound have any existing jural postulates which could be used to resolve the conflict between competing interests?
- Do any new jural postulates come out of this case?

Critiquing the decision

How can we critique the decision? Which theories can we use? Can we use Marx? Not really. You need to think of Marx as a springboard theory. Don't be tempted to try and fit different communities into his model of the bourgeoisie/proletariat model. Classical Marxism only deals with capital and the working class.[11]

Where Marx is important is in giving us a language with which to talk about power imbalance, and we can only find this type of use through the later extrapolations of his theory that we saw in Chapter 12 (see Figure 12.2).

Let's take one example. You can think about others.

- *Hegemony:* Courts could certainly function to protect the interests of the dominant class — people who want to exploit the land for commercial gain — at the expense of others. Is the decision here, relying on the idea of the transfer of customary law into the common law, an example of the dominant class *negotiating* its own interests through a social institution, rather than by the outright exercise of state power?[12]

Critical theory takes issue with the idea that 'facts' exist pre-formed and value free. The line of reasoning adopted by the court here relies heavily on what is accepted as historical or anthropological fact. Critical theory would seek to uncover the origins of these facts — to look behind them and see what values are embedded in them, and what interests are served by constructing them in a particular way.[13]

Critical theory also argues that it is impossible for a theorist to step outside themselves and observe objectively. If theorists are required to lay bare their own position, does that mean that judges should also declare theirs?

Critical Legal Studies (CLS)[14]

Crits argue that the law is indeterminate, and that any result could be chosen and justified to further particular social or political ends. Does *Yorta Yorta* demonstrate the observations about law which crits make?

---

11 See Chapter 8 above.
12 See Chapter 12 above, pp 281–282.
13 Chapter 12 above, pp 279–281.
14 Chapter 12 above.

The anthropological material which the court has relied on creates a false genealogy of broken connection with the land, when (ironically) it was the treatment of the Yorta Yorta people, in the form of forced removal and dispossession, which created the break in the first place.

Look at the strands of CLS thought in Chapter 12, from page 283 on. How many of these themes are evident in this decision? We'll start you off:

- *Law's claimed neutrality cloaks social and political agendas:*[15] Are there any hidden values or value judgments which might be driving the analysis? Does the need to protect certain interests — those of white landowners — actually drive the decision, rather than the presumed dispassionate legal analysis which law claims as its method?

- *Is it open to the court here to 'play with' the law to achieve a certain result?*[16] Professor Stone would never have read the concept of society in the narrow sense that the court did. The court has decontextualised the theory, and put a slanted view on Professor Stone's phrase, turning its original socially progressive tone into a way of thinking about the Yorta Yorta claim which emphasises conventional categories of land ownership. By stressing the break in connection and the re-establishment of law by reference to the later (Common law) legal system, the court seems to be laying the groundwork for placing the Yorta Yorta claims in opposition to the interest and needs of the wider community — a good reason for denying them.

- *Legal categories are not 'real' or necessary. Law could easily be organised into different categories or concepts:*[17] The long-standing problem for native title claims was that they did not fit readily into pre-existing legal categories of land tenure. By constructing the claim around a concept of *broken* connection with the land, law makes it difficult to accept native title into the existing law. This law serves the interests of landowners whose tenure accords with conventional legal doctrine. But crits would say that it doesn't have to be this way, and we could organise interests in land in ways which did not favour one group over another.

- *Law operates as an alienating force in society:*[18] A feature of Indigenous social organisation is its interrelatedness, both within the community and *with* the land. By constructing native title within common law concepts of land tenure, law has proved a profoundly alienating influence on Indigenous communities, breaking up their internal cohesion and fracturing their connection with the land — and building in selective disadvantage for the benefit of conventional landowners.

Consider the fifth and sixth strands of CLS thought. Are these also evident in the way the court is going about constructing its argument? (You can also look at the CLS analysis of contract law on page 284 to get some ideas about how CLS thought might approach these questions.)

CHAPTER 14

---

15 Page 283 above, number 1.
16 Page 283 above, number 2.
17 Page 283 above, number 3.
18 Page 283 above, number 4.

Postcolonial legal theory[19]

There is no problem in making a *general* connection between this case and postcolonial theory. *Yorta Yorta* deals explicitly with the interaction between the social and legal context of Australia's Indigenous inhabitants and the British legal system which was imposed over it at the time of settlement. Obviously, postcolonial analysis would 'disagree' with the conclusion that the lack of continuing connection meant that there was no native title. However:

- It is important in this context to recognise the difficulty which has been signalled in terms of Australia's history.[20] Sovereignty did not revert to the Indigenous inhabitants on decolonisation, but remained in the hands of the European population.

- Davies' caveat – about masking 'continuing colonialism' – is particularly relevant here. There is a marked irony in examining Indigenous social practice for a continuing connection, when any 'break' in the connection is traceable to the dispossession, depopulation and forcible removal of the Indigenous inhabitants from the land in question.

- Are the practices described in the anthropological material – banning of traditional ceremonies, separation of children from their families – traceable to the construction of the Indigenous population in terms of Said's Orientalism ('inferior, irrational, depraved and primitive')?[21]

- Is it possible to look at this process in ordinary postcolonial terms? Bhabha's concept of 'hybridity', for example, assumes a 'new and different process of negotiating meaning for the emergent culture, generating new institutions and political structures.'[22]

- In the absence of a continuing connection, the judges describe the content of 'old' social custom or law as now deriving from the new legal order which validates them. Even if native title had been found in this case, would the legal relationship between the Yorta Yorta people and the land just be an example of the 'continuing colonialism' Davies refers to, or would it demonstrate the postcolonial idea of mutual influence between colonised and coloniser?

- If the nature of such law did change as a result of being adopted (eg changing from an oral tradition to a written one), is this also an example of the mutual influences as colonised and colonisers 'work it out'?

---

19 Chapter 13 above.
20 Chapter 13 above, 'Where does Australia fit in', p 305 – specifically footnote 30.
21 Chapter 13 above, footnote 20.
22 Chapter 13 above, footnote 20.

Case Study: RE KEVIN (VALIDITY OF TRANS-SEXUAL MARRIAGE) (2001) 28 Fam LR 158

The *Marriage Act* requires that marriages be between 'a man and a woman', although it does not define these terms. Kevin and Jennifer[23] had married and sought a declaration from the Family Court that their marriage was valid. At issue was Kevin's sex — he had been born 'Kimberley' and subsequently undergone a sex re-assignment. Chisholm J had to decide whether Kevin was a woman (based on his sex at birth) or a man (based on subsequent medical intervention).

The Attorney-General argued that the issue was one of statutory interpretation, and that on that basis, Kevin could not, as a female-to-male transsexual, marry 'as a man'. His sex was to be determined by reference to the English decision in *Corbett*, in which Ormrod LJ had decided that anatomical or biological criteria were the determining factors. Where genitals, gonads and chromosomes pointed consistently to one sex at the time of birth, an individual was classified as a member of that sex for the purposes of marriage. (As background, later commentators, including other judges, have detected a strongly homophobic tone in some of Ormrod LJ's comments in the judgment.)

Chisholm J, however, declined to consider *Corbett* as binding. Our understanding of the nature of what makes us one sex or another had changed since then, and evidence was led that a fourth anatomical feature, located in the brain, was differentiated according to sex. In some instances, this part of the brain formed with characteristics which contradicted the three indicators which *Corbett* relied on. His Honour also incorporated into the criteria for determining sex the evidence of Kevin, his family and his friends about *how* he had lived his life — that he had always gravitated towards traditionally male behaviours and activities.

Here are some of Chisholm J's observations and comments:

- His Honour considered whether the words 'hetero-sexual character' meant more than simply that one party should be a man and the other a woman. He cited a central passage from Corbett, which held that the criteria for determining sex for the purposes of marriage were solely biological. Where someone was born with male gonads, genitals and chromosomes, no biological condition, and no surgical or hormonal intervention, could create a person who was able to perform 'the essential role of a woman in marriage'. (That is, if these biological characteristics pointed consistently to one sex at birth, then they alone determine a person's sex for life, no matter what happened afterwards!)

- His Honour pointed to the problematic nature of the word 'natural'. In this context, it could have many meanings. He posed the questions: Was a man who could achieve an erection only with Viagra 'naturally' capable of performing sexual acts? Was a person with a constructed vagina 'naturally' capable of intercourse? Was it relevant whether the person experienced pleasure, or an orgasm? He concluded that there was no clear answer to such questions, and that a law that required these matters to be put under the microscope to determine the validity of a marriage would neither be sensible nor respectful of people's dignity.

23 'Kevin', 'Jennifer' and 'Kimberley' were pseudonyms adopted by the court to preserve the applicants' anonymity.

- Chisolm J went on to ask what the phrase 'the essential role of a woman in marriage' meant. Did it require a capacity for sexual activity? If so, precisely which activities? Was a woman who could not have genital intercourse either through illness or disability unable to perform this 'essential role'? Why should it be assumed that the 'essential role of a woman' in marriage is concerned only with sex and biological sexual constitution?

What legal theories emerge from this case?

Modernism and positivism[24]

Not surprisingly, the government took a decidedly positivist stance in insisting that the case was one of statutory interpretation. The *Marriage Act* was a valid law properly enacted, so it was just a question of giving it a meaning. Since the terms man and woman were not defined in the Act, case law would provide their meaning, and the doctrine of precedent should ensure that this meaning prevailed. *Corbett* applies — end of story!

Nevertheless, the existence of a body of scientific evidence allowed Chisolm J to step outside the bounds of *Corbett*. Here is the kind of objective and certain knowledge which is held in such high regard in the modernist tradition. It at least allows a court to depart from *Corbett* on the basis of sound scientific observation and conclusions — not just relying on subjective evidence.

Bentham

You can imagine what Bentham might think about this scenario. If only the government had enacted a code which unequivocally defined all its terms, there would be no need for judicial intervention! Everyone would know what the law of marriage said *and* meant, so the whole court case would have been unnecessary. (Declarations by the court would, we suspect, not be needed at all in Bentham's perfect world.)

- But what would Bentham's censorial jurisprudence conclude about what the law should be? It's very easy for such a small group to be overborne by the needs or wants of the majority in situations like this, and for utilitarianism to create considerable pain for minorities.

- What factors would get built into the equation? Kevin's pleasure in being able to get married and live a normal life? Society's displeasure and the lingering sense that this marriage is somehow homosexual in nature?[25]

---

24 Chapter 4 above.
25 It is ironic that Kevin, having undergone sex re-assignment, remains a woman under *Corbett's* analysis. He would, after all, still be entitled to marry — it's just that, as a woman, he could only marry a man. This would, obviously, produce a marriage which had all the outward appearances of a same-sex marriage! See, for example, Whittle, J, "An Association for as Noble a Purpose as Any", *New Law Journal*, March 16, 1996, 366-369.

Natural law[26]

The most obvious of Finnis' goods here is life. But Finnis' idea of life, including procreation, doesn't apply unambiguously here. It is connected to vitality and 'living well', and procreation is conceived of in terms of 'normal' processes (Chapter 3, p 75). Obviously, Kevin cannot father children, so if he and Jennifer are to have children, they must do so by other means.[27]

- This is not 'life' in the sense that Finnis uses it — it doesn't conform with the true meaning of 'vitality'.

- Has Finnis simply constructed a theory of law which supports a conservative status quo? Does Ormrod LJ's insistence on biological criteria at birth reflect this sort of conservative view of life and reproduction — you have to play with the hand you were dealt?

Look again at the requirements of practical reasonableness.[28] How might the application of the first moral principle — the fostering of law 'compatible with integral human fulfilment' — affect the determination of moral principle, and thus good law, for this case? Remember that this principle denies individualistic self-fulfilment in favour of the fulfilment of the community as a whole.

Pound

We described Pound (pp 212–216) as providing a way of keeping the law moving in step with the needs of society. The change in outcome between *Corbett* and *Re Kevin* certainly demonstrates a change, and the result in *Re Kevin* seems to be more relevant to society in the 21st century. Here are some starting points:

- Does Kevin have an 'interest' within Pound's scheme? This is a law-centred concept, and the claim that transsexuals should be allowed to marry in their post-assignment sex has certainly been before the courts ever since the medical technology has been available.

- But where would you classify this interest in Pound's scheme? Is it an individual interest, designed to allow these individuals to lead a normal and fulfilled life? What interests are opposed to it? Are they social interests only? Does everyone else have an *individual* interest in whether Kevin marries?

- Is it possible to balance these interests in the same plane — that is, individual against individual or social against social? Here we have an instance of a *government* (at a social level) taking on individuals. What would Pound have thought about this?

- Is there an existing jural postulate, or generalised principle of law, which can tell us whether Kevin's interest should be recognised?

---

26 Chapter 3 above.

27 During the hearing of the appeal, Kevin and Jennifer were present in the court, in full view of the bench. As Mark Thomas observed, Jennifer was 9 months pregnant with their second child, both through IVF. On the second day of the hearing, though, Jennifer wasn't there, and her lawyer announced that the couple's second child had been born the night before, so Jennifer couldn't be in court!

28 Chapter 3 above, pp 76–77; Figure 3.6.

American Legal Realism

Look at the nine points about law made by Llewellyn in the 'realist manifesto'.[29] Do these cases demonstrate any of these ideas?

Look at point 3, for example. Society — including its understanding of the nature of sexuality, its capacity to intervene medically as well as people's attitudes to sexuality — changed between *Corbett* and *Re Kevin*. Does *Re Kevin* illustrate the need for law to catch up with social change occasionally? Or point 7 — is this an example of law adapting to a particular (new) field? Does Chisholm J think about his decision having *an effect*?

Critique

Remember what we said in *Yorta Yorta* about using Marx with caution. Again, there are no really Marxist class issues here. But what about the extrapolations?

Chisolm J's approach and result are clearly not a 'blunt instrument' to enforce the values of the dominant class. Has his Honour demonstrated the 'relative autonomy' of the law? (remember EP Thompson).[30]

Critical Legal Studies

- *'Playing' with the law to achieve a certain result:*[31] The fact that Ormrod LJ and Chisholm J can arrive at opposite conclusions using fundamentally the same raw materials suggests this indeterminate nature of law. Each has used the raw materials in a different way (completely within the 'rules') to achieve what for them is the 'right' answer. What underlying values are being supported by each of these approaches? Does one favour liberal ideology about sexuality and marriage, while the other create a more flexible view of how people should (or can) organise their lives?

- *Law could easily be organised into different categories or concepts.*[32] The ascription of individuals into one sex or the other for legal purposes is one of the most common and significant processes of legal categorisation in society. We tend to assume that people are 'one thing or the other' — either male or female. Yet some branches of law have created a third category — intersex — to accommodate people who don't fit into the unambiguous sexual classifications of male and female. Law generally allows these people to 'change sex' not just in practice, but also for legal purposes, like social security entitlements and obligations. Why do you think marriage law should be any different? What values are being protected when the state resists Kevin's desire to marry as a man?

---

29 Chapter 9 above, p 219.
30 Chapter 12 above, pp 276–279.
31 Page 283 above, number 2.
32 Page 283 above, number 3.

Feminism[33]

Underlying the reasoning in *Corbett* was a very clear image of what women are, and what their place in society, and marriage, should be! Which version of feminism has the most to say about this?

- Radical feminism would take issue with *Corbett*'s assumption that women were just there to fulfil male sexual demands.

- Postmodern feminism would argue that *Corbett* has explicitly constructed the idea of *woman* in an essentialist framework — assuming that there was a set of characteristics, including sexual compliance, which defined women (very much to their detriment). Chisolm J's questioning, and ultimate rejection, of this application of an essential (sexual) role for women is consistent with postmodern ideas about the construction of the individual.

Postmodernism[34]

Here are some starting points for postmodern themes:

- Foucault's concept of *power/knowledge*: In *re Kevin,* the court has the power to construct authoritatively what 'man' and 'woman' mean, together with what those meanings imply for the people to whom they apply. Mrs Corbett and Kevin will be able to marry (or not) solely on the basis of the court's construction of the concept of sex.

- 'Truth' — in this case the truth about what it is to be a woman or a man — is contingent, and can be constructed on the basis of what you choose to build into the equation. Stick to the anatomical, and you can't marry. Accept the psychological and you can. Law can't be disconnected from the society in which it arises.

- Does Kevin correspond to the featureless liberal legal subject? What would be the effect if a court were to treat him as if he did? Has the court here taken a more realistic and individual approach to Kevin?

- Kevin's life is dramatically different from most people's — although not perhaps as dramatically as Borges' classification of animals. He has lived most of it with his body looking female and his brain *knowing* that he's male. Can this be read as a 'text'? If so, what is it saying? Is law well adapted to reading the multi-layered 'interplay of signs' (Chapter 10, p 235) that such a text reveals?

- How would you go about deconstructing the idea of 'man' in the context of marriage? What is its genealogy? What assumptions were built into the law of marriage in its early history? How do these play out in this new context?

Where to from here?

You can imagine that there are many other approaches which could be taken to this material on the basis of theories which we have discussed in this book, as well as those which we've had to leave out.

---

33 Chapter 11 above.
34 Chapter 10 above.

For example, in Chapter 1 (p 5), we mentioned the fact that during the hearing of the appeal of Chisolm J's decision in *Re Kevin*, counsel's submissions made frequent reference to the phrase 'equal concern and respect'. So, how would Dworkin take rights seriously in each of these cases? How would they be afforded 'equal concern and respect'? Which are the rights that would need to be taken seriously? Are they 'hard cases'? How would Dworkin's view of utilitarianism deal with the views of people who have no direct stake in the subject matter, but would nonetheless be upset if native title were granted to the Yorta Yorta people, or if Kevin is allowed to marry 'as a man'?

We are now going to turn things over to you. Do you agree with the starting points and ideas which we've put forward in this chapter? Remember, it's not enough to just disagree with us – if you want to evaluate our statements, you'll need to understand the theory we're talking about, as well as the argument we're putting forward. Ask yourself the questions we set out in Chapter 9[35] as the basis for your own criticism. But above all ...

Have fun!

---

35 Page 223 above.

CHAPTER 15

Concluding, Only to Begin All Over Again

Reading 323
Aim. 323
Where you've been and where you're going 323
Keeping up with 'the Joneses' 326
Breaching the theoretical boundaries 328
Further reading. 329

READING

DAVIES, *Asking the Law Question: the Dissolution of Legal Theory*, 2nd edition, Chapter 1, Chapter 8 (pp 349–351)

AIM

This chapter will:

- see if you can sustain, support, and justify your own theoretical position;
- see if you have been able to make the connections between legal theory and the law itself;
- set you on the path towards finding out about other legal theories;
- help you get your bearings when delving into developing and emerging legal theory.

Where you've been and where you're going

Justifying your position

At the beginning of this book, we posed some questions for you to reflect on.[1] We wanted to you think about the assumptions we bring to law, and asked you

---

1 See pp 1–3 above.

to *support or justify* your response to the questions we posed. We also introduced you to the idea that law has a hidden, as well as a secret, language,[2] to which we can only gain access once we know where to source those ideas – through legal theory!

CHAPTER 1

- Do you remember what your responses were to these points when you first read the chapter?
- Could you justify your standpoint, or support the views you held when you first read it?

That was then and this is now. We assume that if you are reading this last chapter that:

- You have worked your way through most or all of this book, and the reading for each chapter from Davies and Lloyd.
- You have come to know something about the different theories we have looked at in this book, including some understanding of their underlying ideas and methods.
- You will have seen some of the ways we can use legal theory to uncover assumptions we may make about law and the legal process.
- You will have discovered how legal theory is used by judges, to support the legal reasoning in their cases, so that it becomes part of the justification of the decision-making process.
- You may have found where you sit in the legal theory spectrum and be able to justify or support your stance.
- You may know how to use legal theory instrumentally, to assist you in supporting or developing a practical legal argument.
- You may be able to construct a well-supported, reasoned argument using legal theory to justify your position on a legal question.
- You may be able to construct an argument within a theoretical school of thought.
- You have acquired an ability to critically examine or analyse your own standpoint as well as those of the theories and theorists you have met.

ARMED WITH THESE ABILITIES, WHAT DO YOU NOW MAKE OF YOUR INITIAL RESPONSES TO CHAPTER 1?

- Do you still hold the same views? If you do, do you have the tools to explain your standpoint? Which legal theories support your viewpoint?
- Have you changed your mind? What made you change your mind? You will also need to explain why you now adopt a different standpoint.

Looking back to see where we have come from can be a disconcerting experience. Murky ideas are now crystal clear, and concepts that seemed unrelated to your own experiences are now obvious to you.

---

2 See pp 4–5 above.

The capacity to read new material and to justify your views is a skill
you can carry to all your law studies, and into whatever form of legal work
(or other work) you will do in the future.

Using your knowledge and understanding

The same goes for using legal theory in legal practice. In the previous chapter, we saw particular cases where the courts used legal theory to support or justify their decisions. When you read other judgments, it will be up to you to find out if any legal theory has been used, either expressly or impliedly. Knowing this will help you understand a key premise on which the judgment was framed. The same techniques can be used to frame the legal argument contained in submissions to the courts.

Legal theory can be used to help reach decisions in cases such as:

- untested areas of law, like *Yorta Yorta* and *Re Kevin*[3]

- reappraising existing doctrines, like *Garcia*[4]

- cases which highlight competing interests within the ideals of liberalism, such as the competition between the right to free speech and the protection of personal property[5]

- moral questions, like obeying or applying an unjust law,[6] or considering whether life support should be continued.

Theoretical approaches inform the policy decisions of government and administrative agencies.

You can use the same techniques to inform the framing and writing of policy submissions.

Legal theory looks at all sorts of 'real live' law.

Legal theory will also be used to critique or critically examine the approaches adopted by the courts, or policy underlying the law. You may cast a sceptical eye over decisions that look like they have formalistically applied the law to reach 'good' decisions, and ask whether the American Legal Realists and crits were right after all.[7] You will find a vast body of literature — books and journal articles — that examines everything from the natural law foundations of copyright law to the liberal foundations for company law, to Marxist critiques of the legal rights of the homeless.

If we step out of legal theory, and into the general law, we may find some theoretical idea or other underlying the principles in case law and legislation. We may now understand why the work of employees becomes the property of employers,[8] or why the law treats intrusions on liberty and freedom as

---

3   See Chapter 14 above.
4   See Chapter 1 above, p 4.
5   Chapters 4 and 8 above — see also Merkel J at first instance in *Brown v Classification Review Board* (1997) 145 ALR 464.
6   Chapter 3 above.
7   Chapters 9 and 12 above.
8   Chapters 3 and 5 above.

repugnant.[9] We may also appreciate why our personal experience, or common sense,[10] may conflict with law's commonsense.[11]

Keeping up with 'the Joneses'

No, we don't mean literally

What we mean by this is, can we trust a new theory to be a good theory, or one which fits into the theoretical framework we want to adopt? And could we understand it anyway without having someone tells us what the theory means?

Let's start with the use of the theory by the courts. You will find that the courts will fairly readily rely on *conventional legal theory*. This type of theory can be used to justify existing legal frameworks, rather than challenge them, or like Dworkin, represent the practices of judging.[12] On the other hand, the courts will not use the non-conventional critical theories, unless they have been adapted to 'practical' settings by academic writers.[13]

> Another reason why courts and practitioners stay within conventional theoretical frameworks is that trying to work out what a new theory says can be daunting. It is much safer to stay within the boundaries of the theory you have learnt (even if it was 30 years before), because you know what it says and what it does.
>
> It is not surprising that we feel far more comfortable when someone tells us what the theory says, and it is so much better when we think the theory makes sense to us.

So what do you do?

Legal theory, as we saw in Chapter 12, keeps on changing and adapting because of the new insights that theorists bring to all sorts of legal situations. The newest ideas are the most challenging for us, because we may not feel confident about what they mean or say, or whether we can trust them. We want someone to tell us if the theory is safe to use!

We feel safe with books, too, but you should be wary of material published on the web that can't be traced to a reputable source, which is 'self-published' or not published by a reputable publisher. The newest ideas and theoretical insights are published as articles, after being 'refereed' (a little like being examined, in order to ensure the articles are 'up to scratch'). Some of the places you will find legal theory articles are:

---

9 Chapter 4 above.
10 Chapters 8–13 above.
11 Chapters 3–7 above.
12 See Chapter 4 above.
13 See Chapter 1 above, in relation to the *Garcia* case, p 4.

- Specialist journals or the publications of legal philosophy associations and societies like *Law and Critique, law-text-culture, Australian Journal of Legal Philosophy, Legal Theory, Law and Philosophy, Oxford Journal of Legal Studies, Australian Feminist Law Journal*, and the *Australian Journal of Law and Society*. The bibliographies in Davies and Lloyd will give you some idea about the breadth of sources you can access.

- University law reviews and journals and special editions will contain theoretical articles: *Law in Context, Griffith Law Review, Flinders Journal of Law Reform, Alternative Law Journal*, and the journal of our institution, the *QUT Law & Justice Journal*.

- You can also trace ideas through the articles and books referred to in books you are familiar with, like Davies and Lloyd, or the texts we have suggested as further reading.

> We hope you can also use some of the techniques we suggested in Chapter 8, to help you decide if the ideas found in articles are valid.

Changing fashions

What if we like a theory and it suddenly looks like the theory is out of favour, or that you somehow missed the end of CLS and thought it was still going strong? What if CST takes off and you had dismissed it as yet another theoretical fashion?

One of the things about theory is that it is just that — a theory. It is a form of guidance, not a prescription. If you are going to be a theorist, you need to know about the movements in the field, but if you are an ordinary punter, you will sometimes miss out on developments or changes in the field. If this happens, you will start to see a change of emphasis in journal articles, or in the kinds of books being published. While some theorists never change their (theoretical) spots, others may move into new theoretical genres. They may not tell us outright, and you will have to be able to read their argument rather than just labelling them by their original title. You will see that the older Duncan Kennedy has tempered the views of the young Duncan Kennedy,[14] while some postmodern theorists may decide to adopt the methods of positivism. If you think they are still writing as postmodern theorists, you will seriously misread what they write! In other words, be wary of names and labels.

> Non-conventional theory will bring out a response in conventional theory like legal positivism,[15] and the whole process of theoretical change and development continues. As we know, all types of theories are competing for space![16]

---

14 See Lloyd, p 1055.
15 See Lloyd, Chapter 6.
16 See Figure 1.2 above, pp 12–15.

What if we left out a theory?

Just because we have left out a theory, or Davies and Lloyd haven't included it and we have,[17] doesn't mean the theory is not of value, or that there is something wrong or right with it. There are lots of theories we would like to talk about, but there is only so much space available in one book! Some important and useful theories covered by Davies and Lloyd which we have not looked at are:

- Economic analysis of the law[18]
- Common law theory[19]
- Historical and anthropological jurisprudence[20]
- Rawls, Nozick,[21] Raz (in any depth), MacCormick and the newer positivists,[22] ethical and other new positivists[23]
- Luhmann, Tamanaha,[24] Unger and Habermas.[25]

Because of the way we have structured this book, we have not looked at some of the important thematic considerations in legal theory — like rights in general, or concepts of justice — in any depth,[26] and you should take the opportunity to think about these issues. We have also limited our treatment of fundamental theorists like Aristotle, Kant and Hegel (and others). We hope you will find the occasion to read further into some of these areas.

Legal theory is a huge domain and it has all sorts of (conceptual, not real) fences placed around its different traditions and patterns of thought.

Breaching the theoretical boundaries

We thought we would end this book with a theoretical bang. Margaret Davies says she ends her book not to end it.[27] We will conclude ours by (very briefly) starting all over again, as this chapter title suggests. We will introduce you to ideas that have been sitting at the legal theoretical margins: the *law and literature movement*, which has been around at least since the 1970s.

Conventional forms of 'law and lit' are based around two strands of thought. One centres around *law IN literature* (or how the law is dealt with by novels, poems, film and so on), and includes explorations of legal forms in 'classics' like Dickens' *Bleak House*, Shakespeare's *The Merchant of Venice*, and Kafka's *The Trial*. Contemporary legal storytelling is examined as well, to engage with

---

17 As we told you in Chapter 1, pp 6–8, we have sometimes supplemented the material in Davies and Lloyd.
18 Davies, Chapter 4.
19 Davies, Chapter 2; Lloyd, Chapter 17.
20 Lloyd, Chapter 11.
21 Lloyd, Chapter 7.
22 Lloyd, Chapter 6.
23 Davies, Chapter 3.
24 Lloyd, Chapter 8.
25 Lloyd, Chapters 8 and 13.
26 Lloyd, Chapter 7.
27 Davies, p 351.

the nature of legal interpretation, judging and authority, and to consider the limits of the role of law. The other strand of thought is centred around *law AS literature* (by adopting literary forms of analysis, deconstruction and the like to legal texts, ie case law). Think of Dworkin's chain novel,[28] as a classic (albeit narrowly focused) archetype of this form. Judges use literary analogies and extracts in (some) judgments, while legal theorists use metaphor, parable and stories to illustrate argument. Think of Lon Fuller's story of Rex,[29] Llewellyn's poetic turns of phrase,[30] and the examples used throughout Davies', such as Valerie Kerruish's critique of Finnis,[31] and Patricia Williams' criticisms of the crits.[32]

Through conventional law and literature, law is effectively seen to be a practice based in the humanities, instead of the social and formal sciences that law has taken to be its natural 'external' home. Law, of course, is based in language, and its practices adopt the forms and practices of theatre. It is thought that the insights of literature will provide another dimension to the practices of law, and an understanding of the effects of law.

So this is where we end. We have taken you to a partial end, and have left you with literature to take up in the further reading.[33] We have ended abruptly, so that you can take up this story for yourselves.

FURTHER READING

Bix, Brian, *Jurisprudence: theory and context*, 2nd edition (Sweet & Maxwell, London, 1999).

Campbell, Tom D (ed), *Legal positivism* (Dartmouth, Aldershot, 1999).

Campbell, Tom & Goldsworthy, Jeffrey (eds), *Judicial power, democracy and legal positivism* (Dartmouth, Aldershot, 2000).

Dolin, Kieran, *Fiction and the law: legal discourse in Victorian and modernist literature* (Cambridge University Press, Cambridge, 1999).

Gearey, Adam, *Law and aesthetics* (Hart, Oxford, 2001).

Goodrich, Peter, *Law in the courts of love: literature and other minor jurisprudences* (Routledge, London, 1996).

Kramer, Matthew H, *In defense of legal positivism: law without trimmings* (Oxford University Press, Oxford, 1999).

Manderson, Desmond, *Songs without music: aesthetic dimensions of law and justice* (University of California Press, Berkeley, 2000).

---

28 Chapter 5 above, pp 126–128.
29 Chapter 3 above, pp 68–69.
30 Chapter 9 above, p 219.
31 Davies, p 86.
32 Davies, p 179.
33 Of course, you will have to work out which listed texts or chapters will be the right ones for you to follow through!

Morison, John & Bell, Christine (eds), *Tall stories? Reading law and literature* (Dartmouth, Aldershot, 1996).

Polloczek, Dieter Paul, *Literature and legal discourse: equity and ethics from Sterne to Conrad* (Cambridge University Press, Cambridge, 1999).

Sarat, Austin & Kearns, Thomas R (eds), *Law in the domains of culture* (University of Michigan Press, Ann Arbor, 1998).

Thornton, Margaret (ed), *Romancing the tomes: popular culture, law and feminism* (Cavendish, London, 2002).

Ward, Ian, *Law and literature: possibilities and perspectives* (Cambridge University Press, Cambridge, 1995).

Index

[page numbers in *italics* refer to a diagram; page numbers in **bold** indicate a major discussion of a topic]

Aboriginal Australians *see* indigenous Australians

abortion, 75, 255

absolute knowledge, 85, 98

absolute power of sovereign, 62, 157

absolute values, 229

abstract theories *see* conceptual theories

accountability, 145

active learning, 28

active reason, 54

Acts *see* statutes

adjudication, rules of, 174, *175*, 175–176

administration, 210–211

adversarial system, *264*, 266

affirmative action, 114

African Americans, 21

Age of Reason, 66, *85*, 86 *see also* Enlightenment, The

alienation, 193, **194**, 283, 284, 287, 315

Althusser, 278

America, *13–15*, 157, 212

American Declaration of Independence, 111, 112, 118, 130

American Legal Realists, *14*, 19, 20, 206, **216–222**, 286, 311, 320

analysis
  Bloom's, *34*, 35, *37*
  conventional, 236
  classical Marxist, 198
  Enlightenment, 86
  in judgments, 27
  modernist, 87, 95
  positivist, 18, 66, 140–141, 142, 144
  postmodern, 229, 249 *see also* deconstruction
  statistical, 207
  see also methods

analytical jurisprudence, 18

Ancient Greece, *12*, 16, 51, **53–55**, 86

Ancient Rome, *12*, 16, **56–57**, 145

Anetts v Australian Stations Pty Ltd, *15*

Ansett (example), 198–199

anthropology, 229, 310, 315, 316

anti-discrimination legislation, 129, 298, 299, 301

anti-Establishment, 187, 188, 197, 281

anti-feminism, 267

Antigone, 51

antithesis, 190, *191*, *193*

application of theory, 5, 32, *34*, 35, *37*, 274

Aquinas, St Thomas, *12*, *15*, 48, 50, 51, **57–61**, 65, 73, 74–75, 79

arguments, 2, 3, 22, 27, 29, 31, 35, 73

Aristotle, *12*, 49, 50, 51, **54–55**, 57–58, 59, 68, 73, 120, 312

Armory v Delamirie, 13

assumptions
  causes of, 17, 92, 93
  denying, 95
  exposing, 1, 21, 35, 96, 186, 204, 241, 242–243, *243*, 244, 288, 304
  not accepting, 3, 207, 259, 267, 321

Athens, 53

Atkin, Lord, 234

Augustine, St, *12*, 48, **57**, 58

Austin, John, *14*, 38–39, 66, 110, **140–142**, 143, **151–164**, 181, 246
  criticisms of, 18, 38–39, 165, 169

Australian Constitution, 103, 112

author, intended meaning of, 231, **234–236**

authority, 154, 220, 229, *247*, *248*

autocracy, 87, 90, 196

autonomy, 89, 91, 111, 114, *115*

Averroës, *12*, 57–58

Avicenna, *12*

bad law, 45, 72

'bad man', 217

balancing method, 215, 313

Balkin, JM, 242, 244

Barthes, Roland, 229, **235**

base, 191, *193*, 276, 277

basic goods *see* goods, Finnis'

behaviour, 144, 147, 177, 288 *see also*
    judicial behaviourism

Behrendt, Larissa, 303

Bell, Derrick, 299

Bentham, Jeremy, *14*, 18, 38, 66, 110,
    140–142, **143–151**, 152, 164, 242,
    246, 318
    utilitarianism, 120, 139, 144, 146, 148,
        318

Bernstein v Skyviews, 15

Bhabha, Homi, 305, 316

biases, 221

Bill of Rights, 112

binary opposition, 240, 245, 266, 304

black feminism, 266–267

Blackstone, William (*Commentaries*), *13*, 66,
    144

Bloody Sunday, 298

Bloom, Benjamin, 33–37, *34*

Blumenbach, Johann, 296–297

blunt instrument approach, 275, 276, 286,
    320

Bolton v Stone, 14

Borges, Jorge Luis, 99, 231

bottom-up view of law, 247, *248*

bourgeoisie, 192–193

Bridges v Hawkesworth, 14

Bruno, Giordano, 93

bureaucracies, 210–211

business law *see* contract law

calculus, 147

capitalism
    assumptions, 97
    development of, 17, 62, 145, **189**, 197,
        279
    facilitating (Weber), 209, *210*, 212
    Marx's view, *192*, 192, *193*, **194–195**,
        275, 278

Carlill v Carbolic Smoke Ball, *14*

Cartesian *see* Descartes, Rene

Cartesian subject *see* individuals, Cartesian

case law *see* common law

categorisation, 54, 99, 179–180, 231, 283,
    297, 314, 315, 320 *see also* types of
    law

Catholic Church, 46, 61, 72–73, 80

Caucasian form, 297

censorial jurisprudence, 144, 146, 318

censorship, 261

certainty, 221, 222 *see also* uncertainty

chain novels (Dworkin's example), 126–128

change
    for Durkheim, 207–208
    for Marx, 190–192
    for postmodernists, 249
    for realists, 219

changing the rules, 174–175, 177, 179

Chisholm J, 317–318, 320, 321

choices, 114, *115*, 117

Church (as institution), *12*, 16, 38, 57, 58,
    86, 92–3, 155 *see also* religion;
    Catholic Church

Cicero, Marcus Tullius, *12*, 50, **56–57**

citizen, 55 *see also* individuals

city-state, 53–54, *54*

civil rights movements, 21, 254, *294*,
    297–299, 301

classes (Marx's), 192–194, 275, 276, 277, 278

classical Marxism, 198, 314

classical positivism, *138*, 141–142, 143, 169,
    312

classification *see* categorisation

cloning, 73, 75

'close analogy', law by, 160–161, 162

clubs, 160

codification, 145, 146, 148–149, *149*, *210*,
    242, 318

cogito ergo sum, 88

Cohen, Felix, **218**, *224*

colonisation/colonialism, 296, 297, 304–306,
    316 *see also* postcolonial theory

colour-blind law, 295, 297, 301

commands, 141, 150, 151, **152–154**,
    158–160, *158*, *159*, 169

commerce, 17, 62, 111, 112, 117, 145, 192, *193*, 197

commercial law *see* contract law

commodity-form theory, 277, 286, 287

common good, 68, *73*, 75, 76, *77*, 78

common law
  assumptions in, 204
  criticisms of, 144–146, 149, *210*, 211, 212
  events, *12–15*
  using, 126, 153, 156, 220, 248

Commonwealth
  Cromwell's, 62
  Hobbes and Locke's, 63, 64

Commonwealth Constitution of Australia, 103, 112

communication, 70, 150, **153**

communism, 186, *189*, *192*, 194, 279, 281

community
  Bentham's rejection of, 147
  in liberalism, 117, 124, 128–129, 130, 131
  in natural law, *45*, 54, *55*, 59, *60*, 68,
    69–70, 73, 312–313

company law, 197, 199

comprehension, *34*, **35**, *37*

Concept of Law (Hart), 71, 167

conceptual theories, 5, *14*, 18, 97, 98, 99,
  100, 141–142

'concrete' norms, 102, *103*

conferring power, 169, 175

conformity, 231

conscience, 48, 76, *77*

consciousness raising, 260

conservatism, 46, 80, 187, 200, 236, 257,
  267, 282, 319

constitutional law, 103–104, *105*, 111, 151,
  161, 174, 176, 236

constitutional monarchy, 64, 196

consumers, 4–5, 244

contemporary social theory (CST), 272, *273*,
  281, *285*, **287–289**

context, 80, 229, 236, *237*, 238–240, 244,
  249, 264, 265

contraception, 46, 61, 70

contract law
  assumptions, 4, 92, 244
  criticisms of, 284
  development, *13*, *14*, 145, 197, 244
  examples, 71, 89, 114, 117, 230, 283

conventional theories, **10–11**, 21–22, 38,
  188, 195, **231**, **236**, 247, 272, 326

Copernicus, Nicolas, 62

Corbett, 317, 318, 319, 321

'core of certainty', 179–180, *180*, *243*

corporations, 4–5

corporations law, 197, 199

corruption, 144–145

Cotterrell, Roger, 206

counter-culture, 187, 188, 197, 281

courts, operation of, 87

crafts of law, 220–221

criminal law, 44, 67, 71, 117, 152, 169, 175,
  196

Critical Legal Studies (CLS), 9, *15*, **20**, 21,
  272, *273*, 281, **282–287**, 289, 299,
  302, **314–315**, **320**

critical legal theory (CLT), 275, 281, 288–289

Critical Race Theory (CRT), 9, 10, *15*, 21,
  294, **299–303**, 307

critical theories, 3, *15*, 19, 20–21, 39, 230,
  271–290

critical theory, 275, **279–281**, 286, 287, 314
  see also Frankfurt School

critical thinking, 37, 199

criticising theories, 36, 50, 79, 222–224

Crito (Plato), 54

crits *see* Critical Legal Studies

Cromwell, Oliver, 62

cultural feminism, 263–266

customary law, 161, 306, 311, 312

Darwin, Charles, 97

Davies, Margaret, 7, 10–11, 21–22, 50, 51,
  79

De Legibus (Cicero), 56

De Re Publica (Cicero), 56

decision-making, 76, 78, 123–124, 144–145,
  236, 325 *see also* judgments

Declaration of Independence (US), 111, 112,
  118, 130

Declaration of the Rights of Man and Citizen,
  111, 112

Declaration of the Rights of Woman and
  Citizen, 254

decolonisation, 305, 306

deconstruction, 22, 231, 236, **241–246,** **248–249,** 266, 286, 287

deduction, 89, 142

deity *see* God

Delgado, Richard, 300–302

delict, 101

democracy, 46, 53, 87, 91, 196

denial, 287

deontological view of rights, 119

Depression, 217, 218

Derrida, Jacques, *228,* 229, 240–241, 245, 249

Descartes, Rene, *13,* 17, 62, *85,* 87, **88–92,** 141

Devlin, Lord, 282

Dewey, John, *14,* 217, *224,* 267

dialectic method, 53

dialectical materialism, 190–191, *191*

differance, 245

difference, 230–231, *232–233,* 237, 258

discrimination, 129, 254, 261, 267, 298, 301, 302, 303

divine laws, 158

divine right of kings, 17, 90, 196

divorce, 154, 175, 230

doctrine of precedent, 145, 247

doctrines, 248

'dog law', 145–146

domestic violence, 116

dominant groups, 197, 260, 277, 278, 295, 302

dominant values/views, 197, 230, 244, 249, 260, 266, 275, 281, 304

domination, legitimate, 211

Donoghue v Stevenson, 14, 153, 234

Durkheim, Emile, *14,* 19, 206, *207,* **207–209,** *223–224*

duty of care, 93, 153, 234, 248

Dworkin, Ronald, 5, 17, 110, 115, **122–133,** 181, **261–262,** *262,* 322, 329

economics
    Marx's emphasis on, 19, 186, 190–191, 192, 194, 195–**196,** 200, 276, 277
    Weber's views, 209, 211–212

emerging theories, *9,* 10, *15,* 21, 272

empiricism, 62, 66, 95, 106, **141, 142,** 207, 217, 218, 281, 288, 289

employees, 198–199

enforcement, 150, 151

Engels, Friedrich, 186, 194

England, 61–66, *210,* 211

English Civil War, 62

Enlightenment, The, *13,* 16, 49, 62, 66, *85,* **86,** 92, 93, 96, 121, 142, 146, 155, 156, 229

Entick v Carrington, 13, 112, 121, 197

'equal concern and respect', 5, 130–131, 322

equality
    of classes, 193
    Hart's, 71
    liberal, **118,** 124, 130, 256, 258, 296
    of men and women, 20, 254, 256, 258
    positivist, 148
    racial, 296, 299
    see also inequalities

equity, 38, 55

essays, 29, 52

essentialism, 266, 268, 302, 304, 307, 321

Establishment, The, 187, 197, 204

eternal law, 57, 59, *60,* 65, 66

ethics, 45

Ethics, The (Aristotle), 54, 55

Europe
    medieval, *12,* 57–61
    modern, *13–14,* 61–72

euthanasia, 75

evaluation, *34,* **36,** *37*

evidence, 87, 96, 116, 122, 142, 209

evil law, 45, 72

experience vs logic, 217

experiences of people of colour, 301, 302

experiences of women, 20, 252, 255, 266, 268

expert witnesses, 123, 143

expository jurisprudence, 144, 149–150

external aspect of rules, 170

external standpoint, 3, 187, 206

Fascism, 279, 281

fact skeptics, *14,* 220, 286

facts, 87, 96, 142–143, 221–222, 314

false consciousness, 260, 268

families, 54, *55*

family law, 230

felicific calculus, 147–148, *147*, 149

feminism, **252–268**, 321

feminist legal theory, 4, *9*, 10, *15*, 20, 254

feudalism, 58, 91, 117, 155, *192, 193*

Finnis, John, 7, *15*, 16, 48, 49, 50, 51, 67,
    72–80, 312–313, 319

'first constitution', 103–104, *105*

first moral principle, *74*, **76**, *77*, 319

first order principles, 60, 61, 78, *78*

formal law, *210*

formal style of judging, 221

formalism, 216, 217, 299, 325

Foucault, Michel, 99, *228*, 229, **246–247**,
    304, 321

Frank, Jerome, *14*, 220, **221–222**

Frankfurt School, 207, *273*, 278, **279–280**
    see also critical theory

free market, 194, 199

freedom, 89, 91, 113, 130

freedom of speech, 130, 261–262

Freedom Rides, 298

Freeman, Alan, 299

French revolution, 46, *85*, 86, 111, 113, 118,
    121

Freudian psychoanalysis, 279

Fuller, Lon, *14–15*, 51, **67–70**, 71, 329

functionalism, 220

Gabel, Peter, 302

Galileo, Galilei, 62, 92–93

gaps in rules, 181

Garcia v National Australia Bank Limited 4,
    325

gender, 241, 260

genealogy, 244, 246, 286, 287, 288–289, 315

generality of commands/laws, 154, 173

Gilligan, Carol, 263–266

globalisation, 306

goals, 114, 117, 118, 128, 129, 131–132

God, 16, 17, 44, 50, 51, 57–59, *60*, 64, 65,
    66, 67, 92, 158

Golden Rule, 76

good, 45

good law, 45, 51, 144, 319

good life, 54, 69, 70, 73

goods
    Aristotle's, 54, *55*
    Finnis', 49, 73, *74*, **74–76**, *77*, 78, 79,
        312–313, 319

government
    liberal views, *13, 91*, 111, 114, 115, *116*,
        118, 121, *121*, 164, 196
    natural law view, 64
    positivist views, 151, 157
    postmodern view, 246–247, *247*

Gramsci, Antonio, 207, *273*, 277, 278, **281**

grand style of judging, 221

Great Depression, 217, 218

Greece, Ancient, *12*, 16, 51, **53–55**, 86

grudge cases (Nazi), 67–68

Grundnorm, 103–105, 141

Guide of the Perplexed (Maimonides), 58

Habermas, Jürgen, *273*, 278, 280, 288

habits, 170

Hale LJ, 204

happiness, 147–148, *147*

hard cases, 125–126, 128

'harm principle', 116–117, *117*

Hart, HLA, *14–15*, 18, 38–39, 67–68, **70–72**,
    167–181, 187, 206, 236, 242, *243*,
    282, **312**

Hedley Byrne v Heller, *15*

Hegel, Georg, *13*, 190, 279

hegemony, 198, 207, *273*, 275, 277,
    281–282, 286, 287, 314

Hellenism, 54

Hercules J (Dworkin's super-judge), 128, 129,
    133, 181

hidden language of law, 3, 38

hierarchy of norms, 101–103, *102*

historical change, 190–192, *193*, 194–195

historical context, 8, *12–15*, 80, 84–86, 236

historical legal record, 127

historical origins *see* genealogy

Hobbes, Thomas, *13*, 50, **62–63**, 64, 72

Holmes, Justice Oliver Wendell, *14*, 19, 217

homosexuality, 73, 75

human condition, 71

human law, 45, 46, 48, 50, 56, 57, **58**, 59, 60, 61, 65, **78–79**, 158, **159–60**, 162

human rights, 45, 46, 48, 66–67, 111, 118, 164 *see also* rights

Human Rights and Equal Opportunity Commission, 130

Hume, David, *13*, 49, 66, **94–95**, *142*, 146

hybridity, 305, 316

hypotheses, 92

idealism, 190, 220, 279

ideals, 133

Ideological State Apparatuses (ISAs), 278

ideology
    or Marxists, 197–198, 275, 278
    for postmodernists, 244

imperialism, 304–305

inalienable rights, 64–65, 118

indigenous Australians, 21, 296, 298, 303 *see also* native title; customary law

individualism, 117

individuals
    Cartesian, 87, 88, **89–92**, *90*, 111, 146, 236, 238, 240
    and CRT, 21, 294–296, 307
    and CST, 288
    Durkheim's, 207–208
    Enlightenment, 92, 114, 117, 236
    Hobbes' and Locke's, 62–65
    Kant's, 119
    and liberalism, 4, 21, 124, 128–129, 130, 256, 262, 294–296
    male vs female perspectives, 264–265
    and modernism, 96, 117, 146, 240, 283
    and natural law, 45, 50, 51, 59, *73*
    and positivism, 140, 147
    and postmodernism, 231, **236–240**, 247, 283
    Pound's, 214–215, *214*, 319
    Weber's, 209

Industrial Revolution, *14*, *189*, 194–195

inequalities, 186, 246, 254, *257*, 258, 259, 261, 284, 300

infrastructure, 191, *193*

Inquisition, Holy, 93

insiders, legal, *177*, 187, 231, 236, *247*, 312

'instinctive' ideas, 87–88

Institute for Social Research *see* Frankfurt School

institutions of law, 220, 221, 275, 288, 302, 312 *see also* legal systems

instrumental use of theories, 4

interdisciplinary theories, 272, 288

interests, theory of, 213–215

internal aspect of rules, 170–171, *171*

internal standpoint, 3 *see also* insiders

international law, 98, 118, 130, 161, 169

interpretation
    Dworkin's, 123–124, 125–126
    Hart's (of words), 18, 242
    postmodern, 234–236, *235*, 241, 242
    of statutes, 113, 317, 318

inter-subjectivity, 280, 287

irrationality, 142, 144, 209, *210*, *211* *see also* rationality

is and ought, 66, 67, 73, 74, 99–100, 142–143, 219

Jaensch v Coffey, 15

Jews in Nazi Germany, 21, 66–67

journals, 327

judges, 144–145, 149, 154, 156, 157, 176, 181

judgments, 87, 123–124, 125, 127–128, 133, 221, 267 *see also* decision-making

judicial behaviourism, 218, 222

jural postulates, *213*, 215, *216*, 314

jurimetrics, 218, 222

jurisprudence (definition), 6

justice, 55, 66, 98, 249, 264

justifying your views, 2, 3, 27

Kant, Immanuel, *13*, 18, 97, **99**, **119**, 120, 279

Kelsen, Hans, *14–15*, 18, 87, 94, **97–106**, **141–142**

Kerruish, Valerie, 79, 329

King, Martin Luther, Jr, 298

kings *see* divine right of kings; monarchy

knowledge
   in critical theory, 280
   good of, **75**, *77*
   modernist, 95, 98, 99
   and power *see* power/knowledge
   of theories, **16**, 29, **34**, *34*, *37*

Kohlberg, Lawrence, 263

Kolb, David, 30–33

Kuhn, Thomas, 96–97

Labor government, 4–5, *15*

labour, 64, 71, 192

Lacan, Jacques, 229, 287

laissez-faire capitalism/liberalism, *189*, 194,
   195, 200

Lamarck, Jean, 97

land rights *see* native title

landowners, 65, 192, 315 *see also* property,
   private ownership

language, 18, 38, 145, 149, 169, **179–181**,
   231, 234, **240–241**, 242, 329 *see
   also* law's hidden language; law's
   secret language

Lat-Crit, 303

law (definitions)
   Aquinas, 59
   Austin, 141, 152, 157–158
   Bentham, 149–150
   Durkheim, 208–209

law and literature, 234, 328–330

law by 'close analogy', 160–161, 162

law by 'slender analogy', 161–162

law-jobs, 220–221

law properly so called, **158**

law strictly so called, 163–164

law's hidden language, 3, 38

law's secret language, 4–5, 309

Leaf v International Galleries, *14*

learning as a process, 28

learning styles, 30–33

learning theory, 25–40

legal philosophy (defined), 6

legal positivism, 3, *9*, *14*, 16, **17–18**, 51, 66,
   67, **94–95**, **137–183**, 188, 212, 216
   see also positivism

legal subject *see* individuals

legal systems
   Bentham and Austin's, 140, 141, 144,
      150, 154
   Fuller's, 67–69
   Hart's, 72, 170, *178–179*
   Kelsen's, **97–99**, 100, 141
   Weber's, 209–212

legal theory (defined), 6

legislation *see* statutes

legitimate domination, 211

Leviathan (Hobbes), 62–63, *63*

Levi-Strauss, Claude, 229

Lewis, CS, 246

'lex injusta non est lex', 61, **79**

liberal (definition), 91, 112–113

liberal feminism, 255–258, 259, 268

Liberal government, *15*

liberal political philosophy, 3, 17, 188

liberal subject *see* individuals, and liberalism

liberalism, *9*, *13–15*, **17**, **109–133**, *193*, 283
   as a basis of thought, 3, 4, 20
   critiques of, 20–21, 133, 195, 283, 301
   see also liberal feminism

liberation movements, 245, 255–256, 282 *see
   also* women's liberation movement

liberty, **113–115**, 148

life
   good of, **75**, 76, *77*, 313, 319
   preservation of, 65

limitations, statutory periods, 120

literature, 234, 328–330

Llewellyn, Karl, *14*, 206, 218, 218, **219**,
   220–221, 329

Lloyd (textbook), 22

Locke, John, *13*, 50, 62, **64–65**, 72, 111

logic, 54, 89, 144, 217

'looking in ourselves', 50–51

Lyotard, Jean Francois, *228*, 229

Mabo, *15*, 161

MacCormick, Sir Neil, 176

Machiavelli, Niccolo, 281

MacKinnon, Catharine, 261–262, *262*

McLoughlin v O'Brian, 129

Maimonides, Moses, *12*, 58

mandatory sentencing, 47–48

Mansfield, Lord, *13*, 145, 197

market-based economy, 91–92 *see also* capitalism

marriage, 175, 246, 317–322

Marriage Act, 317, 318

Married Women's Property Act (UK), 254

Marx, Karl, 5, *14*, 19, 39, 65, 91, **185–201**, 207, 259, 281, 287, 314, 320

Marxism, 9, 10, *15*, 97, 186, **259–261**, 273, **274–279**, 288, 320 *see also* classical Marxism

Marxist Legal Theories (MLTs), **274–279**, 286

materialism, 190–191, 279

Maurice, Michael, QC, 48

meanings of text, 234–236, *235*, 243, *243*, 245 *see also* words

mediated texts, 242

mediation, 266

medieval Europe, *12*, 57–61

metanarratives, 85, 94, 199, 229, 249

metaphysics, 67, 68

methods, 3, 27, 32, 36, 274, 279
  Cartesian, 89
  critical theories, 285
  CRT, 301
  Marxist, 275
  modernism, 88–95, 199
  natural law, 49–51, 67, 74
  positivism, 71, 141
  postmodernism, 20, 22, 249 *see also* deconstruction
  sociological, 206, 207, 209, 213–215
  EP Thompson's, 275

middle class, 62, 195 *see also* bourgeoisie

Mill, John Stuart, **116–117**, 146, 254

Miller v Race, *13*

minimum content (Hart's), 70–72

minority groups, 124, 295, 302, 303, 307, 318

mode of production, 190, 191, *193*

modernism, 9, *13–15*, *17*, **83–107**, 140, 144, 146, *193*, 199, **229–230**, 318

monarchy, *13*, 17, 38, 50, 53, 62, 64, 90–91, 151, 154, 155, 157

Monty Python and the Holy Grail, 90–91, 112, 155, 209, 240

moral dilemmas, 44, 263

moral questions, 71

morality, 68, 69–70, *70*, 76, 95, *139*, 141, 142, 150, 162, 173, 244

Morality of Law, The (Fuller), 67–68

morals, 16, 45, 48, 67, 74, *77*, 80, 124, 130, 263–264, 282

motivation, 147, 150

multidisciplinary theories, 279, 288, 301

murder, 61, 78, 125, 129, 153, 169, 242

narrative method, 301, 305, 307

nation-state, 141, 155

native title, *15*, 297, 310, 312, 316

natural law, 8, *9*, 10, *12–15*, 16, 21, **43–81**, 123, 164, 211, 229–230
  criticisms of, 80, 124, 147, 188
  Re Kevin case, 319
  Yorta Yorta case, 312–313

natural rights, 61–65, 79, 144, 148

nature (Hobbes'), 64

Nazi Germany, 21, 66–68, 69, 72, 97, 123, 279

needs (societal vs individual), 45

negative liberty, 113–114

negligence, 93, 153, 156, 173, 175, 195, 234, 248

neutrality, 249, 267, 283, 295, 315

Nicomachean Ethics (Aristotle), 54, 55

Nietzsche, Friedrich, 244

non-conventional theories, **10–11**, 39, **186–188**, 205, 248–249, 272

non-obligation rules, 171–172, *172*

norms, 98, **99–106**, 141, 311

Northern Territory sentencing laws, 47–48

obedience, *151*, 155, *156*

objectivity
  and CLS, 283, 284
  and critical theory, 280, 314
  and feminism, 266
  and modernism, 87, 93–94, 95, 96, 98
  and positivism, 142, 146
  and postmodernism, 199, 249
  and scientific method, 92, 96

obligation rules, 171–178, *172*, 174, *178*

observation, 92, 95, 106, 142

officials, legal, 177–178, *177*, 312

'open texture' of language, 179–181

opinions, 143

oppression, 195, 259, *260*, 267, 297, 302, 305, 307

Orientalism (Said), 303–304, 307, 316

original thought, *34*, 35, 36–37

Ormrod LJ, 317, 319, 320

O'Shane, Pat, 263

ought and is, 66, 67, 73, 74, 99–100, 142–143, 219

outsider's view of law, 187 *see also* external standpoint

Oz trial, 122–123, 197, 275, 281–282

pain and pleasure, 147–148

paradigm shifts, 97

Pareto, Vilfredo, 281

Parker v British Airways Board, *15*

parliament, 46, 62, 64, 151, 154, 155, 157, 176

Parsons, Talcott, 207, 281, 288

Pashukanis, E, *273*, 277, 286

passive learning, 28

patriarchy, 259, 261, *300*

Payne v Cave, *13*

Penfolds Wine v Elliot, *14*

'penumbra' of doubt, 179–180, *180*, 242, *243*

'persons, property and promises', 46, **61–65**, 72, 173, *214*

philosophies, 2

philosophy, *12*, 38, *193*, 229

physics, 94

Plato, *12*, 53–54

pleasure and pain, 147–148

police powers, 122

policies, 124, 128–132, 204, 215

political (definition), 91

political nature of law, 124, 286

political philosophy, 62

political power, 91, 111, 117, 121, 155, 306

Politics, The (Aristotle), 54

pornography, 115, 123, 130, 261–262, 267

positive law, 142, 159–160, *163*, 211

positive liberty, 114, 115

positive morality, 162, *162*

positivism, 3, *14–15*, **17–18**, 38–39, **137–183**, 219, 242
  and modernism, 84, 87
  and natural law, 67, 71, 72, 123
  and postmodernism, 229, 230
  Re Kevin case, 318
  Yorta Yorta case, 311–312
  see also legal positivism

postcolonial theory, 9, 10, *15*, 21, *294*, **303–306**, 307, 316

postmodern feminism, 266, 321

postmodernism, 5, 9, *15*, 19, **20**, 21–22, **227–249**, 286
  definition, 228–229
  and Marxism, 199
  and postcolonialism, 303–304
  Re Kevin case, 321

poststructuralism, 5, 9, 19, 20, 286

Pound, Roscoe, *14*, 19, 188, 206, **212–216**, *224*, 313–314, 319

power *see* conferring power; political power

power/knowledge, 231, 246–248, *247*, 304, 321

practical reason, 59, 60, 79

practical reasonableness, 73, *74*, **75**, **76–77**, 78, 313, 319

practical use of theory *see* application of theory

practical wisdom, 54

pragmatic feminism, 267

pragmatism, 19, 206, 216–217, 218, 219, *224*

precedent, 145, 247

prejudices, 221

primary rules, 173–174, 179, 312

primary sources, 40

primitive societies, 174, 177, *192*, 208, 312

principles, 124, 125, 128–132, 144

private sphere, 115, *116*, 215

proceduralism, 51, 68, 70

Prohibition of Discrimination Act 1966 (SA), 298

proletariat, 192–193, 194, 195, 200, 279

proof, 96

property, private ownership, 65, 112, 192, 194, 195, 313

property law, 44, 61, 78

property rights, 17, 62, 64, 65, 71, 112, 148, 196, 256 *see also* native title

Province of Jurisprudence Determined, The (Austin), 152, *163*

psychoanalysis, 229, 279, 286, 287

public sphere, 115, 214–215

punishment, 65, 146, 147, 150–151, 154, 196 *see also* sanctions

Queensland Constitution Act (1867), 175, 176

Queensland Criminal Code, 174, 245

Queensland Succession Act (1981), 175

R v Jack Congo, 14

'race', 296–297, 300

racism, 297, 299, *300*, 301, 302

radical (definition), 188

radical feminism, 259–263, 268, 299, 321

radical skeptics, 220, 222

rape, 204, **245–246**, 267

rationalism, 229, 249, 266

rationality, 88, 146, 148–149, 209–210, *210*, *211* see also irrationality

Raz, Joseph, 114

Re Kevin, 5, *15*, **317–322**

reading legal theory, 26–27, **38–40**, 243

reading natural law theory, 51–52

readings, 37, 235, 241

realism, 217–220, 299 *see also* American Legal Realists

reason, 16, 50, 51, 53, 54, 56, 57, 58–59, 60, *60*, 61, 75, 76, 88, 89, 312

reasonable person test, 93–94, 236, 240

received wisdom, 229

recognition, rule of, 174, *175*, **176–178**, *177*, 181, 236, 309, 311, 312

reification, 287

reforms, 4–5, 204, *258*

regulation, 115, 118, 169, 173

relationships
  female perspective, *264*, 265
  for Marx, 186
  for postmodernists, *238*, *239*

relative autonomy model, 275, 276, 320

religion, 38, 50, 51, 67, *77*, 91, 150, *193*, 313 see also Church (as institution)

Renaissance, *13*, *85*, **86**, 92

repressive law, *208*

Republic (Plato), 53–54

restitutive law, *208*

retrospective nature of common law, 145–146

revolutionary changes, 190, 192, 282

revolutions, 46, 62, 63, 64, 68, 72, *85*, 86, 111, 118, 121, 194, 196, 278, 282

reward, 147, 151, 153

Rex (Fuller's parable), 68–69

Riggs v Palmer, 125, 128, 129

rights, *13*
  and CLS, 283, 287
  and CRT, 21, 302–303
  of individuals vs society, 262
  and liberalism, 17, **118–120**, *119*, 124, 128, 130, **131–132**
  male vs female perspectives, 263–264, *264*
  and natural law, 45, 46, 50, 63
  as trumps, 131–132, *262*
  of women, 255–256, 257
  see also civil rights movements; human rights; natural rights; property rights; voting rights

road rules, 140, 173

Robertson, Geoffrey, 187

Roe v Wade, 255

Romanticism, *14*

Rome, Ancient, *12*, 16, **56–57**, 145

Roscorla v Thomas, 14

rule of law, **120–122**, *121*

rule of recognition *see* recognition, rule of

rule skeptics, *14*, 220, 221

rules, 68–69, 71, 126, 144
  for Hart, 170–179, 181
  of sports, 160

rules of adjudication, 174, *175*, 175–176

ruling ideas, 197–198, 200, 277

Rylands v Fletcher, 14

Said, Edward, 303–304, 316

sanctions, 98, **100–101**, 105–106, 141, 150–151, 153–154, 173 *see also* punishment

Saussure, Ferdinand de, 240

scepticism, 67, 87, 89, *300*

Schlag, Pierre, 247–248

science, *13*, 62, 86, 96–97, 247, 296–297, 318

scientific method, 17, 87, 88, **92–93**, 95, 96, 97, 142, 207

SCIG v Trigwell, *15*, 145

'seamless web' of the law, 133

Searle v Wallbank, *14*, 145

secondary principles, 60, 78, *78*

secondary rules, 173, 174–176, *175*, 177, 179

secret language of law, 4–5, 309

secular natural law, 67–68, 73

self-evidence, 49, 51, 73, 74

separation of powers, 64

'separation thesis', 139, 141

Shaw v DPP, *15*

skeptics *see* scepticism; rule skeptics; fact skeptics; radical skeptics

slavery, *192*, 297

'slender analogy', law by, 161–162

Smith v Baker, *14*

social cohesion, 208, 213

social consciousness, 197

social contract, 50, 62–63, 64, 72, *85*, 87, 89, 91, 111

social engineering, 212–213, 215

social rules, 171–172, *172*

social theory, 287–289

socialism, 186

society
    and critical theory, 280
    for Foucault, 247
    and Marxism, 186
    and natural law, 45, 54, 57, 59, 62, 69, 75
    and positivism, 169
    for Pound, 215
    and sociology, 207–208

sociological jurisprudence, 19, 188, 206, 212

sociological legal theories, 9, 10, *14–15*, **19**, **203–226**

sociology, 204–212, 218, 223–224, 229, 272, 281, 286, 287, 289

Socrates, *12*, 53

solidarity, 208

Sophocles, 51

South Staffordshire Water Company v Sharman, *14*

sovereign
    Austin's, 141, **154–157**, *156*, 159–160, 161
    Bentham's, 141, 150, 151, *151*
    Hobbes', 63

'speaking to the sky', 50

speculative reason, 60

sports rules, 160, 171, *172*

standpoints, 3, 20, 40, 88, 95, 249, 283, 324
    see also external standpoint

statutes, *12–14*, 126, 152–153, 175, 176, 234

statutory interpretation, 113

statutory limitations periods, 120

Stefancic, J, 300–302

Stoicism, 56

Stone, Julius, 311, 315

subject *see* individuals

subjectivity, 92, 95, 96, 97, 252, 283, 307

substantive law, *210*

succession law, 125, 129, 154, 175

Summa Theologiae (Aquinas), 58

superstition, 86, 91, 95, 96

superstructure, *192*, *193*, 195, 196, 276, 277

supporting your views, 2, 3, 27

Supreme Court of Queensland Act (1991), 176

syllogistic method, 54, 217

synthesis
    Bloom's, *34*, **35–36**, *37*
    Marx's, 190, *191*, *193*

system *see* legal system

taxation, 64, 148

taxonomy, Borges', 99, 231

technology, 190, 192, 194, 278, 279

teleology, 54–55, 59, *119*, 120, 312

'text', 231, **234–236**, 245, 321

theology, 58

theory of interests, 213–215

thesis, 190, *191*, *193*

thinking, influences on, 2, 16, 46, 84–86, 92, 264–265

thinking skills, 33–37

Thompson, EP, 198, **275**, **276**, 277, 278, 320

time limits, statutory, 120

timelines (use in this book), 8, 11

top-down view of law, 247, *248*

torts, *14–15*, 44, 129, 153

totalitarianism, 279

trace, 245

Trade Practices Act 1974 (Cth), 4–5

traditional laws, 161, 306, 311, 312

trashing, 20, 242, 286

trespass, 121

true law, 57

trumps, rights as, 131–132, *262*

truths, 229–230, 247, 321

types of law, 59, 157–158, 209–211 *see also* categorisation

tyranny, 56, 57, 111

uncertainty, 174, 179–180, *180*, 190, 221, 242, 249, 283

understanding theories, 29–37

Uniform Commercial Code (US), 218

United Kingdom, 157

United Nations, 118

United States, *13–15*, 157, 212

universal law, 55, 56, 57

universal theories, 94, 229 *see also* metanarratives

'unjust law', 48, **79**

unpacking, *243*

upper class, 195

'urtext', 274, 281

US Declaration of Independence, 111, 112, 118, 130

utilitarianism, 120, 124, 130, 131, **139**, 144, **146–148**, 149, *262*

validity
    of constitutions, 104
    of criticisms, 223
    of law/rules, 16, 18, 56, 66, 68, 142, 176, 247, 312
    of legal systems, 68, 311
    of norms, 101–103, 104–105
    of theories, 36, 95

values, 1–2, *77*, 95, 96, 98, 124, 130, 140, 148, 165, 215, 314

views *see* standpoints

virtuous life, 56, 57, 61

voting rights, 65, *253*, 254, 256, 298

vulnerability, 71

Wave Hill walk-off, 298

Weber, Max, *14*, 19, 206, *207*, **209–212**

welfare systems, *189*, 195

Western thinking, 16, 86

Williams, Patricia, 302, 329

wills, 154, 175

wishes (Austin's), 152, **153**

witnesses, 123, 143, 221

Wollstonecraft, Mary, 254

women's liberation movement, 254, 255–256

words, 18, 27, 39, 179–180, 242

working class, 192–193, 194, 195, 200, 279

world views, 79, 80, 85, 87–88, 91, 92

World War Two, 66–67, 97, 123, 164, 168

writing about legal theory, 28–29, 51–52

Yorta Yorta, 309, **310–316**, 322